2/00

NEW MEDIA AND AMERICAN POLITICS

New Media
and
American Politics

Richard Davis
Diana Owen

New York   Oxford
Oxford University Press
1998

Oxford University Press

Oxford   New York
Athens   Auckland   Bangkok   Bogota   Bombay
Buenos Aires   Calcutta   Cape Town   Dar es Salaam
Delhi   Florence   Hong Kong   Istanbul   Karachi
Kuala Lumpur   Madras   Madrid   Melbourne
Mexico City   Nairobi   Paris   Singapore
Taipei   Tokyo   Toronto   Warsaw

and associated companies in
Berlin   Ibadan

Published by Oxford University Press, Inc.
198 Madison Avenue, New York, New York 10016

Oxford is a registered trademark of Oxford University Press

Library of Congress Cataloging-in-Publication Data
Davis, Richard, 1955–
    New media and American politics / Richard Davis and Diana Owen.
        p.   cm.
    Includes index.
    ISBN 0-19-512060-4; 0-19-512061-2 (pbk)
    1. Mass media—Political aspects—United States.   2. United
States—Politics and government—1993-   3. Mass media—Technological
innovations.   I. Owen, Diana Marie.   II. Title.
    P95.82.U6D38 1998
    302.23′0973—dc21   97-52291

9 8 7 6 5 4 3 2 1

Printed in the United States of America
on acid-free paper

To my children—Audrey, Jonathan, Romney, Bethany, and Devin—the next generation, for whom new media will not be new at all

Richard Davis

To Jeffrey

Diana Owen

Preface

Mass communication in the United States is in a state of flux. "New media," such as talk radio, television news magazines, electronic town meetings, tabloids, MTV, and the Internet, convey political information to the public in ways that depart, sometimes radically, with convention. While no consensus has been reached about the wide ranging implications of the new media's political presence, it is fair to say that the new media have substantially altered the way that American journalists operate, politics is conducted, and the public relates to media, politicians, institutions, and political processes.

Debate over the new media's role, significance, and implications for democratic governance has been sparked in academic and journalistic circles. Some argue that new media have the potential to be a positive force in society. New media are the people's media, and as such, they can generate interest in politics among apathetic citizens, facilitate public discourse, and occasionally even stimulate political participation. They also act as a check on the mainstream press, which an increasing number of ordinary people perceive to be an elite domain too closely aligned with politicians and government to play a legitimate watchdog role.

Yet, the new media's political role, indeed their very existence, is determined overwhelmingly by economic market forces to an extent that exceeds even that of the profit-conscious media mainstream. New media offerings depend on near-instant profitability, in many cases, for survival. Talk radio programs, for example, are regularly canceled and replaced with little warning when ratings drop. The economic imperative that drives new media has direct implications for content, and has caused these communication formats to privilege entertainment over substance. New media have been a significant contributing factor in the tabloidization of news and consequently the trivialization of politics. While many new media provide more opportunities for public engagement and discussion, much of the discourse is banal. New media rarely provide channels for genuine participation, but instead substitute ranting and venting for action.

After our examination of the evidence, we find that the latter perspective has the most credence at present. However, new media represent highly diverse forms of communication, and it is difficult to generalize without finding exceptions. Electronic town meetings, for example, have provided successful interchanges between the public, candidates, and officials. In fact, the potential for most new media to be positive forces in the polity is present by virtue of the media formats and technologies themselves. Unfortunately, the public service and democratizing possibilities for most new media are undercut by the singlemindedness of the profit imperatives that drive them.

The new media's political role is complex and dynamic. The goal of this project is to begin sorting out the new media phenomenon. We start by taking up the difficult task of defining new media and distinguishing them from the mainstream press. We discuss the evolution of new media and the context which facilitated its emergence as a political force. We then examine the content of and audiences for new media, the influence of the new media on the old media, and the role of new media in election campaigns and in the policy arena. Our concluding remarks focus on the implications of new media, especially in terms of their ability to meaningfully contribute to a more participatory democratic politics.

This project has benefited greatly from support and assistance from a variety of sources. The College of Family, Home and Social Sciences, and the Political Science Department at Brigham Young University provided funding to complete this project. Students in Political Science 410 at BYU read all of the chapters and offered helpful suggestions and comments on our ideas. Richard Davis thanks the research assistants who assisted in the completion of this project: Amy Bice, Anna Nibley, Stephanie Ord, Vincent James Strickler, and Kristen Winmill. Diana Owen is grateful for the encouragement of her Georgetown colleagues. She also appreciates the support of her friends at the ABA and in the office of Congressman Ben Cardin. It has been a pleasure working with Thomas LeBien, our editor at Oxford University Press, his assistant, Jeffrey Soloway, and Lisa Stallings. We thank the anonymous reviewers for their helpful and insightful suggestions for improving the manuscript. We are appreciative of the Pew Research Center for the People & the Press for making their data available to us.

Completing a major project is never easy, and we are most fortunate to have had the continual encouragement, support, and inspiration of our families and friends.

Provo, Utah   R. D.
Washington, D.C.   D. O.
September, 1997

Contents

1 Defining the New Media, 3
2 An Environment for New Media, 28

ONE   **The Role and Content of New Media**
3 Talking Politics, 51
4 Showing Politics: Tabloid Journalism and
   Entertainment Television, 92
5 Typing Politics: Computer Networks, 110

TWO   **The Audiences and Effects of New Media**
6 The Audiences, 133
7 Audience Attitudes, 164

THREE   **The Effects of New Media on Traditional
Media, Campaigns, and Public Policy**
8 Shaping Old Media, 189
9 Shaping Presidential Campaigns, 210
10 Shaping the Policy Agenda, 231

Conclusion: Popular Voice or Demagogic Tool, 253

Notes, 263

Index, 297

NEW MEDIA AND AMERICAN POLITICS

Defining the New Media

Periodically, the mass media system in the United States experiences significant transformations that signal a new stage in its evolution. New communication forms emerge in the political media realm, sparking elite interest and stimulating public curiosity. These emergent media work, often through trial and error, to establish their place in the political communication hierarchy. At times, a struggle ensues between the old and new forms. Ultimately, each adapts to the other's presence, and the new communication forms are absorbed into the media mainstream.

This process is currently underway for the so-called new media in American politics. Talk radio and television, electronic town meetings, television news magazines, MTV (Music Television), print and electronic tabloids, and computer networks have assumed an enhanced role in the political process. Their emergence coincides with, and in many ways contributes to, the present commercial and entertainment focus of political news.

The arrival of the new media on the political scene raises some key questions. What is meant by the term *new media?* How are the new media different from traditional media, such as daily newspapers, television and radio news programs, and general interest news magazines? What effect does new media content have on audiences?

How have new media influenced presidential campaigns? What role do the new media play in the public policy arena? And finally, what does the future of the democratic process look like with the new media as a political force? This book addresses each of these questions and seeks to illuminate what these new communication forms are, where they came from, and what they mean for American politics.

The New Media Era

New media began proliferating and their political role evolved in the late 1980s. Events such as the Gulf War and the William Kennedy Smith trial sparked talk radio debate and provided material for the increasingly popular television news magazines. Widespread recognition of the new media's presence on the American political scene occurred during the 1992 presidential election campaign. New media were heralded as an innovative and significant force in presidential campaigns

Candidates appearing on talk radio, television talk shows, news magazine programs, MTV, and the internet became the latest fad in campaigning. Ross Perot initiated candidates' implementation of new media strategies by announcing on "Larry King Live" that he was willing to run for president if drafted by the American people. The three major presidential candidates—Bill Clinton, George Bush, and Ross Perot—appeared on "Larry King" a total of thirteen times during the campaign. Bill Clinton was a guest on the "Arsenio Hall Show," wearing sunglasses and playing the saxophone. Talk radio became an important candidate forum in 1992. Bill Clinton and Jerry Brown made frequent talk radio appearances during the Democratic primaries. George Bush was interviewed by conservative host Rush Limbaugh. MTV debuted its own brand of coverage of the presidential campaign with its regular "Choose or Lose" news and public affairs program.

The new media continued to be a force in the 1994 midterm election. Nine talk radio hosts ran for statewide or local office. Although most were unsuccessful, their positions as talk radio hosts offered them instant legitimacy as candidates.[1] Other unsuccessful candidates, such as Oliver North, former New York governor Mario Cuomo, former presidential candidate Jerry Brown, and former New York mayor Ed Koch, moved into local or national talk radio host jobs.[2] Talk radio hosts were credited with mobilizing young, male Republican voters, thus helping to secure GOP control of both houses of Congress for the first time since 1954.[3]

The presidential election of 1996 signaled not only the beginning of a second term for Bill Clinton, but also marked an anniversary for new media. The four years following the 1992 campaign demonstrated that the new media were not a fad, and that they had become entrenched in the political world beyond the campaign context. The new media came of age, suggesting not a transitory status, but a permanence in American political life.

By the 1996 election cycle, the new media were an established part of the campaign process. On September 24, 1995, independent presidential candidate Ross Perot, employing a familiar strategy, announced on the "Larry King Live" show that he would form a third party to compete in the 1996 presidential contest. Senator Bob Dole appeared on "Late Night With David Letterman" to announce his candidacy for the 1996 presidential contest.

The use of talk radio by candidates was routine, if not expected. Republican presidential candidate Lamar Alexander hosted his own monthly call-in television talk show broadcast on more than six hundred cable systems.[4] GOP presidential candidate Bob Dole was criticized for not using talk radio as part of his campaign strategy, even though his wife, Elizabeth, and running mate, Jack Kemp, appeared regularly on local talk radio programs. The campaign implemented an extensive surrogate network of fifteen to twenty personalities a day who were available for talk radio interviews supporting the Dole effort.[5] Television talk show hosts' monologues about presidential candidates, a campaign staple, took on a different character in 1996. The nasty tone of the monologues prompted one commentator to suggest a new low: "What's different here is that there is a . . . coarseness, and there is a personal quality to this stuff, particularly with the president."[6]

Perhaps the most significant new media trend in the 1996 presidential campaign was the extensive use of Internet Web sites by candidates and parties. Internet sites became commonplace for candidates running for all levels of office, from president to local sheriff. Candidates not only posted information but also interacted with voters through computer network-mediated town meetings and chat rooms.[7]

The new media's role is hardly limited to campaigns and elections. Policymakers, interest groups, and political organizations embrace the new media as fresh resources for information retrieval and dissemination, agenda-setting, and public opinion formation. Citizens use new media as a mechanism for accessing the polity.

Talk radio has taken a lead role in fostering a nexus between citizens and politics. The potential power of talk radio in this regard has not gone unnoticed by politicians. In September 1993, the White House invited talk radio hosts to broadcast from the South Lawn. One hundred and twenty-four hosts accepted the invitation and were treated to interviews with an array of administration officials involved in promoting the Clinton health care reform proposal. President Clinton held a press conference with the hosts. Moreover, the president expressed his hope that "this will be the first of a number of opportunities" for talk show hosts to be briefed by the administration.[8] In addition, the annual talk radio show host convention attracted well-known politicians, including Senator Bob Dole and House Minority Leader Dick Gephardt. The convention also featured representatives of the Clinton White House.[9]

Beginning the first day of the 104th Congress, new House Speaker Newt Gingrich allowed talk radio hosts to broadcast from the basement of the Capitol building.[10] They remain, marking another step in congressional accommodation of the media. Acknowledging their ideological bond and his role in their rise to power, the Republican freshman class made Rush Limbaugh an honorary member of their group.[11] Senate Majority Leader Bob Dole attempted to use talk radio to gain support for a balanced budget amendment early in the 104th Congress.[12]

Throughout the early 1990s talk radio grew in popularity, becoming the top AM format in the major media markets in the nation.[13] The controversial aspects of talk radio escalated along with its popularity. Talk radio was attacked by President Clinton, using a talk radio platform, for generating public distrust and hatred. The president later charged talk radio with contributing to national violence, particularly the bombing of the federal building in Oklahoma City on April 19, 1995, which resulted in the deaths of nearly two hundred people.[14]

Politicians also appear regularly on new media venues other than talk radio. President and Mrs. Clinton have been occasional guests on "Larry King Live," news magazine programs, and MTV. On November 9, 1993, Vice President Al Gore and Ross Perot debated the merits of the North American Free Trade Act (NAFTA) before the nation on the "Larry King Live" program.[15] Vice President Al Gore, with his own top ten list on being vice president appeared on "Late Night with David Letterman" and also on "Donahue." Ross Perot was featured as a guest host on "Larry King Live." House Speaker Newt Gingrich met with teens on an MTV discussion program.[16]

The Internet burgeoned with political information. Internet sites proliferated throughout government at all levels: federal, state, and local. While only a few members of Congress were on the Internet in 1993, all had personalized Web sites by 1998. Nongovernmental players also have gone online, including interest groups, news media organizations, and political parties. The Library of Congress's online legislative archive of the 104th Congress, White House speeches and press releases, interest group position statements, political party platforms, public opinion poll results, video of campaign commercials, debate transcripts, and much more are available to the Web-connected public. Usership of the Internet grew dramatically from an estimated 10 to 11 million people in 1994 to 30 to 40 million by the end of 1996.[17]

The new media have acquired staying power in American politics. They also have the potential to grow in importance. The distinct role of particular new media will wax and wane in years to come, but the continuation of their political presence is very much assured. In fact, the term *new media* will become less significant in the near future as these communication formats gain broad acceptance and their roles are viewed as routine, rather than novel.

What Are the New Media?

Defining the new media and their role in American politics is an important, albeit somewhat challenging, task. In this book, we argue that the new media are quantitatively and qualitatively different from the mainstream press. They do not simply represent a variation of the established news media.

New media are mass communication forms with primarily nonpolitical origins that have acquired political roles. These roles need not be largely political in nature; in some instances they are only tangentially so. What distinguishes these communication forms from more traditional ones, such as newspapers and nightly television news, is the degree to which they offer political discussion opportunities that attract public officials, candidates, citizens, and even members of the mainstream press corps. In particular, the new media enhance the public's ability to become actors, rather than merely spectators, in the realm of media politics. Further, to a greater extent than traditional media have historically, the new media place a high premium on entertainment.

The new media have significant potential to educate, facilitate public discourse, and enhance citizen participation. They provide mass audiences with a seemingly boundless array of sources that transcend the time and space constraints of traditional media. In addition, new media technologies easily bypass national and international boundaries, bringing American citizens into contact with diverse cultures and distant happenings to an extent previously unimaginable. As such, new media have the potential to enhance the public's understanding and tolerance of different societies.[18]

However, as we will argue later, new media's promise is undercut by the commercial and entertainment imperatives that drive them. In reality, the political role of new media is ancillary. The new media are political when politics pays. Thus the new media's role in the political realm is volatile. Their educational function is incomplete and sporadic.

The new media constitute a highly diverse range of communication formats. One way of distinguishing between types of new media is to categorize them on the basis of whether they employ old or new technologies. For many forms, the term *new media* is a misnomer. They involve old media technologies that have been newly discovered or reinvigorated as political media. It is the extent of their politicization that is new, not their existence. Thus there is a sense of novelty even in those media that have existed for some time. New media that employ old communication technologies include political talk radio, television talk shows, television news magazines, electronic town meetings, and print and electronic tabloids.

Political talk radio, for example, dates back to the origins of radio itself in the 1920s. Early radio stations featured not only news, but also political broadcasts, such as conventions, presidential inaugurations, and speeches of presidents and other public officials.[19] Television talk programs also are not new. Morning variety talk shows, such as "Today," "Good Morning America," and "CBS This Morning" certainly predate the current interest in "new media." The "Today Show" first aired in 1952, while "CBS Morning News" debuted five years later. Phil Donahue's nationally syndicated talk program premiered in 1970 and featured presidential candidate debates from 1984 to 1994. His program became a significant venue for Democratic presidential primary candidates in 1992.

There are many more examples of particular new media programs that did not exist a decade ago. The nationally syndicated Rush Limbaugh radio program appeared in 1989 and his television show first aired in September 1992.[20] Many other talk radio hosts with large national audiences, such as G. Gordon Liddy and Michael Reagan, have emerged only in the 1990s. MTV's political campaign coverage did not debut until the 1992 presidential primary election.[21]

In addition, new media channels employing traditional media technology have surfaced in recent years. For instance, even though cable is not a new format for broadcasting, new channels designed at least partly for political talk now exist, including C-SPAN, CNBC, The Talk Channel, MSNBC, and The Comedy Channel.

Some formats are genuinely new, having evolved from more recent innovations in communications technologies. The proliferation of online computer networks, coupled with an explosion in the use of home computers, has created new methods for political communication. Fax machines and voice mail operations facilitate citizens' ability to register opinions with politicians and journalists. These new technologies infuse political communication with a new immediacy. The public can now receive and disseminate political messages with increased ease and speed.

An interesting feature of these new technologies is that they combine the characteristics of interpersonal and mass communication forms. Fax machines, voice mail, and e-mail allow the user to disseminate messages from one point to another, and as such constitute interpersonal communication. However, they also can be used to send the same message to many users simultaneously, as is the case with online discussion groups and mass political mailings sent via fax. These communication formats can be viewed as a novel form of print communication, as cyberversions of newspapers, magazines,and letters.

New Media, Old Technology

Political Talk Radio

Political talk radio is prominent on any list of types of new media. The format has proliferated recently as radio stations have turned to "talk" to expand audiences. Talk or news/talk formats on radio have mushroomed in number since the early 1990s.[22] In fact, talk radio has been a boon for local radio stations, especially AM stations. Because listeners increasingly showed a preference for the higher clarity of FM frequencies, AM radio was losing its audience. Political talk radio has become a vehicle for restoring listener interest in AM stations. Although talk radio host Rush Limbaugh contributed to this rise in popularity, talk's political ascendancy was actually occurring before Limbaugh's fame.

Talk radio, as we know it today, had its origins in the 1930s. Politics and talk radio have long been joined. The political implications of radio were recognized early. One early historian of radio proclaimed that since the rise of radio "never in the history of our nation has there been a more widespread knowledge of our government and its modes of operation, nor a more intimate acquaintanceship between the voter, who buys government with his taxes, and those charged with governing."[23]

Political talk radio was a popular forum for politicians in the early days of radio. President Franklin Roosevelt's fireside chats and the positive responses from listeners are legend. Roosevelt was a popular radio speaker. One of FDR's radio speeches during the 1940 presidential campaign was heard by 38.7 percent of all households with radio sets.[24]

One of the first regular political talk hosts was Father Charles Coughlin, a right-wing Catholic priest who used his regular radio broadcasts to attack the New Deal. He frequently spiced his broadcasts with newly coined phrases such as "Franklin Double-Crossing Roosevelt." During the mid-1930s, Coughlin was estimated to have an audience of 10 million people for his weekly broadcasts.[25]

Politicians long have used talk radio to bolster their careers. An early example was Senator Huey Long of Louisiana, who was a frequent orator on national radio broadcasts. On average, he would receive up to sixty thousand letters after his broadcasts. One of his opponents even termed him the best radio speaker in America, "even better than President Roosevelt."[26] Reportedly, Long was planning to use his national popularity for a presidential bid in 1936, until he was gunned down by a disgruntled opponent in 1935.

Several political talk programs were popular during this early period, including "Town Meeting of the Air," "People's Platform," and "American Forum of the Air." "Town Meeting of the Air" included a political debate between well-known political leaders before a live studio audience allowed to ask questions of the debate presenters. The range of participants suggested that surprising diversity was accommodated in national political radio broadcasts. Participants at various times included Wendell Wilkie, 1940 Republican presidential candidate; Senator Robert Taft of Ohio; Norman Thomas, leader of the Socialist party; and Earl Browder, Communist party presidential candidate. The format for "People's Forum" was a broadcast dinner conversation on current political issues by ordinary Americans invited to the CBS studios.[27]

Nationally syndicated radio call-in programs originated in the 1970s with the "Larry King Show." Within a decade, King had more than three hundred affiliates. Other syndicated hosts, such as Bruce Williams and Jim Bohannon, were offered to affiliates by broadcast networks. Politics was not the exclusive focus of these early talk hosts. King, for example, carried a wide array of personalities as guests.

The movement toward a newly constituted political talk radio began in the late 1980s.[28] During the 1990s, news/talk has become one of the highest rated radio programming formats. In some markets, such as Chicago, San Francisco, and Boston, it is the most listened to radio programming.[29] For example, three of the five top radio stations in Boston are AM stations with talk formats.[30] Rush Limbaugh, the best-known talk radio host, reigns over a daily midday program that airs on more than six hundred radio stations and has an estimated audience of 20 million listeners. Most talk radio hosts, however, are local. Popular local hosts include Neal Boortz in Atlanta, Michael Jackson in Los Angeles, and Mike Siegel in Seattle. While Rush Limbaugh focuses exclusively on national political issues, these local hosts provoke debate on a mixture of national issues and personalities, as well as local and state political leaders and policies.

In spite of its popularity, talk radio is surrounded by controversy and its contribution to democratic governance is hotly contested. On the one hand, talk radio has been called a "window on the world for millions" and "the ultimate arena for free speech."[31] But evaluations of political talk radio also have been cast in darker terms. Critics have labeled it "hate radio" and have linked it to violence in American society.

Television Talk

Television talk programming encompasses a broad array of formats. These shows range from those dedicated almost entirely to politics to those only occasionally treating political topics. They also vary widely on the amount of audience interaction that the program accommodates.

Television talk shows, such as "Nightline," CNN's "Larry King Live" and "CNN and Company," "The Charlie Rose Show" on PBS, and CNBC programs like "Equal Time," the "Tim Russert Show," and the "Cal Thomas Show," deal seriously with political topics on a regular basis. "Politically Incorrect," which debuted on Comedy Central before gaining a network affiliation, takes a lighter look at political issues, as host Bill Maher coaxes humorous analyses from guests from government, academia, the press, and the arts.

Other programs regularly include political content alongside entertainment fare. Established network morning variety programs, such as "Good Morning America," "Today," and "CBS This Morning," fall into this category. Fox's "Morning News" program offers more serious political discussion per hour than its flashier counterparts on the three major networks. These programs garner large audi-ence shares at the start of the day and thus are attractive forums for politicians.

In addition, talk shows whose predominant emphasis is on entertainment cross over to political themes with increasing regularity. Programs, such as the "Tonight Show," "Late Night with David Letterman," the "Dick Cavett Show" on CNBC, and the "Charles Grodin Show" on CNBC, have become outlets for political discussion and they can even provide the backdrop for political events. For example, immediately following the 1996 election, defeated GOP presidential candidate Bob Dole appeared on a "Letterman" broadcast from Washington, D.C., and cohosted "Saturday Night Live"—a popular venue for political guests.

Even talk shows whose primary agenda is to provide a forum for bizarre and outrageous confessional tales integrate politics into the mix. These programs play host to political guests and tackle what are in essence public policy issues, such as crime and health care, frequently with a characteristic tabloid spin. "Donahue," "Oprah," "Jerry Springer,"[32] and "Montel Williams" are examples of this genre. The judicial process also receives substantial attention on the talk show circuit. Geraldo Rivera, for example, declared his program the "television show of record" for the O. J. Simpson criminal and civil trials, and featured extensive trial coverage, interviews with legal experts, law enforcement officials, and principals involved with the case, and fielded telephone call-ins from audience members. Since the Simpson case, Rivera has followed other cases, such as the murder in Denver of child beauty queen JonBenet Ramsey, the trial of Timothy McVeigh for the Oklahoma City bombing, and the Paula Jones case alleging Presidential improprieties with similar diligence.

Television and radio talk differ in some important respects. Talk radio is a somewhat more populist forum than television talk. Television talk is centered more intensively on the host and in-studio guests than is most talk radio. Conversely, talk radio relies more on call-ins. Television talk provides a visual advantage for the hosts and guests, and a distinct disadvantage for callers, whose images are rarely projected on screen.

There have been some attempts to create video versions of radio talk that eradicate the differences between the two genres to some extent. Rush Limbaugh's television program is a prime example of this genre, although Limbaugh's television audience was a mere fraction of his radio audience. In addition, C-SPAN and MSNBC regularly broadcast talk radio programs live, although these programs normally consist of nothing more than the host doing his or her show from the studio. C-SPAN's Brian Lamb also hosts a morning chat program in which journalists discuss the day's headlines with callers.

Electronic Town Meetings

The classic New England town meeting has been restyled for the television age. Electronic town meetings allow citizens and politicians to interact directly in a televised forum. During the 1992 presidential electoral campaign, electronic town meetings came into vogue. Candidates at all stages of the election employed the town meeting format as an element of the new media campaign strategy of bypassing the mainstream press. Bill Clinton and Ross Perot were especially successful at making town meetings an integral part of their presidential bids. The second televised debate used a town meeting style and proved to be the format favored overwhelmingly by the public.[33] The tradition of including a town meeting style debate was continued during the 1996 contest.

Yet the campaign uses of electronic town meetings mark only the tip of the iceberg. Town meetings have gained significant popularity among citizens and increasingly are employed for public policy debate.[34] They feature a number of beneficial characteristics that encourage people to participate in them directly or vicariously through media. Citizens are enticed by the spectacle of ordinary people like themselves deliberating about important political issues. Further, individuals who are unable to attend town meetings in person can tune in via television. Often, televised town meetings provide opportunities for the viewing public to participate from home by calling in or sending messages via modem or interactive cable television, where viewers communicate through a computer console attached to the television itself.[35] In fact, television is not the only venue hosting town meetings. There have been experiments with online versions of town meetings in an effort to include more people in the process.

National politics is not the exclusive domain of electronic town meetings. Cable television has broadened the potential market for town meetings. Town meetings have been employed at the state and local levels of government, where some of the most innovative experiments with town meetings have been launched. Currently, town meetings serve primarily as arenas for political discussion and debate. However, electronic town meetings have been used as vehicles for citizen decision-making. For example, Alaskans debated the spending of transportation funds, Oregonians discussed state budgetary priorities, and San Francisco Bay area residents deliberated the region's future using electronic town meeting formats.[36] Town meetings were used in extensive experiments in "deliberative polling" initiated in 1996 at the University of Texas at Austin, where a national random sample of Americans gathered to discuss in detail issues that were raised using a survey instrument.[37]

Television News Magazines

Another old technology/new media format is television news magazines, that is, programs occasionally offering hard news, but generally focusing on feature stories that may or may not be oriented toward politics. The number of such programs has grown in the last decade. From their inception in 1968 with CBS's "60 Minutes," such programming has extended to all networks and even to several programs on each network. Examples of the genre today, in addition to the veteran "60 Minutes," include "Day One" (NBC), "Dateline" (NBC, which features segments hosted by "NBC Evening News" anchor Tom Brokaw), "48 Hours" (hosted by "CBS Evening News" anchor Dan Rather), "Eye to Eye" (CBS), "20/20" (ABC), and "PrimeTime Live" (ABC). Each magazine program strives to develop its own personality in order to appeal to particular audience segments. For example, "PrimeTime Live" is designed to attract a higher educated, slightly less mainstream audience by emulating a video version of *Vanity Fair* magazine. In contrast, "20/20" targets middle America by highlighting human interest stories and Barbara Walters's interviews.[38]

Originally attractive to networks because they are relatively inexpensive to produce and attract respectable audience ratings, television magazines' popularity periodically falls markedly. These programs overdosed on coverage of the O. J. Simpson criminal trial. In addition, serious doubt has been cast on the veracity of stories featured on these shows. For example, "Dateline" staged a fire in a General Motors pickup truck and "Day One" so feared losing a defamation suit filed by two tobacco companies that it paid them $15 million to cover legal fees.[39] A successful lawsuit was waged by Food Lion against ABC for a broadcast on "Prime Time Live" that featured footage depicting unsanitary food handling procedures captured by a hidden camera. When the popularity of these programs has become precarious, networks tinker with their form and content. As is the case with much of talk television, the lines between politics and entertainment are frequently blurred on television news magazines, especially on the more recent additions to the roster.

A good deal of the material presented on such programs is unrelated to politics, but other stories are explicitly political. Investigative reports form the cornerstone of many of the political stories and were the staple of early editions of these programs. They also feature more in-depth stories drawn from the evening news programs or interviews with well-known figures in politics.

Television news magazine programs have offered themselves as forums at critical moments in campaigns. For example, during the 1992 presidential election, Bill and Hillary Clinton used an appearance on "60 Minutes" to downplay the significance of Gennifer Flowers's allegations of an extramarital affair. These programs also can make political news outside of the campaign context, such as in 1990 when, on the ABC program "Primetime Live," the late Justice Thurgood Marshall made derogatory remarks about then President George Bush and White House chief of staff John Sununu. Marshall was criticized by newspaper editorials as being too outspoken for a Supreme Court justice.[40]

MTV

MTV, which began as a marketing mechanism to aid an ailing record industry, has become much more than a screening room for music videos. Over the course of its decade and a half long history, MTV has evolved into a network that provides diverse programming to its more than 60 million viewers.[41] MTV supplements its musical fare with offerings such as "The Real World," an experiment in Generation X group living; "House of Style," a fashion show; and "Beavis and Butthead," an animated cartoon program. Politics, on occasion, becomes fused with the dominant amusement aspects of the programs. Beavis and Butthead, for example, have participated in an animated town meeting with President Bill Clinton.

MTV also has entered the political realm outright with Rock the Vote, a Los Angeles based organization that attempts to get young people involved in politics. During the 1992, 1994, and 1996 election campaigns, Rock the Vote publicized its voter registration and get-out-the-vote drives via MTV. In addition, MTV sponsored forums for all major presidential candidates. Young people asked questions while MTV political beat reporter Tabitha Soren served as moderator. The most famous sound bite from these forums, the question of "boxers or briefs" asked of Bill Clinton, belied the more serious tone of the majority of the discussions, which addressed issues of concern to younger citizens. Candidates now routinely conduct interviews on the Rock the Vote bus as it travels across the nation. In the off-season, Rock the Vote continues to be active, producing programs that deal with a variety of issues, including teen health, crime, and violence.[42]

In addition to Rock the Vote, MTV works to politicize its audience through "MTV News," which updates viewers about current affairs several times throughout the day. MTV also sponsors concerts and other events that highlight political concerns, such as the devastation of the rainforest in South America, the plight of American farmers, and world hunger.

Print and Television Tabloids

Tabloid journalism has been associated historically with weekly newspapers, such as the *National Enquirer* and the *Star,* whose outrageous headlines glare at us from supermarket checkout counters. Television counterparts to these print tabloids have emerged in the past decade. Examples of these syndicated tabloid television news magazine programs include "Hard Copy" and "Inside Edition."

In their print and broadcast forms, these tabloid formats are the "penny press" of the 1990s. The penny press, which arose in the mid-1800s and was designed to reach a mass audience, featured sensational human interest stories, crime, and political scandal. Like the penny press, modern day tabloids feel no obligation to cover political news. The emphasis is on human interest that attracts audiences. On a day when Israel and the PLO sign a peace agreement, the lead story in the tabloids will be a scandal involving a rock star or the latest high-profile murder trial.

Increasingly, however, tabloids find the personal side of politics can be spun into sensational tales that conform nicely to their style. Tabloid stories can spark major political controversy and set the agenda for other media. For this reason, we include tabloids among the new media. The tabloids have been sources of information for major scandals involving presidential candidates, such as those involving the personal lives of presidential candidates Gary Hart in 1987 and Bill Clinton in 1992, or high ranking members of their campaign staffs, such as Dick Morris in 1996. Tabloids have been known to pay large sums of money to individuals who are willing to reveal personal secrets of politicians, which increases their potential to be players in the political realm.

New Media, New Technology

A quickly evolving form of new media are computer networks. E-mail communication and computer online services are not primarily political in nature, but like any other tool, they can be so used. The Internet and various online services, such as Prodigy, Compuserve, America Online, Netscape, and MSN (Microsoft), now provide users with easy accessibility to political information and electronic communication. Entirely online political publications, such as *Slate,* have been tried, but have difficulty becoming financially viable.

A virtual communications revolution is upon us, as the technology becomes increasingly sophisticated and online resources multiply daily. One of the major implications of computer technology is the degree of interconnectedness that it facilities on both the human and mechanical levels.[43] Computer networks allow citizens to converse with one another through personal messages and the more anonymous forum of bulletin boards with relative ease and speed. They provide platforms for registering information that can be shared with people all over the world. On the technical side, computer networks carry text, audio, and visual messages through a complex global highway system that bridges geographical boundaries and stimulates the senses with multimedia presentation. Computer networks can be used in conjunction with other media to facilitate citizen input into the political process, as when e-mail messages accompany televised political broadcasts.

Political information of all types and levels of sophistication abounds on computer networks. Citizens, politicians, political parties, and interest groups can dash off cryptic comments or treatises to be read by a single individual or by millions. Public officials, policymakers, and candidates have recognized the utility of establishing a presence on computer networks to reach constituents. The World Wide Web is host to numerous government and campaign home pages, which provide citizens with mountains of information at the click of a mouse. Members of the executive branch and Congress invite the public to provide feedback via electronic mail.

The degree to which computer technology will influence the political world is unknowable at present, but its potential to be influential is immense. Computer networks raise important questions. Will this new tool become a viable alternative for interaction between policymakers and the public? How is it currently used by policymakers? What can the public learn online? What will future political discussion and policy-making be like with such systems? Does instantaneous communication damage the deliberative nature of representation?[44]

Mixed Media

The boundaries between different forms of new media are becoming increasingly artificial. Some practitioners are crossing lines by communicating to audiences through a variety of old and new media. For example, network anchors and correspondents regularly host television news magazine program segments. In addition, programming innovations combine new media formats. Traditional media, recognizing the importance of keeping current with technology, have taken steps to adapt. Electronic versions of newspapers, which frequently include more details about the stories that appear in print, are available online. Larger news organizations, such as the *Washington Post* and *New York Times*, for example, make available the results of entire surveys to their online subscribers.

Larry King was known as a popular talk radio host before launching his CNN television talk program. Rush Limbaugh appears on both media as well. Don Imus has a regular segment on MSNBC emulating his radio show. New media devotees use computer network home pages to keep up with developments of their favorite programs, such as "Late Night with David Letterman" or "Rush Limbaugh." They connect to online bulletin boards to communicate with one another.

Increasingly, the new media are merging. Television news magazines invite viewers to register their opinions online. *Time, Newsweek,* and other print publications receive many of their letters from readers via e-mail. CNN's "TalkBack Live" program features a complicated mixture of old and new media, which integrates television talk, a talk radio concept, and a computer online service.[45] In July 1995, one NBC public affairs program offered the opportunity for live computer online response by viewers. MSNBC is designed to facilitate online discussions with viewers on a range of arts, news, and societal issues each day.

How Do the New Media Differ from the Traditional Media?

As the foregoing discussion illustrates, it is difficult to generalize about the new media, given the diversity of formats, style, and content. Further, the boundaries between traditional and new media have become somewhat blurred as the two categories of media borrow techniques from one another. In some, although not all, respects, the differences between the two forms of media are a matter of degree, rather than substance.

Nonetheless, it is possible to discuss meaningful differences between traditional and new media. First, they vary in their respective approaches to political news, which, in turn, shapes the content of that news. Further, there is a distinct contrast in their political goals. The new media have a clear anti-institutional bias. As such, they have been less proximate to politicians than the traditional press. Finally, using mechanisms such as regular newsletters and publications, some new media practitioners develop closer linkages to their audiences than mainstream press journalists.

In the current communication environment, commercial incentives drive both the mainstream press and the new media. However, the two media forms are marked by significant differences in the manner in which the profit motive manifests itself. The mainstream press has historical grounding in public service and in the professional norms of journalism, although these orientations may be obscured in the current era. The traditional media have a sense of obligation to cover governmental affairs. The new media rarely claim even the pretense of a public service motivation. Entertainment as it is linked to profits is the primary function of new media. When politics becomes entertainment, it makes its way onto new media. When politics ceases to be profitable, it is dropped from the new media agenda.

The mainstream press' sense of obligation to cover political news is long-established in the print tradition and carried over to electronic communication forms early in their histories. Newspapers were established in this country specifically to carry information about government and commerce.[46] News programs on television and radio originally were required as part of public service programming. Even though news now is profitable, news programs are still a symbol of mainstream media organizations' public service commitment.

Commercial considerations have a greater impact on most new media than on the traditional press. Mainstream journalists who actually gather and report the news are somewhat more insulated from bottom line concerns than are many new media practitioners. New media have not, in many cases, developed the large bureaucratic organizational structures that can serve to remove journalists from direct dealings with advertising and revenue production. Television and radio talk show hosts, for example, are personally linked to the income their shows receive through advertising. They know how many people watch or listen to their programs, and they know that number is their primary responsibility. Some hosts even hawk products on air.

Thus the bottom line for new media is profit-making entertainment fare, even for those programs that feature heavy political content, such as "Larry King Live." (Electronic town meetings are a notable exception here.) Unlike the traditional press, particularly broadcast media, new media rely on a broader, less politically interested audience. The need to provide more than information alone is greater for new media. Entertainment is critical to the new media's ability to retain and increase their audiences.

New media, due to their propensity to cover politics as entertainment, often personalize political news. Human interest stories are standard fare. Well-known personalities, controversies, scandals, and the bizarre make good new media copy, and conform to the entertainment values that govern these formats. Traditional media also have a strong tendency to personalize news—a tendency that has heightened in the wake of the new media's popularity.[47] However, the level of personalization is held somewhat in check by the mainstream press' underlying conviction that it is serving the public interest and its desire to convey this impression to the citizenry, especially in an era when network television news, in particular, is losing popularity among the public.[48]

The new media also differ qualitatively from the traditional media in the populism they not only articulate, but seem to embody. Populist themes are recurrent in new media. The new media are unabashedly anti–big government and anti-incumbent. They also claim to shear away the filter traditional news media have constructed between the governors and the governed.[49] Unlike traditional news media, talk radio, television talk, electronic town meetings, and the Internet appear to give common people the chance to "talk back." The new media's very existence should be able to offer ordinary citizens the opportunity to participate in politics far beyond public opinion polls, public hearings, or voting. Yet, as we will demonstrate, this promise is not fulfilled in reality.

A feature of political discussion that truly sets the new media apart from traditional media is the propensity to make inflammatory statements about political figures, including ad hominem attacks against both individuals and groups. Such rhetoric is designed to attract attention and audiences through its shock value. Some programs thrive on this type of discourse. Rush Limbaugh's success depends largely on this strategy. One example from his tremendous inventory of lines: "I love the women's movement. Especially when I am walking behind it."[50] Limbaugh's attacks on "feminazis," "radical environmentalists," and the "National Association of Liberal Colored People" expands his listenership since it contradicts the norms of political discourse in the traditional media and enhances the entertainment value for his supporters.

Traditional media, governed by standards of ethics including a credo of objectivity, generally eschew such tactics as nonprofessional. The new media, however, are not so restricted. Sitting politicians, especially incumbent presidents, are the most common victims. According to a survey conducted by the talk radio industry's publication in mid-1993, President Clinton was criticized more than any other individual over a three-year period of talk show content. Michael Harrison, the editor of *Talkers* magazine, commented that Clinton "is most likely the most bashed individual in talk radio history."[51] President Clinton retaliated on C-SPAN's "Booknotes" program with Brian Lamb, stating that talk radio creates a "war of words in America where people are always bad-mouthing each other," and which is "not serving the country well."[52]

Ironically, that one-sidedness may be one of the attractions of the new media. It may be a response to the suspicion on the part of many Americans that traditional journalists are biased.[53] Mainstream reporters are accused of subtly injecting their opinions into their copy, but new media hosts are frank in admitting they are biased. David Sawyer, chairman of a Washington communications consulting firm, suggested Americans "perceive journalists as people trying to make it appear as though they're evenhanded, when in fact they are trying to manipulate their own opinions through the process."[54]

New media practitioners are far more likely than those in the traditional media to explicitly use their positions to stimulate the audience politically. This is particularly true for talk radio hosts, who have sought to motivate their listening audiences to engage in specific political activities, such as mail and fax campaigns on various issues. The talk radio hosts' drive to turn back the congressional pay increase in 1989 was an early example of these efforts. Talk show hosts sometimes even tout their political victories. Seattle talk show host Mike Siegel claims responsibility for policy changes, such as giving more power to state auditors to audit state agencies, killing a proposal for a day care center for the workers at a state agency, and a successful tax limitation initiative.[55]

Traditional media, however, have stated goals that seek to improve the political process. The mainstream press' goals are less specific than those of the new media, and they are not designed to foster particular policy outcomes. Instead, they are more broadly directed toward facilitating effective democratic governance. Providing citizens with information essential to their ability to perform their democratic duties is one such objective. They also seek to encourage political participation, such as voting, in a generic sense.

Another distinction is the association of new and old media practitioners with policymakers and candidates. Traditional media have established normalized relationships with politicians that define the news gathered. Traditional media are "fed" regularly through news conferences, press briefings, news releases, pseudoevents, and photo-ops. There is constant interaction between journalists on political beats and the institutions and individuals they cover.[56]

In some ways, new media have maintained greater distance from politicians than have traditional media. The lack of proximity is understandable given the occasional nature of the direct relationship between politicians and new media. The traditional media and politicians have a long-standing symbiotic association, each depending on the other to sustain their livelihoods. The press interacts with politicians on a regular basis, since they constitute the major sources of news. Politicians use the media as a means of establishing public recognition and policy support. While politicians appear as guests and sit for interviews in new media forums, the new media do not use them as sources in the traditional sense. In fact, new media practitioners often take an adversarial position toward politicians, especially incumbent officeholders.

The new media also provide the means for political actors, including candidates for the presidency, to speak, and even to converse, with citizens. In fact, champions of the new media cite the fact that the public has opportunities to achieve greater intimacy and access to political leaders as one of their greatest benefits. However, the new media are mercurial in their relationships. Politicians cannot count on establishing long-term bonds with talk show hosts or tabloid television reporters or be guaranteed a positive reception in new media venues. As Bill Clinton learned, while a candidate can benefit greatly from new media, a sitting president can suffer from their attacks.[57]

New media practitioners also develop an audience following that is not typical of traditional media. The more personal and populist orientation of new media allows program hosts and other participants who work in this genre to cultivate closer bonds to their audiences. The relationship to devotees is established further through other linkages. For example, talk show hosts Rush Limbaugh and Michael Reagan issue monthly newsletters for their listeners, thus generating valuable lists of conservatives around the nation. Other talk show hosts distribute publications to their listeners and, in the process, develop mailing lists. Audience members also are treated to more of their favorite new media stars through videotapes, books, and public appearances.

Blurring the Lines Between Media

While the distinctions that we note between new and old media are apparent in the 1990s, these differences appear to be fading. As such, this eradication of the lines between new and old media is part of the evolutionary process of political media in the United States. It is not so much the case that the new media are attempting to mimic the traditional media, although this has happened to some extent. Instead, traditional media are moving toward new media formats. Many traditional media outlets, interested in retaining their audiences, have adopted aspects of the new media style. In addition, the mainstream press frequently finds itself in the position of having to cover new media events, which adds an entertainment flair to old media programming.

Media coverage of the O. J. Simpson case illustrates this blurring of the line between traditional and new media reporting. The Simpson criminal trial was a natural for the new media, as it featured all of the most exciting features of entertainment journalism. Yet the major broadcast networks devoted a great deal of air time to the trial. They preempted regularly scheduled programming to offer live, continuous coverage on particular days. At other times they interrupted serial programming to announce developments in the trial. In the last six months of 1994, the Simpson trial garnered 431 stories or nearly fourteen hours worth of news coverage on the network evening news programs.[58] The mainstream television networks faced their biggest challenge regarding the Simpson case when the verdict of the civil trial was announced during the president's State of the Union Address. None of the networks cut to coverage of the trial, although ABC printed the verdict in bold along the bottom third of the screen. CNN and MSNBC chose O. J. Simpson over the president's speech.

In spite of the networks' decision not to cut from the president's speech to the Simpson verdict, the rise of continuous news programming, such as that offered on CNN and C-SPAN, may free the major broadcast networks somewhat from their sense of obligation to emphasize political news. People who are most interested in political news can turn to those avenues, which feature it regularly.

At the same time, real time news programming may create a dilemma for the major networks. For example, CNN and Court TV have focused on highly publicized events in the mold of the new media, such as the trials of William Kennedy Smith, the Menendez brothers, O. J. Simpson, and Timothy McVeigh. (William Kennedy Smith was accused of raping a young woman in Palm Beach; the Menendez brothers were convicted of killing their parents in California; O. J. Simpson stood trial for the murders of his wife and her friend, Ron Goldman; and Timothy McVeigh faces the death penalty for blowing up a federal building in Oklahoma City.) The major networks are threatened with losing audience shares. The networks must decide whether they should allow other news organizations to gain viewers at their expense, or whether they should compete by placing greater emphasis on these types of stories. At present, the latter trend appears to be taking hold, as the traditional media increasingly follow the lead of new media in setting the agenda for news. "NBC Evening News," for example, changed its programming formula in the spring of 1997 to what has been termed, "news lite," focusing on longer stories with a human interest flare that do not have strict temporal constraints.

The traditional media also have considered the new media newsworthy, thus enhancing the new media's political status. During the 1992 presidential campaign, for example, the mainstream press began to treat new media appearances by candidates as news. It is likely that far more people watched Bill Clinton play the saxophone standing next to Arsenio Hall on the recurring clips of the incident shown on various news and traditional public affairs programs than watched the original program. The same holds true for Ross Perot's announcement of the formation of a third party in 1995 on "Larry King Live."

Before the 1992 campaign, traditional media dismissed tabloids as examples of nonjournalism, much as the existing elite partisan press in the mid nineteenth century had looked disdainfully on the penny press. The tabloids, with their penchant for covering stories of Elvis sightings and the births of aliens to human parents, were not viewed as a serious source of campaign news. But Gennifer Flowers's charges of marital infidelity against a serious presidential candidate made in a tabloid story were not easy for journalists covering the campaign to ignore, especially when they provided a news peg for recurring rumors about Bill Clinton. Major newspapers, such as the *Los Angeles Times, USA Today,* and the *Boston Globe* gave the story front-page coverage.[59] After initially passing on the story, the network news programs picked it up after morning talk shows and cable programs aired it.[60] In 1996 the story of top Clinton campaign aide Dick Morris's alleged affairs and out-of-wedlock child was broken by the *Star,* which was praised by mainstream journalists, including the *Washington Post*'s Bob Woodward, for its investigative reporting skills.

It is important to note that scandals have been standard fare in the coverage of presidential campaigns long before the 1992 campaign and the attention to the new media's role. The difference was the source. Typically, the information emerged from traditional media investigative reporting or the opposing political camps' negative research efforts, not from the new media. For example, in 1987, the *Miami Herald* had followed Democratic presidential candidate Gary Hart and revealed the Donna Rice affair. A staffer in the Dukakis camp had provided the videotape to traditional media that demonstrated Joe Biden's plagiarism.

Once the story of Gennifer Flowers appeared during the 1992 presidential contest, millions of Americans who bought tabloids were learning about a political news story that the traditional media weren't even covering. The mainstream press' avoidance of the story gave the appearance that traditional journalists were covering up for a presidential candidate by dismissing the source of information about the scandal.

Today, however, traditional media programming is more influenced by new media standards for news. In fact, the interests of the new media can drive traditional media coverage. For example, in 1994 Connie Chung anchored the evening news from a Portland, Oregon, skating rink for nearly two weeks in order to get an interview with Olympic figure skater Tanya Harding, who was linked to an incident involving the beating of skater Nancy Kerrigan. Chung sought an interview with Harding for her primetime interview program. Thus it is clear that the traditional media are making conscious efforts to incorporate more tabloid style stories into their coverage.[61] One ABC News producer refers to them as "rape and pillage" stories.[62]

Commercialism or Populism?

The new media are in a more precarious position in the media system than are traditional media. On the one hand, this is a natural condition of being newcomers. More serious, however, are the contradictory functions that define new media. The new media are faced with a conundrum. They cannot simultaneously be commercial and entertainment-oriented as well as populist in more than rhetoric. As a result, populism is usually sacrificed to commercial and entertainment imperatives. Hence, we argue that although the new media have already, and yet will, reshape the way politics operates in the United

States in the realms of campaigns, governance, and citizenship, they do not represent, as is sometimes claimed, a newly populist media destined to revolutionize political participation.

Outline of the Book

This book is organized to address the following broad questions: What are the new media? What effects do they have on the political process? What does the future portend for American democracy in a new media age?

Even before these questions are answered, we raise another point: Why have the new media even become an issue? In other words, what forces have produced a role for the new media in American politics? Chapter 2, "An Environment for New Media," offers explanations for the rise of the new media.

Part I: The Role and Content of New Media

In this part, we discuss three types of new media in depth. Chapter 3, "Talking Politics," addresses the content of talk radio. How much of it is political? What do talk radio hosts and callers say about politics? Who sets the agenda for talk radio politics, and how is that done? Chapter 4, "Showing Politics," turns to the political role of tabloid journalism and entertainment television such as public affairs/entertainment programs and docudramas. Chapter 5, "Typing Politics," discusses the role of computer networks in facilitating political discussion and information as well as establishing a new communications link between public officials, candidates, and the public.

Part II: The Audiences and Effects of New Media

The audiences for new media are large and highly diversified. More than four of ten Americans say they listen to talk radio at least some of the time.[63] An estimated 20 million listeners tune in regularly to the Rush Limbaugh show. The *National Enquirer* boasts a weekly circulation that exceeds that of *Time, Newsweek,* and *U.S. News and World Report.*[64] The audience for television news magazines is substantial. The CBS program "60 Minutes" has been the top-rated television program in the nation and, nearly thirty years after its debut, still often falls among the top ten most watched programs in a week. Yet "60 Minutes" has been replaced by "Dateline," a more overtly entertainment focused offering, as the most popular television news magazine.

In this part, we turn to the effects of new media. Chapter 6, "The Audiences," explores who listens to, reads, and watches new media and why they do so. What type of person is most likely to listen to talk radio, watch MTV, or use other forms of new media? What are the motivations for using new media, and what kinds of gratifications are received for doing so? Is the audience attracted to new media primarily as entertainment, or are new media more comprehensible sources of political information than the traditional media? Is the primary motive opinion articulation and reinforcement, which may not be achieved with traditional media exposure?

We will argue that the audiences for particular new media are specialized in terms of their characteristics. People who listen regularly to talk radio, for example, differ in their demographic characteristics and political orientations from those who use online media. Further, we will demonstrate that coinciding with the rise in new media is a new set of audience expectations about political communication. These options, such as the ability to take part actively in mediated public discussions, are facilitated through new media and new technologies, such as online resources. These new uses and gratifications of mass media are in part responsible for the new media's success. However, public perceptions about the new media's ability to facilitate discourse that genuinely furthers democratic goals may be somewhat idealized.

In chapter 7, "Audience Attitudes," we address the new media's effects on the audiences' political knowledge, attitudes, and activities. Given the specialized nature of the audiences for particular new media, we anticipate that people who regularly are exposed to a specific new media format will exhibit similar political orientations. Thus we compared the audiences for talk radio, television news magazines, and online media in relation to the following questions: Do people learn about politics from new media? Are people who regularly attend to new media more knowledgeable about politics than the general public? What do new media users feel about established political institutions such as political parties and governmental organizations? Do new media feed public cynicism and further alienate people from politics and government? Are new media users more or less likely to participate in the political process than other citizens?

The empirical research on the new media's effects on audiences is still in an embryonic stage. However, new media promoters and observers have made claims of significant political influence. For example, according to MTV, the network's Rock the Vote campaign increased voter registration among young people during the 1992 presidential campaign. The cable network claimed it got more than 120,000 phone calls during a single two-hour period from young people asking details about voter registration.[65] Some politicians also are quick to credit the new media with enormous political influence. Vice President Al Gore credited MTV with securing the Democratic victory in the 1992 presidential contest.[66] Speaker Newt Gingrich was convinced that talk radio made a difference in the 1994 Republican congressional takeover. A goal of this section is to examine whether claims about the influence of new media are warranted.

Part III: Effects of New Media on Traditional Media, Campaigns, and Public Policy

In Part III, we explore the ways in which new media have influenced the political media environment. Chapter 8, "Shaping Old Media," examines in greater detail the effects new media have on the style and content of the traditional media. Chapter 9, "Shaping Presidential Campaigns," reviews the role of the new media in the electoral process, particularly during presidential campaigns. We begin with a discussion of some major trends in the mass media election campaign, such as the increased focus on media campaign strategies and candidates' personal lives as well as the shrinking sound bite. These factors set the scene for the new media's arrival in presidential electoral politics. We examine how particular types of new media—talk programs, MTV, and online media—have come to play a major role in elections. We argue that the new media have quickly become absorbed into the campaign process to the extent that their presence is no longer remarkable, but instead is established. Although talk formats, tabloids, and town meetings entered the campaign media mix in 1992, 1996 was a watershed year for online media. We will conclude with some speculations about the role of new media in future campaigns.

The final chapter of this section, "Shaping the Policy Agenda," analyzes the new media's influence on the nation's policy agenda as well as the policy-making process. Talk radio hosts have been active in national public policy debates. Their involvement has been most intense and monolithic on positions viewed as clearly populist and anti-establishment.

But do new media affect public policy? If they do have an effect, is it because new media mobilize their audiences, as some talk radio hosts claim? Or do policymakers act because they anticipate public reaction or interpret expressions of opinion through the new media as public opinion? The new media have become widely accepted as a potent political force, at least by many politicians. As demonstrated above, politicians appear on such programs. They also frequently call in to talk radio shows.[67] They participate in electronic town meetings as a means of reaching constituents. But is this more a perception of power than a reality?

Conclusion

In the concluding chapter, "Popular Voice or Demagogic Tool," we review the arguments about whether or not new media outlets make positive contributions to political discourse. We will present alternative perspectives on the implications of the new media phenomenon.

Proponents of new media, some within the ranks of new media

practioners themselves, claim that these formats have the potential to foster democratic ideals by promoting participation among citizens across social, economic, racial, and ethnic strata. In the current situation, surrogates—political elites, media elites, pundits, pollsters, and a small active segment of the population—speak most often for the general public in political affairs.[68] New media can work to reinvigorate citizenship by placing politics on the agenda in a manner that is accessible to average Americans. They can reach out to those poorly represented in society and bring them into the political process. By stimulating interest in things political and by allowing the voices of citizens to be heard and their faces to be seen in the governmental arena, greater participation in politics can result. The increase in turnout during the 1992 presidential contest, the first new media election, is cited as evidence of the possibilities for enhanced democratic participation that these media innovations can hold.[69]

Yet, our review of the evidence leads us to contend that the commercial imperatives behind new media overshadow their potential to become a democratizing force in the American polity. In fairness, this may not be their role, although some new media practitioners like to claim that they are responsible for a new wave of democratic populism. At the current stage of their evolution, new media are not committed to playing a responsible and established part in fostering citizen engagement. They are unpredictable in their political roles, and fail to offer the public truly meaningful ways of becoming more fully integrated into political affairs.

An Environment for New Media

Historically, the American media have undergone distinct periods of intense, almost cyclical transition. The media continually are reacting and adapting to changes in technological, economic market, cultural, and political forces. The changes within the media business that the United States now is experiencing represent yet another stage in an ongoing process of journalistic evolution.

The current news industry environment has nurtured and sustained the new media revolution. In this chapter, we examine the economic, social, and political influences that have caused the traditional media to change course and to alter their role in the American political system. At the same time, we will explore how these factors have allowed the new media to insert themselves into the process.

The new media have flourished in a news industry environment where the fundamental operating principles have changed dramatically. Most important, news is moving further away from the public service tradition. Instead, news organizations' bottom line is now profit. Further changes have been prompted by advances in communications technology. In addition, news organizations must keep pace with changing demographic trends, such as the increase in two-career families. They must adapt to more volatile personal schedules and more varied news needs and tastes.

The Evolution of the News Business

Before we examine the current state of affairs, a brief historical tour of the news industry is in order. Milestones in American media history, as we have noted, have occurred during periods of technological, economic, and sociocultural upheaval, which prompted alterations in the media environment. Traditional journalism has undergone waves of change throughout its history as an independent force in the American political system.

The elite or partisan press dominated American journalism in the early days of the republic. Because type was set by hand, printing was expensive and time-consuming. Thus newspapers and tracts served educated and wealthier men who were either merchants or political activists. News reporting and news gathering as we know it today were virtually unheard of, as was the journalistic norm of objectivity. Specific newspapers were associated directly with particular political parties or leaders. The news, usually in the form of carefully crafted essays, editorials, or announcements, was brought to printers who copied it verbatim and disseminated it to paying subscribers.

The transition from the elite/partisan press to the penny press, which occurred around 1833 with the publication of the *New York Sun,* was precipitated by industrialization, advances in communication technology, and higher literacy rates among the mass public. The profit motive was a driving force behind this transition to a populist press. This period is known as the "commercial revolution" in American journalism. Industrialization had created a need to market goods produced in factories. The penny press survived and flourished by maintaining a high circulation and through promoting advertising. The penny price made newspapers affordable to middle- and working-class citizens.[1]

A flurry of technological innovations permitted this media transformation to take place. Better printing presses allowed more information to be conveyed to more people at a faster pace. In addition, paper production methods improved, increasing availability and decreasing price. Mass circulation, as well as paper production, was facilitated by the development of rail transportation. Finally, the invention of the telegraph in the 1840s revolutionized reporting, as news from faraway places could be gathered quickly.

The effects of technology combined with an increase in literacy rates to create an environment that encouraged the growth of the penny press. Reporters were hired to gather the news. The mass readership base had different tastes in news than that presented by the elite press. As media scholar Michael Schudson notes, news readers were unsophisticated and "their tastes tended to be simple, concrete, particular, and local."[2] Human interest stories and community news were especially appealing to this audience, opening the door for "yellow journalism."

Political factors also came into play in the development of the penny press. A more populist political environment, with an emphasis on the common man and equality of economic opportunity, epitomized the era of "Jacksonian Democracy." The party system was no longer the exclusive bastion of the privileged class. Parties accommodated average citizens, as voting rights were extended beyond white, male landowners. Newspapers began to reflect these political trends and brought political issues of concern to the mass public to prominence. The tradition of "muckraking"—investigative journalism aimed at exposing corruption—grew out of these circumstances. Reporters made their mark by exposing the stark and often bitter realities of urban life and industrialization. Newspapers played a central role in forwarding the Progressive agenda for political reform that developed by the 1890s. "Yellow journalism," a forerunner of the current tabloid-style reporting, was leaving its imprint on the news scene at about this same time. This type of reporting was characterized by a blatant disregard for facts and an emphasis on sensationalism.

Following the era of "yellow journalism," journalists strove for a role as the objective observer of public, including political, life. Their purpose was to record, not to interpret, events as accurately as possible. The reader would be the analyst, not the journalist. This change in the nature of news and the role of reporters was necessitated by the outbreak of World War I. With so many American citizens serving overseas, newspapers needed to provide accurate information about the war and foreign affairs as well as about developments on the home front. This period is marked by the elevation of journalism to the ranks of a profession governed by standards, in particular, objectivity and ethical codes. Journalism schools were established to provide formal training for reporters, and professional organizations were formed.[3]

Radio and, subsequently, television's emergence as news media enhanced the validity of the professional school approach to journalism. Once again, technological advances prompted significant changes in the media environment that influenced the way news was reported. Print reporters had to compete for attention with an audience that was fascinated by television. At the same time, newspaper reporters needed to be accurate recorders of events because viewers could check the veracity of the printed word through television. The audience perceived that the new electronic media were offering unfiltered news. With television, particularly, viewers could see events for themselves without the screening of print journalists.

The journalist as neutral observer definition underwent a transformation in the 1960s and 1970s, although the transition had been in progress for several decades.[4] Many journalists derided the objective role as mere stenography. Even worse, they argued, this role could lead to abuse of the press by politicians. If the press dutifully reported what politicians said without analysis or correction, the public would be deceived and the press would serve as accomplices in the deed. Advocates for a more active role for journalists in conveying the news pointed to the press' stenographic reporting of Senator Joseph Mc-Carthy's communist witch hunt in the 1950s as evidence of the need for an active, interpretive journalistic role.

Television's influence on the news industry and the way it covered politics cannot be overstated. As is the case with the new communications technologies present in the media market today, television forced established media to alter the style and content of their coverage. As television receivers proliferated during the 1950s and 1960s, television news anchors and reporters became well-known personalities in most American homes. Print reporters, in an effort to remain viable in a media environment that was becoming increasingly dominated by television, developed a more aggressive stance in covering the news.

The rise of investigative journalism was aided by critical political events in the 1960s and 1970s. The turbulent political culture of this period provided much raw material to satiate reporters' need for news, and warranted a change in approach. A credibility gap arose from the disparities between the government's promise of a quick end to the Vietnam War and the continuation of the war. Journalists began to doubt the wisdom of the government's policies, and by 1967 news coverage began to acquire an antiwar tinge.[5]

Another cataclysmic event in journalism history was Watergate. The *Washington Post's* investigative reporting of the Watergate scandal produced widespread acknowledgment of the press' role as a public trustee. Press vitality in covering politics suddenly acquired salience in the effective continuance of a democratic political system.

Journalists' definition of their role changed, in part, because journalists themselves changed. Journalism as a career began to attract large numbers of young people. They were lured by the glamour of journalism. Unlike previous generations, however, these newcomers entered journalism through college journalism programs rather than by serving as apprentices. Journalism soon became a haven for professional writers who held college degrees. These reporters were as well, if not better, educated than the political leaders they covered.

Journalists also began to acquire the mantle of expertise on various issues. As news media organizations faced the coverage of complicated policy issues in the 1960s and 1970s, they created issue beats in areas such as science, space, energy, the environment, and economics. They assigned reporters to cover these issues, and these reporters quickly gained reputations as specialists. Specialists were responsible for explaining complex issues to the general public. Reporters increasingly viewed their task as explicating events and issues of the day, not just describing them. Critics contend that when journalists assume the role of experts they drive a wedge between the public and government leaders by cutting citizens out of meaningful dialogue about policy issues.[6]

The creation of a star system within broadcasting also elevated the status of individual journalists as players in the process, not just recorders of events. Well-known news broadcasters began to acquire a level of name recognition and influence known only to a few national elected officials and Hollywood personalities. A 1985 survey found more people recognized Barbara Walters than the 1984 Democratic vice presidential candidate Geraldine Ferraro.[7]

Recognition was not the only product. Star journalists had the potential to use their recognition to attempt to wield influence. In 1968 Walter Cronkite used several minutes of a "CBS Evening News" broadcast to proclaim the Vietnam War unwinnable and to advocate a negotiated peace. In 1977 Barbara Walters served a policy role in solving the Middle East crisis by urging the leaders of Israel and Europe to meet with each other.

Greater national exposure via television, higher social status, the possession of expertise on complicated issues, widespread public recognition and influence, and acceptance of a role as a political presence to safeguard the public's interest emboldened journalists to change their roles from neutral observers of political events to analysts/interpreters and, in some cases, even advocates of various ideologies or, at least, policy options. As a result, news content began to include more interpretation and less description.[8] According to political scientist Thomas Patterson, journalists today are far more likely than their colleagues of the 1960s to set the tone for stories. In addition, political leaders speak for themselves, rather than through mainstream reporters, far less frequently today than in the past.[9]

The rise in interpretive content has been accompanied, if not facilitated, by a compression of the message by politicians. Obviously, assuming the existence of a finite amount of space, a natural outgrowth of an increase in interpretive content would be a decline in the amount of time devoted to politicians or other sources. Moreover, if journalists allow too much of politicians' messages to be transmitted then the press may be viewed as "shilling" for the politicians.

Further, most television news formats do not easily accommodate more than short news reports. In turn, politicians have increasingly practiced news management techniques designed to tailor their messages to conform to the requirements of television. The result is the shrinking sound bite, as politicians' statements are abridged into ever smaller snippets.

This trend has occurred simultaneously with a compression in the overall length of daily newspaper and evening news stories. The number of column inches print reporters are allocated for stories has been shrinking as advertising consumes an increasing amount of space. In addition, print stories are shorter in order to fit more stories into an issue and to maintain the interest of video-age readers who are intimidated by lengthy articles. Television news stories similarly have shrunk in size in order to accommodate more segments and contain more graphic accompaniments to maintain viewer interest. In turn, journalists have further condensed their sources' comments, but not their own interpretations.

At the same time, personal character became a newsworthy item in political reporting. Personality always has constituted a portion of reporting about politicians. The difference is that by the 1980s, personality, as defined by journalists and not by the politicians themselves, had become a central component of political news. The role of personality in campaign reporting is especially pervasive, as we shall discuss in chapter 9.

The movement toward character reporting, with its accent on scandal, proliferated because it reinforced the journalistic role as public trustee. It also conformed neatly with a bottom line approach to news, as it carried the potential to increase audience share among those less interested in politics. However, character reporting also eased journalists' task. Instead of concentrating on complicated policy issues, they could report on character.

The change in the journalists' view of their role has been accompanied by a veritable explosion in interpretive reporting. News media have proliferated with cable and satellite, which has produced twenty-four-hour news networks, all-news radio stations, national newspapers, and lengthy network and affiliate television news programs from early in the morning, through midday, and on into the night. It was not until 1963 that network news broadcasts expanded from fifteen minutes to thirty. Now, for the 60 percent of the nation that subscribes to cable, local, national, and international news and public affairs programming is available on demand at any time of day. It is within this environment of media riches that the new media revolution has taken shape. As we shall see, this latest phase in the history of mass communications is the result of economic incentives, the legal environment, new technologies, American life-styles, cultural tastes, and political orientations.

News for Profit

Perhaps more than any other factor, economic incentives have encouraged the rise of new media. As we have seen, the profit motive is nothing new in American journalism. Its roots were firmly planted in the 1830s. Throughout much of this century, however, traditional news organizations prioritized their public service obligation. Family-owned newspapers' commitment to providing readers quality news outweighed pure financial concerns.[10] Broadcast networks originated news programming to fulfill public service obligations as holders of public licenses. News shows were supported by the more profitable entertainment programming. Documentaries aired during prime time offered public affairs programming, but did not raise revenue.

By the 1980s, economic considerations loomed large in all sectors of the news industry. The cost of covering, producing, and disseminating news increased, as audience expectations rose. New technologies, such as computers, color presses, satellite transmission, and minicams, allowed for a more vibrant, exciting news product to satisfy public tastes. The acquisition of these technologies, however, placed a heavy financial burden on traditional news organizations. Even local newspapers and television stations were expected to invest in new equipment. Local television affiliates prepared to cover breaking news live.

A major shift altering the traditional media's role in politics is the profitability of news. The news media's potential as profit-making ventures had been downplayed when public service norms dominated the business. Over the past two decades, the potential for newspaper and television news to record significant earnings for their parent companies has been demonstrated, even as the news business experiences periods of financial boom and bust. Even all-news radio has emerged as a stable and highly profitable enterprise.[11] Once the profit potential of news was realized, the traditional norms and values that had governed the business disintegrated. For some press practitioners and observers, the substitution of the profit motive for public interest signals a crisis for professional journalism.

Newspapers

The newspaper industry was the first to feel the pressure to be profitable or face extinction. Traditionally, newspapers in the United States had been family-owned ventures that prided themselves on their independence and strong community roots. The newspaper business took a long range view of its financial status. Newspapers would experience financial ups and downs, and they would use revenues from the good times to keep afloat during crises. Journalist James Squires describes the newspaper business in the decade before profit-induced changes were set in motion:

> The newspapers were making money in the 1960s, but none of us knew how much, or cared. To the bliss-minded ignoramus of the typewriter, the salient fact of newspaper economics was that the good ones profited less than the bad ones because good journalism costs more. Even the old journalist-proprietors agreed that the definition of "quality" journalism was journalism practiced selflessly in the public interest. Their elite huddled together in the front seats at the newspaper publisher meetings and looked down their noses at the merely profit-minded.[12]

Marked changes in the newspaper business began to occur during the 1970s, however. Newspapers experienced a decline in their market penetration for only the second time in history. The Great Depression and the advent of radio in the 1930s resulted in a temporary decline in readership. By 1972 television's effects on newspapers' market share were being felt. Changing demographics also adversely affected the newspaper business. As more and better-educated people moved to the suburbs, city papers lost readers. More people were commuting to work by car and found it easier to get their news from television or radio. As a result, the afternoon newspaper disappeared from most markets.[13] In addition, inheritance taxes made it difficult for families to pass newspapers on without going public with their businesses. This paved the way for outside investors to buy out family papers.

The conglomerization trend in the newspaper business was initiated by Gannett Company under the auspices of Al Neuharth. Neuharth presented the newspaper business to Wall Street investors as "a dependable profit machine in good times or bad."[14] Large companies, such as Gannett and Knight-Ridder, which had other media and corporate holdings, bought out newspapers at an amazing rate. The number of media markets with competing daily newspapers diminished significantly through mergers or collapse. Los Angeles, the nation's second-largest media market, housed only a single daily newspaper by 1990.[15]

The corporate newspaper has substantially different goals than the independent, family-owned newspaper. Corporations do not distinguish between newspapers and any other business enterprise. The goal is to make money; serving the public interest is only incidental to the enterprise. Prior to corporatization, newspapers were satisfied with a 10 percent profit margin in good times in a competitive market. Monopoly markets are far more conducive to profit-making. A corporate newspaper operating in a monopoly market is expected to earn profits in the 20 to 35 percent range in an average year. Interestingly, between 1969 and 1990, profit margins rose as readership declined.[16] Newspaper penetration of American households did not keep pace with their growing numbers, although circulation remained robust enough to sustain profits. The number of households in the United States grew by more than 40 percent between 1970 and 1990, while daily newspaper circulation rose by only 1 percent.[17] When competition is eliminated, newspapers have little incentive to improve or even to maintain a quality product as long as profits are guaranteed.

Competitive, family-owned newspapers sought to reach as many readers as possible as part of their community service ethic. In order to maximize their appeal to advertisers, corporate newspapers prefer to target select audiences, consisting of people aged twenty-five to fifty who fall into the upper echelons of education and income. The size of the news hole in papers has been steadily shrinking in recent years, as more space is devoted to advertising. While readers receive less news, they have been paying more for newspapers.

The newspaper industry fell on hard times during the 1990–92 recession. Papers closed down, as advertising revenues dried up and readership fell off sharply. The newspaper business responded to this crisis by laying off personnel and cutting back even further on the amount of news they reported. The industry also stepped up its market research efforts in order to better target their advertising audiences. As a result, newspapers are now driven more by market researchers' assessments of public tastes than by the editorial opinions of editors and reporters.[18]

This trend has contributed to newspapers' greater focus on entertainment. Although most readers claim to want more news about local events, newspapers have enhanced their entertainment offerings to meet what news organizations believe people actually read.[19] Efforts to target specific types of consumers, such as women and young people, have caused newspapers to incorporate specialty sections, such as life-style and food sections, into their product. Life-style and entertainment sections are more compatible with marketing consumer goods such as clothing and cars than are hard news sections.

The wall that divided the editorial side from the business side of the newspaper industry has broken down.[20] Management invests little in investigative journalism. Reporters increasingly come from prestigious journalism schools, and no longer have close community ties. They adopt a play-it-safe attitude in their reporting in order to avoid offending readers or a business interest that is owned by the paper's parent company.

It is clear that the newspaper industry in the post–public service period has experienced profound changes. Newspapers have become more uniform, risk-averse, and national in scope. Yet it can be argued that the adjustment in orientation may have been necessary in order to rescue the printed page from oblivion in a market saturated by electronic communications options. Even so, electronic media were not immune to the effects of profit-seeking in the communications industry.

Television News

Television news has gone through many of the same experiences that newspapers have in the for-profit era, although they were initiated about a decade later. Ownership of television news organizations has been concentrated in fewer hands. Big corporations with multifaceted holdings, such as Disney and General Electric, control major television news stations. Newscasts have been "reinvented" to meet bottom lines, shifting to a greater focus on "infotainment." The result, according to media scholar Edwin Diamond, has been "a news report of lowered aspirations."[21]

Until the 1980s, newscasts were not subject to ratings by organizations such as Nielson. They were exempt because of their public service status and the fact that management felt that news programs gave their networks an aura of respectability. There was little else occupying the evening news times slots, so the network news programs essentially competed among themselves.

Television experienced a period of deregulation during the Reagan years, which altered the environment within which news programs operated. News organizations were no longer a required public service function of the networks. Networks did not risk having their licenses revoked by the Federal Communications Commission (FCC) if they did not dedicate air time to public service. As media critic Jon Katz notes, advertisers became less willing to sponsor news programs as news ceased to function as an ethical rationale for broadcasting.[22]

During the 1980s, the three major networks were acquired by corporations who sought to control costs by cutting by staff and resources. The news product was downsized—or "streamlined," as managers prefer to call it—resulting in less extensive and rich coverage of national and international events.[23] The salaries for well-known anchors and reporters soared, as bidding wars were waged over on-air talent. At the same time, funds for reporting were restricted.

Once the networks found their news divisions could be profitable entities, the race was on for audience ratings. In order to attract larger audiences, formats had to appeal to viewers less interested in politics. Broadcast news, both at the network and affiliate levels, experimented with various formats to attract audience ratings—dual anchors, "happy talk," exclusively positive news, investigative reporting divisions. At the network level, last-ranked ABC News, led by Roone Arledge, aggressively stole journalists from the other two major networks.

News increasingly became a packaged entertainment product rather than print journalism with video, which had characterized early television news. Gradually the print journalists who had populated the ranks of broadcast news were replaced by young reporters fresh from college broadcasting programs. Also, news program executives were increasingly drawn from backgrounds other than news such as business.

However, television news programs have not been immune to changes in the media market. Given CNN, MSNBC, and the growing number of news program alternatives, audiences with heavy work and home responsibilities do not find fixed-time news programs as attractive as they once were. The networks have not kept pace with innovations in news reporting styles and substance. Old-style anchor formats are becoming the dinosaurs of the news business, as more exciting, on-the-spot reporting takes its place. Hard-hitting policy debates and interactive discussions are not accommodated on nightly news broadcasts. This increased competition and shifting consumer demand has hurt the profitability of network news shows. Some analysts contend that there may not be room for more than one fixed-time network news broadcast in the current media marketplace.[24] Others maintain that the three national newscasts will survive by adapting to changes in the media environment, as has been the case historically.[25]

Defining What's News

As the professional values that permeate the news industry in the current era have changed fundamentally from public service to for-profit broadcasts, the very definition of what constitutes news has been altered. News used to be defined by editors and reporters as current information that is necessary and important for the public to know. News was linked to an actual event or happening.

Today, the definition of news is more malleable and is determined to a large extent by market forces. In fact, even veteran journalists have difficulty agreeing on the definition of news in the current environment. News today is event-driven, but it also involves the reporting of public service information, human interest stories, and data-based trends that need not be late-breaking. An increasing proportion of the news product is manufactured. For example, public opinion polls provide the impetus for a large number of news stories. These stories may or may not be linked to a current event. Poll stories can be more economical for news organizations to report than event stories, which require dispatching reporters and equipment to cover them.

In the "news for profit" environment, the media have enlisted the help of public relations and market research experts employing survey research and focus groups techniques to better target their news products. News management does not rely on the talents of a better educated, more diverse class of professional journalists to decide what is news. Further, there is a fear that news content and critique may be limited by the requirement that it not offend the media organization's corporate partners.

The Legal Environment

The rise of new media, particularly talk radio, was furthered by the deregulatory attitude toward communications policy during the 1980s. Public service requirements, obscenity regulations, and ownership limitations all were reduced.[26] The FCC relaxed its standards for licensing, permitting companies to acquire more media properties, which contributed to the proliferation of media forums.

The most dramatic change, however, was the repeal of the Fairness Doctrine in 1987. Adopted in 1949, the Fairness Doctrine required broadcasters to provide a reasonable balance when airing controversial issues. This balance could be achieved by airing opposing viewpoints over the course of several months, but it still acted as something of a check on media one-sidedness.

Freed from the confines of presenting both sides of an issue, broadcast stations were able to air unbalanced programming. Radio and television talk hosts and commentators could express bias without any legal requirement for opposing views to be aired. Prime time public affairs programs could express opinions without worrying about accommodating opponents. Of course, the marketplace still inhibited news organizations from being blatantly one-sided in their reporting. Prior to repeal of the Fairness Doctrine, however, station management was more interested in avoiding controversial issues than in ceding time to various groups. This policy change was not insignificant. For example, political talk radio as it exists today has flourished since the demise of the Fairness Doctrine. However, the astronomical rise of conservative talk radio has prompted some Democrats and liberals to call for a reinstatement of the rule. To date, these efforts have been futile.[27]

Technological Change

As has been the case historically, changes in the media environment invariably have coincided with significant advances in communications technology. Something of a technological revolution has been unfolding globally for the past decade. A plethora of devices—computers, fax machines, cellular phones, and pagers—that enhance the speed, facility, and diversity of communications options have become commonplace. In addition to enhancing the ability to convey information, new technologies have enabled the media to heighten the aesthetic quality of their products through the use of high-quality graphic and audio enhancements. Further, new technologies have altered the ways in which the public receives and experiences political media.

Effects on the Media

Technological innovations have defined and influenced the new media's place in politics as they have redefined the traditional press' role. Some of the effects of technology on the current media environment have worked to transform the business fundamentally. The introduction of satellite technology, for example, has made real-time newscasts possible, treating television news viewers to the high drama of events, such as the Gulf War and the O. J. Simpson car chase, as they unfold. Reporters face new challenges, as they cannot employ the usual fact-checking and source validation techniques that are established journalistic practices when they must report the news as it happens.

Other effects of technology have been more subtle. Once the

province of business, cellular telephones have moved swiftly into broader consumer use. Participating in a radio call-in program has been facilitated by the burgeoning use of cellular telephones. Cell phones have enabled people to call from any location, including their cars when they are stuck in freeway traffic. According to Boston talk show host David Brudnoy the cellular phone has attracted "upscale" callers, business executives who are "floating around in their cars, thirsty for involvement."[28]

Effects on the Audience

Increasingly, Americans seek solitary or family leisure time options rather than the mass entertainment of the past. Technology, coupled with the breakdown of strong community ties that has accompanied today's more hectic and complicated life-styles, has hastened this mass propensity toward "cocooning" in the privacy of one's own home. The proliferation of video tapes and laser discs, as well as home entertainment centers with large-screen television sets and high-quality sound systems that mimic the motion picture effect, has led to a reduction in entertainment in large group settings.

New media use has become an integral part of the search for solitary entertainment. New media are more individually oriented media than other entertainment forms such as motion pictures, concerts, or live theater. Talk radio, particularly, is a highly solitary medium for entertainment. At the same time, talk radio, Internet chat groups, and other interactive communication formats meet individuals' need to belong in society. They foster the formation of pseudocommunities among the insular masses.

Social Change

Life-style

The life-styles of many Americans facilitate new media usage. The increase in the number of working women, the rise in two income families, and hectic work schedules that no longer conform to the traditional nine-to-five pattern are driving some old media formats toward obsolescence. As we have discussed, fixed-time newscasts, which are the staple of the major networks, are no longer strongly viable. The public is turning increasingly to "'round the clock" news options such as CNN, or cable programs.[29]

Citizens are becoming more eclectic in their media use habits and are using information sources that conform to their routines. The average American spends more than forty minutes commuting to work each day.[30] When many commuters used mass transit, as opposed to driving cars, they could read the daily newspaper on the way to work.[31] With the increase in commuting and the length of time the average commuter spends in the car, talk radio offers a listening alternative to music or news. Talk radio audiences who appear to be more intellectually challenged by talk than the standard fare of music are almost captives in their automobiles. The substantial number of callers using car phones provides some evidence that commuters are paying attention to talk radio programs as they ride to and from work. In addition, when tired commuters return home at the end of the day, they may be less likely to settle down to read the evening paper, but instead tune into some form of news on television as their main source of information.

The type of jobs Americans hold has contributed to changing media use patterns as well. The growing professional and service sector, unlike manufacturing, allows time for radio listening. More than one-half of adult Americans say they have a radio at work, and more than 90 percent say they listen to the radio either daily or every weekday.[32] Living arrangements also may contribute to the prevalence of new media. Talk radio may have become more popular because of the large number of Americans who live alone and use talk shows to keep them company. Similarly, the Internet allows individuals to hold conversations with people many miles away from home or work.

Popular Tastes

Coinciding with the transformation in life-style patterns is a change in the public's cultural preferences. Facilitated by an ever-expanding world of technological gadgetry, society today operates at a far faster pace than it did even a decade ago. Information is available in an increasing array of forms and formats, many of them new media. The challenge for citizens is not to find enough information about politics, but to avoid being overwhelmed by a glut of information.

Busier and better-educated Americans have less tolerance for traditional-style media than in the past. Citizens value their leisure time and would prefer that the news be delivered to them quickly and manageably, when and where they want it. Newspaper reading and even network news watching is on the decline, especially among the younger segments of society.[33] Continuous television news programs, all-news radio, and the Internet meet these needs.

The style of much of American news has become faster-paced, fragmented, and personalized. This style conforms to the expectations of a society whose collective attention span has shortened notably. New-style news is part of a larger cultural trend that is evident in entertainment television programming, film, music, novels, magazines, and art. The public gravitates toward news that is presented with the style and feel of MTV, Arnold Schwartzenegger blockbusters, and *People* magazine—news that grabs attention, makes its point quickly, and moves on to the next topic. The entertainment value of new media is a significant draw for audiences whose free time is at a premium, yet who also want to keep informed.

At the same time, Americans are demanding that news coverage be more sophisticated and complete. Especially since CNN's coverage of the Gulf War, the public has become accustomed to up-to-the-minute reports on late-breaking events. Journalists are expected to provide news analysis, and not just to report the facts. The challenge for the news industry is to strike the correct balance between reporting and analyzing, so as not to alienate either the newsmakers, such as candidates, or their audiences.

Reconciling the competing trends of fast-paced, easily consumable, and entertaining news with sophisticated news has challenged media organizations. It has prompted diversification of the news product by established media organizations and has helped new media to flourish. As we shall see in chapter 4, one outgrowth of these trends has been the proliferation of television news magazines on the major networks. In a prior news era, documentaries, and not news magazines, would have provided careful analyses of important events and issues.[34] News magazines both compliment and compete with established news programs. They can provide deeper coverage of topics raised on the nightly news. At the same time, they have the potential to erode the audience base for traditional coverage, as their flashier style conforms to the new norms of audience expectations.

Political Factors

Politicians' Reaction

The new media's infiltration of the political world has been fostered and legitimated by politicians. Tired of struggling with the mainstream press over control of political messages, politicians have turned to the new media so that they can tell their stories in their own words. The fact that political leaders, including President Clinton, court the new media and pay attention to what is being presented in these venues has allowed the new media to gain in political legitimacy. In fact, there is some evidence that legislators and White House insiders use talk shows to gauge public opinion.[35] The Internet, with its interactive capability, increasingly will play this role as well.

Especially during the television age, politicians and the traditional media have engaged in an uneasy game of tug-of-war to determine who would maintain the most control over news content. Politicians have developed sophisticated media management techniques designed to package information in ways that are easily palatable and appealing to reporters, and conform to the technical requirements of their trade. Dramatic pseudoevents that provide political actors the opportunity to utter the requisite sound bites are staged continually and are timed to permit journalists to meet their deadlines.

The winner of the struggle for control has changed intermittently. At the time of the 1992 presidential campaign, however, the balance of power appeared to have shifted to the mainstream media. The press had become almost relentless in its investigations into politicians' character, engaging in what political scientist Larry Sabato calls "junkyard dog journalism."[36] Further, as we have noted, politicians found that their own sound bites were shrinking, while press commentary was increasing.[37] Not only do politicians chafe at journalistic compression of their message but also at its distortion as it passes through the filter of the news reporting process.

Despite the fact that more reporters covered them than had ever done so in political campaigns, and despite the proliferation of news channels with an insatiable appetite for news, by 1992 presidential candidates were seeking alternative means to reach voters. The search was on for media that would not compress their message nor distort it. Better yet, if politicians could find alternative media that did not have the critical approach characteristic of the traditional campaign press corps, their messages would be transmitted without the assumption that it was the product of crass political motives.

The new media have the potential of meeting these goals. New media allow politicians to bypass the traditional press and deliver their messages directly to the public. Research indicates that politicians, when given the opportunity to write their own media scripts, emphasize their own moral self-worth more than their knowledge of politics or personal characteristics.[38] Politicians also can engage in direct dialogue with citizens via talk shows and electronic town meetings. New media hosts, such as Larry King, regularly invite political leaders to appear on their shows. Politicians tend to receive somewhat more friendly treatment when they make personal appearances on new media programs than they do from the mainstream press.

Political leaders realize, however, that the new media can be a double-edged sword. Although President Clinton benefited from new media coverage during the 1994 presidential election, he has suffered its barbs while occupying the White House. On occasion, he has publicly chastised some talk radio hosts and and certain Internet groups for contributing to the public's disillusionment with politics. Thus while new media have allowed politicians greater freedom of expression, new media also are an effective outlet for voicing discontent.

Public Dissatisfaction

Politicians have not been the only ones unhappy with the traditional news media's current role. According to surveys, the public has become disenchanted with media coverage of politics.[39] The press is

perceived as being too adversarial, too cynical, and obsessed with issues of character. It is viewed by a majority of the public as driving
stories on scandal rather than merely reporting them.[40]

Aggravating the problem is the press' rejection of much of this
criticism. Most journalists, unlike a majority of the general public, do
not believe they focus too much on public officials' misdeeds or that
they are too adversarial. A majority, however, admit they may be too
cynical.[41]

Another problem is the remoteness of the press' political coverage to people's lives. David Broder argues people don't find politics
meaningful, at least as it is treated by the press during elections, "because there is no real connection between their concerns in their daily
lives and what they hear talked about and see reported by the press in
most political campaigns."[42]

Perhaps to no one's surprise, people rank their local television
news programs higher than network news.[43] Such programs provide
news that viewers consider to be more relevant to their concerns.
However, since the 1980s, the distinction between local and network
newscasts increasingly has become blurred, as local programs contain
more national and international news.[44]

One component of this dissatisfaction is the perception of media
bias.[45] Most people fault the press for not adequately separating reporting from commentary.[46] There is also public concern that journalists' own worldviews shape too much of what they write. For example, according to a Times Mirror survey, the vast majority of the
public believe reporters' own social and cultural values make it difficult for them to report about religion or family values.[47] Further, political scientist Susan Herbst discovered that a substantial number of
talk radio callers phone in to "police" the public sphere, to correct biases in information and broaden the scope of discourse.[48]

This public dissatisfaction does not necessarily mean people have
turned away from the news media, although there has been a decline
in newspaper readership and network television news viewing. It
means they are disgruntled with what they see or hear, and they may
be receptive to alternative media forums offering more of what they
want in terms of news and information.

News media organizations should be concerned that readers and
viewers actually may not be there in the future. The problem is that
the bulk of the future audience consists of today's young people, who
are, as a group, less aware of and less interested in politics. Those under the age of thirty-five today are much less likely than their parents
at that same age to read a daily newspaper or watch television news.
Their interest in news is greatest for wars or youth-related news, such
as the anniversary of Woodstock or the student revolt at Tiananmen
Square.[49] People under age thirty may be following a news story when
it achieves saturation coverage and avoidance becomes difficult, such
as news of President Clinton's alleged sexual relationship with a

White House intern, or when the news is related to what they may be hearing through entertainment sources.

The lack of attention to news impacts young people's knowledge of issues, personalities, and events. Those under age thirty are far less likely than those over thirty to know about politics. This is especially true of presidential candidates.[50] This news can be particularly significant for candidates seeking to reach segments of the electorate who are not accessible through traditional news media. The most important target of a candidate's youth-oriented themes—new generations of voters—may be contacted primarily through alternative, largely non-political media, such as MTV.

In addition, the mainstream press may not be fulfilling adequately the basic need to keep Americans informed. The traditional press, because of space and time constraints, frequently does not provide detailed accounts of political events. Historical and contextual factors are rarely incorporated into stories. New media provide the opportunity for citizens to learn about and discuss dimensions of issues that are short-circuited by the mainstream press. According to a Times Mirror study, 58 percent of talk radio listeners said they listened because it was "a good way to learn things that I can't find out elsewhere."[51] Listeners may not only be learning new information, they also may hear opinions not expressed elsewhere.

Populism

Media are essential to establishing the relationship between the mass public and political elites. The press is integral to the orchestration of political events, the management of electoral campaigns, and the definition of policy debates. In effect, the media are the "public sphere" within which political discourse takes place.[52] Yet, as media scholar Michael Schudson notes, "The more people participate in politics, the closer one comes to the ideal of a public sphere."[53]

The traditional media in the United States have set rigid boundaries that have cordoned off the public from political leaders, and thus have restricted the public sphere. Political discourse in the mainstream media is formalized and exclusive. It has become the bastion of political and media elite. The public has been relegated largely to spectator status. The new media's rise in American politics has coincided with a reawakening of populist sentiments among the mass public. Citizens, fed up with insider politics, have embraced outsider philosophies and politicians. Ross Perot's respectable showing in the 1992 presidential contest is testimony to the pervasiveness of populist attitudes. Running against the Washington establishment and elite politics, Perot was able to use the new media to ignite a grassroots campaign that brought him 19 percent of the vote.

New media offer the promise of populism, although as we will

demonstrate in the following chapters, it is largely a promise unfulfilled. They are designed to accommodate more unstructured, open
political discourse. The voices of ordinary citizens can become part of
dialogue and debate. The new media can provide the public with a legitimate forum for questioning established strongholds of political
power and policies. Further, through call-in programs or the Internet, new media can allow for the expression of emotion by citizens, an
element that is largely lacking in sanitized mainstream press presentations. The new media also can facilitate the representation of
diverse interests and identities. Talk radio programs, for example,
cater to specific audiences, including blue-collar workers, blacks, and
Hispanics.

It is through talk radio and the use of online media that the populist potential—while not yet reality—of new media sources is most
visible. The populist image occurs on two levels—content and process.
The content of talk radio, for example, evokes populist themes. Talk
radio hosts usually pursue antigovernment, sometimes libertarian
subjects. Problems with the president and Congress are staples of
talk radio discourse. The Internet facilitates discussions that span the
ideological and political spectrum through chat rooms and newsgroups.

The populism motif also is demonstrated through the process—a
process that gives at least the illusion of the opportunity to participate
in the political debate. Although most talk radio callers will not actually talk on the air, the choice of some average individuals to participate enhances the perception of talk radio as a populist medium.
Many Americans believe they can use talk radio to voice their opinions. According to a Times Mirror survey, more than one of ten Americans has tried to call in to a talk radio program. Slightly more than
half of those have made it on the air.[54]

This populist aura varies across new media. Television talk programs and tabloids are less likely to elicit populist responses directly.
Their content may contain populist themes, particularly in public affairs programs featuring investigative reports on government agencies
or programs. However, the process of public affairs programming
does not provide for the direct participation that talk radio or online
sources allow.

Summary

This new era in media history is testimony to the adaptability of the
mass communications system in the United States. American society
has become increasingly diverse in terms of its sociodemographic
composition. Life-styles have become more complex. Information
consumers live in a world replete with technological gadgetry designed to enhance sensory experiences. Commensurately, what citi-

zens need and desire from mass media in such an environment is widely varied. The old media are not equipped to meet the demands of the current audiences for political information.

There has been a decline in the diversity of traditional media as the new media have proliferated. With the corporatization of newspapers, readers have fewer choices about what to read, as newspaper options look more and more alike. Similarly, television network news broadcasts have an almost eery similarity. The play-it-safe attitude that the for-profit motive has inflicted upon mainstream news organizations has taken the fun and the excitement out of traditional media.

Audiences who are attracted to new media find that these communication outlets fulfill certain needs that are not entirely gratified by old media, as we shall demonstrate in chapter 6. The mainstream press is not as easily accessible as new media. Audience members must adapt their schedules to meet that of the news offering. Old media feature fewer populist themes, and they do not accommodate a process that enhances public participation in the political debate. Further, there is no explicit articulation of ideologies.

In spite of these factors, the old media will continue to constitute a significant portion of the American political communications diet. As we shall see in chapter 8, the old media have had to make some concessions to the new media and have had to adapt to the new media environment. However, traditions are an important part of the American culture. The old media have survived more than two hundred years of transition and will doubtless brave many more.

THE ROLE AND CONTENT
OF NEW MEDIA

Talking Politics

If there has been one communications format that has become emblematic of the new media it is talk radio. Once anchoring the night shift of the airwaves, talk radio has been reinvented to conform to the expectations of a new political era. However, the question of whether talk radio truly offers a fresh and effective outlet for elite and public expression is a subject of debate.

In this chapter we will take an in-depth look at the world of talk radio. We will first examine the role that talk radio plays in the broadcast and political realms. As with most media today, the profit motive has become the driving imperative behind talk radio, shaping its political and social voice. In addition, we will discuss the talk radio industry and its various components. Talk show hosts occupy a central position in the industry, as the focal point of entertainment, advertising, and political discourse.

The medium's unique format also serves to further the profit and political objectives of talk radio. A content analysis of a full week of nine nationally syndicated talk programs will provide some empirical evidence of the substance of talk radio offerings, including the roles of guests and callers.[1] Finally, we will debate whether talk radio truly offers a platform for popular expression and serves as a gauge of public opinion, or if these goals are illusory.

The Role and Function of Political Talk

Profit

Talk broadcasting, even political talk, is a business.[2] The bottom line of broadcast talk is concern with the financial bottom line. As such, talk radio conforms to the requirements of the current mass media environment, which dictate that profit-making is paramount.

This should not be surprising because talk radio stations and networks, like other commercial media in the United States, are economic enterprises. Yet these points must be emphasized because advocates of talk radio's role often forget them. Reminding ourselves that talk radio is, at heart, a commercial venture helps us to understand why it operates as it does.

The primacy of commercial objectives of talk radio does not mean broadcast talk is not interested in the airing of views or the discussion of a wide range of issues. However, such objectives are means to an end, not the end itself. The end is profit.

Talk shows that make money survive and those that don't are yanked off the air. This is not an occasional occurrence; rather, it happens frequently in the business. Station owners cater to what the audience will buy. "I can't tell you how many owners have said to me privately, I hate Rush Limbaugh," explains talk radio industry analyst Michael Harrison, "but he's making me money so I love him."[3]

Profit comes from advertising. With the exception of public radio and a few nonprofit outlets, luring advertisers is paramount for radio stations and hosts. Talk radio has an advantage over music in the courtship process with advertisers because the talk format is listened to in the foreground while music often serves only as background. Listeners are more likely to be paying attention to talk than to music.

This does not mean that talk listeners do nothing else. They often listen to talk while engaged in some other type of activity—working at an office, driving a car, or doing housework. Therefore, talk must grab viewers' attention. According to Ray Suarez, host of National Public Radio's (NPR) "Talk of the Nation," a successful talk show must be "informative, engaging, and entertaining. Entertainment is very important because radio is competing with all the other things you can do without looking at a radio—eating dinner, doing the laundry. . . . We need to shout above the fray."[4] Unlike newspapers, magazines, or computers, talk radio still must compete with other activities the individual is doing simultaneously.

Another edge for talk radio in the competition for advertising dollars is the devoted large following of talk fans to particular hosts. Rush Limbaugh's devotees willingly call themselves "ditto heads" and form Rush clubs all over the country. Thus they respond positively when Limbaugh hawks a product. For example, Snapple, a consistent sponsor of Limbaugh's show, as well as Howard Stern's, has experienced phenomenal growth in sales.[5] Many radio hosts get frequent calls from listeners expressing admiration to the host and confessing a pattern of daily listening.

On the other hand, talk is disadvantaged because the talk show audience tends to be older than the ideal demographic for advertisers. Traditionally talk has drawn its audience more from those over the age of fifty than from younger people. These listeners grew up in an age of radio listening, not television viewing. Younger radio listeners are attracted to music on the FM dial. Consequently, talk stations and networks are attempting to adjust talk formats in order to reach a younger audience more appealing to advertisers. Specifically, they are targeting their appeals to the Baby Boom audience, whose preferences are moving from music to talk. Chapter 7 will discuss whether the strategy is working.

Another disadvantage in luring advertisers is talk's content. Advertisers are rarely attracted to controversy for fear they will be boycotted by potential customers. Hence, despite the growing numbers of talk listeners, the subject of talk at times can be so controversial that some advertisers shy away. One such example is Jim Hightower's weekly program on ABC Radio Network, which failed to attract many large corporate advertisers at least partly due to his on-air tendency to attack the policies of large corporations.

Many family-oriented businesses are reluctant to advertise on talk radio programs hosted by controversial figures, such as Howard Stern, Rush Limbaugh, or G. Gordon Liddy, for fear that they may offend potential customers.[6] The threat is real. When Quaker Oats Company advertised a product on the Stern show on a Dallas station in the wake of Stern's criticism of murdered popular Latina singer Selena, the product was pulled from grocery store shelves, and local citizens banded together to boycott it.[7]

Yet, without advertising, talk radio would wither. Since advertising is inextricably intertwined with the audience, nationally syndicated hosts seek to accumulate as many affiliates as possible. Local hosts are no less driven by audience ratings. A local program must make more money for the station than any other potential program in that time slot, either local or syndicated.

But talk radio is far from withering. In fact, talk has become the dominant format in AM radio. Its rise to the top has been assisted by the Gulf War, the William Kennedy Smith trial, and the O. J. Simpson case. Stations that aired the O. J. Simpson criminal trial during 1994 and 1995 from gavel-to-gavel experienced a more than doubling of their audience during that period.[8]

Talk radio has become the salvation of AM radio, which had become the ghetto of radio broadcasting. In some markets, AM talk radio revenues have helped to offset FM radio losses.

As FM stations proliferated during the 1970s, particularly with clear channel reception, the AM market increasingly had been shunted aside. Once the haven for top-forty music, AM was displaced by the better-quality FM stations. AM was left with news, late-night network nonpolitical talk programs, and a declining audience.

The rise of talk radio has offered a starker distinction between FM, which is primarily music, and AM, increasingly dominated by talk. That distinction may become less clear if, as one industry analyst suggests, talk moves aggressively into the FM dial as well.[9] In the meantime, the AM dial is now filled with local and syndicated hosts who fill time on news/talk or all-talk stations. Hosts like Rush Limbaugh, Howard Stern, and G. Gordon Liddy have become household names to AM station talk radio listeners.

A Vehicle for Popular Expression

The problem for talk radio is the assumption on the part of the public, which is often fed by analysts and even some hosts, that talk radio is primarily a tool for empowering the powerless, giving voice to the silent majority. As we have discussed, however, empowerment is a residual, and not a primary, motivation for political talk.

Talk radio has been proclaimed as "an excellent, unstructured outlet for public discourse." This is true, some advocates claim, because callers can "express themselves in their own words."[10] Talk radio also is perceived as performing the function of allowing anyone to talk with policymakers. One talk radio host proclaims:

> How many people actually get a chance to talk to . . . Jimmy Carter or Jack Anderson? As a talk show host, I not only provide that opportunity for my audience each evening, I share in it as well. . . . To think that I and the people at home who are listening are actually going to get the opportunity to talk with the person who might become the next President of the United States.[11]

In even more glorified terms, talk radio has been called "the ultimate arena for free speech."[12]

Not all hosts publicly articulate such a socially responsible role. Some, like syndicated Westwood One Network host Tom Leykis, claim only "a responsibility to the shareholders of Westwood One. That's my responsibility."[13]

The Talk Radio Industry

Industry Representation: The National Association of Radio Talk Show Hosts

The talk radio industry encompasses the syndicate executives, local station owners and managers, and an array of others, including producers and support staff. Talk radio, however, has become a personalized medium centered around the host. As talk developed into a popular radio format and talk programs proliferated, talk hosts began to band together to form a national association to promote their interests within the industry. In 1989 the National Association of Radio Talk Show Hosts (NARTSH) was created.

Befitting talkers' broadening appeal and extensive political content, the group's annual convention attracts more than five hundred hosts and an array of politicians and traditional journalists. The Clinton administration regularly has sent representatives. Congressional leaders such as former Senate majority leader Bob Dole and House minority leader Richard Gephardt also have addressed the group. The Democratic National Committee, the National Rifle Association, GOPAC (the Republican fund-raising political action committee), the *Washington Times*, the National Mining Association, and Citizens for an Alternative Tax System all shared the same exhibit hall during the 1996 convention.

In 1996 President Clinton sent a letter to the group praising them for promoting "healthy debate."[14] White House aide George Stephanopoulos, addressing the convention, stated, "We take talk radio very seriously. The president has been convinced from the minute I've known him that radio is probably the surest way to reach voters and get your ideas out into the public marketplace."[15]

One method for attracting attention to the convention is its bestowal of an annual Freedom of Speech Award. The organization gave its 1995 award to G. Gordon Liddy, which provoked anger among even some hosts. The controversy continued in 1996, as the Freedom of Speech Award was shared by talk show host Bob Grant, Harvard Law professor Alan Dershowitz, and Disney chairman Michael Eisner. Grant had been fired by WABC in New York for making racist comments about blacks. Dershowitz was thrown off the air by WABC for calling Grant a racist. Disney owns WABC. Feminist attorney Gloria Allred staged a protest against NARTSH's decision to honor Grant, interrupting the awards ceremony, and stating that "racist speech should never be honored."[16] Senator Bill Bradley, in his keynote address to the convention, also expressed his distress at Grant's receipt of the award and stressed that talkers need to stamp out racism and promote civility in discourse.[17]

In spite of the attention NARTSH garners at its national convention, its real political clout is questionable. NARTSH is only a loose association of individuals, many of whom are in direct competition with one another for the ear of the audience and differ widely in their political views and approaches to political topics. Moreover, many are not even political talk hosts. It is the hosts as individuals, not host trade organizations, that affect American politics.

The Hosts

Who are the hosts who talk incessantly on tens of millions of radio sets all over the nation? It only seems like they appeared suddenly on the scene. In fact, many have been in broadcasting for years.

Still, they have proliferated rapidly in recent years. In 1990 there were only a few syndicated hosts, one of whom was a new entrant—the still relatively unknown Rush Limbaugh. Now, new nationally syndicated hosts have joined the growing crowd, and more hosts appear locally as stations turn larger blocks of their air time to a talk format.

Entrants since 1995 alone include Oliver North, former New York governor Mario Cuomo, and former U.S. surgeon general Jocelyn Elders. Some of those already in the business have seen their audiences grow exponentially during the 1990s.

The arrival of newcomers, particularly former politicians, has irked those who have made careers of the business. One longtime host starts his show announcing that he is not "a right wing wacko or a convicted felon." Another in the business since 1978 complains, "Now it seems like everybody who can speak English has their own talk show."[18] The notable exception to the newcomers is long-standing host Larry King, whose late night talk program has been in syndication since the late 1970s. Even King has earned new notoriety as his radio program moved into television.

The rise of talk show hosts has been meteoric. A little more than ten years ago, Rush Limbaugh was a talker on a local program in Sacramento, Michael Reagan was a business executive, and Oliver North was still a little-known White House aide running covert operations.

One host, who worries about talk radio's influence, concluded that "we're just commentators or columnists. That's all we are."[19] But who are these commentators or columnists who dominate the AM airwaves and whose presence is increasing on the FM dial?

The Syndicates

There are basically two categories of talkers, the syndicates and the locals. The syndicates receive most of the national attention. They also carry great appeal for affiliates. Syndicated hosts already have name recognition, they have proven ability to attract audiences, and they almost always come free to the station. Only a few hosts, such as Rush Limbaugh and Howard Stern, charge for affiliates to carry their program, and even that development is relatively new. Most other shows negotiate barter arrangements that allow the affiliate to place approximately half the advertising time of the show while the network retains the rest. The arrangement means that no money actually changes hands between the network and the affiliate. Both rely on their advertisers for revenue.[20]

The more popular a show is on a local station, the higher the local advertising rates, and the greater the demand among affiliates for the program. The more affiliates a show generates, the higher the rates for national advertising.

Rush Limbaugh's network can charge for his program because of the high demand to carry the program in a particular market. Other stations without Limbaugh furiously attempt to program around him. Competing hosts during the same time slot will compare their audience draw against Limbaugh to meet station needs for popular counter programs.

Who are these syndicated hosts? We now take a look at a sample of the most prominent of the syndicated talkers.

Rush Limbaugh

The king of the syndicates and talk radio generally is Rush Limbaugh. A native of Cape Girardeau, a small university town in southeastern Missouri, Limbaugh is the son of a local Republican leader and the grandson of a Republican state legislator. He dropped out of college at the age of twenty and bounced from one station to another until he was discovered by Ed McLaughlin, a former network executive. McLaughlin brought Limbaugh to New York in 1988 and gave him a nationally syndicated program.

Limbaugh's appeal stems from his entertaining, often bombastic, style. His flamboyance even makes liberals chuckle. He calls his style a "unique blend of humor, irreverence, and the serious discussion of events with a conservative slant."[21]

A large part of the appeal of Limbaugh's show is his egotism. Limbaugh opens his show with the reminder that his listeners need only listen to him to get their information. In the introduction of one of his books he admits, with no hint of modesty, that "I realized early on just how right I have been about so much." He describes his books as "loaded with insight, brimming with profundity." And he predicts that this age will someday be referred to by historians as the "Era of Limbaugh."[22]

However, Limbaugh's influence may already have peaked. His numbers (both in terms of affiliates and listeners) already have begun to fall off. One cause was his relentless attacks on President and Mrs. Clinton, which may have become too predictable and, thus, boring. Some argue Limbaugh's reaction to the 104th Congress hurt him. For a period, he became an unabashed supporter of Newt Gingrich, Bob Dole, and the Republican agenda, even when the public's support had eroded. His criticism of other candidates, such as Pat Buchanan and Ross Perot, also may have offended some of his audience.

Even with some drop in his audience, Limbaugh still is the most listened to host on talk radio. According to one survey, 37 percent of talk radio listeners tune in to Limbaugh, compared with 10 percent for the next most popular host, G. Gordon Liddy.[23] Almost all political talk hosts compare themselves with Limbaugh. This is true not only for those who directly compete with him, both nationally and locally, but also for those who do not. Many other hosts respect him as a role model and listen to him regularly to scrutinize his style. It is interesting to note that Limbaugh's style is made-for-radio and does not translate well to television. His short-lived television program—a studio version of his radio show—did not succeed in attracting an audience.

Limbaugh's three-hour show is *the* topic of interpersonal conversation about politics for many Americans. Some restaurants have created "Rush" rooms where "ditto heads" (the self-attached label of devoted Limbaugh listeners) can gather to eat and listen. Callers to other talk shows often will make reference to some statement Rush Limbaugh has made. Moreover, all of his books have become national best-sellers.

Limbaugh's political influence has become legend. Some analysts credit his support for the GOP Contract With America with aiding the Republican take-over of Congress in 1994. Republican politicians crave access to his show, with the possible exception of 1996 presidential contender Robert Dole.[24] Such influence even was noted by President Clinton when he criticized the fact that Limbaugh has "three hours to say whatever he wants. And I won't have an opportunity to respond."[25]

G. Gordon Liddy

One of the most remarkable rises in talk radio has been that of G. Gordon Liddy. Once the Watergate figure who refused to talk, Liddy now gabs into a microphone for three hours daily. His show is even more politically oriented and controversial than Limbaugh's. Although Liddy's statements about shooting federal agents and using cardboard figures of the Clintons for target practice has led some affiliates to drop his show, his popularity has risen dramatically since his first broadcast in 1992.

Like Limbaugh, Liddy's fame feeds on controversy. At the same time Liddy received the NARTSH award, he was uninvited to speak to a Republican party fundraiser when press reports, fed by information from the Democratic National Committee, described Liddy's more extreme on-air statements.[26] Liddy's sometimes nasty content has been termed "beyond the pale of civil discourse."[27] Liddy was even singled out for criticism by President Clinton, who said that he had come to realize "what a serious threat these ultra-right activist groups pose to America, and that G. Gordon Liddy is essentially their spokesperson."[28]

Yet none of this reaction to his broadcasts has changed his style.

In fact, all of it has helped Liddy, who calls himself the "G-man" and terms his show "Radio Free D.C." (his show is based in Washington), attract a niche audience eager to hear his fulminations about the crimes of the Clinton administration and the Bureau of Alcohol, Tobacco, and Firearms, in particular.

Ollie North

No nationally syndicated talk show host was better known prior to his talk show career than Oliver North. The featured witness of the Iran-contra hearings, North was a familiar face and voice to millions of television-viewing Americans during the summer of 1987. His appearance before the Iran-Contra committee dressed in his Marine uniform bedecked with medals made him a national hero among conservatives. North moved quickly from a possible prison term to the Republican nomination for the U.S. Senate from Virginia. North barely lost the race to a weak incumbent, Chuck Robb, another ex-Marine.

North launched his radio career soon after his defeat and has seen his show quickly gain popularity. At its inception, the show had only two affiliates—one in Washington, North's home base, and another in Houston.[29] Three months later, he was appearing on 122 stations.[30]

North generated less controversy than Liddy, but he also had acquired a devoted audience of conservatives. Yet, uncharacteristically, the former Marine colonel has included guests such as Mario Cuomo to take calls and debate with North on air. He was not, however, a skilled communicator nor quick on his feet, unlike many other hosts.

Michael Reagan

Michael Reagan, the adopted son of the former president, has been surprisingly successful as a talk show host, given his primary qualification as a relation to the star of the conservative movement. Reagan, now heard on over one hundred stations nationwide, publishes a newsletter that is popular among his listeners.[31] Reagan is highly political, but also one of a few activist hosts who frequently urges listeners to take action on various bills before Congress. Listeners hear Reagan discuss specific bills, including the bill numbers, and then cajole them into becoming involved in the legislative process.

Tom Leykis

One of the few nonconservatives among the major syndicates, Tom Leykis is syndicated with Westwood One and has nearly two hundred affiliates. Leykis's fast-paced style is designed to draw younger listeners, a more favorable demographic for advertisers. "We take shorter calls," Leykis illustrates, "We play loud bumper music. We have nasty promotion liners on the air that position the show as being dangerous or hard core or angry or whatever."[32]

Leykis's approach is less overtly political than Liddy, Reagan, or Limbaugh. He does not adopt the label of a liberal per se. Given the unpopularity of liberals in syndicated talk radio, it is not surprising that Leykis instead has proclaimed himself a "populist."

Alan Colmes

Another nonconservative is Alan Colmes, a New York City—based talk show host since 1978. Colmes started a nationally syndicated program in 1990 on a network called DayNet, which Colmes and other hosts created. DayNet was sold to Major Networks in 1994, but Colmes retained his show, which now has more than a hundred affiliates. Unlike Leykis, Colmes proudly carries the label of "liberal" and often defends President Clinton. Yet Colmes has been unable to become known as the liberal alternative to Rush Limbaugh. Colmes's New York style approach to talk radio limits his appeal in many markets across the nation.

Blanquita Cullum

One of the few women in talk radio syndication, Blanquita Cullum does not discuss that status much. She focuses instead on her role as a popular alternative to Rush Limbaugh among conservative listeners and as a political watchdog. "Many politicians start to behave," Cullum claims, "not because they see the light, but because they feel the heat—the heat generated by talk radio."[33] With her Hispanic background, Cullum is a rarity among syndicated hosts in her appeal to Hispanic listeners.

A former Bush administration political appointee, Cullum was a broadcast personality in Texas before moving into national syndication. Unhappy with her treatment by other syndicates, Cullum created her own network in order to control the distribution of her show. She falls into a group of syndicates still struggling to attract affiliates and take audiences away from the better-known syndicated hosts.

Chuck Harder

Chuck Harder is known as the king of the conspiracy theorists. His rhetoric is some of the most extreme among a group known for vitriol. He talks of President Clinton as the "most criminal president" the United States has ever had. He contends that "the difference between Watergate and Whitewater is a very, very big pile of bodies."[34] Harder has created his own network called the People's Radio Network, which carries his daily program, "For the People." His program airs on more than 270 stations. *Talkers* magazine calls him one of the twenty-five most influential hosts in the United States.

Locals

Nationally syndicated hosts get the most attention from the press, but local hosts can become well-known personalities in their own markets. According to one talk radio survey, a majority of audience members listen to less well-known hosts, including local hosts.[35] Success at the local level can then translate into national syndication. Most syndicated hosts started local and then moved into syndication with a different program. Some local hosts, such as Bernie Ward in San Francisco, maintain both local and syndicated shows.

Some local hosts refuse to make the move. There are distinct advantages to hosting a local show rather than a nationally syndicated one. The local host can cover both national and local issues, while the syndicated host is limited to national ones. Syndicated hosts say they also cover localities, but they must always relate such attention to a national issue.

The local angle is a powerful draw for listenership. The host can discuss issues proximate to the listener. "You can talk about the fact that there are no traffic lights working," explains one local host. "On the syndicated show, you can't talk about that. You can only be very, very generic."[36]

It is imperative that local hosts exploit this advantage because, unlike syndicated hosts, they cost the station money. Local hosts must be paid, while syndicates, with few exceptions, come free, subsidized by advertising revenues.

Despite their costs, local stations, especially the larger ones, maintain a staff of local hosts in order to retain a local flavor for their programming. Local hosts can reflect the personality of the city. Former New York mayor Ed Koch is an example of a successful local host because of his close identification with the community. Koch would probably fail as a national host because his brash personality may be offensive to some and his accent grating to listeners in other parts of the country. But Koch thrives in New York.

Local hosts have the advantage of appealing to a more homogeneous audience. One host, who has done a local program in New York and now is syndicated, explained that "you can get away with a lot in New York City that you can't get away with on a national basis. I'll say something that I think is innocuous, but maybe somebody in the Bible Belt will find it very offensive."[37]

Women Hosts

Few women have broken into the ranks of political talk show hosts. Exceptions at the nationally syndicated level include Blanquita Cullum, Victoria Jones, and Judy Jarvis, whose affiliate lists still pale beside those of Limbaugh, Liddy, Leykis, and Colmes.[38]

Female political hosts at the local level are also rare. Gloria Allred in Los Angeles and Diane Rehm in Washington host popular local programs. Male hosts dominate in the vast majority of markets around the country.

Female hosts believe they get more female listeners than male hosts do, although they do not support that conclusion with empirical evidence. The dearth of women talk radio hosts may attract women listeners to those few women hosts. "A lot of women listen to me because . . . just like anybody else it's nice to have a woman to listen to," suggests one female host.[39] The position of female hosts in this male-dominated industry is awkward. Female hosts sometimes are assigned to be sidekicks to a main host who is male. As one female host explains, "It's kind of like a Mutt and Jeff routine where you're supposed to be slightly dumber than the guy, and if you start asserting yourself too much, then they [station management] say, 'Well, you're really taking over.' But if you actually listen back to the tape, what you're actually trying to get is equal time."[40]

Female hosts sometimes face hostility from callers who are male. "They really like to get into it with a woman," explains Victoria Jones. "And they really like to try and best me in an argument, which, of course, they're not allowed to do. If they did that my whole shtick would go down the drain."[41]

Female hosts also operate in a climate of overt hostility fostered not only by executives, but also by some other hosts. Rush Limbaugh, G. Gordon Liddy, Don Imus, and Howard Stern are not discouraged from making sexist remarks on air.

The presence on the set of Howard Stern's long-standing partner, Robin Quivvers, for example, at times appears to give Stern license for misogynist or racially offensive remarks. "The male management laugh at that," one female host complains. "They think it's very funny. . . . That makes it even harder then for the female host to have credibility, whether she wants to go on the air and talk about a political issue, or if she wants to talk about an issue of sexual politics."[42]

Female hosts split along ideological lines much like male hosts do. For example, Blanquita Cullum self-identifies as a conservative, and she uses her contacts as a former official in Republican administrations. Judy Jarvis, however, calls herself a political independent and stresses that she doesn't "carry water for either party."[43]

The Black Experience on Talk Radio

Black hosts are common at the local level, particularly on stations that appeal to black communities within large metropolitan areas. One black commentator even calls talk radio a natural for the black community. "First, radio is oral, which fits in with the black rhetorical tradition. And second, its specific and specialized, so that we can talk to one another about what we care about."[44] The best-known local black host was former Virginia governor Douglas Wilder, whose talk radio crossed racial lines. Local black hosts, however, rarely have transcended the gap between black and white communities.

Syndicated black hosts are even more rare than women hosts. Even rarer is the syndicated black liberal host. The exception that proves the rule is former U.S. surgeon general Jocelyn Elders. Black hosts are usually considered to be communicators with local black communities and not with whites.

Two conservative hosts who have broken the race barrier are Ken Hamblin and Armstrong Williams. They have succeeded because their programs are attractive to the demographic talk radio seeks—conservative, young, professional, white male listeners. They appeal to that audience because they themselves are conservative.

Hamblin, who is carried by the Entertainment Radio Network, is heard on more than a hundred stations around the nation. He terms himself "the black avenger" and hosts a three-hour show full of controlled anger. In fact, the toll free number for Hamblin's show is "1-800-I'M ANGRY."

Hamblin is not only staunchly conservative on most issues (one exception is abortion), but he often is derogatory toward the poor black community, particularly its leadership. He rails against affirmative action, welfare, the criminal justice system, and blacks who adopt the role of helpless victim. He frequently takes calls from whites who agree with him.

With views that are unpopular among many in the black community, it is not surprising that Hamblin's show has been criticized by black leaders. He was dropped from a Salt Lake City radio station after the local chapter of the NAACP protested. National black leaders have urged the Federal Communications Commission to ban his show and the *Denver Post* to stop running his regular column.[45] But Hamblin's style has remained the same.

An ideological soul-mate, although less acerbic, is Armstrong Williams. Williams, who is carried on the Salem Radio Network, hosts a program called "The Right Side with Armstrong Williams." A former aide to Senator Strom Thurmond and to Clarence Thomas, Williams, like Hamblin, is seeking to increase the ranks of black conservatives by offering himself as a role model.

Conservative black hosts receive cover in discussing race-oriented issues that conservative white hosts do not enjoy. "They [conservative black hosts] say things that white people think but may not feel they have the moral authority to say," according to Michael Harrison, editor of *Talkers*.[46] Network and station owners find them appealing because they broaden the racial composition of syndicated talk show hosts while still appealing to the conservative listenership talk radio has attracted. Also, these hosts help these predominantly young, white, and male listeners assert that although they are conservative, they are not also racist.

The Revolving Door

Until talk became famous during the 1992 presidential campaign, the ranks of talk hosts were populated largely by career talkers. Talk was a career that emanated from working as a deejay, a broadcast news reporter, or less likely, a local print journalist. Talkers usually were career broadcasters.

For some hosts, talk radio today has become less a career and more a stepping stone either from political office or toward it. Many of the newer entrants to talk radio come directly from politics. Some hosts, such as former New York governor Mario Cuomo, former San Diego mayor Roger Hedgecock, and former representative and presidential candidate Bob Dornan, moved from elective office to talk radio. Others, such as syndicated hosts G. Gordon Liddy, Blanquita Cullum, and Jocelyn Elders, came from backgrounds as political appointees in presidential administrations. Still others, such as Oliver North and Michael Reagan, just take advantage of national notoriety.

Political talk is not merely a one-way ticket, but a revolving door. Reverend Pat Robertson left his combination religious/political talk program, the "700 Club," to run for president, but then returned after being defeated. In a three-year period, New Jersey Governor Christine Todd Whitman went from defeated Senate candidate to radio talk host to governor. Ross Perot guest-hosted "Larry King Live" in between presidential bids. Both Jesse Jackson and Oliver North are widely rumored as future candidates for office.

Political aspirants in the talk show business often are dismissed by longtime professionals as people who possess the attitude that "if you can't make it in other fields, become a radio talk show host."[47] One host called politician/talk hosts "incredibly tedious" and "still trying to follow their own political agendas."[48]

Yet for network executives and local station owners, politicians are appealing as talk show hosts because they come to the medium with wide name recognition and a base of support, as well as familiarity with political issues. Moreover, they have succeeded in politics at least partly because of their ability to use mass media.

These characteristics also can be detrimental. Politicians' movement to talk radio usually comes because of electoral defeat. Mario Cuomo, Bob Dornan, and Douglas Wilder became talk show hosts after losing bids for reelection or higher office. Oliver North lost his bid for a U.S. Senate seat from Virginia.

Politicians also can find it difficult to adjust to the medium. Often they have failed. Douglas Wilder lasted only a short time as a Richmond, Virginia, talk host. Mario Cuomo had trouble getting affiliates for his syndicated program. David Duke and former Los Angeles police chief Daryl Gates were fired after they failed to attract an audience.[49]

One reason for politicians' inadequacy is the difference between the two occupations. Politics is more about compromise while talk radio feeds on confrontation. Seattle host Mike Siegel argues that "when you're a talk show host, your job is to create provocative conversation. A politician is trying to bring people together. They're almost 180 degrees diametrically opposed."[50]

Another difference is the approach to issue discussion. As one talk host explained, "Politicians come to this primed for logical debates . . . they're issue oriented people. And doing a talk show is a different thing."[51]

The "different thing" is the medium. Talkers must be entertaining more than informative. They must emphasize the show business aspect of the job.

Politicians are likely to see talk radio hosting as the opportunity to debate, at great length, the policy issues of the day. Yet audiences are not necessarily interested in such content. Local hosts, particularly, must be willing to handle the complicated substantive policy issues as well as those human interest issues politicians would consider more trivial, but which stimulate widespread audience interest.

Mario Cuomo came to the job tentatively, worried about how it might affect his treatment of issues. "The danger is it gets to be entertainment. You start having to speak in shorthand."[52] Even though Cuomo had received plaudits for his frequent appearances on radio call-in programs in New York, his reluctance to become a full-fledged alternative to Rush Limbaugh suggests Cuomo's realization that he was no longer on familiar turf for a politician.

The Host's Ideological Bias

Although talk radio is now widely viewed as a haven for political conservatives, it has not always been so. Some conservative or moderate hosts, such as Judy Jarvis, Jerry Williams, and Michael Harrison, have liberal roots. Many of those who were broadcasting in the 1960s and 1970s were using the talk radio forums in those years to oppose the Vietnam War or support the civil rights movement.

Talk radio has been remarkably flexible in its ideological bent. Talk radio has moved with the times, from right-wing Father Charles Coughlin in the 1930s to antiwar protests in the 1960s and 1970s to conservative antigovernment themes of the 1990s. This ideological shifting supports the conclusion that ratings govern ideology and not the other way around. The accusation is less that hosts shift to reflect the perceived prevailing public sentiment (although that may be true also) as much as it is that talk radio executives promote certain hosts at particular times and avoid other hosts with less popular stances. As host Alan Colmes has put it: "Every programmer wants to put on the next Rush."[53] An important part of that formula is to find a host who is perceived to be in synchronization with the times and, therefore, politically popular.

The prevailing sentiment among many hosts, especially conservatives, is that liberal hosts just can't make it in syndication because their views are not popular. Liberals find it difficult to attract large corporate advertisers because they fail to enlarge their list of affiliates and, hence, their audiences. Jim Hightower, for example, while he was on the air, relied on union groups and liberal-oriented interest groups for advertising support.[54] Mario Cuomo's lack of success is suggested as a classic example, as is the dropping by the ABC network of the Jim Hightower show. Former Virginia governor Douglas Wilder could not even get a national show off the ground.[55] And Tom Leykis, who is popular, eschews the label "liberal."

The causes of the conservative bias in talk radio elude even the talk radio industry. San Francisco host Gene Burns argues that talk radio is conservative because it is in "an adversarial position to the established order. . . . The liberals have been in control of the machinery of government and people who were frustrated wanted to lash out at the liberals." Alan Colmes thinks the talk radio format offers advantages to conservatives because they are angry. "Liberals are preachers of tolerance, love, and compassion."[56]

However, Leykis and Alan Colmes are examples of successful nonconservative hosts who are programmed partly because they provide balance, but also due to sheer entertainment value. Their success also suggests that nonconservative hosts can find audiences in certain markets. Leykis, for example, is the top host in the Los Angeles area. Their audience reach negates the argument that only conservative hosts are popular.

Even among the conservatives, there are varying shades of ideological difference. Some, like Chuck Harder and local host Chuck Baker of Colorado Springs, are radical conspiracy theorists. They speak to an audience deeply suspicious of power and power holders, regardless of their ideological or partisan hue. Tales of black helicopters and road sign markings designed for UN vehicles to invade the United States are welcomed by them as evidence of secret collusion.

Some talk show hosts define themselves as populists rather than ideologues. The late Frank Rizzo, a Philadelphia host and former mayor, once explained his show as alluring because " there's another message people want to hear. There's a lot of issues that should be directed to the row house people. The little people. This is the group I relate to."[57]

Still, most hosts eschew populism or conspiracy theories. They are economic and/or social conservatives. Hosts such as Rush Limbaugh and Blanquita Cullum view themselves clearly as conservatives, not populists. They further economic or social conservative agendas rather than a populist agenda of government reform geared toward greater public involvement.

The contrasting types of hosts do not easily take to one another. When one host at the September 1993 White House gathering of talk radio hosts pressed Donna Shalala, secretary of Health and Human Resources, to admit that President Clinton had a disease that was being hidden from the public, other hosts booed him down. One host remembered, "I just sat there saying, I really don't want to be associated with this group of people."[58]

Unlike traditional journalists, political talk show hosts are usually identified by their ideological bias. Hosts label themselves conservatives, liberals, or more frequently, "moderates" or "independents." Some networks, such as ABC, Major Radio Network, and Westwood One, carry both liberal and conservative hosts. But others cater only to conservatives. The small Pacifica Network is an example both of a leftist radio network and of the lack of commercial success of left-wing radio.

Not only is ideological bias the sine qua non for publicity for many hosts, but for some it truly governs their approach to the show. Few hosts make an effort to be evenhanded in their discussions of issues. "I don't see it as my role to be fair to both sides in my presentation," states one host.[59]

Responding to the criticism of unfairness, some hosts argue the callers will offer opposing perspectives. Hence, balance can be achieved. Balance, however, is not the main objective. Hosts are being paid to express opinions. With the exception of the few noncommercial radio outlets, ideological or partisan expression must be linked to profitability. The goal is appealing to the marketplace.

Additionally, it is not coincidental that the conservative views of hosts are reflected by many of the owners of networks and local affiliates. Local affiliates are the most resistant to the expression of opposing views, which, given the present conservative bias of talk radio, usually constitute liberal views. Some stations in largely conservative areas do not attempt balance, but program only conservative hosts.

The balancing of liberal and conservative hosts on a station might help promote fairness and attract more listeners. Still, several stations have successfully moved to all-conservative formats in line with commercial strategies. One talk analyst suggested that mixing liberals and conservatives is a bad strategy for the sales force "almost as much as clearing Howard Stern on a religious station."[60] But from the perspective of public affairs debate, such a business strategy is likely to hurt liberals even more since an all-liberal station would be considered by the industry a potential commercial disaster.

Yet owners are not going to sacrifice the bottom line. The economics of radio broadcasting prevail over ideological considerations. Owners and executives may be able to weigh in on certain issues to direct the programming, but perpetuation of ownership is more important than fostering a particular ideology.

Station managers become highly responsive to what audiences will buy. In light of that fact, managers and hosts perceive ideological conservatism as a hot commodity. They point to one critical statistic to support that conclusion: the high ratings of conservative hosts such as Limbaugh, Reagan, and Liddy.

However, these perceptions of conservative ascendancy and the failure of moderates may be changing. Increasingly, hosts are calling themselves "independents" and distancing themselves from particular parties or candidates. This may signal a shift to political independence. Judy Jarvis calls herself an independent "like 80 percent of the American public."[61] Some other syndicated hosts, such as Jim Bohannon and Bruce Dumont, have eschewed ideological labels.

Nor are even the most partisan of hosts immune to the dynamics of audience choice. Hosts who are too ideological in changing times must change or lose their audience. Even Rush Limbaugh appeared more moderate in the 1996 election in order to maintain his widespread national audience. Furthermore, some hosts who are nonconservative, such as Leykis and Colmes, have gained a large national audience despite the current conservative trend.

Overall, owners take a hands-off approach to hosts if they are making money. Tom Leykis, ties *his* control (rather than that of executives) over the show's agenda to his financial success. "If we're gaining stations and increasing revenue and increasing market shares, nobody cares."[62]

Yet for many hosts a conservative bias is viewed as desirable because it is perceived as reflecting the current audience. Michael Harrison, the editor of the industry publication, *Talkers,* believes views on talk radio mirror the popularity of views in society. "Partisanship is more motivated by economic interests as opposed to political ones."[63]

The operative question is whether the appeal for the audience stems from the ideological content of programs or their entertainment value. One piece of evidence supporting the latter conclusion is the discrepancy between host and public opinion. Poll after poll suggests Americans are more moderate in their political views than the conservative talk show hosts, such as Rush Limbaugh and G. Gordon Liddy, that many listen to. If these audiences do not necessarily agree with the host, could their draw be due to other reasons, such as the entertainment value of political talk?

Another demonstration of the power of the bottom line is the rarity of political activism and the distance station owners place between themselves and politically active hosts. The ideological bias of many hosts leads some to become policy activists rather than just talkers. These hosts differ from the majority of their colleagues who merely take verbal positions on issues.

However, this activism must support the financial status of the program, not undermine it. At times, such activism may be bad for business. Too much attention to an issue the audience is unconcerned about, or worse, disagrees with, will cause audiences to wither.

As a further protection to the bottom line, many stations routinely air disclaimers at the end of the program distancing the management from the host, the callers, and the guests. The implied message is that these programs are for your enjoyment, but if you are offended, take it out on the host and not on the station.

Thus, economics prevails over ideological bias. Owners are far more interested in the bottom line than in the party line. Although conservative hosts are more popular than nonconservatives, the rise of nonconservative hosts suggests owners may be perceiving a moderating trend in the audience that will be reflected in the hosts promoted both at the local and syndicated levels. Few owners are interested in using their position to stimulate political activism.

The Talk Show Host Personality

As we have stressed, talk radio is primarily in the entertainment business. The host provides the main entertainment for every show and must maintain the audience day after day, week after week, for as long as possible. One talker described his job as "a one man act, three hours a day, five days a week."[64] Understanding the nature of the personality traits that underlie a successful talk show host is a prerequisite to explaining talk radio's content. It helps illuminate how talk radio, even political talk radio, is at heart an entertainment medium.

One overriding characteristic of talk show hosts is the ability to sound passionate. According to Greg Dobbs, a Denver host, you must "have passion for everything you bring up."[65] Although the average citizen possesses intense fervor about a few issues, the talk show host does not have that luxury when her or his goal is to sustain enthusiasm for issue discussion on a daily basis. Rush Limbaugh himself admits that there are "some days I don't care if anybody knows what I think. But you gut it up and do it."[66]

Station managers encourage hosts to be provocative on the air, rather than to remain neutral or acknowledge the worth of varying opinions. "I might actually think that an issue is complicated enough that there are two sides to it," Victoria Jones confesses. "But in the world of sound bites, . . . a lot of stations do not like you to go on the air and say 'I'm of two minds about this issue and I'd like to discuss it with you.' They just want fire and brimstone. You have to have an opinion or you don't do the issue."[67]

In conveying this passion, the hosts also must talk incessantly and try to make sense while they are doing it. According to one host, "You have to come up with jokes, you have to be quick on your feet, you've got to think of quips, you've got to deal with the caller who thinks you're a dope."[68] All of this must be done at once.

To fit the personality, the host must be highly animated. "Actually, offstage, and I do regard this as a stage, I'm fairly quiet," states one host.[69] Sometimes hosts admit that their anger is not necessarily emotion, but serves commercial purposes. One talk show host once told callers that his anger is a form of play.[70]

The host also must be willing to be superficial, that is, to address a wide range of issues while spending a limited amount of time on each one. Talk programs usually shift focus hour by hour (and sometimes even more frequently) in order to avoid losing listeners who are not interested in the topic. The array of brief conversations with callers reinforces the frantic shifting of thoughts from one conversation to another. As one host admitted, "Maybe having a short attention span is part of me doing this job."[71] The result frequently is an artificial passion about issues the host does not really care about it, and a superficial knowledge of many issues addressed.

Hosts—Entertainers or Politicians?

Given the requisite traits for hosting a talk radio program, there should be little doubt about what talk radio hosts really are. Yet the questions persist: Are they journalists tracking down stories, political commentators whose responsibility it is to explain and interpret current issues and events, or primarily entertainers?

Even though they are primarily entertainers, sometimes talk show hosts do take their political role very seriously. Rush Limbaugh has called talk radio "the portion of the media that the people trust the most."[72] Yet Limbaugh also calls himself primarily an entertainer.[73] Other prominent hosts echo that self-description.

The problem for determining what talk radio hosts are is important particularly when talk radio is perceived as something other than what it is. If listeners perceive talk radio programs as public service-oriented, similar to public radio, then their response to the medium will be remarkably different than if they view it as primarily entertainment.

Such a misperception by the audience can be attributed, at least partly, to the rhetoric that has accompanied the rise in public attention to talk radio. Call-in programs, which prevail in talk radio and are also a common component of television talk, have been praised for their potential as venues for public discussion. One host contends that "talk radio is giving a voice to the previously mute majority, and the people have spoken."[74] Boston talk host David Brudnoy attributes to talk radio many public service roles:

It can expose ideas for what they are, bring important facts to light, give a hearing to all sides of an issue. . . . It can move people to get involved, locally or nationally, in the issues of the day. It can prompt a listener to invade the arena of ideas—and the politics they generate—and to become a player, a participant, a citizen.[75]

But there is also recognition that the potential is not the reality.[76] Some observers argue that the expectation is all wrong. According to Michael Harrison, talk radio is not a new vehicle for promoting democracy. "Talk radio's job is simply to be a viable and interesting medium that depends upon public acceptance or disapproval for its future."[77]

Yet, talk radio still may become such a vehicle, even if there is no such intent. This is particularly true if individuals perceive it to serve such a role for them. Further, talk radio's populist potential is enhanced when politicians pay attention to citizen discourse on radio programs.

However, such a role is fraught with problems, given the structure of talk radio. Talk radio scholar Murray Levin calls talk radio "potentially democratic" but argues it is not actually democratic because the content is determined by the host: "Political talk radio is structured by the ideology of the host. His political philosophy and moral disposition determine the agenda, channel the ebb and flow of talk, and motivate some to call more than others. Freedom of speech can be instantly abridged with the flick of a switch."[78]

Talk radio hosts themselves, however, claim that they merely offer an outlet for listeners to express their views. Listeners, they claim, set the agenda. As Larry King notes, "People want two-way talk. They say, 'We want to talk to our government.' "[79]

However, despite the rhetoric of talk radio as a public opinion forum, with the bottom line of profits, advertisers, and listener ratings, talk radio is still primarily an entertainment medium. Thus it must respond to entertainment imperatives far more than political ones.

For example, talk radio hosts seek to avoid issues, processes, or even people who are dull because they do not attract audiences and therefore contribute to the station's bottom line. One talk show host lamented that there is a "whole universe of people who never tune in talk shows and yet who are voters, who are important citizens, who are part of the community organizations . . . but, who are not in the talk show audience." Yet, he admits that if they were included in the format, eventually talk shows would "probably screen them out as too dull."[80] Talk radio must be understood as an entertainment medium where hosts are entertainers responsible for doing whatever is necessary to build audiences.

Yet talk radio cannot be dismissed as purely an entertainment medium and, therefore, unrelated to the study of politics. Millions of Americans rely on talk radio programs as a significant source of news and information about public affairs. It is essential to understand talk radio as an entertainment medium with political effects. Such a discussion should commence with an appreciation of how talk radio operates.

Talk Radio Operations

Format

Most talk radio programs follow a rough script that has become familiar to audiences. Talk radio programs routinely follow an established pattern: an opening monologue by the host, often followed by the introduction of a guest, who then interacts with the callers. Many hosts include guests for part of the program and then take calls alone for the rest of the program. Others rely more heavily on guests. Still others use guests infrequently. With or without guests, the host still serves as the star of the program. The host is more like Geraldo or Oprah than Dan Rather or Judy Woodruff.

Advertising

One major difference between talk radio hosts and other media personalities is their direct association with advertising. While television network news departments' movement toward entertainment is commonly known, broadcast journalists still are more independent of ratings concerns than talk radio hosts.

Although their stories are placed beside bedroom furniture or farm implement ads, print journalists are separated from advertising in that they are not expected to write ads or place their name on advertisements. Even network news anchors or reporters, although they may introduce commercial messages, rarely actually deliver them.

Both national and local talk radio hosts do more than carry commercials on their programs. They often read them live (and sometimes ad lib through them), thus increasing the level of attention to the commercial. Like early television game show and variety program hosts, today's talk radio personalities are linked to specific products.

Unlike traditional journalists, including most of those in broadcast, in the course of a multihour program, local hosts move frequently and seamlessly between discussing a pending bill in Congress and hawking for a local auto dealership. Even for hosts with ethical objections to the shifting roles, it is difficult to overcome the allure of an extra bonus for doing a live commercial on behalf of a sponsor. A live spot by Rush Limbaugh is considered golden for many advertisers.

Opening Monologue

The host's opening monologue carries enormous significance in the program. It is at that point that the host must lure the listener in with promises of controversial topics and interesting conversation with well-known figures.

In the opening monologue the host sets the tone for the remainder of the program. Many hosts have a subsequent monologue at the beginning of each hour reinforcing the topic of the day or introducing new topics for discussion. Opening monologues are opportunities for hosts to express their opinions and invite reaction. One host, typical of others, said he makes "my opinions the centerpiece of the show."[81]

The opening monologue ranges from just a few minutes to fifteen or twenty minutes depending on the interests of the host and the reactions of the callers. The lack of calls, which is sometimes a problem at the local level, means a longer opening monologue, especially in the absence of a guest.

Talk show hosts are encouraged to express opinions to stimulate callers. The most popular ones are strongly opinionated on the air. The opening monologue, then, often becomes an attack on some unpopular person, group, or institution. Popular targets are Bill and Hillary Clinton, Congress, and the news media.

Various interest groups also come under attack. Rush Limbaugh is a master of group denigration. He gave widespread currency to phrases such as "feminazis," his term for militant feminists, watermelons (i.e., environmentalists who Limbaugh considers "green on the outside but red on inside"), militant vegetarians, and animal rights extremists.[82]

The length of opening monologues (either at the beginning of the program or at the beginning of program segments) varies considerably depending on the host. Table 3.1 demonstrates that Jim Bohannon and Ollie North devoted little time to an opening monologue in the week we studied. However, G. Gordon Liddy monopolized the time, taking nearly half of his program for monologues, and Limbaugh and Harder took one-quarter of the time.

Discussing Issues

One of the remarkable features of talk radio is time, as demonstrated by the length of host monologues. While broadcast journalists squeeze complicated stories into ninety-second or at most three-minute packages and print journalists are allocated a shrinking news hole, daily talk hosts are faced with the opposite dilemma of filling ten to fifteen hours of time per week.

Often the perception by critics of talk radio is that the medium addresses issues in a highly superficial manner. This view of superficiality is echoed by traditional media, according to Michael Harrison, editor of *Talkers*, "Television and newspapers always accuse talk radio of catering to the stupid people in our country and catering to unintelligent points of view, which I find fascinating."[83]

TABLE 3.1 Percentage of Time for Host Monologues, Guests, and Callers

Segment	Bohannon	Colmes	Harder	Leykis	Liddy	Limbaugh	Majors	North	Reagan	Average
Host Monologue	2	14	25	12	48	25	19	6	22	16
Guest(s)	67	37	58	36	13	11	0	35	35	38
Callers	31	50	17	51	38	65	81	58	43	45
Total	100%	100%	100%	100%	100%	100%	100%	100%	100%	100%

TABLE 3.2 Host Topics Addressed by Callers

Addressed by Caller?	Bohannon	Colmes	Harder	Leykis	Liddy	Limbaugh	Majors	North	Reagan	Average
Yes	35.5	54.7	33.3	61.4	27.3	44.8	40.5	94.3	56.7	57.9
No	64.5	45.3	66.7	38.6	72.7	55.2	59.5	5.7	43.3	42.1
Total	100%	100%	100%	100%	100%	100%	100%	100%	100%	100%

74

The hosts themselves say their listeners want to spend large amounts of time discussing issues and, therefore, the hosts take more time than other media to do just that. "We do not suffer the constraints of a conventional news story," explains one host. "This gives us the freedom to spend more time looking at issues and exploring them in greater depth and complexity."[84] Another host compared his coverage of a local issue with how the traditional news media would have covered it and concluded that "you could put Brokaw and Rather and Jennings together, and they don't get into that kind of depth."[85]

The time discrepancy between traditional and new media is confirmed by Greg Dobbs, a former ABC News reporter and now a Denver talk host, who prefers the amount of time provided by talk radio to convey information. As a reporter, Dobbs had to compress his reports into segments as short as ninety seconds. Now he can take up to three hours to tell the story.

However, just because talk radio possesses large blocks of time to discuss issues does not mean that such discussions are more substantive. Talk radio programs often cover a wide range of topics. The exception is the overriding issue that callers choose to discuss over and over again, and listeners want to listen to. These topics are rarely public policy oriented. They are more likely to be human interest stories such as the O. J. Simpson trials and the sex scandals involving President Clinton.

Agenda Setting

Despite the rhetoric of talk radio, which proclaims itself the medium that allows Americans to express themselves, talk show hosts almost always determine the agenda for the show. Some indicate flexibility in their willingness to shift topics, particularly if one does not attract calls. One host remarked that he will switch topics because callers "will often bring up topics that I wasn't prepared to do . . . but if that's what they want to talk about, I'm there to kind of serve them and you got to give them what they want."[86]

Hosts usually have a predetermined agenda. As one host explained, "Ninety-five percent of the time [the agenda] is what I've chosen to talk about, however arrogant that sounds. . . . And if somebody calls with another subject altogether the screener has instructions to tell them that's not what we're doing right now."[87] As another host put it, "They've got to talk about what we're talking about or they don't get on."[88]

Callers generally respond to the host's agenda. As Table 3.2 illustrates, a majority of the callers discussed the same topics the hosts raised. The agreement was strongest for Oliver North, which suggests that his screener is more effective in eliminating callers who call to discuss other topics.

Some hosts have qualms about setting the agenda all the time. NPR host Ray Suarez admits that he doesn't "necessarily want to be the one to raise all the topics." Yet he will tell the screener that he wants a topic to be raised and waits for the screener to identify a caller who wants to make that point. Then he goes to that caller.[89]

Still, hosts are not free to raise any issue any time. They are constrained by perceived listener interest, the ability to attract callers, and current events. In order to maintain freshness, usually talk show hosts determine the agenda for a program no sooner than twenty-four hours before the program. Talk radio's agenda is very "event-driven."[90]

Routinely the host and the producer meet several hours before the program and determine the agenda for that day. The most difficult part is the choice of topics. Moreover, it is a recurring decision because, absent an overriding story such as the arrest of a Unabomber suspect or the O. J. Simpson trial, the material must remain fresh daily.

Talk radio's agenda is easier to set when such an overriding event or issue saturates the traditional media's news coverage. One example is the 1994 midterm elections, which attracted high notice from the audience, even resulting in an increase in voter turnout over the previous two midterm elections. Political talk programs reaped the benefits. During the fall of 1994, ratings rose for many syndicated talkers, as hosts debated the upcoming elections.[91]

The O. J. Simpson criminal trial was another seminal event that occupied talk radio time for more than fifteen months. However, the trial also harmed some hosts whose programs were reduced in length because of their station's live coverage of the trial.

The overriding topic need not be of long duration as is the case with an electoral campaign or a lengthy, well-publicized trial. The event can be the illness or death of a famous person or a controversial Supreme Court decision. These topics are easily identified. Denver talk host Mike Rosen calls them "water cooler topics," that is, those that will be discussed around the office water coolers throughout the nation.[92]

Water cooler topics do not occur every day. When a water cooler topic is not available for discussion, the decision-making process becomes more subjective. "It's probably a lot more art than science," admits one host.[93]

One key to such decisions is listener interest, which, in turn, often is defined as "what will get the most phone calls." Although the shows are rated periodically by Arbitron, the immediate measure of audience interest is the telephone.

Talk show programs, like other new media, lean heavily toward issues close to home, simple to digest, and inclusive of personalities. The O. J. Simpson criminal trial, then, was ripe for talk shows.

A few hosts, however, seek out issues that are not addressed by everyone else. One talker, who hosts a Sunday evening program, said he chooses topics from the Saturday papers because it is "the least read paper, and yet it includes all the important news that's come up on Friday, and also it's news that no national talk show has had an opportunity to really dive into."[94]

Issues of deeper policy significance, particularly in foreign policy, usually are perceived as unlikely to appeal to listeners. During the debate over U.S. military involvement there, one host summarily dismissed Bosnia as an issue because "there aren't three people in America who care about Bosnia."[95] One of the authors observed a talk show where the host spent the first hour on U.S. involvement in Bosnia and received few calls. For the second hour the subject was switched to whether parents should allow their children to be tattooed, and the phone lines lit up.

Talk shows vary considerably in the extent of political content they showcase. Syndicated shows, such as Rush Limbaugh, G. Gordon Liddy, and Michael Reagan are more likely than local ones to concentrate on politics. However, other syndicated programs such as Don Imus and Howard Stern are only partly or accidentally political. Many other hosts, especially at the local level, treat topics unconnected to politics. Judy Jarvis expresses the views of many hosts that "if we did an all political show, it wouldn't be very entertaining."[96] Some hosts argue that most of what they do is political because almost everything is political in some way. But even though the host may take a human interest story and insert a political theme, the base appeal is not politics, but human interest. Reflecting this conditional approach to political topics, one host calls her talk show issues "the dinner table conversation with a good smattering of politics, if politics is the issue of the day."[97]

In fact, in the era of the Fairness Doctrine, nationally syndicated talk radio began as a medium devoted more to other kinds of talk than political discussion. A growing number of talk radio programs are almost wholly unrelated to politics. Instead, they address themes such as social relationships, computers, pets, car repair, and personal finances. According to Charles Brennan, a St. Louis talk radio host, political topics do not receive automatic priority. "If something happens that affects people, . . . or if there are taxes, [or] if there's a sensible issue that's fine, but we're not like 'Washington Week in Review.'"[98]

Since the determination of listener interest is hardly scientific, the hosts usually rely on other sources for guidance. Ironically, many of their ideas for topics come from the news media. One host said he and his cohost draw many of their topics from what "we see on television or read about in the newspaper or think about while driving to work or steal from another talk show."[99]

Newspapers, particularly, are critical sources for talk show preparation. One survey of talk radio producers in two major markets found they relied to a great extent on the morning newspaper for topics.[100] Rush Limbaugh claims he reads nine newspapers a day.[101] Other hosts say they read half a dozen or more newspapers daily, usually drawing on national newspapers such as *USA Today*, the *New York Times*, the *Washington Post*, and the *Wall Street Journal*. Some conservative hosts also rely on the *Washington Times*.

That day's newspaper stories become critical components of the host's opening monologue and, therefore, the springboard for discussion of the host's selected issue. G. Gordon Liddy even reads on air lengthy sections of selected articles from major newspapers, such as the *Washington Post*, the *New York Times,* and *USA Today.*

Fifty-seven percent of the information sources hosts mentioned on their shows were from newspapers (see Table 3.3). One host admitted that he relies so much on the local morning daily that he has dubbed the paper "the official program guide to the 'Morning Meeting,'" which is the title of his show.[102]

Newspaper stories serve as "talk show fodder." However, even within newspaper coverage, the hosts are selective. Hosts often play off the more outrageous stories regarding human behavior, governmental malfeasance, or incompetence.

Ironically, while the traditional news media have been criticized for emphasizing negativity, bizarre behavior, or conflict, talk radio, when drawing from newspapers, tends to focus on those very story types, making the information gleaned from talk radio even more distorted from reality.

Another source of talk show topics is the mountain of faxes programs receive daily from a wide variety of sources, including private

TABLE 3.3 Mentioned Sources in Hosts' Monologues

Newspapers	
New York Times	14%
Wall Street Journal	7
Washington Times	7
Washington Post	5
L.A. Times	5
USA Today	4
Other	15
Subtotal	57%
Television News	7
Government Documents	7
Wire Service Stories	4
News Magazine Articles	4
Other	21
Total	100% (N=100)

citizens. These sources are rarely noted on-air, but can affect the choice of topics or guests. Frequent faxers to talk radio hosts are Free Congress (a conservative Washington think tank), the Republican National Committee, and the House Republican Conference (the party organization for Republican members of the U.S. House of Representatives).

Still another source is the industry publication, *Talkers,* which includes listings of the hot topics on talk programs around the country. According to the editor of *Talkers,* "We publish this information for people to get a handle on what's being talked about if they want to know what to talk about."[103]

In formatting the show, some hosts segment their programs into political and nonpolitical sections. Local hosts usually avoid carrying a full two- or three-hour program of political topics, which would likely alienate less politically interested listeners.

Local hosts routinely include a mixture of traffic, weather, interviews with local personalities as well as local and national politics. Topics affecting daily life evoke the strongest reactions. One host explained that discussing local drivers will "light up the switchboard faster than the most egregious political violation."[104]

Hosts rely less frequently on "open mike" programs, that is, sessions allowing people to express their views freely without restraints or host agenda-setting. Such programs are shunned by many hosts because they do not serve the interests of the program. They rob the host of the power to direct the show to enhance listener appeal. Mike Rosen, a Denver talk host, explained that "you can't let your callers set the agenda. . . . I can't let callers dictate what we'll talk about. . . . If you do they'll take over your show . . . and you're gone."[105] One Houston station tried airing large blocks of "open mike" programs, but found that younger listeners tuned out. When the station returned to exercising more control over the subject matter, the younger audience returned.[106]

One talker called open mike programs "poison" because they attract people who do indeed want to say what's on their mind, but to whom other people really do not want to listen.[107] "An open line is like a full moon," one host has complained. "It is a green light for all the crazies to come out of their rubber rooms."[108]

The agendas for talk radio programs are audience-driven in the sense that they must meet entertainment values and reinforce, and even expand, listenership. Still, listeners (or callers) almost always are left to respond to the host's agenda. Political imperatives are less important than entertainment. But within the broad rubric of entertainment, the host (in conjunction with producers) has wide latitude to determine the direction of the program.

Censorship

"The essence of talk radio is to give people a punch in the solar plexus," proclaims Boston host Jerry Williams.[109] But the reality is that talk radio often pulls its punches due to commercial imperatives or station owners' interests. Since talk radio, with few exceptions, is a product offered by private enterprise, hosts (as employees) are rarely free agents. Local hosts are governed by owners and the advertisers they depend on for revenue. Even the syndicates are not free; they operate under the management of broadcast networks. Few own their own networks; but even they are in turn responsive to their advertisers.

Hosts seem intuitively aware of their limits. They need only to remember incidents where hosts have been dropped by owners after offending them. One example is Jim Hightower, whose program was canceled by ABC Radio Network in September 1995 after the network claimed Hightower's program drew poor audience ratings. However, immediately prior to the cancellation, Hightower had criticized the Walt Disney company, which had just purchased ABC.[110] Moreover, Hightower was well known for attacking large corporations, some of which were potential or current sponsors of ABC network programming.

Many hosts insist they are free to discuss whatever topics they wish. However, the fact that even they express surprise they have not had more encounters with management suggests they exercise a great deal of caution. Some admit they employ self-censorship on topics they believe might offend station or network management.

Ideological bias is less the issue than economics, that is, sensitivity to advertisers and offense to listeners. Due to the influence of advertisers, companies are more sensitive targets for hosts than many politicians who need the hosts more than they are needed. "You can go after a politician a lot easier than you can a person who spends $5 million a year advertising on your station," one host contends.[111]

Station executives, however, are susceptible to politicians with power over the station's future. Certain elected officials who can directly affect broadcast communications policy are more difficult targets for talk radio. House Democratic leader Richard Gephardt once called the general manager of a St. Louis radio station in the middle of a talk radio interview derogatory of Gephardt, prompting the executive to tell the host to cut short the interview.[112]

Listeners' values also intrude in the process. Due to the potential for giving offense, few local hosts around the country could mimic Howard Stern's raunchy style. This sensitivity leading to self-censorship is more common among major regional stations attracting a broad-based audience than niche stations within markets.

Self-censorship comes in the form of avoiding certain topics or guests known to be offensive to management. Self-censorship is usually operative because externally imposed censorship is always a reality. One example was a show on a St. Louis talk program that had scheduled a guest critical of Monsanto, a major company in the St. Louis area. When Monsanto complained to the station management about the upcoming show, station executives insisted the guest be dropped from the schedule.[113]

Although such overt censorship, or more subtle self-censorship, occurs, it usually escapes the audience. Listeners are unaware of the internal battles within a station and are rarely aware of what the station chooses not to discuss and why.

Callers

Hosts continually assert that the callers are an integral part of talk radio. The reasons, however, have little to do with gauging public opinion.

After a host completes the initial monologue and announces the telephone number once or twice, he or she hopes the telephones will begin to ring. When they do (if they do), a call screener (often the show's producer) answers the call and types onto a terminal certain information about the caller, such as her or his first name, the city she or he is calling from, the gender of the caller, estimated age, and a one- or two-line summary of the comment the caller wishes to make. This information is simultaneously relayed to the host through a computer screen in the studio. The host's screen also may tell him or her how long the caller has been on hold. The screener usually can type notes to the host about upcoming breaks or additional comments about callers.

As a result, the screener becomes the filter for input from callers. That filter is hardly neutral. Put bluntly, the screener's job is to enhance the listener appeal of the program, not to facilitate the expression of opinions by the callers.

While talk radio is promoted as a format for the expression of public opinion, this role is secondary. It is true that average citizens can call the toll-free numbers provided and converse with the hosts or articulate brief expressions of their opinions. That is not, however, their primary purpose on the program. Further, callers do not constitute a representative sample of public opinion.

Rather, the callers function as an integral aspect of the program's entertainment value. According to Rush Limbaugh, "the primary purpose of callers on my show is to make me look good, not to allow a forum for the public to make speeches."[114] The caller's key function is to keep people listening. If listeners tune out because of boring callers, the show is over.

Since the callers' exchange with the host is a critical part of that appeal, the screener and the host attempt to control the type of caller who is granted time to talk. According to one host, it can be devastating "to the survival of the station to put the wrong callers on."[115]

The dilemma for talk radio is the prevalence of older listeners in the audience and therefore among the callers. Talk radio does not appeal as much to those under thirty as it does to those over fifty. Moreover, the established superstations in various metropolitan areas are likely to have built a devoted traditional audience, which is older. Talk radio programmers usually want a younger audience, preferably between the ages of twenty-five and forty-nine. In pursuit of a more youthful audience, talk radio structures the format to appeal to those who are younger. Callers, particularly, serve that role.

Hence, those callers who do not enhance the station's efforts to reach that goal are most likely to be discriminated against by the screener. They include callers who sound like they are over the age of fifty. A producer for a local host admitted that she screens out callers who sound like they are over fifty. "In talk radio we want to put the best speakers on," she confided.

Our content analysis of talk radio programs revealed that those who are estimated to be over fifty are less likely to talk on the air than those under fifty. Less than one fifth of the callers on air for the Limbaugh, Liddy, Leykis, and Colmes programs were estimated to be over the age of fifty (see Table 3.4). Given the large number of calls to Limbaugh, Leykis, and Colmes, such a difference becomes significant. While Harder seems to take many more over-fifty callers than the norm, (and North, Reagan, and Bohannon are near the median), the other hosts seem to take very few over fifty callers.

This table of age and gender differences also explains that, for most of the hosts, those who were estimated to be over fifty were given less time on air than those who were estimated to be younger.

TABLE 3.4 Age and Gender Differences: Number of Callers and Caller Time on Air

Host	Number of calls	% Female	% Over 50	Mean No. Minutes Air Time	Mean Time % Female	% Over 50
Bohannon	59	25	30	2.44	2.40	1.91
Colmes	84	14	19	2.09	2.10	1.96
Harder	24	33	50	2.19	2.11	2.07
Leykis	71	34	11	2.64	2.57	2.70
Liddy	21	33	19	4.05	5.42	5.40
Limbaugh	61	18	10	3.21	2.98	3.18
Majors	48	21	26	4.62	4.82	3.30
North	91	24	33	2.35	2.39	2.56
Reagan	31	16	32	4.26	4.95	4.11
Total	54.4	24.2%	25.5%	3.09	3.30	3.02

The difference was starkest with Majors, who gave those in the older cohort on average almost two minutes less than the mean length of a call. Bohannon, Colmes, Leykis, and Reagan gave less time to that age group. It is possible that these callers were more succinct than younger ones. But it is more likely that these callers were urged to make their point quickly and get off the air.

Two of the hosts granted more air time to those over fifty than to the average caller. North and, especially Liddy, moved in the opposite direction. The fact that one third of North's callers were estimated to be over fifty suggests perhaps even a deference given to callers in that age group. Liddy gave far more air time to those estimated to be over the age of fifty, but they represented a small fraction of the total number of callers.

Another group discriminated against on talk radio is women. We have discussed the dearth of female talk show hosts, rendering talk radio a bastion of male domination. The bias in favor of male callers also may be attributed to the predominance of males in the audience. The content analysis starkly demonstrates that female callers on air were less frequent than men. In fact, a large majority of callers to these programs were men. Less than 20 percent of calls on air to the Colmes, Limbaugh, and Reagan programs were women. Only on the Leykis, Liddy, and Harder programs did female callers reach one-third of the total. This result corresponds to a 1993 study, which found male callers are nearly twice as likely as female callers to actually talk on the air.[116]

With the exception of Limbaugh, hosts did not allot female callers less time on air. Liddy spent significantly more time on the air with women, as did Majors and Reagan, although to a lesser extent.

Since those who called the programs but did not get to talk on air are not examined, this study cannot conclude whether callers over age fifty and women were discriminated against in the screening process. However, given the demographic for talk radio, discrimination is the most likely possibility. Surveys of talk radio listeners find that more than 40 percent are over fifty and about the same percentage are female.[117] Perhaps listeners in these groups are considerably less frequent callers. One study found that men were twice as likely as women to call. However, another, more recent study found no significant gender difference.[118] And, according to an unpublished study by Susan Herbst, 33 percent of those who said they had called in to a radio or television talk show were fifty or over.[119] Overall, discrimination based on age and gender seems apparent in the determination of who gets on the air.

The disparities among programs suggests discrimination by certain hosts such as Colmes, Reagan, and Limbaugh, or a more limited female listenership for these hosts producing fewer female callers. According to one female host, men are more likely than women to call in about politics.[120]

Apparently, those over fifty and women are not the only ones whose participation is routinely minimized. Some hosts admit that those callers who are less articulate or incapable of stating their position or question succinctly often are screened out. For syndicated shows or popular local shows with large numbers of callers, the screening process places a premium on interesting or provocative callers. As Tom Leykis admitted, "If they're not fascinating, we don't put them on the air." Leykis is hardly apologetic about screening callers in this way because, as he put it, "I'm not in the public service business. I'm in the advertising business."[121]

As some callers are shunted aside, others are accorded priority. Policymakers or individuals who are being discussed on the air are given priority to join the discussion if they call.[122] Those who are considered experts in the area are placed ahead of other callers.

Not only are callers filtered, but, where possible, they are sorted to increase the appeal of the programming. The screener or the host can determine the direction of the conversation. On one program, one of the authors observed a host ignoring a caller who, as indicated by the producer's typed message on the monitor in front of the host, disagreed with the host's opinion throughout the program. Other callers were taken until time ran out. Apparently, the host had made a determination he did not want to take an opposing call at that time.

Still, hosts insist they are quick to put people who disagree with them on the air. Such calls, they say, are more interesting for the listener. Some talkers criticize hosts who screen out callers who disagree. Denver host Mike Rosen states, "I think a lot of Limbaugh's audience is made up of people who agree . . . and the absence of guests with whom he disagrees, and very few callers with whom he disagrees. That kind of a package makes it a less interesting show for people who disagree with him."[123] The content analysis reveals that Rosen was correct about Limbaugh, but this generalization also can be applied to most of the other hosts as well.

Put succinctly, callers who agree with the host appear on air more often than those who disagree. The disparity was greatest with hosts such as Liddy, Harder, and Reagan. At least 70 percent of the callers to Liddy's and Harder's programs agreed with the host. During a week of listening to Harder's programs, only one caller appeared on air who disagreed with the host's position (see Table 3.5).

What we do not know is whether those who called were more likely to agree or whether the screening process on these programs eliminated dissenting callers. The first explanation may place less of the onus for a homogenous program on the hosts. But on-air treatment of callers may discourage callers who disagree. Some hosts hang up on disagreeing callers. For example, Oliver North has been known to not only hang up, but also to play the sound effects of a shredder while doing so. Limbaugh has used the sound of a toilet flushing when hanging up on a disagreeing caller.

Once callers do get on, they are encouraged to be succinct and to the point. The caller has a brief time to express his or her views. Rarely does a host's interaction with a caller exceed two to three minutes. In fact, it is unusual for the caller to stay on the air in an extended conversation with the host. However, this can occur if the entertainment value of the exchange is high. One of the authors observed as syndicated host Ken Hamblin kept a caller on through two commercial breaks because the caller was directly challenging Hamblin and creating an interesting dialogue.

One host explained that "it's not how long, it's how good." "If it's interesting and informative and entertaining, they can have plenty of time. But if they're taking a long time and it's not very interesting, then there's no reason to keep them on the air, because the air time is very valuable."[124]

Hosts frequently are pressured to get callers on and off quickly to accelerate the pace of the show. Greg Dobbs, the former network news reporter, admitted that his programming director presses him to create a faster paced show with less time given to individual callers.[125]

Alan Colmes includes a segment called "Radio Graffiti" where callers are allowed to express their views in one sentence. The rapid movement through the calls is the epitome of brief caller statements. It is designed to sustain listener interest and has become a highlighted feature of the show, even a signature piece for Colmes.

As a result, callers are not primarily on air to offer a vehicle for expression, or for policymakers or the station management to measure public opinion. Rather, they serve as a tool to enhance the appeal of the program. One talk analyst concludes, "The caller then becomes a commodity, a product that must suit listeners as the station defines them."[126]

The reality of this usage is not surprising, except when talk radio is touted as a populist medium designed to allow free expression by common people. According to one talk host, in talk radio "there is no great concern for some type of ideal of free speech" because such an ideal, if followed, could "cause people to tune out."[127]

Moreover, although some hosts like to equate callers with listeners, they realize the groups are very different. Some hosts talk about measuring the mood of the audience through the calls they receive. Others, such as Seattle host Dave Ross, are aware of the differences: "I think the people who don't call . . . have lives, you know. They're too busy to call, they haven't got the time. . . . I don't say that to be against the people who do call, but there are those who are political

TABLE 3.5 Host/Caller Position Agreement

Agreement?	Bohannon	Colmes	Harder	Leykis	Liddy	Limbaugh	Majors	North	Reagan	Average
Yes	39.5	38.2	73.1	32.1	70.0	46.0	54.0	42.5	61.2	46.8
No	11.6	40.0	3.8	25.9	13.3	30.2	12.7	23.9	20.4	22.4
Can't Tell	48.8	21.8	23.1	42.0	16.7	23.8	33.3	33.6	18.4	30.8
Total	100%	100%	100%	100%	100%	100%	100%	100%	100%	100%

Note: Agreement percentages calculated only when the host had taken a position (favorable or unfavorable) on an individual, institution, ideology, or policy and the caller also discussed that same reference.

TABLE 3.6 Guest Agreement with Host

Agreement?	Bohannon	Colmes	Harder	Leykis	Liddy	Limbaugh	Majors	North	Reagan	Average
Yes	44.8	37.5	84.2	60.0	66.7	—	—	86.7	69.2	69.7
No	10.3	37.5	—	6.7	16.7	—	—	6.7	7.7	9.1
Can't Tell	44.8	25.0	15.8	33.3	16.7	100.0	—	6.7	23.1	21.2
Total	100%	100%	100%	100%	100%	100%	—	100%	100%	100%

Note: No guests appeared on the Majors show that week.

activists, and those who, frankly, have more important things to do. They're taking the kids to soccer practice or out in the garden doing gardening."[128]

Hosts distinguish between caller-oriented programs and those directed at the listener and usually affirm that their programs are the latter, not the former. If the host allows any caller free expression and focuses primarily on the caller in the interaction, then the program will lose its listener base. According to one talker, he always remembers his listeners: "If I'm having an argument with a caller, I don't believe I'm going to persuade the caller. I'm talking past the caller. I'm talking to the listeners."[129]

Guests

Some hosts, such as Rush Limbaugh, claim that they alone provide listeners all they need to know. For most hosts, the appearance of guests helps stimulate caller conversation and listener interest. But who are these guests and why are they chosen?

Speaking of the decision-making process in inviting guests on the air, one host explains: "I like people who are provocative, controversial, entertaining, concise."[130] Guests are usually spokespersons for causes, well-known personalities, or particularly for local programs, those who were willing to come on the program.

According to the content analysis, the most common type of guest was a media personality. Second most common were identifiable interest-group representatives. Actually, there may be even more spokespersons for various interest groups since some groups will recommend experts who reflect the groups' viewpoint but are not overtly identified with the group. Some hosts rarely feature guests at all. In thirty-one percent of the daily programs analyzed no guest appeared on the program.

Guests also share another trait—they usually mirror the opinions of the host on the topics they are discussing. As Table 3.6 demonstrates, on most of the topics discussed, the hosts and guests agreed. The host with the most guests in agreement with him was Oliver North, who had only one guest during that week who disagreed with North on the topic they were discussing. For example, in discussing a Supreme Court decision on affirmative action, host Oliver North invited former federal judge Robert Bork and a man who claimed he was a victim of affirmative action. Both guests agreed with North's criticisms of affirmative action. Chuck Harder, the conspiracy theorist, included no guests who disagreed with him, while the most liberal host, Alan Colmes, had just as many guests who disagreed with him as agreed.

Thus hosts can orchestrate guest appearances in order to offer a range of views. The resulting discussion could promote public understanding of varying public policy positions. Clearly hosts do not do this. Instead, most of those studied used their guests primarily as an echo chamber for the host's own views.

As was the case with callers, this conclusion is made without knowledge of hosts' efforts in attracting prominent potential guests with dissenting views to participate in the program. Some hosts say they invite these people but are rebuffed. How much hosts attempt to achieve such balance is unknown. The most biased hosts may still want to include occasional dissenting guests in order to avoid the charge of exclusiveness. On the other hand, guests who may fear they will be treated poorly by an unsympathetic host and hostile callers cannot be faulted for avoidance of such a program.

Talk Radio as a Medium for Political Discourse

An Ideal Forum?

The virtues of talk have been touted by its advocates. Talk radio has been championed as the new town meeting or the new neighborhood. Talk host Ellen Ratner calls it "America's back fence" and Ken Hamblin calls his show the "last neighborhood in America." Evoking images of a bygone era of gentle communication and personal interaction, he compares the discussion on his show to coming "to the back fence."[131]

Yet talk critic Howard Kurtz offers a more ominous conclusion: "From Imus in the morning to Koppel late at night, America has become a talk show nation, a boob-tube civilization, a run-at-the-mouth culture in which anyone can say anything at any time as long as they pull some ratings."[132]

As this chapter has demonstrated, talk radio is not a neutral carrier of public opinion. Public opinion expressed on broadcast talk is a filtered product. Its very existence is due not to any sense of social responsibility, but to commercial imperatives. What entertains and what sells are more important than the political imperatives of representation and free speech. The product is skewed toward the hosts' biases with other participants—guests and callers—primarily mirroring the host.

Such a reality should come as no great surprise. Broadcast talk, with the exception of public radio, is, at heart, a commercial enterprise, not a political or governmental one. Commercial enterprises only remain in business if they pay attention to the bottom line of profit. Profit is tied to both advertising and listenership, not to devotion to an abstract goal of public service, especially in the current mass media environment. Moreover, talk radio exists in a competitive environment where attracting audiences and creating a niche within the market become paramount concerns. Even Rush Limbaugh, the king of talk radio, is not immune to commercial considerations in determining the direction of his program. Other, lesser-known hosts are governed even more by such concerns.

Obviously, the rhetoric that surrounds talk radio, that is, a rhetoric of a populist medium, has been employed in order to enhance its audience. That advertising appeal is particularly effective in an era of widespread cynicism and frustration with other means for public expression.

Acknowledging these facts aids us in understanding why talk radio falls short of the much-vaunted forum for public debate. For example, talk radio has been criticized for its inflammatory rhetoric. Feminists are labeled "feminazis," environmentalists are called "wackos," and public officials are treated to a range of insults. Even hosts themselves are not immune from such verbal assaults. One host called another a "vile puss bag" and a "worm." The second retaliated by accusing the first of being "a racist," "a bigot," and "a despicable talk show host."[133]

Such rhetoric also can be viewed as having a cathartic effect on listeners. As one host pointed out, "The popularity of talk radio reminds us that Americans still prefer talking to fighting."[134]

But vitriol does nothing to contribute to problem resolution. In fact, such inflammatory rhetoric not only does not help achieve political compromises, it actually hardens political positions and ignites greater political conflict. Yet talk radio relies on such rhetoric to attract listeners. It is a paramount consideration of an entertainment business.

Merely urging talk radio to be more responsible or more fair is doomed to failure. There is little incentive to do so and strong disincentives to placing political considerations above commercial ones. One solution to the problem would be government action. Political responsibility could be imposed on talk radio through regulation. Talk radio could be required to fulfill certain political roles. Such requirements on the broadcast industry existed prior to the demise of the Fairness Doctrine and other regulations designed to mandate public affairs service. Talk radio stations could be compelled to air programs promoting a range of political views. No single program would be required to provide balance, but the panoply of programs offered by a station would have to cover a broader array of positions. Moreover, at least some percentage of talk radio programs airing on a station would have to be political.

Such requirements would allow current hosts to retain their political biases. The balance would be achieved through a holistic approach to a station's programming. The programs of some current hosts, probably the least popular, would be canceled. This type of policy would open the way for other programs to emerge, encouraging greater balance.

We are not naive enough to believe that in the current political climate such changes would pass the U.S. Congress. Yet, absent such changes, it is highly unlikely talk radio will place the political needs of the democratic system above its own commercial interests.

Politics and the Characteristics of Talk

Admittedly, talk radio is a forum where political discussion occurs daily, even hourly. More than that, through its unique form it has transformed the process of public discussion that occurs within its boundaries.

One change prompted by talk radio has been in the interpersonal nature of discussion. Talk radio has fostered political discussion as an anonymous activity. Some see this as an advantage because callers become more candid with the host and listeners than they would be otherwise. According to talk show host Alan Colmes, people "will say things anonymously on a talk show without identification that they wouldn't say to their best friend sometimes."[135]

Anonymity is fostered by physical distance, which, in turn, can be an advantage. The expression of views rarely leads to direct violence between the discussion participants. "Nobody's going to firebomb your house or cut the tires on your car," boasts Ken Hamblin.[136]

But this anonymity and physical distance also can diminish personal accountability. Callers can make statements about others, including the host, over the air they may not make if they met in person. Hosts can treat callers rudely because there is no face-to-face encounter. Thus talk radio contributes to the lack of civility that has been developing in our society, both among citizens generally and among political leaders.

Although talk radio offers the illusion of intimacy in its casualness and anonymity, it actually is much less intimate than other forms of interpersonal communication. One talk show host admitted, "There's no face, no person there, no hugs."[137]

Debate also is transformed in that there is no presumption of both sides being given a fair hearing on the same platform. While voters have become used to candidate debates at all levels of American politics where the candidates occupy the same platform at the same time, talk radio is very different. Talk hosts are openly biased and usually structure their programs accordingly. Opposing views are granted diminished or no exposure.

Talk radio has been viewed by many of its supporters as an alternative to a liberal news media. The talk radio audience does tend to be more politically conservative than the media audience generally, as will be discussed at greater length in chapter 7. Hence, the talk radio executives and station owners program for that audience.

Therefore, talk radio has altered the public debate by giving increasing public attention and credibility to a new conservative media. However, it is important to realize that if Tom Leykis suddenly gained a larger audience than Rush Limbaugh, the economics of talk radio would lead executives toward what would be perceived as the new wave of talk show hosts—young, brash, and politically somewhat left of center rather than conservative. This would occur because broadcast talk, even political talk, is a business.

Talk radio is a new forum for political discussion, but talk radio also is a business governed by commercial imperatives unrelated to and superior to political ones. In the role of such a forum, it falls short as an ideal mechanism for political communication in a democracy.

Talk radio is not a panacea for public frustration with politics as usual. In fact, because of its characteristics, it even may make communication toward problem resolution more difficult, further heightening public cynicism. That does not bode well for America, but it will make a great show for talk radio.

Showing Politics

Tabloid Journalism and Entertainment Television

One of the most vehement criticisms levied against the new media is that they trivialize serious issues of governing by infusing politics with entertainment. Social commentators have envisioned a frightening future where entertainment dominates politics. In a culture where "all politics is entertainment," Neil Postman laments that Americans are "amusing themselves to death."[1] Oliver Stone's *Natural Born Killers* depicts a chilling vision of a society held hostage by entertainment media gone berserk.

While these characterizations are at present exaggerations, the trend toward more sensational presentations of politics is real. The concern is greatest when the role of the tabloid press and television programs in the new media revolution are considered. As we will discuss shortly, the inextricable blending of politics and entertainment is a fact of American life that precedes the Founding. The most recent development is that tabloid newspapers and television programs have assumed an enhanced position in the political process, and politicians and the mainstream press cannot help but take them seriously.

Several factors have facilitated this trend. During periods when news interest is lagging, news organizations can use their existing television tabloid infrastructure to generate public interest in current events and public officials. Entertainment publications and television

programs have discovered that when their stock story lines involving
sex, scandal, and crime are applied to politicians, they can command
national attention. Tabloids are in a unique position to investigate and
break these more sordid political stories, as they conform to the news
values of the medium. The public, however, has different expectations
regarding the mainstream press. Since 1987, when the *Miami Herald*
came under fire for staking out the home of presidential aspirant Gary
Hart and uncovering his affair with Donna Rice, the traditional media
have been wary of initiating sex scandal stories.[2] Further, when
tabloids do the dirty work, they often do a better job of it than the traditional media. In the Gary Hart incident, the story did not become legitimate news until the *Star* tabloid acquired a photo of Hart and Rice
cavorting aboard a boat named the *Monkey Business.*

Acting in this manner, tabloids can set the agenda for other media. In addition, they can force candidates to react to the charges.
They can, as was the case with the Gennifer Flowers episode during
the 1992 presidential campaign, set off a media "feeding frenzy" that
can significantly alter the course of political events.

In this chapter, we will explore the nature and content of tabloid
journalism. We will briefly discuss the tabloid tradition in America.
Next, we will offer a definition of what constitutes tabloid journalism
and compare print and television genres. The recent increase in the
appeal of tabloid news will be discussed. Finally, we will debate the
pros and cons of tabloid news.

An American Tradition

Americans have a long-standing fascination with rumor and scandal
inherited from their British ancestors. Colonial newssheets and
broadsides contained tales of tragedies, disasters, and the lives of famous people. In fact, the first American newspaper was closed
for printing gossip about the French king.[3] During the penny press
era in the 1800s, sensational stories became a mainstay of newspapers seeking to appeal to a mass, rather than an elite, audience. The
"yellow journalism" practiced by the likes of William Randolph Hearst
and Joseph Pulitzer regularly featured news that was more fiction
than fact, although it is important to note that less of the news reported during this time period was sensational than is commonly
believed.[4]

Tabloid newspapers were established during the middle period of
the penny press era. The precursor of today's tabloid newspapers was
the weekly national *Police Gazette,* published in 1845, which featured
shocking crime tales. In 1919 America's first real tabloid, the *Illustrated Daily News,* debuted as a small format paper with short stories
and many pictures. Rapidly, other tabloids appeared on the scene, as
the format gained popularity with the public.[5] Tabloids thrived until

World War I when a pall was cast over the nation and the need for accurate news of current affairs became imperative.

Tabloid papers experienced their heyday from the late 1970s to the mid 1980s, before they faced real competition from television. Over the past several years, programs incorporating the style and technique of the pathbreaking "A Current Affair" have sprung up on network and cable television.

Although the American tradition of tabloid journalism continues to evolve as it makes its way into different realms of media technology, the basic story themes have remained constant. Many of these themes have their origins in folklore, such as the hero who didn't die; children raised by animals; ghosts; monsters; extraterrestrials; and fairy tales about princes and princesses.[6] As these themes indicate, the basic goal of tabloids has been unabashedly to entertain. The situation is no different when tabloids enter the political scene.

What Constitutes "Tabloid Journalism"

In the new media era, the lines between tabloid news and serious journalism have become increasingly obfuscated. Tabloid type stories regularly appear in the mainstream press. Further, political reporting in even respected publications and on network news programs is far from devoid of entertainment content.

It is possible, although somewhat difficult, to identify some characteristics that set tabloid fare apart from serious news. Tabloid news frequently is considered synonymous with sensational news. Journalism textbooks generally define sensationalism as "news of conflict which centers on violence and crime and flaunts basic ideas about what is important, right, and wrong."[7] However, a more accurate definition of sensational news contains a more specific accounting of the subject matter covered and the treatment of these subjects, especially as it relates to the techniques used in reporting and the style of coverage.

Sensational news subjects include coverage of unexpected events containing some inherent entertainment value.[8] Common topics are wars; sex; crimes, especially murders and violent acts; trials; natural disasters such as fires, floods, and earthquakes; accidents; family problems; and other tragedies.[9] Psychic tales and stories focusing on the occult also feature prominently. Tabloid reports specialize in coverage of the private lives of the rich and famous as well as the lives of ordinary people who have extraordinary or awful experiences. Print tabloids have traditionally focused their "common person" stories on members of the working or lower classes, who constitute their primary target audience. Notably missing are stories about people who fall between these two extremes, members of the middle and upper middle classes. Such a noticeable class bias is not as evident for most tabloid television programs, which reach more diverse audiences.

While the subjects that permeate print and electronic tabloids are fair game for mainstream news organizations, it is the treatment of these subjects that renders tabloid news distinct. The tabloid style evolved over time during the era of the penny press. Early print reports of tabloid subjects differed little in expository style from "hard news" accounts. Stories were written in often laborious prose in lengthy paragraphs. Sometimes they were not even introduced by headlines.[10]

Sensational news developed its unique stylistic imprint as a result of changes in communications technology and the emergence of journalism as a profession. The thrust of these changes occurred roughly between the years 1820 through 1860, with the 1840s marking the turning point. The telegraph increased the speed with which information could be disseminated and bridged distances between news sources and publishers. News was transmitted over the wire as succinct bursts of information, which, in turn, were reported in short stories consisting usually of no more than a paragraph or two. In addition, writing styles were becoming less formal at this time. News stories were tightened and shortened, as the public's appetite for more varied news increased and space considerations in newspapers became an issue.[11]

Reporting techniques also contributed to tabloids' sensational style. During the mid nineteenth century, the journalism profession began to develop the tools of the trade that exist today. The techniques of documentary, observation, and interview became central to the reporting of an ever-widening array of stories. Penny press reporters found that police, lawyers, criminals, and members of the lower classes who populated tenements and asylums were a fertile source of lively information that could be crafted into sensational stories. Articles were peppered with colorful and frank dialogue frequently written in dialect. In addition, the settings for stories, which were often in the seamy underside of society, were carefully integrated into reports. In a sense, the reporter became a tour guide, providing the reader with compelling glimpses into bizarre, frightening, and fantastic situations.[12]

More recent trends in reporting have contributed to the establishment of tabloid journalism's trademark form. "Checkbook journalism" is the increasingly prevalent practice of paying for information. Almost twenty years ago, "60 Minutes" created a controversy by paying H. R. Haldeman twenty-five thousand dollars and G. Gordon Liddy fifteen thousand dollars for interviews pertaining to Watergate.[13] "Checkbook journalism" has escalated in the past few years, especially among print and TV tabloids. Legal scholars claim that the Supreme Court's 1991 decision striking down the Son of Sam law, passed in 1977, which prohibited criminals from earning income from the sale of their stories, prompted the current "pay for news" trend.[14]

Tabloids offer large cash rewards for individuals willing to tell their stories. This practice often results in the tabloids scooping mainstream news organizations who do not have the financial resources to compete with them.

"Checkbook journalism" has permitted the tabloids to play a bigger role in the political sphere than they would ordinarily. For example, the *Star's* $150,000 payment for Gennifer Flower's allegation of her affair with Bill Clinton allowed the tabloid to break the biggest story of the campaign season.[15] The old media were forced to follow the tabloid's lead and cover the story, although they lacked direct access to the main source.

The tabloid reporting style is designed to heighten readers' and viewers' sensory experience with the news. The details of stories are presented in graphic form. Tabloid news is written in dramatic, engaging, and readable prose presented in short paragraphs and set off with attention-grabbing headlines and visual accompaniments. TV tabloids feature quick cuts between plots and subplots, highlighting conflict and crisis. While there are stylistic similarities between print and television tabloids, there also are differences. We turn now to an examination of these two tabloid genres.

Print Tabloids

Politics constitutes one of the smallest categories of news covered by the tabloid press. Yet, the political significance of tabloid papers is on the rise for a variety of reasons. The most conspicuous is that when the tabloids go after a political story, it is usually a big one, and tabloid coverage can have considerable repercussions. In addition, tabloids reach a large audience that is not served by the mainstream press. The tabloid audience is swayed by political news presented in this medium. Regular readers of the *Star,* for example, were more greatly influenced by the Gennifer Flowers incident than were better-educated devotees of the mainstream press.[16] Finally, print tabloids convey some core political values to their readers.

We can trace the lineage of the current breed of tabloid papers to the *National Enquirer,* which provided the model for subsequent entries into the market. Founded in 1926 as the *New York Enquirer,* a newspaper specializing in sensational stories, it was floundering when it was purchased and renamed in 1957 by Generoso Paul Pope who became a legend in the tabloid news business. Pope rapidly increased the sales and popularity of the *Enquirer* by selling it in supermarkets. To convince supermarkets to go along with his scheme, the *Enquirer's* content was cleaned up to include celebrity gossip and health features, rather than the more lurid stories it originally carried. Other tabloids, some owned by the same parent company as the *Enquirer,* provided diversity in content.[17]

The circulation of supermarket tabloids is difficult to gauge, but it is substantial. Readership reached its peak in the mid 1970s and early 1980s, but it has declined somewhat as a result of the incursion of television tabloid programs. Estimates of the total circulation of the six top tabloids range from 25 to 50 million readers per week. These figures include the 11 million people who purchase the papers and the additional people to whom they are passed on. The tabloids themselves like to claim over 200 million readers per week, a figure based on the number of people who glance at them as they are waiting at the checkout counter. Actual circulation figures are impressive. Subscriptions constitute less than 10 percent of tabloids' weekly readership base. The majority of people who purchase tabloids buy them weekly at the supermarket checkout counter.[18] The *National Enquirer* has the largest circulation of any newspaper in America (3.8 million) followed by the *Star* (3.4 million), the *Globe* (1.2 million), the *Weekly World News* (816,000), the *National Examiner* (805,000) and the *Sun* (350,000). By comparison, the *Wall Street Journal's* 1.8 million readers and *USA Today's* 1.4 million top the circulation charts for the mainstream papers.[19]

Tabloids reach a segment of the citizenry who do not generally tune into political news. As we will discuss later, tabloids appeal to readers' sense of fun, their desire for excitement, however vicarious, and their need to feel connected to community by sharing common knowledge. The audience is quite diverse and includes a cult following of college students and intellectuals.[20] The average readers are middle-aged, working- and middle-class white women with a high school education. About one third of readers are men. In addition to the tabloids, these people enjoy publications such as *People* magazine and *Reader's Digest*. Most, although not all, readers tend to have a healthy skepticism about the content of the paper and can distinguish the extraordinary from more realistic content.[21]

Readers of tabloids are indifferent, if not hostile, toward politics. Christopher Clausen notes, "It may be said that the rejection of the political as an object of attention separates tabloid readers from followers of the traditional press."[22] Packaging the political as gossip and scandal brings campaigns and current affairs into the purview of this segment of the population. Thus tabloid papers are a potentially potent political force, even if few papers have begun to exploit this power.

Not all tabloids are created equal. Each tabloid has its distinctive niche. Some tabloids make an effort to base their articles on actual people and incidents, such as the *National Enquirer* and the *Star*, although both carry stories that are remarkable, to say the least. The *Star* tends to focus on stories of often minor celebrities, soap operas, and common people, and is somewhat lighter in tone and subject matter than the *Enquirer*, which has a raw, sometimes violent edge to its reporting.[23] Presently, these two periodicals (which share the same owner) are working to change their tabloid image and liken themselves to *People* or *Parade* magazines.[24] The decision to include more political stories is part of this effort.

Other tabloids admit to being purely for amusement and include stories that may or may not be entirely manufactured. The *Globe*, *National Examiner*, and the *Sun* often use staged photos to add veracity to their questionable reports. The *Weekly World News* advertises the fact that it specializes in outlandish fabrications, many of which involve Elvis and aliens.[25]

This diversity among the tabloids is reflected in the individual papers' approaches to politics. Intense competition for readers also influences tabloid political reporting. For example, tabloids had different spins on the Gennifer Flowers's affair. The *Star* used its exclusive access to Flowers to focus its stories on her latest revelations about her relationship with Clinton. The *Enquirer* decided to impugn Flowers's reputation by reporting on her penchant for dalliances with married men, while the *Globe* ran stories alleging Bill Clinton had affairs with three black prostitutes which resulted in a "love child."

One reason why the tabloids do not become more involved in reporting politics is that political news does not sell. Interestingly, only the *Weekly World News*, the most outrageous of the "Big Six" tabloids, has a regular political columnist who specializes in right wing diatribes. This commentary is as lively and unreliable as the other contents of the paper.[26] In addition, tabloids usually have to pay for information about any scandal that will cause a stir. Thus they weigh the costs and benefits of reporting a political scandal carefully.

As tabloids increasingly have become a source of information for the mainstream press, they have taken unprecedented steps to safeguard their competitive edge. Journalists from outside of the tabloid world routinely call to find out information about upcoming stories and have run them before the tabloids hit the newsstands. As of 1996, American Media, which owns the *National Enquirer*, the *Star*, and *Weekly World News*, requires its employees to sign a confidentiality agreement that prohibits them from disclosing any information to competing publications. This agreement continues for five years after the employee leaves the company. The agreement states:

> I promise to safeguard the confidentiality of all facts I receive and all information I obtain, proprietary and otherwise, including but not limited to information about the Company, its practices and procedures, investigative and research techniques, reporting procedures and editorial analysis. During the period of my employment and for 5 years thereafter, I further promise not to write, speak, or give interviews about, either directly or indirectly, on or off the record, my work at the Company . . . for purposes of publication in any media in any way, directly or indirectly, without prior written approval of the Company.[27]

Steve Coz, *Enquirer* editor, stated that this pledge was necessary because tabloids have gained new respectability in the post–O. J. Simpson era. "We've grown, we've evolved, and the conventional press is becoming more tabloidlike in their approach to stories," he asserted. When the mainstream media more routinely break tabloids' advance stories, sales suffer.[28]

Aside from reporting political scandal, print tabloids make more subtle political statements through the values that underlie their stories. The tabloids have a strong moral code, central to which is a belief in the sanctity of marriage. Politicians who violate this code are readily condemned. In addition, equality between the sexes, races, and classes comes through in much tabloid fare, as everyone is fair game and receives the same treatment for violations of the moral code, regardless of their status in society.[29]

Entertainment Television

Print presentations of extraordinary news items can go only so far in titillating the audience. Television is far more successful in bringing sensational tales to life. Tabloid newspapers began to lose some of their popularity to television beginning in the 1950s.[30] However, it wasn't until the early 1980s that Rupert Murdoch and others more fully exploited entertainment news televisions' mass appeal. As the network system began to disintegrate and more channels became available for program distribution, tabloid TV programs multiplied. Beginning with "A Current Affair" and "Hard Copy," these programs explored territory similar to that covered by the supermarket press.[31]

The boundaries of what constitutes entertainment news programs can be cast rather widely. Talk shows, news magazines, and "reality" shows constitute three major varieties of entertainment news programs. There are significant variations in the content of programs within these categories, and some carry more overtly political stories than do others.[32]

Talk Shows

Talk shows, such as "Donahue," "Oprah," and the notorious "Geraldo!" and late night offerings, including "Letterman" and "Leno," are established American television fare. While these programs have predominantly become outlets for public confessions and celebrity publicity, they do on occasion showcase politics. For example, Jay Leno's opening monologue invariably contains barbs aimed at the politicians involved in the most recent political fiasco. At times, current affairs topics are covered. Geraldo is attempting to make his program more serious and legitimate in the wake of the O. J. Simpson trials, and deals with legal and political issues nightly.

Interviews with politicians constitute the most important political component of these shows. These programs provide the opportunity for politicians to reshape their images, as they do not have to conform to the expectations of the mainstream media. Bill Clinton's appearance playing the sax on "Arsenio" is an unforgettable moment in campaign history. Al Gore showed America that he wasn't entirely uptight when he presented his top ten list of the best things about being vice president on "Letterman," culminating with "Secret Service code name—Buttafucco."

The flexibility of the format allows talk shows to accommodate a wide range of political events. For example, Phil Donahue has hosted debates between candidates on his program that employed a variation on a town meeting format. Political leaders have answered questions from audience members and callers talk-radio-style on programs such as "Oprah."

Television News Magazines

Television news magazines have proliferated at an amazing rate since the late 1980s. In 1984, there were only two news magazines in primetime.[33] At present, there are close to twenty regular programs on network and cable. There are numerous explanations for the rise in entertainment news programs. Market factors are primary among them. Until the 1980s, television news divisions were considered public service enterprises; they could lose money without repercussions from management. When the competition for market shares intensified with the onset of cable television, news divisions were expected to be profitable. The production costs for entertainment news programs are substantially lower than for primetime sitcoms or dramas. For example, it costs approximately $500,000 to produce one hour of an entertainment magazine program compared to $1.8 million for an hour of a sitcom.[34]

Further, entertainment news programs have earned good ratings, which insures them advertisers, even as some major companies balk at the thought. The turning point came in 1988 with Geraldo Rivera's controversial two-hour special on NBC—"Devil Worship: Exposing Satan's Underground." This graphic portrayal of criminal behavior sparked by satanic beliefs drew over 50 million viewers and was the highest-rated pseudonews program in history. While NBC ultimately questioned its own decision to air the program during primetime, the ratings coup triggered the succession of new news magazines by the networks.[35] The high ratings have continued, although there has been some drop-off because of market saturation. At times during the 1994 television season, as many as four news magazine shows were rated in the top twenty.[36] Close to 7 million viewers tune in to "Inside Edition" nightly, and over 6 million regularly watch "Hard Copy."[37]

Finally, news magazine shows do well in syndication. "Inside Edition" and the now-defunct "A Current Affair" have ranked in the top ten syndicated shows.[38] "Inside Edition" broke records as the fastest selling syndicated program in 1993.[39] Network executives insist that local markets' preference for these programs has been a factor in the three major networks' decisions to produce their own news magazine shows despite their concern for maintaining solid journalistic standards.

There are three distinct calibers of news magazine programs, ranging from those that rely more heavily on serious news reporting and maintaining journalistic standards to those that are less inclined to be serious or ethical. "60 Minutes" is the precursor of the programs in this genre, and it is something of an outlier. Unlike the newcomers to the genre, it retains more of a hard news outlook. The second category of news magazine attempts to maintain the semblance of serious reporting while inserting a hefty dosage of entertainment into the mix. The networks each have their own primetime news magazine entry in this category—ABC's "20/20" with hosts Barbara Walters and Hugh Downs, CBS's "Eye to Eye" with Connie Chung, and NBC's "Dateline" with Stone Phillips and Jane Pauley. Finally, there are the more explicitly tabloid versions of news magazines, including "Hard Copy" and "Inside Edition." The distinction between the last two categories is becoming less clear, as the tabloid magazines work to clean up their act, while the network news magazines increasingly employ tabloid-type journalistic tactics.[40]

Many news magazines borrow the "60 Minutes" formula of exploring three or four stories in some depth, with segments running for approximately fifteen minutes. The difference lies in the method and mode of presentation, as well as in the choice of stories. While news magazines employ investigative techniques, they do not feel constrained by established professional journalistic norms and ethics. "60 Minutes" reporters often assume a confrontational style, but they generally are armed with carefully checked facts. In contrast, the new breed of news magazine show tends to play fast and lose with the evidence. They regularly employ re-creations of events, which may be difficult to distinguish from actual footage even when they are identified as reenactments. People appearing in interviews are coached and spend time with makeup artists to create the appropriate image.[41] They make use of "trained seals," people who are paid several hundred dollars to go on camera as experts or witnesses in order to add credibility to stories.[42]

Television news magazines use methods that blend artistry with information and are designed for maximum dramatic impact. They employ stylized visual techniques, sometimes mimicking MTV, which include quick cuts, black and white film, fades, and point-of-view shots. The language of entertainment news magazines is frequently sensational and ideologically loaded. It is aimed at keeping emotions high by evoking vivid imagery. Words like "shocking," "horrible," "ruthless," and "brutal" are standard news magazine lexicon. The verbal and visual images created by these programs are enhanced by musical accompaniments that set the appropriate mood.[43]

As the number of entertainment news programs has proliferated, the competition for ratings and viewers has intensified. Even the network primetime entries have covered sensational stories involving the likes of Lorena Bobbitt, Michael Jackson, and Tonya Harding. These stories appear side by side with hard-hitting journalistic efforts that deal with important issues and expose real societal problems. That news magazine segments are a very mixed bag is illustrated by the fact that a number of entertainment news programs have won Peabody Awards for excellence in reporting for individual segments.

It is interesting to note that even "60 Minutes" includes a heavy dose of entertainment in its more recent programming mix. Journalist James Fallows found that of the nearly five hundred stories aired between 1990 and 1994, more than one-third focused on celebrity profiles, the entertainment industry, or exposes of "petty scandals." Only around one-fifth of the segments deal with economics, the real workings of politics, or other issues of national significance.[44] As is the case with talk shows, interviews with political personalities constitute a substantial share of the political content on entertainment news programs.

Reality Programs

"Reality programs" are the final category of entertainment news offerings. Law enforcement programs, such as "C.O.P.S.," "FBI: Untold Stories," "Top Cops," and "True Stories of the Highway Patrol," have proliferated over the past few years. These programs depict law enforcement officals on the job. Another variety of "reality program" asks viewers to take part in the process of solving crimes. "America's Most Wanted" and "Unsolved Mysteries" are examples of this type of show. Both kinds of programs liberally mix live and dramatized footage.

"Reality programs" espouse a clear political agenda. They promote law and order values. At the same time, they feed public fears about crime and victimization. Further, these programs create and reinforce negative stereotypes of particular societal groups. Criminals inordinately are members of minority groups, especially blacks and Hispanics. Law enforcement officials are overwhelmingly white.[45]

Tabloid Appeal

Whether we like it or not, politics as offered through entertainment forums is followed by millions of Americans. Entertainment appears to be an effective means for getting information across. But what explains the appeal of tabloid news?

Media commentator Joshua Gamson asserts that entertainment news appeals to Americans' sense of fun. While public outcry against tabloid journalism has increased in recent years, readership and viewership remains robust. People satisfy their morbid curiosity about sex, crime, and violence through tabloids.[46] Gamson suggests that people want to hide their guilty pleasures.[47]

The appeal of entertainment news is predicated upon the public's desire to feel connected to society. Much ink and airtime is devoted to issues of popular culture and family life, however brutal the depictions sometimes may be. This helps to promote a common conversation among members of a society that may be too atomized.[48]

In featuring this type of material, tabloid journalism fulfills certain psychological needs. Most people's lives lack a great deal of excitement. Anthropologist Elizabeth Bird finds that tabloids provide individuals with a vicarious escape from their mundane routines. They are a source of enjoyment, inspiration, and inclusion for many Americans. As Bird states, "They are interested in stories about family breakdown because it makes them feel better about their families. There's a fantasy element in there about watching the exciting lives of beautiful people but seeing that what they are really looking for is a perfect family life. . . . They feel a bit superior to these people who they kind of admire at the same time."[49]

The Entertainment News Debate

The explosion in tabloid journalism has sparked debate among scholars and media practitioners. Journalists, in particular, have had to confront the fact that tabloid values have affected the way they practice their craft. Some journalists, such as Jeff Greenfield, have publicly denounced this trend, claiming that it has contributed to the declining civility and quality of political discourse.[50] CBS president Howard Stringer feels that tabloid news is "the dark at the end of the tunnel, and it is a journey to nowhere paid for with all our reputations."[51] Others, such as Diane Sawyer, who straddles the line between hard and entertainment news in her work, defend tabloid media. She contends that entertainment news programs can provide an effective forum for examining critical societal issues.[52]

Critics and defenders of the genre can be divided into elitist and populist camps. Critics contend that tabloid journalism devalues politics by lowering the standard of public debate to conform to entertainment norms. Defenders believe that entertainment politics has a democratizing effect and that it has the capacity to bring people who are at the political margins more fully into the process. We now examine the arguments against and for entertainment journalism.

Problems

While the lines between entertainment and news have always been somewhat fuzzy, it has been easier in the past to separate one from the other. As news organizations' public service incentive has been compromised by profit motives, entertainment values have come to dominate. In this type of media environment, public discourse is compromised. Political news is crowded out by sensational stories.[53] Debates about issues and leaders are reduced to gossip.

When news and entertainment—fact and fiction—become interchangeable, the public loses its ability to distinguish one from the other. When mainstream news organizations and entertainment news media are covering the same stories, the source of the information does not necessarily register with the audience member. As the information blurs together in the public conscience, individuals are less willing and able to trust the information that they receive about politics.[54] This contributes to the public's political skepticism, as citizens do not know who or what to believe. The fact that network news personnel have now crossed over the line to entertainment news programming compounds this situation. Most notably, Dan Rather, who once condemned the networks for "putting more fuzz and wuzz on the air," has caved in and appeared on "Eye to Eye" and other entertainment news shows.[55]

Joshua Gamson contends that the public has acquiesced to "news as play" and that this is linked to a decline in political efficacy. Social historian Stan Schultz concurs with this position. Audience members feel powerless to affect public policy.[56] When the public perceives its role in the polity to be inconsequential, it no longer feels the need to acquire meaningful information.[57] Thus tabloid journalism capitalizes on this public withdrawal from the world of serious politics.

Cultural critic Elayne Rapping also argues that tabloid television programs, especially, have ominous political implications. Society is presented as a more dangerous place that it is in reality. The pervasive message underlying tabloid media fare is that "the world is out of control; we are at the mercy of irrational forces, of deranged, sex- and drug-crazed criminals, or heroes and leaders who are degenerate, corrupt, and powerless against their own inner demons and outer temptations." These programs parade before us a continuous stream of the most contemptuous, hideous, and violent outlaws who could strike anyone, anywhere, at any time.[58]

Violent crime is a mainstay of entertainment journalism. Tabloid newspaper and television's quest to keep a steady flow of new and unusual crimes in front of the public eye has brought the seamier side of community life to worldwide attention.[59] Many reports are designed to appeal to the viewers' emotions, fears, and fantasies of revenge, rather than to expose societal ills.[60] Further, the notoriety awarded to the offenders has raised concerns about the possibility of encouraging "copy cat" criminals.[61]

Coinciding with the tabloid trend, mainstream media focus inordinately on crime and violence. As the homicide rate in the United States declined by twenty percent between 1993 and 1996, network news crime coverage increased by 721 percent, according to a study conducted by the Center for Media and Public Affairs. The O. J. Simpson case placed crime stories high on the network agenda, and they did not abate in the aftermath of the trial. In 1993, crime stories became the most frequently reported category of news, followed by health reports and economic news. Crime stories, especially murder cases, continued to dominate the news in the first half of 1997.[62]

Stories about political officials are interspersed haphazardly with lurid tales of society's criminal underclass. They are reported using the same stylistic conventions designed to maximize shock value. These factors work to erode citizens' faith in their leaders and the political process.[63]

Tabloid journalism, with its focus on extreme and pathological behaviors and confessional tales, may erode society's moral boundaries, as well. The differences between right and wrong may be erased.[64] Tabloid journalism has contributed to the tendency for individuals to use public confessions about personal demons to excuse criminal behavior. An example of this is the Menendez brothers' claim that as victims of sexual abuse they were justified in murdering their parents.

Another criticism of tabloid journalism is that it debases humanity by treating life as a commodity. Entertainment news media have an insatiable need for a constant supply of stories, which they are willing to fulfill by exploiting personal tragedy. Stories are bought and sold. Once they become the property of a news organization, personal stories are frequently fictionalized, as raw material is melded with dramatic touches.[65] The ultimate progression is from real life tragedy, to tabloid or entertainment news media, to movie of the week, with the distance from reality increasing with each step in the process.

Some critics contend that the negative aspects of tabloid journalism have directly influenced the political process. Jeff Greenfield claims that the success of tabloid journalism has sparked candidates to employ similar techniques in their campaigns. Sociologist Todd Gitlin notes, "Their lurid style has been copied by presidential campaign commercials. They cheapen everything."[66]

Possibilities

Not everyone agrees that tabloid journalism is inherently detrimental. Some argue that the democratizing effects of merging entertainment and politics outweigh the negatives. Tabloid journalism reaches members of social classes who are traditionally excluded from high-brow political communications media.

One benefit of entertainment journalism is that it can render complex political situations accessible to average citizens.[67] News magazines have the ability to introduce the public to key political players, provide background material on issues, and construct coherent narratives that explain complicated political happenings. For example, the legacy of the Vietnam War is something that is difficult for many Americans, especially younger people, to comprehend. News magazines have focused on the personal stories associated with the war, which are meaningful to many viewers.[68] Further, television news magazines have attempted to clarify the Clinton's complicated involvement in the Whitewater affair, often with greater success than network news.

Interviews conducted by pseudonews media frequently are longer, more detailed, and less pretentious than those carried by the mainstream press. The public has the opportunity to become better acquainted with its leaders, evaluate their character, and learn about issues. Seasoned interviewers ask tough questions and often receive frank answers. For example, as congressional hearings were in progress, Hillary Clinton was interviewed by Barbara Walters on "20/20" about problems she has faced since coming to Washington, especially her involvement in firings at the White House travel office. Even before the program was aired, excerpts from the interview were featured on network news programs, CNN, and in newspapers such as the *Washington Post*.

In addition, tabloid newspapers and entertainment television news programs offer an anti-establishment forum for the expression of views. The news agenda set in these media highlights issues that may not always be represented or treated in the same way in the mainstream press. The political wants and needs of lower- and working-class people are more likely to be portrayed in these media than in prestige newspapers and on the network evening news programs.

The entertainment press sometimes fulfills public service functions. Some of the problems and scams they expose appear inconsequential. However, others are significant and tend to represent the interests of average citizens. For example, "Inside Edition" investigated the traffic deaths and injuries that resulted from Domino's Pizza's policy of guaranteeing delivery within thirty minutes. The story brought national attention to the dangers associated with this practice and resulted in Domino's adopting safer policies.[69]

The style of news reporting in the entertainment press may have some advantages over mainstream news media. Particularly when dealing with political scandal, mainstream media, especially newspapers, tend to search for the sociological significance of events. These often ineffectual attempts at analysis more frequently serve to

lessen the value of news rather than enhance it. Tabloids and entertainment media focus more directly on the facts of the case and give a
clear accounting of who did what to whom. As Peter Shaw states,
with the tabloid press, "one is witness to the very chronicle of society
that the prestige press attempts to hide or disguise with its pieties."[70]
For example, the traditional media explored the feminist implications
of Lorena Bobbitt's attack on her husband. Skater Tonya Harding's involvement with the attack on her competition, Nancy Kerrigan, was
analyzed from the perspective of the pressures of sports and her
problem childhood.[71]

Entertainment media also can act as agents of socialization and
social control. As we have discussed, tabloid media have established
value codes that underlie their presentation of news. These include
upholding the virtues of societal institutions such as marriage and
obeying the law. By telling the stories of social deviants and passing
judgment on their actions, society reinforces, and at times reevalu-
ates, its shared standards and values.[72] Tabloid journalism holds political leaders to the same ethical standards as ordinary citizens, and
it can act as a check on the behavior of elites.

Some argue that entertainment media educate the public in a way
that mainstream media do not. They allow for frank discussions of
difficult topics and problems, especially those involving family life.
Talk shows, for example, may provide a public service as guests "go
public" with their problems and give advice to others facing similar
situations.[73]

Summary

As journalist Jonathan Alter notes, "Fifty years from now, long after
Kato Kaelin has given up his lounge act, the mid 1990's will be remembered as the golden age of tabloid news."[74] Fads in journalism
come and go in response to market, societal, and cultural factors. The
United States has gone through periods where sensational political
news has gone in and out of style.[75] Recently, the trend has been toward greater sensationalism.

The death of Diana, Princess of Wales, her companion, Dodi
Fayed, and their body guard in a Paris car crash momentarily placed
the issue of the tabloidization of news on the press's and the public's
agenda fueled by speculation that *paparazzi* who were stalking the
Princess played a role in the accident. The debate centered around
the issue of when and if media intrusiveness is justified when it compromises the privacy of even a very public person. Some journalists
argued that this incident created the opportunity for mainstream
media organizations to reevaluate the meaning of newsworthiness and
distinguish themselves from the tabloid press.[76] Yet, others maintained that the press is merely catering to audience demands.[77]

Reform proposals ranged from establishing voluntary codes of press behavior to legislative efforts aimed at restricting the press's ability to violate individuals' privacy, especially in the case of minors.

Questions about whether the death of Diana would cause the mainstream media, especially, to downplay sensational and personal stories were answered quickly. In effect, the press created a "feeding frenzy" surrounding the discussion of its own remorse, and failed to stimulate a debate with meaningful repercussions.[78] Less than a month after the internationally broadcast funeral, old and new media were saturated with graphic coverage of sports commentator Marv Albert's sexual assault trial. Even respected newspapers, such as *The Washington Post*, ran stories about the trial, sometimes on the front page. However, the *National Enquirer* tabloid did not cover the story. "We've left it to the networks to cover," stated editor Steve Coz. "Marv Albert gives the networks an excuse to run sex and violence." The *Enquirer*'s reason for not running the story were entirely audience-driven. The largely female readership is unfamiliar with Albert.[79]

At the time of Princess Diana's death, mainstream news organizations made public gestures toward reevaluating their goals, objectives, and the nature of the information they report. Their first test came shortly in the wake of Diana's passing, as first daughter Chelsea Clinton left home to attend Stanford University. President and Mrs. Clinton took unprecedented steps toward ensuring Chelsea's privacy by formally asking the press to keep its distance while their daughter completed her degree. Some mainstream news organizations, including *CBS Evening News*, pledged, after covering the first day photo opportunities, not to include Chelsea in another story until her graduation.

It is important to note that there are many more outlets for political news now than ever before in history. Although entertainment news is pervasive, there are still plenty of outlets for hard news. Entertainment print and electronic journalism adds diversity to news offerings. Entertainment news supplements, and does not replace, traditional sources of news. Robert MacNeil, former cohost of the "MacNeil/Lehrer NewsHour," a television news program aimed at educated, high socioeconomic status viewers, perhaps summed the situation up best when he noted that the American appetite for news stretches across a vast spectrum. He believes, however, that tabloid journalism will ultimately reach its limits. Referring specifically to tabloid talk shows, MacNeil notes, "After they look at demonic possession and sadomasochism and fetishes, where can they go?"[80]

MacNeil's projections could be on target. Facing a decline in ratings, there is an inclination among entertainment television programs to provide higher-quality programming. Further, an increasing number of entertainment political reporters are coming from the ranks of mainstream journalism and prestigious journalism schools, bringing with them better standards of reporting. Thus the future may look brighter for those who are concerned about the negative effects of entertainment programming on the American political process.

Typing Politics

Computer Networks

Twenty-five years ago the term *modem* did not even appear in dictionaries. Now it is an indispensable device for millions of Americans and others worldwide who rely on one or more modems daily. Modems connect people to online computer services such as CompuServe, Prodigy, America Online, or MSN, and to hundreds of thousands of World Wide Web sites and home pages throughout the world. Once online, users shop, arrange their personal finances, plan vacations, purchase airline tickets, play games, or do a multitude of other activities. The computer screen has the potential to become as central a fixture in American homes as the television.

Increasingly, computer networks have become tools for political communication as well. Users gather political information, express their opinions, and mobilize other citizens and political leaders. The information superhighway is fast becoming an electronic town hall where anyone with a personal computer and a modem can learn about the latest bill introduced in Congress, join an interest group, donate money to a political candidate, or discuss politics with people they have never seen who may live half a world away.

Even more amazing is the fact that this revolution has unfolded over such a brief period of time. So brief, in fact, that the repercussions, both for commercial enterprises and politics, are only now beginning to be felt.

Where did this technology come from and what effect will it have on political life? In this chapter, we examine the political uses and content of the Internet. We begin with an historical overview of the origins of the Internet and discuss how the system has evolved into a far-reaching and multifaceted political tool. We examine the ways in which news organizations and politicians use the Internet. In addition, we assess the importance of the Internet as a mechanism for gauging public opinion. Finally, we speculate about the future of cyberpolitics.

The Origins of the Internet

The genesis of this global computer communication network was the creation of the Internet. The Internet, used originally mostly for national defense purposes, began as a computer science research tool in the late 1960s. It came into being in 1969 at the University of Southern California and was designed to connect various local computer networks through "gateways" or linking systems. Throughout the 1970s, government agencies became involved in supporting the expansion of this new system. Research institutions and governmental bodies interested in facilitating research through computer networking, such as the National Science Foundation, NASA, and the Department of Defense (DOD), were the early users and funders of the Internet.[1]

The DOD split off the network of military research sites while the commercial use of the Internet began to flourish in the late 1980s with the support of the National Science Foundation. In the late 1980s, academic institutions and research institutes constituted a large proportion of Internet users and supporters. By the mid 1990s, however, commercial users predominated.

Government funding, which constituted the bulk of Internet support, has gradually diminished while computer access providers have become the backbone of what has become the most promising and popular aspect of the Internet, the World Wide Web. With the introduction of the Web, the Internet, which once was strictly limited to noncommercial purposes, is now a great commercial highway filled with advertising and various for-profit companies seeking new ways to expand markets.

The Internet can be used to glean all kinds of new information. Already through the Web an individual can search for a new car, locate a house to purchase, rent a recreational vehicle, find a toll-free number, play interactive games such as chess or battleship, or join a discussion group on pyrotechnics, computer software, or numerous other subjects. Prospective travelers can check exchange rates, read maps of cities around the world, or peruse the latest U.S. State Department travel advisories. Travelers manqué can take a virtual photo tour of a museum or watch a video of a far-away place.

Although the Web includes extraordinary amounts of free information, it has become primarily a commercial tool, supported largely by advertising much like other forms of mass communication in the United States. According to 1996 surveys of online users, 15–20 percent said they had nearly doubled the amount of products or services they had bought via the Internet over a six-month period.[2]

Universities and other academic institutions are major Internet sites, and many companies and nonprofit organizations have now joined the Internet through Web sites. But increasingly, users are accessing the Internet at home, which allows them more time to use it for personal interests.[3]

For those who connect on their own, the Internet is reached through access services available locally or through the major online access providers, such as CompuServe, Prodigy, America Online, and the Microsoft Network. These services supplement Internet offerings with their own specialized databases, games, or other activities.

Aided by increasingly sophisticated browsers that help a user sort through mountains of information, the World Wide Web has become the growth area of the Internet. Included in the Web and the latest browsers is technology that supplies extensive graphics, audio, and video. Users can surf the Web and choose from a dazzling array of visual images.

As computer networking has expanded beyond simple text retrieval, usage of the Internet and the World Wide Web has increased dramatically. Regular surveys of Internet use since 1994 have found increases both in the number of people who are users and the amount of time spent online. By 1996, estimates of online users ranged from 27 million to 35 million people.[4] One market research company has estimated the Internet user population grew by 132 percent in a single nine-month period.[5] Growth has slowed more recently, suggesting that Internet usage, like other new communications technologies, will never reach 100 percent of households.

For those who do use the Internet, time spent online has increased. According to a 1996 survey, one half of users said they are online at least ten hours a week. One-fifth said they stayed online more than twenty hours per week.[6] Further, while early users of the Internet tended to be younger and have higher socioeconomic and educational profiles, newer users are older, less educated, and less economically privileged.[7]

Increasingly, companies and other institutions are adopting networking systems requiring employees to master e-mail and the Internet. Universities are establishing courses on the Internet and granting certificates to those who successfully master Internet skills. Many organizations have determined that they will be left behind if they do not link to the Internet. One analyst summed up this attitude: "Debating whether or not you want the Internet in your office is like the conversations a century ago, when people were saying, 'I don't need this gadget called a telephone that other people are hooking up in their homes.'"8

Computer Networks as Political Tools

Entertainment, finance, and interpersonal communication are not the only uses for these computer networks. The Internet also has become a political tool for millions of Americans. The Internet fulfills four political functions, each of which will be discussed in turn. The Internet is used: (1) to access news and political information, most of which was previously less available; (2) to link public officials and citizens through government and other political Web sites; (3) to provide a forum for political discussion, especially through Usenet groups organized around various topics; (4) to act as a public opinion gauge with the potential of offering immediate reaction to events and decisions.

News and Political Information Source

The communications revolution of the twentieth century has restructured the news gathering and reporting business. Across the board, the mainstream news media have adjusted to the revolution in communications technology. This revolution has affected each medium differently.

The Internet, however, unites different media—broadcast and print—into one medium, the personal computer. Through the Internet, the various receivers—television, radio, print copy—potentially can be replaced by a single source. Now anyone with a personal computer, modem, and the appropriate audio and video equipment and software can read a book, peruse articles from a newspaper or a news magazine, listen to radio broadcasts, or even watch television news stories without flipping a page or turning a dial. Pressing keystrokes or clicking at icons on a screen is the only requirement.

The existence of such capabilities does not mean these other media will go the way of the dodo bird. First, it will be a long time, if ever, before print copies of books, newspapers, and news magazines are eliminated. Although print copy may be provided by the computer, Americans are not yet used to reading computer screens while eating breakfast. Curling up next to a warm fire with a computer does not evoke the same feelings as reading a favorite book. Yet the tide of change is surely coming in the way many Americans obtain news and information. The traditional news media, rather than being drowned under it, are seeking to ride the wave.

An ever increasing number of newspapers, news magazines, radio news shows, and television news programs now provide their regular news services via the Internet. Even the sources of news, the wire services, are accessible. Both the Associated Press (AP) and Reuters wire service stories are available to many computer network users. The news is more current than daily newspapers, and often allows the user to predict what will be printed in the morning paper.

In the early 1990s, local newspapers such as the *San Jose Mercury News* became experimental sites for online textual retrieval of newspaper stories. By 1992 *USA Today* placed abstracts of its stories online and three years later included the full text. Most metropolitan dailies, such as the *Dallas Morning News*, the *Houston Chronicle*, and the *San Francisco Chronicle,* now are available in cyberspace. Even many smaller local newspapers, such as the *Casper* (Wyoming) *Star Tribune*, the *Syracuse* (New York) *Herald Journal*, and the *Tacoma* (Washington) *News Tribune* have joined the rush to online text retrieval.

News magazines also have entered the Web. *Time* allows Internet users to read the full text of articles in the current issue. Users can see the cover and select articles from the sections of the issue, including "Milestones" and "People."

The major broadcast networks have established Web sites that allow a variety of services. The MSNBC site, a cooperative site between NBC and Microsoft, offers the latest news and features as well as a chat room, among other choices. PBS has gone online. Its premiere public affairs program, "Frontline," has a page describing the topics of upcoming programs, with special pages for the "NewsHour with Jim Lehrer" online.

Television news and information sites go beyond scheduling information or descriptions of programs. Actual broadcast news can be obtained. Full-video clips of the latest stories can be retrieved from CNN's Web site.

Radio programs also have their online counterparts. ABC radio news offers a twenty-four-hour news service complete with audioclips of latest news. National Public Radio has placed online its full programs or clips from its feature news programs—"Morning Edition" and "All Things Considered"—on a somewhat delayed basis. By downloading the appropriate software, a user can choose various segments of the NPR programs and listen sans radio.

Local television and radio stations also have created home pages. Las Vegas residents who miss one of their local news programs can read the news scripts from KLAS-TV on the Internet. Interestingly, Las Vegas natives who live elsewhere can keep informed about Las Vegas news by doing the same. Other stations offer video clips of recent stories.

United States news media are hardly alone in adopting the Internet as a vehicle for news delivery. Newspapers, wire services, and even radio broadcast news outlets in other parts of the world have established home pages allowing users to access the full text of articles from the latest issue or to search the newspaper's archives of back issues. The *Irish Times,* for example, includes sample articles from each daily issue, including not just hard news, but also editorials and other sections. Full-text news stories from the Tokyo newspaper *Asahi Shimbun* can be accessed in either Japanese or English. The *St. Petersburg Press,* an online English language version of the popular Russian newspaper, even includes classified announcements. Users can search the archives of the South African *Weekly Mail and Guardian.* Broadcast news also is available. Internet users can listen to Canadian Broadcasting Company Radio News or the German broadcast network Deutsche Welle.

International organizations also offer news. Press releases and radio broadcasts from the United Nations can be heard. Amnesty International and the World Council of Churches place their news releases online.

Hard news is not the only type of political information available. Public affairs programming is appearing more frequently. C-SPAN has placed on its home page audio of speeches aired on the broadcast network.

Other types of new media also have gone online. Radio talk is available through Internet talk radio. Users can hear a selection of talk radio programs from around the nation. Some radio hosts sponsor their own home pages on the Web. Through their Web sites, nationally syndicated hosts such as Michael Reagan, Alan Colmes, and Ken Hamblin offer another contact for fans. Some, such as Reagan, rely on e-mail messages from listeners as well as calls. Other pages, such as the Unofficial Rush Limbaugh home page and the Howard Stern fans home page, have been established not by the hosts, but by devoted fans. The Limbaugh page features information about the popular host as well as a review of his famous tie collection and a listing of his " thirty-five undeniable truths."

Television talk programs such as "Late Night with David Letterman," the "Tonight Show," and "Late Night with Conan O'Brien" can be accessed via computer. Letterman's Web site includes an archive of his famous top-ten lists. Tabloids are even available online. The *National Enquirer* offers glimpses of its current issue, including images of the famous people it covers.

The Internet also has become an information tool not only for the consumers of news, but also the gatherers. Journalists have found the Internet a useful tool for connecting to a multitude of news, public affairs, and other political sources.[9] As we will discuss in chapter 8, the use of Internet information sources can create problems, as fact and fiction are often difficult to discern online.

News and political information will come from a variety of sources, such as corporations, industry sites, and a variety of interest groups. Individuals use these sources to get news because often they feel that other media deliberately won't carry the news contained here. One Web site, the "Sovereigns Content Page" describes itself as containing "news and events that the international media does not print." These include topics such as One World Government, the right to bear arms, sovereignty, and AIDS. As more and more groups move onto the Internet, news will be available from a wider array of sources, seemingly further weakening reliance on traditional news media by Americans.

However, news organizations' quick adaption to the Web suggests they will not allow that to happen. Moreover, speed in news delivery, reach in newsgathering, and credibility still offer the traditional media organizations advantages in the competition with alternative sources.

Not all of this news and information is free, however. Fee services, even for news and information, have become standard for some news organizations, such as the *Wall Street Journal*. With all of the information that is available online gratis, however, pay-for-news operations generally have not been profitable. Despite this growth in the availability of news, consumer demand for Internet news and information services still lags behind other uses of the Internet.

Linking Governor and Governed

Political media, traditional or new, constitute only a handful of many offerings on the Internet. Unlike other forms of new media, the control of the technology is not in the hands of media organizations. Also, unlike other media the Internet has no need of a filter. Space or time limitations are almost nonexistent, at least at present.

Since the Internet technology is not controlled by news organizations, access by nonmedia groups is direct and unfiltered. This explains why political organizations such as government agencies, state governments, interest groups, and candidates have found the medium useful as an unfiltered tool for communication.

The Executive Branch

The Clinton White House has been a pioneer in use of the Internet, while the Bush administration never established a presence there. The Clinton administration opened a gopher site in January 1993 that later expanded to a full-color home page. The Web site of the White House opens with an image of the White House and offers a menu for the user to pursue interests in the First Family, the White House itself, or presidential policy. Users who want to know more about the First Family are treated to a scrapbook of pictures of the Clintons engaged in various activities from feeding the homeless in a soup kitchen to vacationing on Martha's Vineyard. The presidential cat, Socks, even provided an audio of a "meow." Users also can conduct a virtual tour of the White House or the Executive Office Building and hear an audio message from the president welcoming them to the historic structure. The tour includes the featured rooms of the usual tour as well as a peek at the Oval Office. For the more issue-oriented, the White House site offers access to presidential announcements, transcripts of daily press briefings, and the texts of major documents such as the annual budget, proposed administration bills, and major agreements and treaties (e.g., NAFTA and GATT). The site has been highly popular with Internet users. By mid 1996 it was receiving approximately 900,000 hits a month.[10]

Many agencies also have established sites on the Internet, including all the cabinet level departments and many of the bureaus within those departments. The sites are similar in their inclusion of information such as addresses and phone numbers, texts of press releases and reports, and mission statements. Some include speeches and congressional testimony by the secretary. Some sites offer more specific user information. The Treasury Department educates users on how to file an electronic income tax form and the Education Department offers instruction on applying for grants or contracts. The Central Intelligence Agency (CIA) offers views of declassified satellite imagery, political reports on other nations, and the sale of CIA maps and atlases. Users can search the latest CIA World Factbook. Those planning international travel can tap the State Department's site to read the latest foreign travel advisories. The most visually entertaining site belongs to NASA. Users can follow the space shuttle in flight through real-time data images from NASA's television cameras or a 3-D tracking display. Or, with video capability, the user can see an animated video of the shuttle in flight or watch daily video clips transmitted from inside the shuttle.

Congress on the Web

When Newt Gingrich became speaker of the House in January 1995, he outlined a technological future for the House promising that "every amendment, every conference report would be online and accessible to the country."[11] The House of Representatives has accelerated toward that future in its online offerings. This movement actually was initiated in the 103rd Congress when Representative Charlie Rose of North Carolina was appointed to create and supervise a House gopher. The gopher included listings of members along with committee memberships and party leadership lists. Some documents were included in the gopher. A few members began to acquire e-mail addresses.

In 1995 the House took major strides toward using the Internet as a tool for disseminating political information. The U.S. House of Representatives Web site now offers an electronic library literally at users' fingertips. The House has uploaded all texts of bills, resolutions, and amendments introduced on the House floor. Internet users can read the texts of newly introduced bills. The user overwhelmed by legalese can access prepared descriptions of the bills.

The effect is potentially revolutionary for followers of legislation. Today, any user can have the capability formerly held by lobbying firms and interest groups of checking the current status of any bill or amendment. Committee actions, including hearings and markups, are described. The user can access transcripts of committee hearings.

Some committees also possess their own home pages. The home page of the House Committee on Government Reform and Oversight, for example, informs users of pending committee meetings and action. It also lists the committee's legislative accomplishments, including a summary of recent bills passed by the committee and subsequent action by the full House, the Senate, conference committees, and the president. The House of Representatives' Web site describes current floor proceedings, including a minute by minute summary of floor action. For the actual content of the debate and action, the user can access the *Congressional Record* online.

Information about individual members has progressed far beyond e-mail addresses. All members of Congress now have separate home pages usually including background information on the member, committee assignments, as well as a listing of legislation either sponsored or cosponsored by the member.

Congressional information is not limited to the official Web sites of the two houses. Other sites, such as Thomas, the Library of Congress's site; C-SPAN; or CapWeb, an independent site, offer legislative information. Through the nonofficial sites, the user can find additional information the member or the institution may not be anxious to reveal. This includes ratings of the members of Congress by various interest groups and political action committee money contributed to their electoral campaigns.

The plethora of information at these sites now allows any user with a personal computer and a modem to follow legislative activity. Although few Americans will be more than casual users, the availability of this information allows even those with infrequent interest in legislative activity to have a readily accessible source when such interest is aroused. Even members of Congress themselves have been aided by this change. Since Speaker Gingrich has required that a bill be placed online before it is voted on, members can see the text of a bill before they are required to assent to it.[12]

State and Local Governments

States have established information sites on the Internet similar to those at the national level. Several state legislatures, for example, now provide information resembling what the House of Representatives'

Web site offers. Common features of such Web sites are various types of directories of members of the legislature. Some state legislatures offer more extensive data, including a description of that day's legislative action, journals of chambers, and the status of a bill. State legislative leaders realize users do not know bill numbers. To facilitate constituent information about legislation, search engines have been incorporated in many sites. Users can conduct searches through texts of bills by topic.

Information about individual members is growing. Arizona legislators' home pages list all the bills they have sponsored. Rhode Island's site publishes the full text of press releases issued by individual members. Moreover, constituents can use the Internet to interact with legislators. E-mail correspondence is growing and will soon become an expected component of a legislator's communication with the district.

State Web sites usually include individual pages featuring various state agencies such as Health and Social Services, Public Safety, Transportation, and Education. Routinely, the sites will include listings of various state departments and programs with phone numbers and descriptions of the agency's mission. Some offer more specific data for citizen use. Wisconsin's Department of Health and Social Services includes names of contact persons for various services such as Medicaid and child care. Nearly half of the state governments post available job listings within the state. For example, Utah's home page of the Employment Security Division links to job postings by various major employers within the state. The Texas Department of Transportation page offers information about vehicle registration as well as news about road conditions in the state. Users can even view city maps and click on roads to learn about specific traffic problems that day.

The judicial branch also is included in the Web sites of some states. Ohio's state government page, for instance, includes decision announcements by the state's supreme court.

Local metropolitan areas are placing online information and links to agencies responsible for city services, such as regulations on animals, gun permits, garbage disposal, as well as information about city ordinances. The home page for the city of Seattle, Washington, includes links for a wide range of city services such as homeless shelters, marriage licenses, rat control, and pothole repair.

Governments also offer more than descriptive information about public services. Many are now using the Internet to post announcements about meetings and decisions of governmental bodies. Even tribal governments have gone online. The Oneida Nation of New York's Web site includes facts about tribal government services and tribal news, but also audio samples of the Oneida language and texts of treaties with the U.S. government.

State and local government information falls into three categories: general information about government activity, specific tools for individual use of government services such as employment or health care, and information useful for facilitating public involvement in state or local policy-making.

What has not occurred is widespread use of this technology for direct democracy. Many Web sites include e-mail addresses or even surveys where users can express opinions. But there has not been more than an experimental reliance on computer networks for expression of public opinion about policy.

Interest Groups

Computer network technology has had profound impacts on the operation of interest groups at the national level. The Internet has lowered the cost of monitoring politics, organizing group members and other interested individuals, and reaching more individuals who are like-minded but unknown to the organization.[13]

The research costs for interest groups have dropped with free electronic information services such as Thomas. Groups can search for the current status of bills, preview committee schedules, and peruse committee prints and other congressional information in minutes with minimal cost. One scholar has summed up the effect on congressional behavior: "The computerization of data and its ready accessibility render the terms 'obscure paragraph' and 'hidden provisions' obsolete."[14]

Lobbying also has become less costly. Because groups now can send letters and fact sheets via the Internet to large numbers of recipients simultaneously, they avoid the cost of hand-dialed fax transmissions, which costs both in terms of time and long-distance charges, and the expenses of even more obsolete postal fees. Moreover, e-mail transmission can achieve nearly instantaneous results in terms of both reach and response. Contacted individuals can take minutes to do what used to take much longer through nonelectronic means.

Various groups, and even coalitions of groups such as the National Coalition Against Censorship, the American Arts Alliance, and the United States Industry Coalition, also have established their own Web sites as regular information sources for their members or other interested individuals.[15] In addition to the publications and regular mailings, the Internet has become another connection between interest groups and their related constituencies.

These sites serve valuable information purposes. The information is similar to the nonelectronic news that groups send to members. The National Organization for Women Web site includes articles from the organization's monthly newsletter, and the AFL-CIO site includes labor news drawn from its regular publications. The information contained on these sites can be quite political: information about pending legislation, discussions of the efforts of various members of Congress, and lobbying efforts of the group. The Christian Coalition's site allows supporters to review legislative scorecards for members of Congress on issues of importance to the group.

The emphasis is not merely on education, but also on mobilization of the constituency. The AFL-CIO site includes instructions on how to organize a union or become a union organizer. To facilitate contact with federal government officials, both the National Rifle Association (NRA) and the AFL-CIO sites include directories of members of Congress, including their e-mail addresses.

Through such Web sites, organizations can convey more lengthy and detailed information at much less cost than through direct mail. The John Birch Society site allowed users to read a lengthy report on the "real story" on the Oklahoma City bombing. The NRA site not only describes pending federal legislation, but also includes files on all fifty states, facilitating user knowledge of proposed changes in laws in their own states or communities.

Many organizations use their site to recruit new membership. Addresses of local or state chapters are included to encourage direct contact with more proximate headquarters. Casual viewers of sites are encouraged to join the organization through membership applications the user can print and mail through regular mail. The Rainforest Action Network even includes an online membership application complete with a method of online payment.

Use of the Internet is hardly limited to traditional mainstream interest groups. Alternative groups in the American political spectrum have incorporated the Internet as a medium for communication. Socialists "chat" on "SocNet: The Socialist Party Online," the discussion group for American socialists. Right wing use of the Internet has proliferated as well. Users who tap into the Stormfront White Nationalists home page, which has as its slogan "white pride world wide," can download images of a Nazi flag. In militia newsgroups, subscribers discuss the mystery of unmarked black helicopters at U.S. military bases and the virtues of various types of semiautomatic weapons.

Interest groups have found the Internet to be a useful tool for disseminating information, maintaining contact with their own members, recruiting new members or at least reaching a sympathetic audience, and mobilizing their constituencies for political action. They offer like-minded individuals another means of obtaining information and collectively acting to achieve political goals.

Candidate Use

The Internet came of age as a campaign tool in 1996. A search of three candidate Web site lists immediately following the November general election found 521 congressional candidates with Web sites.[16]

The Internet was employed for the first time in a presidential campaign in 1992. The Clinton-Gore campaign placed full texts of speeches, advertisements, position papers, and biographical information about the candidates on the Internet. However, Lamar Alexander was the first to utilize the Internet for campaigning. Alexander participated in an interactive session with online users. Subsequently, a bevy of other candidates such as President Clinton, Senate Majority Leader Bob Dole, Representative Bob Dornan, Senator Arlen Specter, talk show host Alan Keyes, and Senator Richard Lugar created campaign home pages. Supporters of potential candidates have even created home pages to stimulate interest in a prospective campaign. Colin Powell was the subject of a Web site before he announced he would not run for office.

The Web sites typically included biographies and pictures of the candidate, speeches, and issue position statements. Some contained special sections for the press. Pat Buchanan's, for example, offered a press-friendly calendar of upcoming media events.

Some of the campaigns utilized the interactive nature of the medium to solicit user opinions on policy issues. Users could complete questionnaires and send them to the candidate's organization. Or users could send their own spontaneous e-mail message to the candidate. Buchanan's home page allowed users to read messages from other e-mail writers.

For some campaigns, the Internet became a fundraising tool. Bob Dole's campaign included an online donation form and offered a free "Dole for President" mousepad for those giving at least twenty-five dollars. The Internet also was used to identify supporters. The Dole campaign created an e-mail subscription list that sent periodic reports on the progress of the campaign to Dole partisans. The user also could sign up to be a volunteer or receive a free bumper sticker from the campaign. On Lamar Alexander's home page, users could find a list of local organizers in their area they could contact in order to volunteer.

The Internet has the potential of serving as an equalizing medium for all candidates. While the candidates who are regularly featured by the media are included, other candidates also have established home pages. Advertising those home pages, however, becomes a problem. Often lesser-known candidates must rely on organizations that cover politics, have established well-recognized and advertised home pages, and are willing to offer links to the candidate's home page.

However, the advantage is not as great as it may appear. Users need to know sites exist before they will turn to them. Third and minor party candidates lack the advertising capabilities of major party candidates. Republican presidential candidate Bob Dole used his debate with President Clinton to advertise his site. No other candidate had such an advantage.

Users following the 1996 presidential campaign could access the home pages of various organizations covering politics, such as *Congressional Quarterly*, C-SPAN, the *National Journal*, and the American Political Network. These organizations, with home pages linked to candidate home pages, offer users the ready access to candidate information. If these links screen out other candidates, then the "dark horse" candidate is disadvantaged.

Minor party candidates did obtain a measure of equality through the links from these established sites. The Web site of the *National Journal* and the American Political Network linked to sites of several lesser-known candidates, including contenders for the major party nominations, minor party candidates, and independents. Other candidates were at least given space to advertise their names, addresses, and party affiliations, if any. Prior to the 1996 primary season, that site listed over one hundred candidates.

Candidates such as Charles Doty, a Tulsa, Oklahoma, minister running for the Republican nomination; Charles Collins, a Florida rancher also running as a Republican; and William Winn, an independent from Mesa, Arizona, created home pages including biographical information as well as platform positions, organization addresses, and press releases from their campaigns.

The candidates' own home pages were not the only sources of information about contenders on the Internet. During the 1996 campaign, for example, others unrelated to the campaigns set up competing home pages about the candidates. Some of these sites were created by supporters, such as the unofficial Colin Powell sites that urged Powell to run for president. Others, however, often contained hostile information. One example of a site critical of most of the candidates was "Real People for Real Change," an independent political action committee with a Web site that aired accusations about the moral character of presidential candidates, both announced and potential. Some sites targeted particular candidates. During the primaries, one such home page parodied Pat Buchanan's official home page using subtle differences such as a Nazi flag in the background.[17] Another site, known as Newtwatch, continued to carry derogatory information about House Speaker Newt Gingrich even after he decided not to launch a presidential bid.

The Internet as Political Discussion Forum

The Internet has launched a multitude of political discussion groups who correspond about a range of topics from Rush Limbaugh to the Socialist party. Groups are organized around individuals such as Ross Perot, G. Gordon Liddy, and Ronald Reagan; around political parties including the two major parties as well as Libertarians; or around ideologies such as progressivism or socialism. Some exist for specific purposes, such as the "Impeach Clinton" group. Others discuss policy areas such as gun control or limitations on militias.

One major problem with the discussion groups is participants can hide behind a veil of relative anonymity. Individuals may or may not use their names with postings. Some even use fictitious names such as "John Q. Public" or "Awesome1" that further mask their identities.

There is somewhat less anonymity than talk radio because the individual posting a message also provides their e-mail address. But such addresses can be anonymous if the individual is using an address from an online service rather than from a particular institution. An address such as "jsmith@pucc.princeton.edu" would identify the sender as affiliated with Princeton University. On the other hand, a posting from an online service such as America Online or Prodigy can mask the name and the location of the sender.

Users can employ extreme rhetoric or make vicious ad hominem attacks on well-known figures or other users while avoiding personal responsibility. The absence of personal contact in the discussion coupled with the ease of rapid (and sometimes ill-considered) response, allows such group discussions to become bitter. One commentator of the Internet society concludes that "on-line discussions too often break down into a kind of name-calling that would not be tolerated in a real-life meeting or social setting."[18]

Another limitation of the political discussion groups is their fragmentation. The groups attract like-minded individuals kibitzing on a narrow range of topics. Although the Internet has the potential of drawing into political dialogue individuals from a wide range of backgrounds, regions, and ideologies, in fact the discussions via the Internet are more likely to be as narrow or perhaps even narrower than those across the backyard fence.

Those with differing views gravitate to their own discussion groups. Rather than communicating with each other, they talk past one another in the ether. These discussion groups appear more designed to reinforce existing beliefs than foster dialogue between competing views. A conspiracy discussion group passes on information about current rumors such as black helicopters flying around the U.S. or the latest Whitewater development.

Occasionally those in opposition to the group's political slant will wander into the discussion and contribute a contrasting view. But the intrusion usually is quickly countered, sometimes with vehemence, by the regulars. For example, on one conspiracy group bulletin board, an individual opined that "government can't pull off a conspiracy because it is too complex for them. Watergate proved that." But the intruder was quickly answered that "the government is just a front organization. It's purposely kept bozo-esque to throw us off." But even such disagreements are far less common than messages that merely confirm the prevailing group opinions.

The Internet as Public Opinion Gauge

An e-mail revolution has been launched in the mid 1990s. E-mail is be-coming the equivalent of the free rural delivery earlier in this century. The bandwagon so popular that millions of Americans are signing onto online services just to keep in touch with family, friends, and as-sociates across the country and around the globe.

Government entities also have been caught up in the e-mail craze, although much more slowly than large companies. Even the e-mail connections within government tend to be used more for internal communication than with the public. Since 1993, Congress, the White House, and many government agencies have begun to offer e-mail as another communication link for the general public. Usage has increased over time.

Early in the Clinton administration, the White House appointed a new director for e-mail and electronic publishing. The Clinton admini-stration has circulated the president's public e-mail addresses on ma-jor online services as well as the Internet. By summer 1993, the White House was receiving about eight hundred messages per day.[19] As use of the address became more common, however, the White House became backlogged with e-mail that was stacked on the floor and left unanswered. There was no system of handling the influx of e-mail messages.

The White House's system has become more sophisticated over time. E-mail sent through the White House's Web site now appears on a standard form and can be categorized easily. To help White House staffers identify the type of letter received, senders are asked to choose from a menu of options, such as seeking assistance from the White House, extending a speaking invitation, or expressing agree-ment or disagreement with a White House position. Senders also must choose a policy topic and an affiliation (such as veteran, stu-dent, civil servant, or senior citizen). This sorting allows the White House to organize reading of the mail and forwarding to appropriate departments.[20] Interest in sending e-mail has exploded with the Web site. In one six-month period, half a million public e-mail messages were sent to the president and the vice president.[21]

In 1993 the Congress also began experimenting with external e-mail communications. The two houses acted separately, with the House of Representatives moving more quickly to implement a public e-mail system. A sample of members volunteered to create e-mail ad-dresses and try out the system. Only a handful of senators, such as Edward Kennedy of Massachusetts, Charles Robb of Virginia, and James Jeffords of Vermont, and three dozen members of the House opened e-mail addresses and encouraged public response.[22]

By 1995, both houses rushed towards e-mail. The House gave e-mail addresses to all members while most senators received them.

Public use of the opportunities of e-mail contact with members of Congress increased dramatically.

E-mail has become the high-tech equivalent of the post card mass mailing on specific issues. During the 104th Congress, for example, e-mail was one strategy, used in conjunction with post cards, letters, and phone calls, by organizations who wanted to encourage members to vote against overriding the presidential veto on the partial birth abortion bill.

Members also face enormous problems with the influx of e-mail messages. Given the limitations on staff, they don't have the capability to answer hundreds of new forms of mail pouring into their offices. Moreover, they don't want to have to answer mail from large numbers of people outside their districts. Yet that is precisely their dilemma. "What's happening is that with the new software programs today," explains Representative Sam Gejdenson of Connecticut, "16,000 kids at a college can send me a letter with a push of a button. I don't have the ability to go through all of that."[23] Members of Congress are unsure about how to handle a large volume of mail from nonconstituents.

Even constituents may become a problem for congressional offices, given the greater ease of communication. According to one congressional e-mail system analyst, "Congressional offices are already so stretched out, and their people are so stressed out. There's the fear that this will take those offices to a whole new level of dealing with the constituent computer hacker."[24]

Members' offices tend to use a variety of methods for responding to e-mail messages. Some constituents who have expressed what the staff considers to be a valid concern via e-mail will receive a return e-mail message. More frequently, a traditional letter will be sent through the regular mail.

The Internet in the Democratic Process

Predictions of computer networking as the final act toward direct democracy have become common. Now the public can interact with political leaders, and each other, in a great national town hall. Linking the citizenry to government through computer will offer the interactive capability missing in past media. Voting and public policy resolution can be achieved at the touch of buttons with little cost to the state or the citizen.

This new medium possesses its own new challenges as a tool for American democratic expression and policy-making. One such limitation is the assumption of public knowledge. How many citizens as users will avail themselves of the opportunities to acquire greater knowledge of public policy or candidate positions? Or will there be a tendency toward entertainment rather than political information? Why should people become suddenly more interested in politics merely because political information is more readily accessible to them? Aren't Americans more prone to respond the same way two characters on the television comedy "Cheers" did to new technology on a 1993 episode? Norm is amazed as he stares at a bank of big-screen television sets linked by satellite to various information sources. His friend, Cliff, explains their real effect: "Well, Normie, this is the information age. We can get up-to-the-minute stock prices, medical breakthroughs, political upheavals from all around the world. Of course, we'd have to turn off the cartoons first."[25]

Also, public opinion about current policy issues will be easier to obtain, but that will tend to a more rapid response. With this technology, the nation will move further from the Madisonian view of a respectable distance between the governed and the governors to allow public passions to wax and wane without concomitant spasms in public policy. Such movement is not inherently bad, however. But neither is it a panacea.

Internet communication facilitates quick responses by users. At a touch of a few keystrokes, opinions can be expressed and communicated far and wide. Yet such rapid reaction should not be the lodestar of public policy resolution. The public's initial response to a public policy problem may not be the most reasoned. Yet there may be intense pressure on representatives to reflect immediate public reaction. One danger, then, for reliance on such opinions is the shrinkage in the amount of time allowed to ponder the implications of decisions.

A related problem is creation of the mechanisms of the Internet for registering political opinions. Surveys conducted on the Internet have been unscientific and therefore unrepresentative even of the user population, much less the citizenry in general. Unless widely respected polling agencies can be enlisted to offer a neutral structure, the potential for manipulation of public expression via the Internet is great. Coupled with the preceding danger, the implications of false readings of the public pulse and immediate responses are clear, and clearly troublesome.

But in a larger sense, the problem with the Internet's use for this purpose lies not so much in whether the Internet serves as an immediate public opinion gauge but whether such expression is granted a weight it may not deserve. Proponents of the Internet often call it a "digital democracy" that is "broad and diverse enough to serve as a sort of surrogate town hall meeting." The Internet falls far short of this goal.[26]

First, the Internet is not an inclusive medium. Other new media—such as talk radio and television talk—can lay a stronger claim to being inclusive, but the Internet is still a middle-class plaything. Internet users are not representative of the total population. Users are predominantly more well to do than the population as a whole. Users tend to have incomes well above the average, are professionals or

managers, and are much better educated than the population generally.[27] One estimate is that the average user of an online service pays
approximately two hundred dollars per year, in addition to the estimated two thousand dollars for the hardware (personal computer,
modem, and sound and video cards) necessary to access Internet
data.[28] Such costs are out of the question for poor and working-class
Americans.

Users also may not be representative in their partisanship. According to two 1996 surveys, 25–29 percent of online users called
themselves Libertarians.[29] Users may be more likely to be Republicans and Independents than the public at large.[30] The problem with
gauging public opinion by Internet opinion is similar to the *Literary
Digest's* telephone poll in 1936. The *Literary Digest* poll incorrectly
predicted the Republican presidential candidate, Alfred M. Landon,
would be the winner over Democrat Franklin D. Roosevelt based on a
sample of people from telephone books and automobile registration
lists. The sample was biased in favor of middle and upper income voters who were largely Republican. The vast majority of citizens do not
subscribe to the Internet at this time. Although this may change, a minority still will be ignored. The cost of owning a computer and sub-
scribing to an online service always will eliminate some members of
the community.

Advocates of the Internet as a public opinion bellwether may argue that the combination of generational adjustment to computer use
and the Internet and declining costs as use increases will reduce to an
almost insignificant number those who cannot have access to the Internet. But it remains to be seen whether Internet use will become
like radio and television, which have saturated the U.S. public, or like
cable, which despite its widespread availability, is still avoided by a
significant minority of Americans. People may be wired, but that does
not mean they necessarily choose to be connected. They may be resistant to a monthly fee for such a service unless it can produce material benefits.

Moreover, many people become frustrated by the technical
hurdles—jargon they must master to set up personal computers,
modems, and online services; inability to get technical support when
something goes wrong; long delays in modem transfers; and the ne-
cessity of a separate telephone line into the house to avoid tying up
the family telephone. According to one estimate, more than 40 percent of customers *drop* online services each year.[31]

Some of these obstacles will be overcome through technological
innovation. MSN, the newest major online service, already has eased
the technical challenges of connecting to the Internet. Modem transfers will become less timely as speeds increase.

Then there is the overall chaos of the Internet. The absence of
structure, which computer aficionados cherish, repels average con-

sumers who expect more organization and guidance for rapid information access. Some companies are attempting to bring order to the Internet by organizing interests, such as book orders, in common sites.[32] But such structure is still in the distance.

The inequities between the resource-rich and -poor will be transferred to the Internet not only in terms of the receivers of information, but also the senders. Well-to-do groups such as the Chamber of Commerce or the National Association of Manufacturers still will have an advantage in the quality of home page they can establish, as well as the ability to advertise their address through other media to attract users. Such failure to be a presence on the Internet may be costly. The president of a small industry association argues that Internet access "may become a matter of survival" for such groups in the future, who, if they do not link up to the Internet, "may be information have-nots."[33]

However, one scholar has opined that small, resource-poor groups such as welfare groups or civil liberties organizations actually may be well served by the Internet because they are more likely to move faster to the Internet due to the lack of reliance on other structures for constituency reach and lobbying.[34] Admittedly, the group must break the initial barrier of possessing the hardware and Internet access, but once beyond that barrier the group may be able to play on a fairly level playing field with other groups.

Yet public knowledge of and interest in accessing these sites may be lacking. For example, the availability of information by fringe candidates or groups may become readily accessible, but that does not mean it will actually be accessed once the novelty of that access wears out.

The Internet has altered how political players interact with each other. However, it has yet to revolutionize such interaction. The most common usage has been information transmission and retrieval. Computer networks eventually will revolutionize the way information is shared and gathered. It will ease the burden of information gathering for average Americans and facilitate opportunities for political expression. It also significantly reduces the costs for individuals to communicate with policymakers and makes it easier for politicians and their staff to gain access to potential constituents. With the self-publishing capabilities of the Internet, political ideas one would have written privately to someone else can now be disseminated to hundreds of thousands simultaneously at virtually no cost. The Internet e-mail message of the 1990s is the equivalent of the broadsheet of the 1790s.

However, that does not mean computer networks will automatically enlighten millions of Americans and justify direct democracy. With a plethora of other available uses for the Internet such as entertainment, pursuit of personal hobbies, financial record-keeping and transactions, and interpersonal communication with distant friends, relatives, or co-workers, it is unlikely regular consumers will be unusually drawn to political databases, except perhaps during major political events, such as elections, and in crisis situations. For those who already engage in political activism, the Internet is an improvement in political communication. For others who are not, it more likely will serve other purposes they consider more important.

Nor does the Internet mean that cyberspace will provide a national unity via communications media that has been lacking since the three major networks began losing audience members to cable. Those days are gone and as long as the technology exists will not return. Cyberspace will connect like-minded individuals in disparate geographic locations through newsgroups and linkages to common Web sites. At a minimum it maintains societal fragmentation, but it may even accelerate such a process by involving those who were not previously formally connected to groups.

Yet, undoubtedly, electronic networks already have and yet will impact the way in which politics is conducted in the United States. They become an effective supplement to existing communication means. The former White House director for e-mail and electronic publishing, Jonathan Gill, predicts that "politicians who don't use the Internet won't get elected in a couple of years because people are going to expect candidates to communicate with them. . . . You will see in 10 years elections won and lost because of the way computer information was used."[35]

Similar predictions were made thirty years ago about the role of television. Whether computer networks will have a similar impact in becoming a required medium for political communication remains to be seen.

THE AUDIENCES AND EFFECTS OF NEW MEDIA

6

The Audiences

Coinciding with any significant alteration in the mass media system are changes in patterns of public media consumption. By providing more choices of format and greater variety of content, the political media product has become increasingly diverse in the new media era. With more sources competing for shares, the media target their products to reach specific groups. Thus the mass audience has become highly fragmented.[1] Identifying who uses particular communication forms and why has become a difficult task.

Yet the importance of understanding the audiences for mass communication cannot be underestimated. This knowledge can enhance our ability to address essential concerns about the new media's role in a democratic polity. Political information is packaged in formats designed to appeal to a wide range of audience tastes, potentially enhancing the media's power in politics. But do the new media make politics more accessible to citizens who previously have been disengaged? Or do they offer more varied outlets to individuals who are well vested in society and who are already interested and involved in politics?

This chapter and the one following take some steps toward addressing these issues. The goal of this chapter is to examine the nature of the audiences for new media. We begin with a discussion of recent developments in patterns of mass media use. Are the new media eroding the traditional media's audience base? Is there an overlapping audience for old and new media? Are the new media establishing an audience niche of their own? The evidence, as we shall see, lends support to the suppositions behind these questions. In addition, we will develop basic profiles of the audiences for talk radio, television talk shows, electronic town meetings, television news magazines, MTV, tabloids, and online media. Finally, we will examine the reasons why citizens use new media compared to traditional media.

Analyzing Audiences

The audience is one of the most central concepts for communication research, yet it has traditionally been one of the most theoretically and operationally challenging for scholars.[2] Critics dismiss the idea of the media audience as a single, heterogeneous entity defined by the potential to be reached by mass communication in a society.[3] Given the complexities of the media system in the current era, it is especially important to establish the distinguishing characteristics of individuals who attend to particular media and to identify multiple media audiences. The audiences for specific kinds of mass communication share social and political traits, common bonds, interests, and concerns that may become particularly relevant during periods of heightened politicization, such as occurs during a presidential election or a time of political turmoil. Through their use of the same media source, audience members acquire like knowledge, and they can develop similar beliefs, attitudes, values, and behavior patterns.[4] Audiences may be passive or detached in their relationships to mass media, or they may actively process, interpret, and create meaning from media messages.

Operationalizing the concept of the audience is difficult. One way of getting a handle on the complexities of audience dynamics is to begin by identifying the background characteristics, such as sex and age, of the group of individuals who attends to a specific type of media.[5] We take this step in this chapter. Because these factors on their own do not offer a rich enough description of and explanation for particular audience segments' media use, the next step is to examine their common orientations to political and social life. In this way, the potential of the audience to make sense of the political world they experience largely through mass communication can be considered seriously.[6] For example, the partisan lenses through which some individuals view politics might draw them to particular formats, such as talk radio, where they can use partisan cues to help them interpret content and even to participate in political discussion. We examine the political orientations of the audiences for certain new media in the following chapter.

It is important to note that there are problems associated with the identification and measurement of media audiences. Are media audiences national or local entities? Further, should exposure or attention to mass media be used as the criteria for determining who belongs in a particular audience category?[7] In this study, we make use of national survey data to examine audience makeup, as we are interested in providing a broad overview of the new media's reach. In addition, we use media exposure variables to identify audience members. People who are exposed regularly to the communication form are considered to constitute the audience for a particular medium.[8] Measures of attention were not available for most new media we analyze here.

Patterns of Mass Media Use

The traditional media still attract more readers, viewers, and listeners than any new media source. As Table 6.1 demonstrates, the proportion of citizens who regularly use the traditional media mainstays of daily newspapers, network and local television news, and radio news is substantial. Approximately 70 percent of the public claims to read a daily newspaper routinely. Local television news (65 percent) has a notably larger regular viewer base than network television news (45 percent). Network news has experienced a marked decline in audience share in recent years, a fact that we will discuss further shortly. Regular readers of mainstream news magazines, such as *Time* and *Newsweek,* are far fewer in number.

The habitual audiences for particular new media are small to moderate in size. Television news magazines, such as "60 Minutes"

TABLE **6.1** Regular Use of Traditional and New Media

Media	Regular Users (%)
Traditional	
Daily Newspaper	71
Network TV News	41
Local TV News	65
Radio News	51
Print News Magazines	15
New	
Talk Radio	13
CNN	26
Daytime TV Talk Shows	10
TV News Magazines	36
MTV	7
TV Tabloids	19
Print Tabloids	5
Online	21*

*Percent who ever go online.

Source: Pew Research Center for the People & the Press, May, 1996.

and "Dateline," are the most popular of the new media offerings, with 36 percent of the public tuning in regularly, followed by CNN (26 percent) and television tabloid programs (19 percent) such as "Hard Copy." Talk radio's popularity has dwindled somewhat since the early 1990s. Thirteen percent of the public claimed to be regular listeners in 1996, down from 23 percent in 1993.[9] Daytime television talk shows such as "Oprah," MTV, and print tabloids have the smallest regular audiences. The proportion of the public that goes online is approximately 20 percent, although the number using the Internet extensively for political purposes is much less.[10]

Although the new media audiences are smaller than the audiences for mainstream newspaper, television, and radio news, they are not insignificant. In fact, the addition of the new media to the communications mix coincides with some shifts in patterns of mainstream media use. The most remarkable trend is a decline in the audience for network television news.

According to the Roper Center, network news has lost almost half of its nightly audience over the past twenty years. In 1975 approximately 48 percent of all households watched network news every evening compared to 26 percent in 1997.[11] The Pew Research Center has tracked the precipitous decline in nightly network television news viewership since 1993. In 1993, 60 percent of respondents claimed that they watched one of the three network news broadcasts regularly, compared to 48 percent in 1995 and only 42 percent in 1996. The greatest decline in network television news viewership has occurred in the 1990s, which coincides with the proliferation of new media options.

The Pew Center found a similar trend for viewing local news broadcasts, although the popularity of these programs exceeds that of network news. Sixty-five percent of those surveyed considered themselves to be regular consumers of local television news in 1996, which was down from 72 percent in 1995. Local news is better able to maintain its audience because of the desire for people to keep in touch with community affairs and the closer connection they feel to the anchors, who are often local celebrities. In addition, the new media have been less attuned to local news than national and international happenings.

Not all old media are losing audience members, however. Newspaper and radio news audience figures have held steady in recent years. The Pew study found that 50 percent of respondents had read the newspaper the day before the survey. Forty-four percent of the public had heard the news on radio the previous day.[12]

Since television news long has been considered the main source of political information for the mass public, this marked and rapid decline in network news viewership gives rise to speculation about its causes. In the past, television news has survived periods when public evaluations of the news product were unfavorable without sacrificing audience shares.[13] In fact, even as public satisfaction with television news dropped over the years, viewership remained stable or increased—until now.[14] However, for nearly three decades, network news had few rivals on air. Television news was nearly the only option in the early morning, early evening, and late evening from the 1950s to the 1980s.

Structural factors may be responsible in part for network news' audience attrition. As we discussed in chapter 2, fixed-time news broadcasts increasingly do not fit into the schedule of busy citizens. In fact, 48 percent of the people who told the Pew Research Center that they watch less network television news claimed that they had no time to watch or were too busy.[15] However, this popularity deficit also may be the result of problems facing the media industry in general. The struggle to meet commercial imperatives has forced television news programs to engage in highly visible ratings wars. Gimmicks and more sensational reporting aimed at heightening viewership may be backfiring. The public, in particular, seems concerned that journalists have lost their sense of decency and civility in the pursuit of news stories. For example, over 80 percent of the respondents to a Roper Center poll maintained that reporters are insensitive to people's pain when covering disasters and accidents, and that the media too often invade people's privacy.[16] Similarly, the Pew Research Center found that 64 percent of the public believes that television news programs unnecessarily intrude in people's private lives.[17]

In addition, television news has not been immune to the "bad news is news" credo that pervades journalism. The heavy negative component of television news programming may be driving audience members away. While these problems are endemic to many political media sources today, they are magnified in the thirty-minute evening newscast. Sensational and highly negative stories that are compressed to conform to the time and space requirements of a standard news broadcast may be perceived as superficial, uninformative, or especially nasty by a public that has an increasing array of alternative options.

A possible explanation for the decline in television news viewership may lie in the conflation of "old" and "new" media forms. As we will argue in chapter 8, the mainstream press has adopted many of the techniques and strategies of the new media, including injecting a heavy dose of entertainment—even tabloid—content into their reports. While no longer occupying a distinctive, somewhat elitist, niche in the reporting world, the traditional media are second-rate imitators of the new media in this regard. Television news does not break and report political scandals with the same panache as the *Star*. Evening news broadcasts do not accommodate heated, lengthy discussions of political issues that is the promise of talk radio at its best.

Instead, television news may be losing its hold on the American public in part because it is no longer essentially different from, but also not quite the same as, the new media.

Traditionally, the public has considered television news to be the most reliable source of information, especially when compared to print media. Yet the public's confidence in television news and the people who deliver it has been dwindling. In the wake of incidents such as NBC News' erroneous accusation of Richard Jewell as being responsible for the Olympic Park bombing in the summer of 1996, the public has a difficult time believing in news reports. Further, only 5 percent of the respondents to a 1997 Roper Center poll stated that they trusted all of what network television news anchors have to say, and only 1 percent rated television news reporters' ethical standards as "very high."

Another trend that has potential importance for the rise of new media is the fact that the number of traditional news outlets regularly relied on by the public is diminishing. The Pew Research Center examined the proportion of people who received their news "yesterday" from newspapers, television news, and radio news. In 1996, 52 percent of the public used two or three of these sources compared to 64 percent in 1994. Thirty-three percent of citizens consulted only one traditional news source in 1996, up from 28 percent two years earlier. Finally, the percentage of people who did not use any of the three mainstream media rose from 8 percent to 15 percent.[18] The question remains: As the public moves away from mainstream media, are they moving toward new media?

Audience Dynamics in a New Media Age

The New Media Factor

While it is hard to establish a direct causal connection between the rise of new media and the decline in network television news viewership or the tendency of the public to consult fewer mainstream media sources regularly, speculation is not unwarranted. The new media have sparked changes in the dynamics of citizens' media usage. While there are still citizens who rely predominantly on traditional media, there are significant segments of the media audience who rely on a combination of traditional and new media, and even those who rely solely on new media.

It is important to keep in mind that some new media are closer in form and content to mainstream media than others. Further, some forms of new media are similar to one another, while others are more unique. Perceptions about the similarities and differences between mass media can play a role in citizens' patterns of media use. Audience members may be likely to use specific types of media that conform to their tastes and meet their expectations in terms of their similarity in style and substance.

In order to gauge whether people think about some media in similar terms while distinguishing them from other forms, we performed a factor analysis. Factor analysis allows us to determine if the public perceives specific dimensions of mass communication. A dimension— or factor—includes media that people believe share some underlying connection or similarity. Table 6.2 presents the results of a factor analysis of the five mainstream media sources and the eight new media sources we examined in Table 6.1. The analysis supports the contention that the public find some types of media to be closely related and distinct from other forms of media, as four factors emerged. The dimensions represent (1) predominantly traditional news media; (2) predominantly new media that is news oriented; (3) entertainment/ tabloids; and (4) radio.

From the first factor, which we have labeled "traditional news media," we can see that the public considers television news magazines to be part of the same dimension as local and network television news and newspapers. We might anticipate, therefore, that individuals who are heavy users of traditional media incorporate television news magazines into their media repertoire. As the second factor, "new news media," indicates, the public distinguishes between traditional sources of hard news and new media counterparts, such as online sources and CNN. MTV also is present on this factor, although it is associated with the "entertainment/tabloid" dimension as well.[19] The MTV audience, as a younger demographic, is more oriented toward

TABLE 6.2 Factor Analysis of Traditional and New Media Sources*

	Traditional News Media	New News Media	Entertainment Tabloid	Radio
Local TV News	.718			
TV News Mags	.697			
Network News	.684			
Newspaper	.452	.330		
Online		.579		
CNN		.566		
Magazines		.550		
MTV		.509	.589	
TV Talks Shows			.767	
TV Tabloids			.714	
Print Tabloids			.622	
Talk Radio				.837
Radio News				.796
% Variance	18.36%	13.67%	10.20%	9.42%

*Table entries are rotated factor loadings.

Source: Pew Research Center for the People & the Press, May, 1996.

new media information sources than traditional ones. There is some crossover on the "new news media" factor with conventional media as news magazines, such as *Time,* and to a lesser extent, newspapers, load on this factor. An "entertainment/tabloid" factor emerged that is composed entirely of new media—MTV, television talk shows, and television and print tabloids. Finally, talk radio and radio news comprise their own factor.

The fact that audience members group particular old and new media together in this way helps to explain some of the patterns of audience orientations that we will observe. We can expect citizens who rely heavily on television news, for example, to be more inclined to incorporate television news magazines into their regular media diet than tabloids or talk radio. Further, there is a contingent of people who regularly use new media forms, such as young people who watch MTV and go online, and who are less likely to employ mainstream media. It will be interesting to track these trends over the long term to see if these generational differences in media use persist.

Overlapping Audiences

In today's saturated mass communications environment, many Americans are multimedia users who incorporate both traditional and new media sources into their political media diet. For some citizens, who might be characterized as "news junkies," the new media *supplement* their use of traditional sources. These people, for the most part, maintain their established media monitoring habits while adding a new media component to the mix. "News junkies" welcome new sources of information and innovative formats, as following politics is something of an avocation for this group. Their overall media consumption actually may increase as a result of new media. "News junkies" may or may not be dissatisfied with the traditional media product. If they are dissatisfied, they continue to follow the mainstream press because their old habits are well-established and they have a strong desire to keep informed.

Another category of old/new media users *substitutes* some new media sources for traditional media. This group may spend a similar amount of time following politics via the media now as they did prior to the advent of the new media revolution, but the sources they depend on for news have shifted. It is these people who may be responsible for the decline in the number of mainstream media sources relied on regularly by the public. The members of this audience segment are likely to have found that certain new media more neatly accommodate the demands of their daily routines than traditional media, such as network television news. Further, they may be expressing their dissatisfaction with some mainstream formats by switching to new media. These citizens may find new media more entertaining and even more uplifting than traditional offerings.

In an effort to examine the extent to which the audiences for traditional and new media overlap, we constructed a table that presents the percentage of people who are regular users of mainstream media against those who are regular users of new media. As Table 6.3 demonstrates, the new media are more likely to supplement, rather than supplant, mainstream media use for the highly engaged segment of the public who habitually follow the news—the "news junkies." For people who regularly follow the traditional press, the new media offer additional sources of information more often than a functional alternative to mainstream news.

Further, regular new media users are heavy consumers of traditional news media. People who attend frequently to all eight of the new media we examine here are likely to read a daily newspaper. As the row percentages in Table 6.3 indicate, eighty-eight percent of tabloid readers,[20] 83 percent of CNN viewers, 82 percent of television news magazine watchers, and 79 percent of talk radio listeners regularly read the newspaper. MTV and daytime talk show viewers are the least likely to read the newspaper, although the proportion is still quite high. Seventy-seven percent of people who go online are avid newspaper readers, in spite of the fact that much of what is available online is similar to the newspaper product.

The propensity for people who rely regularly on new media to tune into local television news is high. The one exception is for people who go online, as only 59 percent watch local news habitually. There is, however, wide variation in the inclination to watch national news.

TABLE 6.3 Overlapping Audiences for Traditional and New Media (%)

Column% Row%	Newspaper	Network TV	Local TV	Radio News	Magazines
Talk Radio	14	13	14	21	11
	79	41	69	81	13
CNN	30	36	30	28	44
	83	58	74	56	26
TV Talk	9	10	11	9	8
Shows	65	42	70	45	12
TV News	41	55	46	38	53
Magazines	82	63	84	54	22
MTV	7	7	7	7	8
	69	42	68	55	18
TV Tabloids	20	25	24	17	21
	75	55	82	47	16
Print	6	5	6	5	6
Tabloids	88	47	82	51	19
Online	37	37	33	37	43
	77	37	56	59	21

Source: Pew Research Center for the People & the Press, May, 1996.

In general, individuals who attend to new media regularly are more likely than the general public to view national newscasts. The exception, once again, is those people who go online. Only 37 percent of online users regularly tune in to national news. Those who frequent online sources appear to be more oriented toward print, as opposed to broadcast, media. The opposite is true for regular television news magazine and CNN viewers, who are the most likely to also monitor network news, reflecting their greater orientation toward television as a medium.

Radio as a communication form has its own group of adherents who follow politics through the medium's various offerings. Not surprisingly, talk radio fans also rely heavily on radio news for political information.[21] However, regular users of other new media are notably less inclined to follow the news on radio.

Printed weekly news magazines cater to a more specialized audience with a desire for in-depth coverage of top stories and special features. They reach fewer citizens than any of the other mainstream media we have examined. However, regular users of CNN, TV news magazines, MTV, and print tabloids, as well as people who go online, are more likely than the general public to read magazines regularly. Talk radio listeners and daytime talk show viewers are the least inclined to read magazines.

It is clear that individuals who gravitate toward new media are highly inclined to monitor traditional media. When we examine the percentage of mainstream media users who regularly use new media (the column percentages in Table 6.3), however, we find substantial differences based on the specific type of media being considered. The three forms of new media that are most attractive to mainstream media users are TV news magazines, CNN, and online sources. These findings are not surprising, given the fact that these sources are most similar in style, form, and content. This observation also conforms to the results of the factor analysis, which indicate that the public places these new media sources—TV news magazines, CNN, and online sources—on the two dimensions that overlap with mainstream media other than radio news. It is interesting to note that regular viewers of network news are more inclined to tune into TV news magazines and CNN or to go online than are local news viewers. Further, readers of news magazines such as *Time* and *Newsweek* are also heavy consumers of these three types of new media.

Radio, especially talk radio, again stands out as unique in this analysis. Mainstream media users are more likely to watch television tabloid programs such as "Hard Copy" than to listen to talk radio. The percentage of regular readers of newspapers and magazines and viewers of TV news programs who also listen to talk radio habitually is small. In fact, only 21 percent of people who listen to radio news often also follow talk radio. The number of frequent users of traditional media who attend regularly to daytime TV talk shows, MTV, and print tabloids is minuscule.

While the new media are difficult to avoid given their pervasiveness, our analysis suggests that citizens generally are somewhat more likely to rely on traditional media to the exclusion of new media sources than to become more focused users of new media. There is increasing evidence, however, that public dissatisfaction with the mainstream press has caused people to turn away from political news, even if they once had well-established monitoring habits. The *Washington Post* contracted a research firm to conduct in-depth interviews with a random sample of Baltimore residents who do not read the newspaper every day. The study showed that lack of interest in traditional political news stems from the way media organizations define and package the news. People who avoid mainstream media characterize the news as "boring," "repetitive," and "monotonous." Some members of the public feel alienated from the political system, of which they believe the media are an integral part.

A partial explanation for this trend offered by the participants in the *Post* study is that people find the news irrelevant to their lives. Working-class Americans find it difficult to relate to a new breed of highly paid, elite-centered journalists. Our observations throughout this book suggest that new media are filling that void. As such, much of the political information these citizens receive may be acquired unintentionally through entertainment programming. For example, tabloids, as we discussed in chapter 4, speak to the concerns of a segment of the population that is normally neglected by other media. As Howard Kurtz reports, "Many people who don't bother with newspapers listen to talk radio or watch daytime talk shows or tabloid television. These programs deal in a more emotionally charged way than the mainstream press with such issues as sex, race, welfare and affirmative action."[22]

We have some circumstantial evidence to support the contention that people who don't rely on the mainstream press spend some time attending to the more entertainment saturated of the new media. Table 6.4 presents the percentage of regular users of new media who rarely or never use traditional sources. The percentages are highest for new media that represent a substantial departure from the mainstream. For example, 35 percent of daytime talk show viewers, 31 percent of MTV fans, 26 percent of television tabloid watchers, 23 percent of online source users, and 22 percent of talk radio listeners rarely or never read a newspaper. The findings are similar with regard to network television news if we add readers of tabloid newspapers to the list. The pattern differs for CNN and television news magazines. Overall, a smaller percentage of the audiences for these new media formats does not follow newspapers or television news. Most regular users of new media watch local television news. The percentage of

TABLE **6.4** Percentage of Regular New Media Users Who Rarely or Never Use Particular Traditional Media

	Newspaper	Network TV	Local TV	Radio News	Magazines
Talk Radio	22	29	12	19	50
CNN	17	19	9	44	38
TV Talk Shows	35	23	10	54	53
TV News Magazines	18	17	6	45	45
MTV	31	26	16	45	44
TV Tabloids	26	19	4	52	47
Print Tabloids	12	25	10	49	49
Online	23	29	15	41	37

Source: Pew Research Center for the People & the Press, May, 1996.

new media followers who avoid radio news and print magazines is much higher than for newspapers and television news. A notable exception to this generalization is, not surprisingly, the small number (19 percent) of talk radio listeners who don't follow radio news. In addition, only 38 percent of devoted CNN viewers and 37 percent of people who regularly go online rarely read magazines, which demonstrates a far greater orientation toward news magazines than the general population.

New Media Audience Profiles

The foregoing analysis demonstrates that there is some overlap between the more generic audiences for mainstream media and the more specialized audiences for new media. We now develop profiles of the audiences for specific new media genres by examining demographic factors, including sex, age, race, education, and income. As we shall see, there is wide variation in the types of people to whom different new media formats appeal.

Talk Radio

The audience for today's political talk radio differs markedly from the listeners and callers of a previous era. In the 1960s and 1970s, talk radio focused less on political and more on personal issues. Audience members were frequently isolated individuals with few social or political ties. Talk radio provided electronic companionship to lonely, isolated, single, and immobile citizens.[23]

Talk radio today, given its commercial incentives, would not survive if it catered to the clientele of yesterday. The new talk radio audience members are not social isolates who hail from the lower echelons of the educational and economic charts. Instead they are individuals who are highly integrated into society.[24]

Contrary to popular impression, talk radio is not a monolithic medium, as we discussed in chapter 3. Talk radio programs span the political and ideological spectrum, although the preponderance of the shows lean right. Further, talk radio shows differ in the extent to which they address national or local issues. Finally, there are various breeds of talk programs. The stereotypical talk show features a charismatic host who takes strong, antiestablishment positions and encourages callers to do the same. Rush Limbaugh's radio show is the best example of this type of program. However, there are also radio talk programs whose discourse is more conversational, less ideological, and more informational.

Call-in programs on public radio, which are run by educational institutions or nonprofit organizations, offer a substantively different alternative to commercial talk radio. The audience for public radio has been growing rapidly, quadrupling since 1980. National Public Radio (NPR), the nation's largest public broadcasting system, maintains an audience of 17 million weekly listeners, while its closest competitor, Public Radio International (PRI) claims a weekly audience of 16.7 million. In response to the growing popularity of public radio, new stations have been established, and new programs have been launched, including an increasing number of call-in shows.[25]

We expect some differences in the audiences for particular types of talk radio broadcasts, given the diversity of the programming that is available. The audience for public radio, for example, is generally thought to be more upscale educationally and economically than the audience for other radio offerings. Data from the Pew Research Center allow us to examine the general audience for radio call-in programs as well as the specific audiences for Rush Limbaugh's commercial radio program and National Public Radio (NPR). NPR features a variety of talk radio shows with a call-in component. Nationally, NPR airs "Talk of the Nation" with Ray Suarez, who also cohosts "All Things Considered."[26] NPR's local affiliates have incorporated an increasing number of talk programs into their schedule. In Washington, D.C., for example, these include the "Derek McGinty Show" and the "Diane Reame Show." The "McGinty Show" also is broadcast on cable television on occasion. It should be noted that not all of NPR's programs are political, nor do they all feature call-ins. However, the case of NPR provides an interesting contrast in audience composition to the Limbaugh case.

Talk radio's audience reach is substantial for a "new" medium. Political scientist Michael Traugott and his coauthors found that there was little variation in the relative size of the talk radio audience in a thirty-five month period from May 1993 to March 1996.[27] Thirty-six percent of the respondents to the 1996 Pew Center study listen to talk radio at least sometimes. Approximately 13 percent tuned in "a lot," which is somewhat lower than the high of 22 percent that Pew reported in June 1994.[28] NPR attracts a respectable 31 percent who tune in a lot or some of the time, with 13 percent being frequent listeners. As we would anticipate, fewer survey respondents listen to Rush Limbaugh's program; 18 percent of the respondents listen sometimes or more frequently, with 7 percent constituting devoted fans who listen a lot. This is still an amazing number, as nearly 20 percent of the public listens to this one host.

As Table 6.5 depicts, there is a gender gap in talk radio listenership that is evident for all three of our indicators. Men are substantially more likely to tune in than women. Sixty percent of talk radio listeners are men, compared to 40 percent who are women. The sex differences are more pronounced for the Rush Limbaugh audience, which is 67 percent male. The situation is slightly more balanced for NPR, as 56 percent of listeners are men as opposed to 44 percent women.

These findings are not surprising. Radio, in general, is essentially a male domain. Men dominate as DJ's, newscasters, voice-overs in advertisements, sportscasters, and weathercasters.[29] This domination continues in the talk radio realm, as female hosts are few and men outnumber women as callers to programs.[30] Rush Limbaugh's pro-

TABLE 6.5 The Talk Radio Audience

	Talk Radio (%)	Rush Limbaugh (%)	NPR (%)	Nonlisteners (%)
Total	13	7	13	39
Gender				
Male	60	67	56	42
Female	40	33	44	58
Age				
18–29 years	18	18	15	22
30–49 years	47	37	51	36
50–64 years	19	22	18	20
65+ years	16	23	16	22
Race				
White	85	95	83	87
Black	11	2	11	8
Other	4	3	6	5
Education				
<High School	13	18	11	24
High School	27	26	23	32
Some College	33	27	30	28
College	27	29	36	16
Income				
<$20,000	24	22	19	32
$20–29,999	17	11	15	20
$30–49,999	25	32	32	28
$50–4,999	14	12	16	12
$75,000+	21	23	19	8

Source: Pew Research Center for the People & the Press, May, 1996.

gram and others like it foster an environment that is openly hostile to women. Limbaugh bashes prominent women on air, such as Hillary Rodham Clinton and female members of the Cabinet. Other hosts, such as Atlanta's Neal Boortz, regularly rail against overweight "welfare queens" and place the blame for sexual harassment on women.[31] NPR, however, may offer a more female-friendly forum, especially as women hold prominent positions as hosts of news and cultural affairs programs.

The audience for talk radio is concentrated in the thirty to forty-nine year age range. In fact, talk radio's reemergence as a popular format was largely in response to Baby Boomers' developing preference for talk over music as they age.[32] A greater percentage of young people are nonlisteners than are talk radio listeners. Rush Limbaugh's audience is somewhat older than the general talk radio audience and regular NPR listeners. Twenty-three percent of his listeners are over sixty-five years of age, compared to 16 percent for talk radio generically and NPR.

The audience for talk radio generally and NPR does not differ significantly in racial composition from the nonlistening public, although some critics claim that talk radio is predominantly a white medium. In fact, black talk radio has been an effective force in some cities, including Boston, Chicago, Los Angeles, and New York, where hosts have inspired listeners to speak out and even to take action on issues of concern.[33] There is, however, a significant difference in the racial composition of the Limbaugh audience compared to listeners in general and NPR regulars. Limbaugh fans are almost entirely white—95 percent. Limbaugh's message clearly does not appeal to minority group members, who are sometimes the target of his attacks.

The present day talk radio audience is somewhat better educated and wealthier than its nonlistening counterparts. As we would anticipate, given the higher-brow nature of much of its programming, NPR listeners are somewhat more educated than the general talk radio audience. Thirty-six percent of those who regularly tune into NPR have at least a college education. The gap between NPR listeners and Rush Limbaugh's followers is the largest when we compare those with at least some college. Sixty-six percent of NPR listeners have at least some college education, as opposed to 56 percent of Limbaugh fans. The income level of listeners to all types of radio programs is higher than that of nonlisteners. Thirty-two percent of nonlisteners earn less than twenty thousand dollars per year, and only 8 percent make more than seventy-five thousand dollars. Approximately 20 percent or more of regular talk radio listeners have incomes lower than twenty thousand dollars, while close to 20 percent or more earn over seventy-five thousand dollars.

The demographic profile of callers to talk radio programs is similar to that of listeners. Callers tend to be largely white, male, older, college educated, and earn a substantial income. As is the case for talk radio listeners generally, demographically callers are not people who traditionally have been denied access to societal resources for making their voices heard.[34]

Television Talk Shows

As is the case with talk radio, television talk shows are a diverse genre. On one end of the spectrum are programs with heavy political content, such as "Larry King Live" and "Hardball with Chris Matthews." These programs appeal largely to political junkies and Washington insiders. At the other end are talk programs, such as "Oprah!," "Jenny Jones," and "Jerry Springer," which are predominantly entertainment shows. Political content is intermittent on these programs, and it often comes in subtle forms. For example, legal rights may be discussed as a family dispute is being showcased. In some instances, hosts openly advocate political positions. During the 1996 presidential race, Rosie O'Donnell made her support of President Clinton and her opposition to Bob Dole clear, even refusing to run a Dole commercial during her time slot. Oprah Winfrey refused to grant Bob Dole an appearance on her program, and was readily forgiven by the Dole campaign, fearing that to publicize the snub might alienate Oprah fans. Needless to say, these programs cater to a far different clientele than the "Larry King" genre, as the subsequent analysis confirms.

Table 6.6 compares the demographic composition of the audiences for political talk television shows in general, "Larry King Live," and daytime talk shows.[35] As we shall see, the profile of individuals who are motivated to watch political talk shows generally is similar to that of "Larry King" fans. However, this audience is quite different from those who tune in regularly to daytime talk programs.

The audience for television talk shows generally has the potential to be quite sizable, as 36 percent of the public are positively disposed toward viewing them. The audience composition for television talk shows is almost equally split between men and women, as is the case for "Larry King Live." The audience for daytime talk, however, is predominantly female.

Differences in the age composition of the audiences for "Larry King Live" and daytime talk television are quite stark. Daytime viewers are a much younger crowd. Thirty-eight percent of viewers are under thirty years of age, while almost 75 percent are under fifty. Political talk show viewers tend to be concentrated in the thirty to sixty-four year age range.

The "Larry King" program appeals to largely white, educated individuals situated in the middle to upper middle classes. In sharp contrast, daytime talk shows have a substantial black following (33

TABLE 6.6 Television Talk Show Audience

	Political Talk Shows (%)	"Larry King Live" (%)	Daytime Talk Shows (%)
Total	36	20	10
Gender			
Male	52	51	34
Female	48	49	66
Age			
18–29 years	15	15	38
30–49 years	44	35	35
50–64 years	26	29	14
65+ years	16	21	13
Race			
White	86	84	60
Black	6	11	33
Other	8	5	7
Education			
<High School	10	6	39
High School	28	33	36
Some College	30	27	18
College	32	34	7
Income			
<$20,000	18	24	52
$20–29,999	19	17	14
$30–49,999	25	32	23
$50–74,999	21	21	5
$75,000+	17	7	4

Source: Americans Talk Security Foundation, Roper Center Archive, 1993 (Political Talk Shows, "Larry King Live"); Pew Research Center for the People & the Press, May, 1996 (Daytime Talk Shows).

percent). These programs reach a disproportionate number of people with a high school education or less (75 percent). The majority of frequent viewers (52 percent) earn less than twenty thousand dollars per year; over 90 percent make less than fifty thousand dollars.

Electronic Town Meetings

Town hall meetings have come to connote a wide range of formats for accommodating political discourse. They range from video and online versions of the traditional town meeting, to television talk shows, to political debates. The electronic town meeting format has been used in a variety of ways. The electronic town hall format, especially town meetings that resemble television talk shows, are quite popular among the public. The format has been employed by established news programs, such as "Nightline" with Ted Koppel, to facilitate public discussion of issues, such as race relations and journalistic practices. Electronic town meetings are often featured as special events, especially during elections, where the format can be used for candidate debates or to raise referenda issues. While some interactive public forums can suffer from low participation rates, and thereby can be accused of being unrepresentative,[36] nationally broadcast town meetings, which have become a staple of American presidential campaigns, are more successful in reaching a fairly broad spectrum of the public.

Data from the Americans Talk Security Foundation examine people's willingness to watch televised town meetings sponsored by the networks that feature experts on important issues, audience participation, voting, and call-ins. As Table 6.7 depicts, 11 percent of the public is strongly predisposed toward viewing televised town meetings of this type. There are no sex differences among those who favor town meetings. However, they are most popular among white, older, better-educated citizens. In fact, 38 percent of those who are inclined to tune in to town meetings hold at least a college degree. The audience is rather evenly dispersed among income categories, although only a small percentage earns over seventy-five thousand dollars per year.

TABLE 6.7 Electronic Town Meeting Audience

	Town Meeting Viewers (%)
Total	11
Gender	
Male	51
Female	49
Age	
18–29 years	7
30–49 years	33
50–64 years	22
65+ years	38
Race	
White	87
Black	11
Other	2
Education	
<High School	7
High School	22
Some College	33
College	38
Income	
<$20,000	28
$20–29,999	20
$30–49,999	26
$50–74,999	20
$75,000+	7

Source: Americans Talk Security Foundation, Roper Center Archive, 1993.

Thus, lower and middle-income individuals are receptive to electronic town meetings, which offers some encouragement regarding their democratizing potential.

Television News Magazines

Television news magazines such as "60 Minutes," "Dateline," and "20/20" garner a significant share of regular viewers, especially as these programs have proliferated over the past few years. They offer audience members greater depth in their story coverage. "48 Hours," for example, showcases a single story topic in its hour broadcast. Often, the nightly network newscasts serve as advertisements for news magazines by using short news segments as a means of whetting the audience's appetite for a longer treatment to follow. The stories frequently are packaged in a dramatic, human-interest style wrapping.

Table 6.8 provides a demographic profile of the audience for television news magazines. This format appeals more to women than to men, especially given the more personal style of reporting as well as

TABLE **6.8** Television News Magazine Audience

	Television News Magazine Viewers (%)
Total	36
Gender	
Male	40
Female	60
Age	
18–29 years	12
30–49 years	39
50–64 years	24
65+ years	25
Race	
White	85
Black	10
Other	5
Education	
<High School	16
High School	34
Some College	30
College	20
Income	
<$20,000	25
$20–29,999	19
$30–49,999	27
$50–74,999	14
$75,000+	14

Source: Pew Research Center for the People & the Press, May, 1996.

the substantial number of female correspondents and anchors. The audience consists largely of middle aged to older citizens. Regular viewers are concentrated among high school graduates and people with some college education, and among individuals in the lower to middle income brackets.

MTV

MTV's political product, like its music product, is packaged to appeal to a young, hip audience. Politically, the station has been described as a "kind of *Rolling Stone* of the air,"[37] interspersing politics with music, art, and celebrity gossip. News reports are eclectic and fast-paced, designed for a generation with a short attention span, cutting quickly from Madonna's latest escapade to Capitol Hill to Eastern Europe. At times, MTV will offer long format, in-depth broadcasts of important or breaking events that incorporate the opinions of artists and young people, such as coverage of the Los Angeles riots that included the reaction of black rappers. These formulas have worked well, and over time MTV has increased the amount of political content in its programming. The network discovered that viewers did not typify the stereotype of Generation X as disinterested and alienated, and instead represented a political market waiting to be tapped. For a good number of people under the age of twenty-five, MTV is a primary news source.

Media critic Jon Katz explains that MTV news is cutting into the network news market because it recognizes the heterogeneous and multicultural nature of American society. "Forty years ago, when television was born, television news consisted of middle-aged white men reading 22 minutes of news into a camera. Today, network news consists of middle-aged white men reading 22 minutes of news into a camera."[38] MTV caters to a young audience whose concerns, such as sex, AIDS, jobs, racism, and the environment, are cast differently than for older citizens. In fact, MTV executives make a conscious effort not to broadcast news items that they feel won't engage a young audience, including much Washington insider politics. MTV political segments also differ from network news in that they are almost twice as long—three to four minutes in length.

In its political presentations, MTV does not strive to simulate a 1960s' style music-led counterculture movement, as some critics feel it should. Nor does MTV want to make its viewers feel guilty or ashamed for not taking part more in politics. Instead, MTV recognizes that Generation Xers do not share the same sense of rebellion as their predecessors. The station attempts to forge the missing connection between Gen X and politics, to identify and define issues that are of most concern to this generation, and to provide information about how to become involved for those who wish to do so.

The MTV approach dovetails nicely with its audience, which consists predominantly of young, white, middle-class suburbanites. In terms of the voting age population, close to half of MTV's viewers are under thirty. However, viewers are clustered at the lower end of this spectrum. Twenty-seven percent of eighteen- to twenty-one-year-olds report that they view MTV "a lot" while an additional 25 percent watch "some of the time," constituting over 50 percent of this age group.[39] Thirty-four percent of those twenty-two to twenty-nine tune in at least sometimes, as is the case for 25 percent of the twenty-six- to twenty-nine-year-olds. The drop-off is marked for people between the ages of thirty and thirty-four, as only 19 percent watch often or sometimes.

Table 6.9 presents demographic data for regular MTV viewers. MTV's audience consists of more males than females, perhaps as a result of the "Beavis and Butthead" syndrome. Many of MTV's videos and feature presentations objectify women in ways that might depress the station's female viewership. The audience is predominantly white, but it does include a sizable proportion of minority viewers—25 percent. MTV has made a concerted effort in recent years to include

TABLE 6.9 MTV Audience

	MTV Viewers (%)
Total	7
Gender	
Male	60
Female	40
Age	
18–29 years	46
30–49 years	30
50–64 years	9
65+ years	15
Race	
White	74
Black	18
Other	8
Education	
<High School	28
High School	39
Some College	25
College	8
Income	
<$20,000	38
$20–29,999	21
$30–49,999	22
$50–74,999	9
$75,000+	10

Source: Pew Research Center for the People & the Press, May, 1996.

more music that appeals to particular racial and ethnic groups, such as reggae, rap, and hip hop. Given their age, it is not surprising that the majority of MTV viewers have not completed a college degree. In fact, only 8 percent of the MTV audience hold a college diploma.

Print and Television Tabloids

As we discussed in chapter 4, print and television tabloids appeal to a different type of audience than is the target of most hard news organizations. While much tabloid content focuses on the scandalous, the lurid, and the bizarre, a notable proportion is devoted to stories about and issues of concern to members of the working and lower classes. The style, tone, language, and pitch of print and television tabloids is geared toward inclusiveness. Tabloids reach a portion of the citizenry that frequently feels alienated by mainstream media and by politics generally.

The percentage of individuals who admit to being regular readers and viewers of tabloid offerings is relatively small—5 percent for print and 19 percent for television. As Table 6.10 demonstrates, the audi-

TABLE 6.10 Print and Television Tabloid Audience

	Print (%)	Television (%)
Total	5	19
Gender		
Male	41	39
Female	59	61
Age		
18–29 years	16	17
30–49 years	31	38
50–64 years	26	24
65+ years	26	22
Race		
White	86	76
Black	11	18
Other	2	6
Education		
<High School	32	26
High School	41	39
Some College	18	26
College	8	9
Income		
<$20,000	33	34
$20–29,999	20	25
$30–49,999	28	26
$50–74,999	13	8
$75,000+	6	7

Source: Pew Research Center for the People & the Press, May, 1996.

ence for both tabloid formats is overwhelmingly female. Audience members tend to be over thirty years of age. Racially, the audience for print tabloids is predominantly white, while television tabloids have greater minority appeal. There is a slight difference in the educational profile of print and television tabloid regulars. A strong majority of print tabloid consumers—almost 75 percent—have a high school education or less, while 35 percent of television tabloid viewers have at least some college. Finally, the audiences for both types of tabloids are most heavily represented among lower- and middle-income categories.

Online Media

Keeping tabs on the number and characteristics of users of online media, such as the Internet and e-mail, is somewhat difficult given the fact that the technology and public access to it is continually changing. Early profiles of online users indicated that they were largely younger, better-educated individuals who were comfortable using computer technology. As the cost of the equipment decreased, access to affordable online services increased, and technical difficulties became less prevalent, the size of the online community grew and its characteristics changed. Older, less-educated people began to use online services with greater frequency.[40]

Approximately 20 percent of the public goes online at least every once in a while. According to a 1996 Pew Research Center study of online users, about 21 million citizens, or 12 percent of the voting age population, use online sources for political information. Of those who go online, 74 percent connect to the World Wide Web at least sometimes, and 47 percent use the Internet for political news. Four percent of the public consulted online sources during the 1996 election.[41]

Table 6.11 depicts the demographic breakdowns of people who go online at least once every few weeks. It also contains information about people who engage in online discussions of politics and who contact any groups, organizations, or public officials about political issues or public policy questions. According to these data men are more likely to enter cyberspace than women. This is especially true for use of online resources to engage in politics. Sixty-nine percent of people who take part in online discussions are men, as are 68 percent of individuals who use e-mail for political communication. However, the gender gap in online media use is closing. While trends indicate that more older people are going online, these resources are still largely used by younger and middle-aged citizens. It interesting to note that 36 percent of people who engage in online political discussions are under the age of thirty—a group that is normally considered to be politically alienated and disengaged. Perhaps online sources offer a user-friendly political forum for Generation Xers. The vast ma-

TABLE 6.11 Online Users

	On-line Users (%)	Political Discussions (%)	Political E-Mail (%)
Total	20	7	8
Gender			
Male	62	69	68
Female	38	31	32
Age			
18–29 years	26	36	28
30–49 years	57	49	55
50–64 years	14	13	15
65+ years	3	2	2
Race			
White	86	83	83
Black	6	6	5
Other	8	11	12
Education			
<High School	15	26	11
High School	27	26	27
Some College	32	26	31
College	26	23	31
Income			
<$20,000	18	25	17
$20–29,999	15	19	16
$30–49,999	14	9	10
$50–74,999	26	26	22
$75,000+	28	22	35

Source: 1996 Pew Research Center Survey of Technology.

jority of online users are white; blacks are underrepresented in this forum. Online resources, while appealing to more educated and wealthier adults, also reach other citizens. More than half of those who engage in political discussions online have a high school education or less. However, these people are not as likely as those with at least some college to send political e-mail messages.

There are a variety of reasons to be optimistic about the prospect that cyberspace ultimately might become a more inclusive space politically, although at present it still supports an upscale clientele. First, demographic trends in usership indicate that online sources are becoming more readily available to lesser educated and disadvantaged socioeconomic groups, although women and blacks are underrepresented online. President Clinton has urged that school children in poor districts be taught computer communication skills. Older citizens, who were not weaned on computers, are mastering the technology and going online. In addition, identifying characteristics such as race, sex, age, and class are masked online unless users reveal them. Grammar and terminology used in written communication may be the only clues to an individual's identity, and these may be difficult to pick up. Thus the potential for conversation to occur without prejudices formed on the basis of racial, sexual, or class characteristics is enhanced online.

Uses and Gratifications of New Media

The foregoing discussion indicates that the audiences for new media are as diverse as the communication forms themselves. New media provide a widely varied range of informational resources in terms of the amount of politics covered, presentational style, and pitch. As such, audience motivations for attending to new media may be different than for traditional media. The audience movement away from some mainstream sources, such as nightly network news, may signal that citizens have developed a new set of expectations regarding media. Thus we turn now to an examination of why people use new media.

The Uses and Gratifications Approach

Uses and gratifications approaches for studying audience orientations toward mass communications emerged from studies of print and radio conducted in the 1930s and 1940s. The goal of this research was to examine why audience members deliberately seek out some forms of communication while ignoring others. Researchers were interested in identifying the functions served by specific content, such as comic strips, soap operas, and political news, disseminated through particular media, like newspapers, radio, and film, and how they met audience expectations.[42] The scope of uses and gratifications studies was expanded to accommodate the advent of television.[43] In the new media era, it is again time to rethink the uses and gratifications of political communication.

Underlying uses and gratifications theories is the assumption of an active audience that turns to particular forms of mass communication in order to satisfy specific needs. Elihu Katz, Jay Blumler, and Michael Gurevitch provide the classic formulation of the major tenets of uses and gratifications theories. Uses and gratifications perspectives focus on "the social and psychological origins of needs, which generate expectations of the mass media or other sources, which lead to different patterns of media exposure (or engagement in other activities), resulting in need gratifications and other consequences, perhaps mostly unintended ones."[44]

Several basic assumptions underlie uses and gratifications approaches. Unlike hypodermic effects models, which assume that audience members are passive receptors of media messages, uses and gratifications theories posit that individuals have substantial control over the communication process. Much communication behavior, including media selection and use, is goal-directed, purposive, and motivated. Individuals take the initiative in selecting and using communication vehicles to satisfy basic needs and desires. A wide range of social and psychological factors influence people's communication behavior. These include individuals' environmental surroundings, their social circumstances and group associations, their potential for interpersonal interaction, and their psychological state. This is not to argue, however, that all audience members are equally active at all times, or that some media use is not habitual, ritualized, incidental, or dependent upon individuals' moods.[45] Finally, media compete with other forms of communication, such as interpersonal discussion, as a means of satisfying individual needs. Thus media are not the only sources of need gratification.[46]

Among the primary functions served by mass media are (1) information-seeking or surveillance; (2) reinforcement of personal values, opinions, and identity; (3) social interaction and integration; (4) social compensation and companionship; (5) entertainment and enjoyment; (6) escapism, diversion, and passing time; and (7) mood management and emotional release.

Individuals' motivations for using mass media vary based on the medium, such as television, newspapers, or radio, referenced. The specific content associated with a communication outlet is also important for determining media uses and gratifications. Rush Limbaugh's talk radio audience, for example, may be very differently motivated than the audience for NPR's call-in programs, as the variations in audience characteristics outlined above suggest. In addition, recent studies indicate that audience uses and gratifications associated with watching CNN's "Burden of Proof" legal talk program and an Internet newsgroup discussion of the Million Man March are particularized.[47]

People may expect certain things from a particular medium or program, and their expectations may or may not be met. Whether or not gratifications are received from a source can influence future use.[48] For example, an individual may turn to talk radio for information about the latest breaking news story, be disappointed by the lack of current news, and refrain from tuning in again. Conversely, a person who wants to hear the opinions of other citizens on topical issues might find talk radio to be a highly satisfying medium and would be likely to listen with some regularity.

Why People Use New Media

New media formats and technologies have rendered media effects potentially stronger and more complicated in the present period than at any time in our history.[49] Thus the uses and gratifications of new media are more diverse and complex than those associated with traditional communications formats. Individuals have a greater number of more varied communication choices. As such, the motivations people have for using new media, in keeping with the multifaceted functions they perform, are enhanced.

Audience members seek and receive conventional forms of gratification from new media formats. The primary motivation for listening to talk radio is information seeking, as is the case for many forms of new media, including electronic town meetings, news magazines, and online sources. Listeners want to keep abreast of issues, learn about what others think, find out more about things they have heard about elsewhere, and provide reinforcement of their own political views. Entertainment, personal interest, and passing the time are also motivating factors for talk radio listeners.[50] Less important reasons for tuning into talk radio include gathering information for conversations and enjoying the host.[51]

Yet even information seeking and surveillance functions are cast in a different light where new media are concerned. Unlike the mainstream newspapers and news programs, which make claims of objectivity, talk programs and Internet chat rooms unabashedly accommodate bias in their discourse, thus providing more direct reinforcement or rejection of the audiences' political views. New media thus facilitate bonding between like-minded individuals.

Further, the Internet has become not just a means for surveying information, but a widely used research tool. The 1996 Pew Technology Survey indicates that the online audience uses computer technologies to do research for school (41 percent), for work (72 percent), and to get financial information about stocks and bonds (44 percent). Seventy-two percent of the online public uses online sources to get news and information about current events, public issues, or politics. The information sources that are available to the public, such as databases on congressional legislation, public opinion polls, government agencies, and interest groups, are the same sources used by journalists. The Internet has become a resource that is widely used by reporters researching stories and even by academics writing books on new media.

The intensive infusion of entertainment and information that is characteristic of most forms of new media also alters the audiences' expectations and their motivations for reading, listening, or watching. While the entertainment function of tabloids, news magazine programs, and daytime talk shows is what draws the audience in, political learning is an ancillary, but not unimportant consequence of exposure, even if this political learning is unconventional in style and message. Scandal stories that reveal the seamier sides of politicians' lives can raise and answer questions about character. Confessional tales of domestic violence can be accompanied by information about assistance programs and legal recourse. People may watch these programs as a means of seeking advice about how to handle situations in their own lives.

In addition to the wider scope of the uses and gratifications of communication, the relationship between audience members and new media is, in many case, a more instrumental one than is the case with mainstream media, where ritualistic use is prevalent. Individuals' involvement with mass media can range from detachment to a strong association. In the case of new media, a substantial amount of use is purposive, as citizens make deliberate decisions to engage particular media. For example, according to the 1996 Pew Technology Survey, 67 percent of people who go online are looking for specific information, 20 percent are browsing, and 12 percent engage in both activities.

Some new media require the active participation of the users, such as going online, asking a question during an electronic town meeting, or sounding off on a call-in program. The degree of involvement or interactivity with media is linked to the level of an audience member's media consumption and the strength of the effects of the communication.[52] People who have a highly active relationship with a particular medium, such as callers to talk radio programs, may be more likely to establish a regular habit of attending to the medium and are more likely to be influenced by content than those whose acquaintance with the communication source is more casual.

In addition, new media have the capacity to create strong psychological bonds between users and the communication source. Communication researchers Byron Reeves and Clifford Nass have amassed convincing documentation to suggest that people respond socially and naturally to technology, even though it may not be reasonable to do so. Individuals form personal relationships with their television sets and their computers. They treat computers as if they are people, talking to them, ascribing personalities to them, and reacting to them emotionally when computers hand out praise or criticism during an interactive session. These researchers conclude that the human brain has not kept pace with the quickly evolving technology, and thus people have difficulty distinguishing what is real from what is mechanical or artificial. Reeves and Nass use the following story to illustrate their point (which also illustrates the significance of merging entertainment and politics):

> In a recent U.S. congressional hearing, entertainer Shari Lewis answered questions from senators about television violence and children. She brought her hand-puppet, Lamb Chop, with her. At one point in the hearing, Lamb Chop the puppet made a statement (through the projected voice of Shari Lewis) about television violence. A senator then said, "Miss Lewis, do you agree with Lamb Chop?" . . . None of the senators laughed right away. Everyone sitting in the hearing room seemed to think it was perfectly reasonable for a puppet to give testimony, and it was perfectly reasonable to ask the puppeteer if she had a *different* opinion than the puppet.[53]

Reeves and Nass's findings imply that the connection between online users and the technology may be especially binding, even though the

Internet is considered by some to be the most disembodied form of mass communication.

Psychological bonds also can be forged by the fact that new media encourage what political scientist Susan Herbst has termed "the communication of emotion." Talk programs, for example, not only allow people to express opinions, they can convey their feelings, as their words are infused with affect.[54] People can express anger, happiness, sorrow, agitation, satisfaction, and disgust in a public forum. The expression of deep emotions by the audience is facilitated by hosts who routinely engage in the *construction of controversy* on talk radio programs, taking adversarial positions to callers and guests in an effort to stimulate affective responses.[55]

New media can help individuals find their place in a fragmented and anomic society by fostering the development of pseudocommunities. In the past, talk radio served as an oasis for people who were bored, immobile, and highly alienated from society.[56] Similarly, talk radio today creates political communities of like-minded individuals, sometimes on a national scale. Online communities form within chat rooms, where conversations about politics between nicknames in cyberspace can lead to meetings between people in human space.

Citizens have greater control over the content of new media than of mainstream media. The interactive nature of many new media formats allows people to respond to, shape, and alter messages.[57] This characteristic contributes to perhaps the most significant political function associated with certain new media—the perceived potential to facilitate active citizenship. Historian David Thelen laments that much conversation about politics and government is beyond the reach of average Americans. Pollsters and pundits, through the practices of opinion management, leave the impression that the public's views are being considered in the policy arena, while in actuality they are left out of the process. Citizens no longer have individual voices. Instead, the public is transformed into abstractions, such as "soccer moms" and "angry white males," whose thoughts and words are extrapolated from polling data and then largely dismissed by pundits and policymakers. Further, citizens lose the abil- ity to "come to public judgment," to formulate deep and reasoned opinions, as they are denied the opportunity to deal with issues in more than cursory terms.[58]

Thelen argues that the basic challenge for democracy is for citizens of all types to engage in meaningful dialogue in their own space and in their own words, devoid of the intervention of opinion managers. In spite of the barriers to genuine public speech articulated by members of the mass public, citizens are anxious to tell their own stories. In fact, citizens will find and use any available mechanisms for expression and do not fear challenging dominant norms that are presented via the media mainstream. For example, members of Congress receive a tremendous amount of mail in which constituents, using their own words and terms, reconstruct policy arguments that have been defined by the media via elites.[59] Communications scholar Roderick Hart also finds evidence of a reservoir of "political energy," which is exemplified by writers of letters to the editors of newspapers, but which needs to be cultivated more vigorously among the mass public.[60]

Mainstream television news programs support the culture of opinion management, of elites talking and listening to elites and putting words into the mouth of the collective public. New media, however, are widely perceived to have the capacity to tap into the well of public political energy and to foster dialogue between citizens. A major explanation given by callers to talk radio is that it allows them to articulate their views publicly. The same is true for people who frequent online bulletin boards and chat rooms. A study of the reasons why individuals posted to a bulletin board on CNN and *Time* magazine's AllPolitics Web site revealed that people prefer an active role in shaping political dialogue to having their "views" stated by experts. In fact, some posters aspire to be pundits themselves, as the following quote from the study indicates, "Not only can you express your views here, they can be read by thousands of people. For all of us George Will and Mary McGrory wannabes, this is great!" People who engage in online political discussions also believe that their postings make a difference and that they learn things themselves. Another study respondent stated, "People make up their minds on a number of issues based on the things they have read here. I've been educated tremendously by the information other people have posted here." Others report changing their opinions based on online discussions.[61]

Yet users of new media may have idealized perceptions about the utility and impact of their communication via these channels. The citizenship-oriented uses and gratifications associated with new media, in fact, may signify promises unfulfilled, even as avid audience members continue to speak out, deliberate, argue, and discuss. For example, the public rarely directs policy even in new media venues. Instead, citizens follow the lead of political discussions that are initiated by elites who set the agenda through traditional media venues. Further, few policymakers pay attention to discussions that take place in new media forums, such as on talk radio or in Internet usergroups. In fact, many members of Congress discount e-mail correspondence, especially mass mailings.[62]

We will return to the issue of the real and perceived democratizing potential of new media in the concluding chapter. For our purposes here, it is important to note that some members of the media audience *feel* that new media offer unique opportunities for expression. Whether these feelings are borne out in actuality is a matter of debate.

Summary

Accompanying the diversity of the media product has been a greater segmentation of the media audience. While audience members are shifting away from some mainstream media, such as network news, they are not gravitating toward any one new medium. The audiences for new media are more specialized than for the mainstream press. The new media meet a variety of more specific audience communication needs in more novel ways than old-style news formats. Given the choices, citizens can now more sharply tailor their media habits to suit their life-styles, tastes, and needs.

The democratizing potential offered by new media has not gone unnoticed by the public. Although critics rightly point out the limitations of formats such as talk radio and online chat rooms, citizens are using these forums in an effort to reclaim their voices and to control their own opinions. At present, these efforts have been less successful in influencing public policy or the political process than democratic theorists would hope. Whether the situation will change for the better in the future is subject to debate. It is clear, however, that new media have reshaped audience expectations about the nature of political communication. Mass media, in order to be considered legitimate, must accommodate some measure of public discourse by average citizens.

Audience Attitudes

As we have seen, there are a variety of characteristics that set the audiences for new media apart from other citizens. They are demographically more specialized than the audiences for newspapers, television news, and radio news. They use new media to gratify particular needs, some of which are not met satisfactorily by the mainstream press. New media users welcome the opportunity to obtain a different variety and style of information that is offered through these sources and to participate in discussions that occur in a public forum. Further, the information disseminated via new media and received by audience members is often opinionated, even highly ideological, in content.

Given these conditions, do the political orientations of the audiences for new media differ from those of other members of the mass public? Further, do the audiences for specific forms of new media have particular political identities and attitudes? In this chapter, we address these questions by comparing the political attitudes of audiences for talk radio, television news magazine programs, and online sources to those held by the general public. We selected these three formats for analysis because they represent diverse new media experiences.

Studies of the talk radio audience indicate that listeners and callers have distinct political orientations that set them apart from the majority of citizens. For example, they are more strongly ideological than nonlisteners. Unlike the social isolates of talk radio days past, the new talk radio audience has a stronger sense of citizen duty and is more participatory than the general public.[1] We intend here to fill out the emerging political profile of the talk radio audience.

As we have discussed in previous chapters, television news magazines are a pervasive and popular format. Because these programs are widely accessed by the public, the TV news magazine audience is more similar to the general public than the audiences for some other forms of new media, such as talk radio. The public considers these programs to be more similar to mainstream news media, as our factor analysis in the previous chapter indicates. Television news magazine programs are not a radical departure technologically or substantively from mainstream media offerings. Yet, as we shall see, devoted viewers are not mirror images of the general populous.

Finally, online media, as the newest technology, merit our attention. Early indications are that the online community may share some core political orientations. People who use the Internet for political purposes appear to be more libertarian and more adamant about support for basic freedoms, such as speech, press, and assembly, than other members of society. It is conceivable, however, that as the technology becomes more widely available, the political character of this group may shift.

We will examine the political knowledge levels, ideological leanings, partisanship, trust, efficacy, political interest, and participation of the audiences for these new media. Data from the 1996 American National Election Study (ANES) were used in our analysis of the talk radio, television news magazine, and online audiences.[2] The ANES asked a series of questions about talk radio use, allowing us to identify people who listen to talk radio with some regularity. This group consisted of 37 percent of the sample. The study also included a question about how often respondents watched television news magazines such as "Prime Time Live." We combined people who responded "every week" and "most weeks" to form a category of frequent viewers, which constituted 30 percent of the respondents. The ANES included a question regarding online media use, which asked whether or not the respondent has access to the Internet.[3] Twenty-six percent of the ANES respondents had regular Internet access. Throughout our analysis, we compare the talk radio, television news magazine, and online audiences to the general public, which we operationalize as all respondents to the survey.

Political Knowledge

Studies and anecdotal observations repeatedly confirm that the American public is poorly informed about politics. Even as levels of educational attainment have increased over the past three decades, factual knowledge of politics has not escalated commensurately.[4] Political learning from mass media is generally limited, as the public does not recall much from news broadcasts, even in the short term.[5]

People's lack of interest in information that is not directly relevant to their daily lives has been cited as a reason for low political knowledge levels. However, the nature of the news product itself might contribute to the problem. Sound bite journalism, which has become the norm for much political reporting in mainstream televised media, does not provide sufficient substance or context about issues and events, and thus does not make a great impression on the audience. The highly negative character of much news reporting does little to encourage people to pay attention. Finally, the heavy emphasis on drama and personalization in the presentation of news stories serves to undercut their significance.[6]

Whether the new media further exacerbate or work toward remedying this situation has yet to be determined. On the one hand, many new media may contribute to the trivialization of political information because of their heavy entertainment focus. The new media introduce an additional concern—the spread and consumption of misinformation—as fact-checking practices are not routine. Yet entertainment does not necessarily preclude learning, especially when it is used to stimulate interest. Traditionally, alternative sources of political information, such as "Meet the Press" and the "NewsHour with Jim Lehrer," that present detailed discussions of issues have been more "highbrow" and insider-focused. The new media may facilitate political engagement, as they make information more accessible to more people through their more populist orientation.

It is difficult to determine whether or not the new media contribute directly to meaningful political learning. Measuring knowledge, especially using survey data, is problematic, as it is impossible to take into account the many kinds of information that validly represent political knowledge. Attributing knowledge gain to specific sources is even more challenging. However, we can examine whether people who listen to talk radio, watch television news magazines, and go online exhibit higher or lower levels of basic knowledge about politics than the general public.

Table 7.1 presents the percentage of people who correctly identified the majority party in the House of Representatives (Republican), the majority party in the Senate (Republican), Vice President Al Gore, Speaker of the House Newt Gingrich, Supreme Court Chief Justice William Rehnquist, and Russian President Boris Yeltsin. In general, the audiences for new media were more knowledgeable about these basic political facts than the public overall. Users of online media were the most informed. A higher proportion of online users (35 percent) than other citizens correctly identified William Rehnquist,

TABLE 7.1 Political Knowledge of Talk Radio, Television News Magazine, and Online Media Audiences

	Audience (%)			
Knowledge	General Public	Talk Radio	News Magazine	Online
House Majority Party	76	91	88	91
Senate Majority Party	72	91	91	94
Al Gore	89	98	97	99
Newt Gingrich	60	76	72	83
William Rehnquist	26	26	17	35
Boris Yeltsin	67	84	82	83

Source: 1996 American National Election Study.

which was the most difficult of the questions for respondents to answer. Regular news magazine viewers were just slightly less informed than talk radio listeners and online media users.

It may be the case that talk radio listeners and users of online sources, especially, are more politically aware in general than other citizens. The demographic profile of these audiences presented in chapter 6 indicates that they would exhibit advanced levels of political acumen based on their educational attainment and socioeconomic status. These people also regularly attend to other forms of mass media. They may enhance the depth and breadth of their political knowledge via their use of new media channels.

In order to test this hypothesis, we performed a multiple regression analysis which predicted political knowledge based on talk radio, television news magazine, and online source use controlling for the effects of age, sex, education, income, and race. As one would expect, education is the strongest predictor of political knowledge. However, the findings reveal that listening to talk radio and using online media are still significantly related to increased levels of political knowledge, even when these demographic variables are taken into account. The relationship is strongest for online sources. Television news magazine watching does not hold up to the introduction of demographic controls. The relationship to political knowledge, in fact, becomes negative.[7]

Political Orientations

Ideology

We expect to find that the audiences for new media have more strongly defined ideological orientations than the general public. In fact, some new media users specifically turn to these sources as a means of learning the opinions of other citizens and reinforcing their own views. Particular new media, especially talk radio, are viewed as ideological alternatives to the media mainstream, with its veneer of objectivity.

Studies repeatedly have indicated that the talk radio audience leans rightward ideologically.[8] Our analysis of these 1996 data continues to support this finding. As Table 7.2 indicates, the talk radio audience contains only a slightly lower percentage of liberals than does the general public. However, talk radio devotees are much more conservative than citizens at large, as 57 percent profess to lean right compared to 42 percent of all respondents. The audience for television news magazines is more reflective of the public overall than are talk radio listeners. As is the case for talk radio fans, a slightly smaller proportion of regular news magazine viewers call themselves liberal than is true for the general public. News magazine viewers are, however, almost equally as conservative as the public (45 percent), although not nearly as conservative as talk radio listeners. In contrast, people who go online are ideologically polarized. Only a small percentage (21 percent) falls into the moderate category, while 32 percent consider themselves liberal and 47 percent label themselves conservative. A higher percentage of online media users call themselves liberal than is the case for other citizens or talk radio and TV news magazine devotees.

We can see these ideological similarities and differences reflected in the opinions of talk radio, news magazine, and online audience members on a number of issues addressed by the study as depicted in Table 7.3. These include equal rights, equality of opportunity, and moral and life-style issues. In general, the views of the talk radio and television news magazine audiences were similar, although news magazine viewers were very slightly more inclined toward the conservative position. The online audience differed markedly in its views from the general public and the other new media users.

On issues of equal rights and opportunities, talk radio and television news magazine audience members are somewhat more inclined to believe that that there is not a problem or that the government has

TABLE 7.2 Political Ideology of Talk Radio, Television News Magazine, and Online Media Audiences

	Audience (%)			
Ideology	General Public	Talk Radio	News Magazine	Online
Liberal	26	22	22	32
Moderate	32	21	33	21
Conservative	42	57	45	47
Total	100	100	100	100

Source: 1996 American National Election Study.

TABLE 7.3 Opinions on Selected Issues for Talk Radio, Television News Magazine, and Online Media Audiences

Issue	Audience (%)			
	General Public	Talk Radio	News Magazine	Online
Not a Problem People Don't Have Equal Rights				
Agree	37	41	43	30
Neutral	19	43	20	20
Disagree	44	39	37	50
Total	100	100	100	100
Gone Too Far Pushing Equal Rights				
Agree	54	57	56	58
Neutral	14	13	15	16
Disagree	32	30	29	26
Total	100	100	100	100
Best Not to Be Involved in Helping Others				
Agree	35	35	39	26
Neutral	17	17	20	18
Disagree	48	48	41	56
Total	100	100	100	100
Fewer Problems More Traditional Families				
Agree	85	87	89	77
Neutral	8	6	7	11
Disagree	7	7	4	12
Total	100	100	100	100
Newer Lifestyles Bad for Society				
Agree	70	73	76	61
Neutral	14	12	11	16
Disagree	16	15	13	23
Total	100	100	100	100

Source: 1996 American National Election Study.

become too involved in this area. A slightly higher proportion of these citizens agree with the statements, "We have gone too far in pushing equal rights in this country" and "It is not really that big a problem as some people have more of a chance in life than others." The online media audience is more likely to disagree with these sentiments than either the general public or the talk radio and news magazine audiences. A similar, although not identical, pattern exists for the issue of providing assistance to those less fortunate in society. Respondents were asked if they agreed or disagreed with the statement, "It is best not to get too involved in taking care of other people's needs." The talk radio audience's views reflect those of the general public. Thirty-five percent of the public and talk radio listeners believe that it is best not to be involved in helping others, while 48 percent disagreed with this sentiment. Television news magazine viewers were slightly more inclined to agree with the idea of not getting involved than was the general public. Once again, people who go online were more likely to take a more progressive stance. A majority of online users (56 percent) disagreed with the statement that it is best not to get involved in helping others.

Another set of issues deals with moral concerns and life-style choices. As Table 7.3 demonstrates, the chasm between the talk radio and television news magazine viewers on the one hand and online media users on the other persists in this realm. Online users diverge the most from the main of public opinion. A strong majority of Americans believe that, "This country would have many fewer problems if there were more emphasis on traditional family ties." Eighty-five percent of the public agrees with this view, as does 87 percent of talk radio listeners and 89 percent of news magazine viewers. A smaller percentage of online media users feel that family values should prevail, although a substantial majority (77 percent) agree with the statement. Similarly, 70 percent of the general public agrees with the view that "the newer life-styles are contributing to the breakdown of our society." A slightly higher percentage of talk radio listeners (73 percent) and news magazine viewers (76 percent) feel the same way. However, 61 percent of online media users' views are in accordance with the statement. Once again, people who go online assume a notably less conservative stance.

Partisanship

Party Identification

The new media audiences differ somewhat from the general public in terms of their partisan identification (see Table 7.4). As we might expect because of their more conservative ideological orientations, the talk radio audience is significantly more Republican (37 percent) than citizens overall (28 percent). Evidence of the talk radio audience's

TABLE 7.4 Political Identification of Talk Radio, Television News Magazine, and Online Media Audiences

	Audience (%)			
Party Identification	General Public*	Talk Radio	News Magazine	Online
Democrat	39	32	42	35
Republican	28	37	26	34
Independent	25	25	25	27
No Preference	7	6	7	4
Total	99	100	100	100

*Not 100% because of rounding.

Source: 1996 American National Election Study.

Republican orientation is reinforced by the fact that 31 percent of listeners believe that the Republican party is best able to deal with the most important problems facing the nation, compared to 21 percent of the general public who feel this way. Only 17 percent of talk radio listeners feel that the Democratic party is the most competent.

Television news magazine viewers come close to resembling the public overall in their identification with political parties. They are only slightly more likely to claim Democratic party affiliation (42 percent) and less inclined to call themselves Republican (26 percent). The percentage of Independents and those who have no par-tisan preference—slightly over 30 percent—is virtually constant across the general public, talk radio, and TV news magazines categories.

Users of online media differ somewhat in their partisan preferences from the general public and from the other new media audiences we have examined. The approximately 70 percent of online users who identify with a political party split their allegiances about equally between the Republicans and the Democrats.[9] In keeping with the patterns for all of the other categories of citizens we are examining, 31 percent of online users are Independent or have no partisan preference.

Attitudes Toward Political Parties

The American two-party system is remarkable for its endurance. Yet over the past two decades, there has been an erosion in support for political parties among the mass public. People now are less likely to identify with the Democratic or Republican parties, they are less enamored with political parties as institutions, and they desire less intervention by parties in the political process.[10] As we can see from the discussion above, new media users are no less likely to declare themselves Independent than the general public. But are new media users more dissatisfied with political parties than other citizens? Do new media users, more than the general public, prefer alternatives to the existing political party system?

The mass media have been accused of contributing to the rise in antiparty sentiments in the United States, although some media-related consequences may have been unintentional. Perhaps the most visible encroachment of the media on political parties' turf has occurred in the electoral arena. The parties' attempts in the 1970s to reform the presidential nominating system to facilitate greater citizen representation and participation unwittingly transferred power from parties to the media. The emphasis on primaries, as opposed to caucuses, for selecting delegates to the national nominating conventions made it necessary for candidates to appeal directly to the public, as opposed to party regulars. These developments gave rise to candidate-centered, as opposed to party-directed, elections, as candidates campaigned through the media largely to the exclusion of party mechanisms. The media have assumed roles that were previously reserved for parties, including recruiting and screening candidates for office, structuring the campaign process, organizing the issue agenda, and informing and mobilizing voters.[11] Thus the media undermine the electoral function of parties, which may leave the impression among the public that parties are unnecessary and obsolete.

In addition, the mass media foster the growth of negative attitudes toward parties through their political reporting. Especially in recent years, the media have chastised politicians for what they consider to be excessive partisanship, which has precluded cooperation in government and effective policymaking. The situation has been highlighted in a period of divided national government. The press' coverage of partisan cleavages and bickering in Congress during the reign of Speaker Newt Gingrich has been particularly critical.[12]

The new media play a role in undermining party salience as well. Outsider candidates for all levels of office use new media to launch their campaigns, following Ross Perot's "Larry King Live" tactic in 1992. Talk show hosts throw their hats into the electoral ring, capitalizing on their skill with the medium. In addition, discussions of parties and politics on call-in programs and investigative reports on news magazines, especially of questionable fundraising tactics, emphasize the dubious, even scandalous, practices of the two major party organizations.

The ANES included a question about the American party system. When asked whether they support the continuation of the two party status quo, candidates running for office without party labels, a multiparty system, as Table 7.5 depicts, a majority of the public favors some alternative to the existing two-party system. Only 42 percent of citizens prefer a continuation of the current situation. Television news magazine viewers are the most supportive of the status quo, while talk radio listeners and online users are less favorably disposed toward

TABLE 7.5 Attitudes About the Future of the Party System of Talk Radio, Television News Magazine, and Online Media Audiences

Preference	Audience (%)			
	General Public	Talk Radio	News Magazine	Online
Continue two party system	42	40	48	38
Candidates run without party labels	32	28	29	30
Growth of multiparty system	26	32	23	32
Total	100	100	100	100

Source: 1996 American National Election Study.

this option. Of the other alternatives, 32 percent of the public prefers to have candidates listed on the ballot without party labels, while 26 percent favors the proliferation of third-party options. The talk radio and online audiences differ from the public generally, in that they are more likely to embrace the multiparty option over the idea that candidates should run without party labels. The pattern of preferences for news magazine viewers is similar to that of the mass public.

Attitudes Toward Government: Trust and Competence

The erosion of public trust of government and political leaders is not a recent development. Trust has been on the decline since the mid 1960s, reaching all-time lows in the 1990s despite a minor reprieve during the early 1980s.[13] Citizens have lost faith in the government in Washington, they are less fond of political institutions, and they distrust the people who are holding office at all levels. The rise in public cynicism has raised cause for concern, as a lack of trust can undermine democratic values and strong community ties among citizens as well as dissolve social capital.[14] Citizens' frustration and dissatisfaction with government may cause them to withdraw or abstain from the political process by not voting or participating in community affairs, for example.

The sources of discontent are many, varied, and frequently contradictory. Public expectations regarding government are not being met, yet there is no consensus on what the role of government should be. Some citizens feel that the government has gotten out of hand—that it has become so large that public control and direction is almost impossible. Many believe an elite professional class that is impervious to public sentiments now rules the nation. For many, there is too much government intervention in too many aspects of society.[15] The conventional wisdom is that the government is populated by corrupt politicians who are unable to deal with the major problems facing the nation, the states, and local communities.[16] This situation is compounded by the fact that some citizens today, rather than registering concern over the size and scope of government, are making increased demands on government, especially in the economic sphere.

The media have been blamed for exacerbating public distrust and cynicism. News stories about government and politicians focus an inordinate amount of attention on problems, infighting, and scandals. Little coverage is given to the things that work in government, many of which are routine, or to the accomplishments of political leaders. The personalized nature of news coverage draws attention away from policy issues and focuses it on the human foibles of political leaders.[17]

Joseph Cappella and Kathleen Hall Jamieson provide rare empirical validation for the speculation that the media encourage public distrust. They argue that the press' focus on political strategies, conflict, and politicians' motives fosters public cynicism about leaders, their performances, and institutions. When the news is framed in terms of issues, contrary to current journalistic culture, it is less likely to spark cynical reactions.[18]

Negative media coverage is not limited to the mainstream press. Pundits make their living casting aspersions at politicians and the policy-making process. Some new media formats thrive on their unrelenting criticism of government. In the aftermath of the Oklahoma City bombing, and after taking many hits from talk radio hosts and callers, especially Rush Limbaugh and G. Gordon Liddy, President Clinton called into a talk radio program to voice his concerns about the medium. He accused talk radio of generating public cynicism and intolerance because of its unrelenting barrage of negativity.[19] Talk radio is not the only source of negative messages. Television news magazine stories feature investigative reports that showcase government corruption. Various Internet sites host ongoing discussions of the problems of government and the failure of leaders.

However, are users of new media more distrusting and dissatisfied with government than the general public? Is President Clinton correct in assuming that talk radio listeners will be especially cynical? The new media audiences are exposed to extra heavy doses of negative press about politics through mainstream and alternative sources. This could breed increased cynicism, or it may have a limited or negligible effect. We examine our data for some answers.

As Table 7.6 demonstrates, there is little evidence that people

TABLE 7.6 Trust in Government for Talk Radio, Television News Magazine, and Online Media Audiences

Attitude	Audience (%)			
	General Public	Talk Radio	News Magazine	Online
Trust Government				
Most of time	32	30	37	33
Sometimes	67	69	63	67
Never	1	1	1	—
Total	100	100	100	100
Most Faith In				
National	30	27	31	31
State	37	41	37	39
Local	33	33	32	30
Total	100	100	100	100
Least Faith In				
National	48	54	44	49
State	18	18	18	20
Local	34	29	38	32
Total	100	100	100	100

Source: 1996 American National Election Study.

who attend to any of the three new media sources we examine here are any less trusting of government in a general sense than the mass public. It may well be the case that citizens' faith in government is so diminished in general—only 32% of the public trusts the government most of the time—that any new media effects would be difficult to discern. Regular viewers of television news magazines are slightly more trusting of government than citizens in the other categories. There are some differences between types of media users in the degree of trust exhibited for particular levels of government. In general, people place the most faith in state government and have the least confidence in the national government. This pattern is the most pronounced for talk radio listeners.

There are, however, variations, based on media use, in attitudes toward government performance and the role government should play in society. Table 7.7 contains the responses to a variety of questions tapping opinions about government. The talk radio and online audiences differ most from the general public. News magazine viewers' attitudes are more reflective of those of citizens overall. Very few of those surveyed believed that the government was doing a good job handling the problem that they identified as the most important one facing the nation. A majority of talk radio listeners (54 percent) and online media users (57 percent) actually rated the government's job performance as poor. The television news magazine audience was somewhat more benign in its evaluation than the general public.

The survey included a series of items that tapped the peoples' attitudes toward government intervention in society and in economic affairs. The question required respondents to choose the one of two statements that comes closest to their opinion. The first item provided the following two options: "The less government, the better," or "There are more things that government should be doing." The second question asked them to choose between "We need a strong government to handle today's complex economic problems," and "The free market can handle these problems without government being involved." Finally, participants were asked to select either "The main reason government has become bigger over the years is because it has gotten involved in things that people should do for themselves," or "Government has become bigger because the problems we face have become bigger."

The pattern of responses to these questions supports the contention that the reasons behind the lack of political trust are complex, and they are often conflicting, as members of the public want and expect very different things of government (see Table 7.7). In general, the public believes that government should play a role in handling society's problems. Fifty-five percent of the public feel that government should do more, while 62 percent advocates stronger government to handle complex economic problems. The talk radio audience, however, consistently gave the anti–big government, free market

TABLE **7.7** Attitudes Toward Government for Talk Radio, Television News Magazine, and Online Media Audiences

Attitude	General Public	Talk Radio	News Magazine	Online
	\multicolumn{4}{c}{Audience (%)}			
Most Important Problem				
Good Job	7	7	10	6
Fair Job	44	39	52	37
Poor Job	49	54	39	57
Total	100	100	100	100
Less gov't better	45	57	46	53
Gov't should do more	55	43	54	47
Total	100	100	100	100
Need strong gov't to handle problems	62	49	63	58
Free market can handle problems without gov't	38	51	37	42
Total	100	100	100	100
Gov't bigger— too involved	50	61	50	54
Gov't bigger— problems bigger	50	39	50	46
Total	100	100	100	100
Gov't wastes taxes				
A lot	60	63	65	58
Some	38	35	34	41
Not much	2	2	1	1
Total	100	100	100	100
Gov't run by few big interests	72	73	69	67
Gov't run for good of all	28	27	31	33
Total	100	100	100	100

Source: 1996 American National Election Study.

responses to these questions. Fifty-seven percent of talk radio listeners believe in less government, 51 percent feel that the free market can handle problems without government assistance, and 61 percent contend that government has grown because it is interfering in things that people should handle for themselves. These findings are much in keeping with the conservative ideological orientations of hosts and listeners, and reflect the antigovernment banter that fills the airwaves.

The television news magazine audience is almost identical in its reflection of the public's attitudes on these issues. Online media users, while diverging somewhat from the mainstream of public opinion, are less consistent in their views than the talk radio audience. Online users are slightly more inclined to believe that government is too big and interferes in places where it does not belong. Yet 58 percent of the online audience feels that we need a strong government to handle economic problems.

The final set of indicators that we examine here taps whether people believed that the government wastes tax dollars and whether they felt that government was run by a few big interests or for the good of all citizens. There is little variation on these measures based on new media breakdowns. As is the case with general trust of government, the negative responses are high across the board. Approximately 60 percent of citizens believe that government wastes taxes "a lot," while virtually no one responded "not much." Nearly three quarters of the public believes that government is run by a few big interests. A slightly smaller percentage of the online audience felt this way.

Political Efficacy

Political efficacy refers to an individual's belief that she or he can influence the political process and have an impact on political leaders. Efficacy is closely tied to political trust, in that individuals who are more trusting of government tend to believe more strongly in their ability to effectively influence politics than other citizens. Efficacious citizens also are more likely to participate in the political realm.[20]

The concept of political efficacy is frequently divided into separate components. Internal efficacy refers to individuals' perceptions that they have the necessary skills to be successful political actors and represents the degree to which they feel they can personally influence politics. External efficacy deals with whether people believe that the government is responsive to attempts by ordinary citizens like themselves to affect the government.[21] Dividing efficacy into these two components is a common practice, although there is disagreement about how the concepts should be measured.[22] For purposes of this analysis, we will divide the indicators available in the survey into two categories that reflect internal and external dimensions. To tap internal efficacy, respondents were asked if they agreed or disagreed with the following statements: (1) "Public officials don't care much about what people like me think," (2) "People like me don't have any say about what the government does," (3) "Sometimes politics and government seem so complicated that a person like me can't really understand what's going on." The questions employed to measure external efficacy indicate whether a person believes that the government is responsive to citizens' input. The two items are: (1) "Over the years, how much attention do you feel the government pays to what the people think when it decides what to do?" and (2) "How much do you feel that having elections makes the government pay attention to what the people think?"

Citizens' use of new media raises some interesting issues related to political efficacy, especially with regard to the more interactive formats that thrive on public expression. Are new media users more or less efficacious—in terms of both internal and external efficacy—than the general public? It may be the case that people who use new media regularly have a strong sense of political efficacy. Their attention to new media is another manifestation of their sense of connectedness to the political world. In fact, research has demonstrated that people with higher levels of personal efficacy, which is closely related to political efficacy, were most likely to view and phone into television call-in programs featuring candidates during the 1992 presidential election contest. The finding was especially robust for African-American users of television call-in programs.[23]

Alternatively, the new media's popularity may be attributable, in part, to the fact that some citizens do not feel that they can influence the government via conventional methods, such as voting, mounting petition drives, or contacting public officials. Thus individuals who have low levels of political efficacy may turn to new media out of a sense of frustration. As we shall see, members of the audiences for talk radio, television news magazines, and online media sources vary in the degree to which they feel politically efficacious.

Research conducted in 1993 found that talk radio callers and listeners had a strong sense of civic responsibility and commitment, but they felt they had a limited capacity to influence government. The talk radio audience scored higher on measures of citizen duty than the general public, but lower on political efficacy indicators.[24] As Table 7.8 indicates, these findings are not replicated in the current analysis. In general, the mass public is not especially efficacious. The overall perception is that public officials do not pay attention and are not responsive to citizens. The talk radio audience has a somewhat stronger sense of internal political efficacy than the general public. Talk radio listeners are more likely to disagree with the statement that public officials don't care what they think, although their scores on this indicator are closer to the mass public than for any other item. They are less likely to feel that people have no say in government or that politics is too complicated for people like them to follow.

The talk radio audience closely reflects the general public as well as the television news magazine and online audiences on measures of external efficacy. Very few people—less than 20 percent—believe that the government pays a good deal of attention to public input. Citizens are somewhat more inclined to think that elections make government leaders pay attention to what they want. Approximately 45 percent of the public believe elections make government officials pay a lot of attention. The percentage of new media users who score high on external efficacy measures is just slightly higher than for the general public.

There are a variety of explanations for the disparity in findings between the two studies. One possibility is that methodological factors are responsible, given that two different data sources were employed.

TABLE 7.8 Political Efficacy for Talk Radio, Television News Magazine, and Online Media Audiences

Attitude	Audience (%)			
	General Public	Talk Radio	News Magazine	Online
Don't Care				
Agree	61	60	61	52
Neutral	15	12	15	15
Disagree	24	29	24	33
Total	100	100	100	100
No Say in Gov't				
Agree	45	38	45	32
Neutral	10	8	10	10
Disagree	45	54	45	58
Total	100	100	100	100
Politics Too Complicated				
Agree	61	54	62	49
Neutral	10	9	11	10
Disagree	29	37	27	41
Total	100	100	100	100
Gov't Pays Attn				
A good deal	16	18	19	18
Some	63	61	59	67
Not much	22	21	21	15
Total	100	100	100	100
Elections Make Gov't Pay Attn				
A good deal	43	46	46	45
Some	42	41	42	44
Not much	15	13	13	12
Total	100	100	100	100

Source: 1996 American National Election Study.

The 1993 study used data from a national survey conducted by the Times Mirror Center for the People and the Press in a nonelection year, which is a time when politics may appear more remote to many citizens than when a campaign is in full swing. However, the efficacy items included on both surveys are nearly identical. The talk radio audience for the 1993 study was divided into listeners and callers, but both groups exhibited similar trends with regard to efficacy. It may be the case that the people who constitute the talk radio audience have changed since 1993, especially given the ebbs and flows of listenership. However, the demographic characteristics associated with the talk radio audience in 1996 identified in chapter 6 are consistent with those found in earlier periods.

A reasonable alternative explanation—although one that is impossible to test here—is that in the three-year period between studies talk radio users have gained an increased sense of their own political power through their use of talk radio and their perceptions about the power of the medium. Political talk has received a great deal of publicity since the 1992 campaign. High ranking public officials, such as President Clinton and Speaker Gingrich, have spoken on talk radio and both have attested to its ability to influence public sentiment. Talk show hosts work hard to instill this perception in their listeners, whether their power over politics is real or imagined. Over time, members of the talk radio community may have developed a stronger sense of their own political efficacy because of their association with a medium to which an influential political role has been ascribed. They themselves, or people like them, can actually be part of a political discussion and sometimes can even talk directly to leaders who are guests on talk programs.

Regular viewers of television news magazines are almost identical to the general public in their sense of internal political efficacy (see Table 7.8.). Television news magazines do little to include the public in their presentations, except through very short segments that report viewer correspondence. Further, the political content of these programs is not overwhelming, nor is it presented in a way that might enhance the viewer's sense of political potency.

The online audience is the most internally efficacious of all the new media groups, including the talk radio audience. On every indicator, online media users demonstrate a notably greater sense of their own ability to influence the political process than the general public. Their upscale demographics might account partially for this finding.

Political Interest and Activity

Regularly attending to a political talk program, viewing a magazine program where political interviews and issues are raised, and going online to seek political information are indicators of political interest in and of themselves. Calling into a talk program, sending an e-mail to express an opinion about a magazine program segment, and participating in an online discussion are forms of political participation. But do people who routinely use talk radio, television news magazines, and online media limit their political engagement to media-related activities, or are they more uniformly interested and participatory? We examine both general and campaign-specific forms of political engagement in our exploration of this issue.

Interest in Politics

It stands to reason that people who regularly use new media would be more interested in politics than the mass public in general. As we demonstrated in chapter 6, talk radio listeners, news magazine viewers, and people who go online also are likely to habitually attend to the mainstream press for political information. Their somewhat higher levels of political knowledge and efficacy also point to their concern about the political world.

The data in Table 7.9 lend empirical verification to these asser-

TABLE 7.9 Follow Government and Public Affairs for Talk Radio, Television News Magazine, and Online Media Audiences

	Audience (%)			
Awareness	General Public	Talk Radio	News Magazine	Online
Follow Gov't and Public Affairs				
Most of time	23	32	29	27
Some of time	40	44	44	41
Now and again	26	20	20	23
Hardly ever	11	4	7	10
Total	100	100	100	100
Discuss Politics With Family or Friends				
Yes	78	88	81	93
No	22	12	13	7
Total	100	100	100	100

Source: 1996 American National Election Study.

tions. A larger proportion of the audiences for talk radio, television news magazines, and online media follows government and public affairs more closely than the general public. Of new media users, talk radio listeners are particularly attentive to political affairs, followed closely by news magazine viewers. People who go online are slightly less interested. Sixty-three percent of the general public follows governmental activities most or some of the time, compared to 76 percent of talk radio fans, 73 percent of news magazine watchers, and 68 percent of online media users.

In addition to their enhanced interest in public affairs, new media audience members are more likely than the public in general to engage in political discussions. As Table 7.9 depicts, most citizens claim to discuss politics with family and friends (78 percent). However, the proportion of online media users (93 percent), talk radio listeners (88 percent), and television news magazine viewers (81 percent) who talk about politics with others is notably higher than the norm.

Campaign-Related Involvement

We expect that the general interest in politics exhibited by new media audience members will carry over to the campaign context. This expectation is especially warranted, given that the 1992 presidential campaign was the catalyst which sparked the new media's political ascendancy. While the 1996 contest did not stimulate the same level of public and media enthusiasm as the previous presidential election, new media devotees still rivaled the general public in terms of their interest in the election, level of voter turnout, and tendency to engage in discussions of candidates with other people for the purpose of trying to change their vote choice. However, they did not participate more frequently in other forms of electoral activity.

According to the data employed here, only 32 percent of the general public admitted to being "very much interested" in the lackluster 1996 election (see Table 7.10). The talk radio (43 percent) and television news magazine (42 percent) audiences were somewhat more interested, while online media users (33 percent) were less engaged by the campaign. Consistent with prior research,[25] we found that new media audiences are much more inclined to be registered and to turn out to vote than the general public. Eighty-five percent of talk radio listeners, 82 percent of television news magazine viewers, and 86 percent of online media users went to the polls on election day in 1996.[26]

In keeping with our finding that new media audience members are more likely than the general public to discuss politics, these individuals also are significantly more inclined to talk about the campaign with others. Twenty-nine percent of citizens reported that they tried to convince another person to vote for a particular candidate. Forty percent of talk radio listeners try to persuade others, compared to 34 percent of each of news magazine viewers and online media users.

New media audience members do not stand apart from the general public in other areas of campaign involvement. Very few Americans take an active part in the campaign process other than voting, attending to media, and discussing the election. A small percentage wear a button or display a bumper sticker for a candidate, attend a candidate meeting or rally, work for a party or a candidate, or contribute money to a party or a candidate. Talk radio listeners and

TABLE 7.10 Campaign Involvement for Talk Radio, Television News Magazine, and Online Media Audiences

Involvement	Audience (%)			
	General Public	Talk Radio	News Magazine	Online
Interest				
Very much	32	43	42	33
Somewhat	52	49	46	55
Not much	16	8	12	11
Total	100	100	100	100
Talk with others about candidate	29	40	34	34
Button/Bumper Sticker	10	13	12	14
Attend Meeting or Rally	6	9	7	12
Work for Party or Candidate	3	4	2	5
Contribute Money	6	8	5	9

Source: 1996 American National Election Study.

online media users are very slightly more inclined to participate in the campaign in these ways than is the general public.

Involvement in Political and Community Groups

Based on prior surveys, there is some evidence to suggest that people who regularly use new media, particularly interactive formats, engage in political activity other than voting to a greater extent than other citizens. Talk radio and online media users are much more likely to contact a public official about a problem by writing a letter or sending e-mail than the general public. There also are indications that new media devotees are active in community affairs.[27] They attend city council meetings, join political organizations, and do volunteer work.

The survey included a battery of questions asking respondents about their involvement in a wide range of organizations, including political, community, labor union, business, and church groups. These questions allow us to probe the issue of the community involvement and integration of the new media audiences more deeply and to identify areas where these citizens might be most engaged. The results for our comparison of new media audiences appear in Table 7.11. We find, overall, that there is a slightly higher tendency for new media audience members to become involved in organizations, especially online media users. However, the differences in the levels of involvement between the mass public and new media devotees is remarkable in only a few instances.

TABLE 7.11 Organizational Involvement for Talk Radio, Television News Magazine, and Online Media Audiences

	Audience (%)			
Organization	General Public	Talk Radio	News Magazine	Online
Political Groups				
Party/Cand	3	6	4	4
Issue	6	9	5	9
Lib/Con	0.2	0.3	0	0.2
Community Group	13	14	13	22
Work Problem	23	30	27	31
Civic Associations	2	2	1	3
Volunteer Work	42	46	45	52
Elderly Groups	12	12	16	5
Children's Groups	16	18	14	26
Needy	10	10	15	13
Educational	18	20	20	32
Labor Unions	14	15	10	17
Business Groups	18	21	12	30
Church Groups	58	64	65	56

Source: 1996 American National Election Study.

These data indicate that few Americans are involved in political groups that are associated with parties and candidates (3 percent), issues (6 percent), or ideological positions (0.2 percent). New media users are just slightly more likely to join these groups than the general public. Issue groups, in particular, appeal to talk radio and online media users.

Participation rates are significantly higher for community-oriented organizations, some of which can play political roles. Forty-two percent of citizens claim that they do volunteer work, while 23 percent have banded together with others to work on a community problem. A somewhat higher proportion of the talk radio, news magazine, and online audiences has engaged in these activities. If we take participation in community-oriented organizations as a whole, what stands out is the higher rate of involvement of people who go online. Online media users are the most likely to join a volunteer organization (52 percent) and take part in a community group (22 percent). They are also inclined to work with children's groups (26 percent) and educational organizations such as the PTA (32 percent). However, they are the least apt to work with the elderly (5 percent). A possible explanation for this pattern is found in the demographic characteristics of online users, as many of them are in the age bracket often associated with parenting younger children. Other than volunteering and working on community problems, the talk radio audience does not have a significantly greater tendency to join community groups than the mass public. News magazine viewers are just slightly more inclined to work with the elderly and the needy than other citizens.

New media users are not much more likely to belong to a labor union than the general public. However, online users are almost twice as involved in business groups as are citizens overall. The fact that the Internet is used widely by businesses, and many people access it through the work place, may contribute to this fact. Finally, the talk radio (64 percent) and television news magazine (65 percent) audiences are more involved in church groups than other citizens. While a majority of online users belong to church groups (56 percent), the proportion is lower than for other new media users.

Discussion

The foregoing analysis comparing the political orientations of talk radio, television news magazine, and online media users drives home the point we have been making about the diversity of the audiences for new media. To at least some degree, the political content of new media reflects the political orientations of those who attend regularly to a particular format. It is a well-established fact that the talk radio audience, for example, is far more conservative than the general population, which is in keeping with the conservative banter that dominates the airwaves. The greater ideological diversity among on-line media users, especially the disproportionate number of liberal self-identifiers compared to the mass public, reflects the fact that dis-cussion groups and chat rooms can and do accommodate intense and highly polarized political discussion.

Our analysis highlights the fact that new media users are some-what more politically aware, knowledgeable, and active than most citi-zens. Without adequate longitudinal or panel data to track new media users, however, it is difficult to determine the source of this enhanced political engagement. Do the new media arouse individuals' interest in politics, or do people gravitate toward new media because they al-ready are politically engaged and seek new outlets for information and expression? The answer is probably a little bit of both. Given the upscale demographic profiles of the audiences for talk radio and on-line media, especially, we would expect to find among them a higher proportion of politically active citizens compared to the general pub-lic. For those already immersed in politics, new media offer fresh op-portunities for involvement in novel ways. We may further speculate that new media can work to make regular users feel more efficacious over time.

On the other hand, the new media's greater accessibility may at-tract some people to the political fold who have previously been left out. Talk radio has been used to target specific populations, such as blacks and Hispanics, in order to foster political initiative. Computers that allow citizens to register opinions about community issues and communicate with local officials online have been installed in working-class bars. However, the extent to which new media actually facilitate democratic practice by promoting a politics of inclusion is unclear. The regular audiences for the more politically viable forms of new me-dia, such as talk radio, electronic town meetings, and online sources, are not underprivileged in terms of social status, economic well-being, or educational attainment. As such, the circumstantial evi-dence seems to suggest that for now new media are more likely to provide yet another resource for people who already have real or po-tential political clout.

THE EFFECTS OF NEW MEDIA ON TRADITIONAL MEDIA, CAMPAIGNS, AND PUBLIC POLICY

Shaping Old Media

On January 18, 1996, CNN interrupted its regularly scheduled programming with "Late Breaking News." The marriage of Michael Jackson and Lisa Marie Presley was ending. The impending Jackson-Presley divorce became the topic of CNN's "Talkback Live" program, which immediately followed the announcement. Audience members registered their opinions about the breakup live, by phone and via electronic mail. For days, this story preempted news about issues of national and international importance, including Congress' battle over the federal budget, as reporters, legal experts, and the public debated questions surrounding the divorce.[1]

This incident—a particularly outrageous example of the hundreds that we could have employed—illustrates just a few of the ways in which the new media have transformed the old media. As we have discussed in chapter 4, entertainment stories that traditionally had served as tabloid fodder now feature prominently in "hard news" forums. "Late Breaking News" has become an overused catch-phrase, as it is no longer reserved for urgent, important developing stories. Further, the public's role as media commentator has become more formally established. Finally, information is disseminated via a wide array of formats initiated by the same media source.

The new media's impact on the mainstream press has been

substantial and wide ranging. Yet it is not simply the case that the new media's high-profile presence has forced the old media to change. Rather, as chapter 2 demonstrates, shifts in social, cultural, political, and economic conditions created a media environment in which change was inevitable.

In this chapter, we will analyze the old media's response to the new media. The traditional media's modes of operation, the techniques used in reporting, the style of journalism, and the content of stories have undergone significant transformations in the new media age. We will explore how the new media have precipitated changes in the rules of the game under which the old media operate. A "star system," whereby an elite corps of celebrity journalists make news as they report it, has emerged. While this trend cannot be directly attributed to the new media, it is a manifestation of a media system that increasingly emulates the entertainment business. The new media encourage and enhance the role of celebrity news personnel. In addition, practices regularly employed by the new media, such as paying for news, have begun to infiltrate the traditional press. We will discuss how these developments have precipitated changes in the news agenda and altered the form and substance of stories. Further, we will examine how the old media have integrated new media techniques and technologies into their reporting repertoires. Finally, we will ponder the implications—present and future—of these developments.

New Rules for a New Media Age

Even before new media rose to prominence, trends in professional journalism foreshadowed what have become trademarks of the modern era. Increasingly, journalists themselves became an integral part of news stories and events. As political scientist Larry Sabato observes, "Journalists now take center stage in the process, creating the news as much as reporting it, changing both the shape of election-year politics and the contours of government."[2] Further, politicians speak far less often for themselves today than in the past, as journalists interpret their words and actions.[3] Celebrity journalism represents an outgrowth of this pattern.

Celebrity Journalism

The news media industry increasingly has assumed the trappings of the entertainment industry it has come to emulate. One of the characteristics of the new media is that they are driven by personalities. As we discussed in chapter 3, the popularity of talk radio hosts largely determines the success or failure of a show.

This "cult of personality" has infiltrated the old media, as an elite corps of "celebrity journalists" has emerged. The star system, while not a new phenomenon in journalism, has taken on new and, to some, troubling dimensions.

"Celebrity journalism" has its origins in the days of radio. Prior to the advent of electronic communications, print journalists operated under a shroud of relative anonymity. During World War II, a group of American correspondents working overseas used radio to broadcast news of the conflict. Known collectively as "the Murrow Boys," they included Edward R. Murrow, Eric Sevareid, and Howard K. Smith, among others. Their radio coverage of the war brought them instant celebrity of the kind reserved for Hollywood stars. They hired agents, went on the lecture circuit, and were featured regularly in gossip columns. Media stars were paid fees by sponsors to hawk their products on air. They used their fame to branch out into other areas of the entertainment industry, such as writing novels and screenplays and hosting pure entertainment programs, such as celebrity interview shows.[4]

While radio catapulted "the Murrow Boys" into the public spotlight, it was television that propelled the star system to new heights beginning in the early 1950s.[5] Television allowed viewers to become even more directly acquainted with reporters than did radio. This relationship was solidified further as citizens associated reporters with the fascination they held for the new medium and its exciting visual means of conveying information.

The entertainment component that television encouraged in news reporting has been magnified in the new media era. While the old media give star journalists legitimacy, new media add luster. Even the "Murrow Boys" realized that conflict played well on radio and television, and arguing about politics could engage audiences.[6] Celebrity is enhanced when media stars have more of a free rein to express themselves, which often means locking horns with other media stars, public officials, or citizens. The new media provide celebrity journalists with the opportunity to showcase themselves outside of their traditional media roles.

Celebrity journalists follow a similar path to stardom, which includes landing a prestigious traditional press job, doing the political talk show circuit, and branching out to entertainment media forums. Televised political talk shows are the proving ground for celebrity journalists. The number of these shows has increased in recent years to over thirty on major networks and countless others on cable stations.[7] The Saturday night and Sunday morning free-for-all political talk show circuit, which includes programs such as "The Capital Gang" and "Meet the Press," allows aspiring and established media celebrities to hone their inside-the-Beltway skills.

New media forums such as talk radio present more and varied occasions for stars to appeal to the public appetite for entertainment. As we discussed in chapter 4, network anchors regularly double as hosts of television news magazine programs with tabloid undercurrents, such as "48 Hours," "Dateline NBC," and "Primetime Live." Some of these crossover appearances find established journalists frequenting unlikely venues. For example, Dan Rather is a regular guest on the "Imus in the Morning" talk radio program. Media stars even make cameo appearances in feature films, such as *Dave, My Fellow Americans,* and *Rising Sun.*[8]

The star system has created a paradox in the financially troubled news business. While media organizations are downsizing their news divisions and laying off staff, celebrity journalists command salaries in the millions of dollars. This situation has created two classes of journalists—an elite upper class of press "personalities" and the majority of working reporters.[9]

One factor that sets star journalists apart from the pack is their ability to parlay their celebrity status into a lucrative side business of paid speaking engagements. Exceptions to this rule include Tom Brokaw, Peter Jennings, Dan Rather, Ted Koppel, Bob Schieffer, Jim Lehrer, and Brian Lamb, who either decline fees or donate them to charity. Some media stars, such as Sam Donaldson, Larry King, and Cokie Roberts, have commanded lecture fees of as much as fifty thousand dollars—more than some journalists earn in an entire year, and they can make hundreds of thousand of dollars in extra income in a year.[10] Even *U.S. News & World Report* editor James Fallows, who decried the practice in his book, *Breaking the News,* has earned yearly lecture fees of over forty-five thousand dollars, largely from academic institutions.[11] Star journalists frequently are represented by agents, such as the Washington Speakers Bureau, who negotiate their outside deals. Some news organizations, such as *U.S. News and World Report,* have their own booking agents, as they believe that these appearances are good publicity.[12] Bad publicity about the high fees paid to star journalists has resulted in some media celebrities limiting their appearances and lowering their fees.

Critics fear the star system has contributed to the declining quality of news. Reporters' celebrity status institutionalizes the entertainment component of news. Further, when media stars spend a significant amount of time operating in the new media environment, they tend to adopt new media habits and styles of reporting. Because the system works on the premise that it is not so much information that is important, but the person who is delivering it, reporters who have a specialized areas of expertise now need to become instant experts on a wide range of stories and issues. Programs like the "Capital Gang" and the "McLaughlin Group" require their participants to be ready to speak on a variety of unrelated topics at a minute's notice in order to appear current. Conversations during a given show can range from a discussion of the federal budget to Bosnia to the NBA basketball draft.

Because media stars lack detailed information about many topics, discussions tend to focus on strategy rather than substance. Instead of providing the public with useful information, politics is presented as a game, a struggle, rivalry. Issues matter little, except as they serve as the focal point for disagreement. Banal shouting matches masquerade as sincere debate about issues.[13] For example, the debate over the federal budget in the 104th Congress was presented on the talk circuit as a power struggle between President Clinton and Speaker Newt Gingrich, rather than in terms of specific policy provisions.

Margaret Carlson, a *Time* magazine columnist who has been a participant on the "Capital Gang," sums up the situation. "What I write in *Time* magazine are things I've thought through, I've studied, I've gotten every point of view. . . . What's good tv and what's thoughtful analysis are two different things. That's been conceded by most producers and bookers. They're not looking for the most learned person; they're looking for the person who can sound learned without confusing the matter with too much knowledge. I'm one of the people without too much knowledge. I'm perfect."[14]

Another concern is that celebrity journalism poses a serious threat to the credibility of the mainstream news business. Some critics allege that correspondents who are paid hefty sums by special interests favor these groups in their coverage. They contend that the power of media stars to influence public opinion far outweighs that of politicians. David Gergen, who is a mainstay of the speakers' circuit, finds evidence of a more subtle effect, that is, the isolation of journalists from the public they are supposed to be watchdogs for. "You just talk to these well-groomed, well-heeled business folks. You're traveling in a bubble. It tends to encourage a pro-establishment viewpoint."[15] The news agenda itself is narrowed, as the topics that tend to be raised for discussion are those that are of interest to political and business insiders.

Further, a potential conflict of interest arises when celebrity journalists are earning large sums of money for personal appearances in front of the same interest groups they condemn for buying favors from politicians through campaign contributions and other perks.[16] For example, "Prime Time Live" was ready to air an expose about a trip to Key West, Florida, for thirty congressional staff members paid for by the American Insurance Association and other insurance groups until it was revealed that anchor Sam Donaldson had received first-class airfare to New York City, hotel accommodations in the Waldorf Astoria, limousine service, and a thirty-thousand-dollar fee for speaking to the same organizations.[17]

Celebrity journalists defend their status by claiming that they are private citizens, not elected officials. They argue that they do not have power over the public purse, nor are they in the position of making laws or public policy, therefore, they are not compromising the public trust. Media stars also contend that when they speak to interest groups they appear as celebrities, and not as journalists. The motives of groups are to provide a source of entertainment for their members, and not to influence the speaker, they argue.

The star system has prompted people in government and media to call for reform. Al Hunt of the *Wall Street Journal* has proposed that journalists be required to disclose outside income from groups that lobby Congress before they are given congressional press cards. West Virginia Senator Robert Byrd has taken action to put this requirement into effect. Reacting to a "Prime Time Live" crew's attempts to ambush him outside of his home, Byrd introduced a nonbinding resolution that would require reporters to reveal their outside income in financial disclosure forms before receiving credentials. The resolution passed by a vote of 60 to 39. Byrd would like to make the rule mandatory, although that has yet to occur.[18]

Some media organizations, such as the *Washington Post* and the *Wall Street Journal*, prohibit reporters from giving paid speeches to industries or trade associations that lobby Congress, although they permit college appearances. Other organizations, such as ABC News and CBS News, require that all speaking engagements be cleared with a supervisor.

Partisan Pundits

A separate set of concerns surrounds a corps of celebrity journalists who move from political jobs into the newsroom. David S. Broder identifies a trend where people who have held prominent political positions circumvent the usual process of working their way up the newsroom ladder to become high-profile pundits. These political advisers turned pundits, whose ranks include George F. Will, a close associate of Ronald Reagan, and George Stephanopoulos, an intimate of Bill Clinton, tend to populate the same media venues as other celebrity journalists. They are usually based at a mainstream political media organization and use new media to heighten their celebrity.

At times, these pundits have difficulty abandoning their prior political roles, and they will offer advice to politicians publicly via both old and new media. David Broder notes that their partisanship is frequently in full view, and that their actions blur the line between advisers and journalists. For example, *New York Times* columnist William Safire, a former speech writer for Richard Nixon and Spiro Agnew, wrote that House Speaker Newt Gingrich had called him for advice about how to handle the situation surrounding the ethics charges that were levied against him. Safire reported that he advised the Speaker to step down "for the sake of the country, the conservative cause, the Republican Party, and even his own long-term career."[19]

George Will stepped in and out of his journalistic role when he editorialized on the Reagan campaign in 1980, helped prep Reagan for the presidential candidates' debate, and then returned to commenting on the Reagan campaign. Susan Molinari, the highest ranking Republican woman in the House of Representatives, left her elected office in 1997 to anchor a Saturday morning program for CBS News. This move has led to speculation that Molinari will be using this position to launch a campaign for higher office. The easy fluctuation between politics and press has raised concern. Such a revolving door may be known to political insiders, but usually is not reported to the readership who expect journalists to maintain some level of independence from those they report on.[20]

Broder argues that it is essential for a division of labor to exist between journalists and government officials. He elaborates on the dangers of eradicating these lines:

> More and more of the prominent figures in journalism display the mindsets and play the roles of partisan advisors more appropriate to the political world from which they came, flouting the values of detachment, skepticism and caution about leaps of judgment that are vital to the craft they have joined. And fewer and fewer opinionmakers accept the notion that those in government have responsibilities beyond doing what the public (or the pundits) want. Both journalism and politics are subverted by these trends.[21]

Checkbook Journalism

The practice of mainstream media reporters compensating sources for information is not new. Until recently, the magnitude of this compensation was rarely more than the price of lunch or dinner. Today, however, the issue of paying top dollar for news—checkbook journalism— has become a troublesome reality for the traditional press. Tabloids routinely and unabashedly reward their sources with cash, gifts (such as fur coats and electronic equipment), first-class travel, and other payoffs. The old media increasingly find themselves in competition with tabloids for the same sources of information. Mainstream journalists are faced with the prospect of paying up or losing out.

The proliferation of high-profile cases where tabloids compensate sources handsomely has created expectations of payment among informants. Information about Tonya Harding and Nancy Kerrigan, Lorena and John Bobbitt, Michael Jackson, and O. J. Simpson was sold for extraordinary prices. It was the Amy Fisher case, in which a Long Island teenager was convicted of shooting the wife of her boyfriend, Joey Buttafucco, that set off the pay-for-news craze. In 1989 Buttafucco was paid $500,000 by Fox's "A Current Affair" for an exclusive interview.[22] The precedent established in these cases has created a situation where sources, in some cases, will withhold information if they do not receive remuneration.

Tabloid news and television news magazine organizations contend that in spite of the high cost of news, checkbook journalism is an economical way of producing a story. An exclusive interview with a key player in a major story easily costs less than half of what it takes to produce a conventional segment, as the interview can be taped in the studio and does not require a crew to track a story on location. Further, these interviews frequently can be used for two or three days.[23]

Critics contend that checkbook journalism threatens to undermine the fundamental credibility of news.[24] Fringe figures become a part of the process. A seedy group of semiprofessional information brokers, who wait for a big story and then trade intelligence for cash, whether they have direct involvement in the case or not, has emerged. In fact, information brokering has become a new subfield of the legal profession, as lawyers specialize in handling clients with news for sale.[25]

This situation was documented in a "Frontline" examination of the Michael Jackson case. As soon as allegations of Michael Jackson's inappropriate relations with young boys became public, a cadre of informants who had worked other high profile cases flocked to Hollywood to cash in. News organizations across the globe joined the bidding frenzy for exclusives with people whose direct connection to the case was tangential, at best.[26]

The popularity of home video cameras has added another twist to the pay-for-news story. Amateur photographers are shopping their home video footage around to news organizations, even in local markets.[27]

In spite of their expressed opposition to checkbook journalism, the mainstream media have found that it is almost impossible to avoid compensating sources for information while maintaining a competitive edge. Network news programs even have had to pay off local reporters to gain access to their sources. Mainstream news organizations generally are not as open or crass as tabloids about the payments they make to sources.[28] They have devised methods to camouflage payments, such as calling the sources "consultants." They also will cover travel, accommodation, meal, and entertainment expenses for informants who participate in interviews and even for family and friends who accompany them.

Aside from engaging in the practice, the mainstream press has devised some strategies for dealing with checkbook journalism. One approach is to maintain a policy of not paying for news, and then raise the issue of how much money sources have received from other media. The goal is to cast doubt on the opposition's story while maintaining that your story is not tainted.

Another strategy is to concede defeat on the scoop, and to do a more thorough follow-up story. Some reporters find that sources who are paid sometimes are soured by the process afterward and are willing to tell more later.[29] Walter Cronkite has suggested that journalists be forced to disclose the amount of money they have paid to sources. For example, during television broadcasts, the amount will be superimposed on the screen throughout the interview.[30]

The problems caused by checkbook journalism have implications for the judicial process as well. Potential witnesses compromise their testimony by selling their stories to the press. In fact, some defendants can benefit from this practice, as the government's case is weakened when key witnesses sell information to tabloids. Defense attorneys can challenge the witnesses' credibility and claim that their client has been unfairly tried in the press.[31]

Here are just a few examples of the impact of checkbook journalism on the judicial process:

- A key witness' testimony in the trial of William Kennedy Smith, accused of raping a young woman at the Kennedy family's Palm Beach estate, was called into question by jurors as she was forced to reveal on the stand that she had taken money for interviews by "A Current Affair." Anne Mercer was paid $25,000 for the first interview and $15,000 for a follow-up. She had turned down an initial offer of $150,000 by "A Current Affair" because she had not given her statement to the police. William Kennedy Smith was acquitted in this trial.[32]

- Two of Michael Jackson's bodyguards, Leroy Thomas and Morris Williams, who had filed suit against Jackson claiming that they had lost their jobs when they learned of his pedophilia, were paid $100,000 for interviews with "Hard Copy." The deal included an additional interview with the "Maury Povich Show" for no extra cost. The case eventually was settled out of court.[33]

- Jill Shively, who told a grand jury that she saw O. J. Simpson in the neighborhood on the night Nicole Simpson and Ron Goldman were murdered, was paid $5,000 by "Hard Copy" for her story, after her $100,000 asking price was turned down by "Inside Edition." Holding her subpoena for the cameras, Shively proclaimed that Simpson looked like "a madman gone mad, insane." She also received $2,600 from the *Star* for a print interview. Prosecutors refused to call her during the trial, indicating that her credibility was damaged.[34]

- During the preliminary hearing for the Simpson case, two of the prosecution's opening witnesses, Allen Wattenberg and Jose Camacho, revealed that they had split $12,500 from the *National Enquirer*. These witnesses were the co-owner of and salesperson at Ross Cutlery, the store where Simpson allegedly purchased a knife shortly before the murders.[35]

- Bidding for an interview with O. J. Simpson house guest Kato Kaelin began at $100,000 by the *National Enquirer* and quickly was raised to $250,000. While Kaelin claimed during the trial that he did not accept money from any news source, there is some post-trial evidence to the contrary.

The problems created by checkbook journalism continue even after the trial. Jurors serving in high-profile cases increasingly expect compensation for post-trial interviews. For example, after the second trial of Rodney King, reporters for the *Los Angeles Times* turned down interviews with certain jurors because the jurors refused to talk to the press without being paid.[36]

Law enforcement officials are attempting to deal with this situation by telling witnesses not to accept money for information before a trial as it compromises their testimony. Attorneys try to mitigate the damage by introducing evidence that was gathered by police before the witness was paid by a media source and trying to corroborate their stories with those of other witnesses. However, most prosecutors believe that the jury will always have doubts about information that has been sold to the press.[37] Formal action has been taken by the state of California, which has passed a law prohibiting witnesses from selling their stories until one year after the crime has been committed or until a final court judgment is rendered.[38]

While the majority of the analyses of checkbook journalism are critical, there are some observers who defend the practice. They maintain that information is a commodity, and that there is no reason why the source of information should not be compensated. Both old and new media make money from the information they disseminate. Defenders of checkbook journalism argue that the press asks people to surrender their privacy and submit to sometimes embarrassing questions. Sources should be rewarded for their time and effort.[39] Further, many of the stories that result from checkbook journalism involve ordinary people who have had bad experiences. Central figures in these stories frequently incur substantial legal debt. The money they make by selling their stories can be used to cover the cost of adequate legal representation.[40]

Reporting Techniques in the Entertainment Age

The increased use of monetary payoffs to sources is not the only way in which reporting has been influenced by new media rules. The new media's presence, combined with economic constraints on the industry and technological advances, has prompted changes in the fundamental techniques of reporting employed by the old media.

Erosion of Individual Coverage

One of the trademarks of the old media industry was the ability of individual news agencies to investigate stories on their own, to take their own pictures, and put their own individual stamp on coverage. Newspapers and television news programs would compete to report the latest scoop and provide the best coverage. Increasingly, the traditional media have abandoned their insistence on providing their own unique coverage and have come to rely on information gained secondhand.

This trend is the result of a variety of factors. In an era when news must be profitable, cost considerations have caused media organizations to scale down their news gathering operations. The news is taking place in more diverse, exotic, and distant places. Reporting from around the world not only requires expensive equipment to send feed to the United States, but journalists reporting from foreign locales must have special skills, including an understanding of the language and culture.

According to media critic Jon Katz, the Gulf War was the event that caused mainstream media, especially the nightly network news, to abandon their quest to have the latest and greatest in coverage. For a short period in 1991, the Gulf War became a national obsession. A large part of the appeal was that Americans could watch the war unfold before their eyes on CNN. They could debate the war with political experts and other citizens on talk radio. They could register their opinions about the war on Internet bulletin boards. Print formats and network news broadcasts could not compete with real time news and public debates, try as they might. By the time the Gulf War had ended, each of the major television network news operations had suffered losses in the neighborhood of $55 million per network, and they had failed to draw an audience.[41] The fixed-time network news format with its focus on the news anchor, instead of on field correspondents, did not accommodate the kind of exciting and ever-present coverage that CNN specialized in during the war.

The Gulf War fiasco demonstrated to network news organizations that it was no longer financially feasible to insist on covering stories on their own, and that it was acceptable to use feed provided by other media or by private citizens using video cameras. For many news organizations, the cost of sending correspondents around the globe, and even around the country, has become prohibitive. Traditional media organizations have begun pooling coverage of White House and other briefings. Further, while each of the three major television networks used to sponsor its own exit poll during presidential elections, they now share data from a single source.

Fact-Checking

As the speed with which the news media seek to report information to the public has increased, some tried and true news practices have been compromised. Verifying the facts of a story, frequently with multiple sources, has been a standard practice of professional journalists for decades. In an era when the news can unfold on television before your eyes, fact-checking becomes difficult, if not impossible. With the tape rolling, reporters must rely on their own immediate and hurried observations; quick, on-the-spot interviews with witnesses; and even rumor to supplement the visual feed with commentary. In the rush to report the latest information on the alleged relationship between President Clinton and former White House intern Monica Lewinsky, the multiple source rule frequently was eschewed. Established news organizations, including the *Dallas Morning News* and *The Wall Street Journal,* ended up retracting parts of stories they had released when the facts could not be verified.

The inability to verify facts, or the quality of sources, while broadcasting a real-time news event has resulted in some embarrassing moments for veteran journalists and anchors. For example, during the O. J. Simpson car chase, ABC News anchor Peter Jennings conducted a live interview with one of shock-jock Howard Stern's staff members who pretended to be an eyewitness to the event. This trick has become part of Stern's repertoire, as it has worked to fool reporters on several occasions.

The media face a dilemma when reporting real-time news. They need to weigh the benefits of relaying a story to the public as it happens against the possibility of reporting information that may not be accurate. In the new media era, the decision increasingly is to go with the story and correct the facts later if necessary. Real-time dramas grab public attention, and the fallout from these events usually lasts for several days, if not weeks. Following the drama can become a national obsession, as the O. J. Simpson case demonstrates, creating an attentive audience for news organizations.

In addition, new technologies have enhanced opportunities for the mass dissemination of misinformation. The Internet provides a wealth of material for news stories. However, there is nothing to prevent incorrect information from being posted. Reporters who use the Internet as a source may inadvertently spread misinformation via other media. When this occurs, rumor can be mistaken for fact.

An example of inaccurate Internet information making the media rounds involves the crash of TWA Flight 800, which exploded off the coast of Long Island. A theory that the aircraft was downed by a U.S. Navy guided missile launched from a ship that was in the area of the crash was posted on the Internet by an America Online subscriber who was a retired United Airlines pilot. The subscriber said that he had received his information from someone who had attended a high-level briefing in Washington.

The story was picked up by the wire services and then broadcast by Marcia Kramer of WCBS-TV in New York. Kramer added that the FBI was being denied full cooperation in investigating this theory by the Pentagon. The story received widespread play on television and radio and in newspapers across the country.[42] After flight investigators refuted the rumor, it died temporarily until it was resurrected a few months later by journalist Pierre Salinger, who allegedly used the same Internet source for his information.

The News Agenda

The old media's news agenda has been influenced significantly by the new media. The standards for determining what constitutes news have been altered in several respects. News values have increasingly become dictated by entertainment standards as the need to be economically competitive supersedes public service considerations. Media "feeding frenzies" constitute a habitual part of the reporting process. At the extreme, supermarket tabloid exposes of the personal lives of politicians set the mainstream news agenda with growing regularity. In addition, the overall tone of news has become increasingly negative and critical of government and political leaders. Finally, the new media themselves are a source of news.

Feeding Frenzies and Bad News

The press historically has prided itself on protecting the public interest by serving as the public's watchdog—overseeing the actions of political leaders and exposing wrongdoing. However, Larry Sabato identifies three periods in recent press history that show the progression from a more government-friendly media to an appropriately aggressive press on to a pervasive mean-spiritedness.

According to Sabato, from 1941 to 1966, "lapdog" journalism," prevailed, where reporters served and reinforced the status quo. Journalists protected the private lives of political leaders, such as President John F. Kennedy, whose extramarital affairs were well known to members of the press corps.

The second stage, "watchdog journalism," was a result of the Vietnam War and Watergate, and extended from 1966 to 1974. Reporters took their investigative role seriously, yet they focused on public rather than private transgressions.

The final period which began about 1974 and extends to the present is labeled "junkyard dog journalism" by Sabato. "Feeding frenzies," where the rules of the game are "anything goes," subject the personal lives of politicians to harsh scrutiny, whether or not this information is relevant to governing.[43]

Commentator Adam Gopnik identifies the underlying dynamic of these trends as a switch from an "access culture" to an "aggression culture" in journalism. In earlier days, reporters would show greater discretion in their reporting in order to maintain access to their sources. At times, reporters would develop close associations with politicians, and they recognized that political leaders had human failings that did not need to be published.

The "aggression culture" has brought a nasty edge to reporting. For the most part, aggressive journalism does little to foster reform. The press spends an overabundance of time analyzing the personal motives and behavior of politicians, rather than the implications of their policies. These connections are often spurious.[44] For example, the fact that President Clinton is known to give himself strokes when playing golf has been reported as an indication of his personal dishonesty, which carries over into the political realm.

It is difficult to pinpoint one particular cause of this transition to an overly aggressive "junkyard dog" press. The new media are frequently blamed, especially for the tabloidization of mainstream news. Fearing that it might lose audience shares to new media, the old media has become more entertainment oriented in its reporting. The fact that journalists, especially those with star power, regularly cross the lines between old and new media serves to further ingrain entertainment values into hard news reporting.

However, the advent of the "junkyard dog" era predated the rise of new media, although the new media have exacerbated the situation. Some observers contend that aggressive journalism, coming in the wake of major political scandals, is a reaction to politicians' attempts to manage the news and the rise of "spin control." In the television era, most political events are pseudoevents, staged to present political leaders in the most favorable light. Reporters use aggressive tactics in order to subvert politicians' attempts to manipulate the news agenda.[45]

Attack journalism requires reporters to rely less on political leaders themselves as sources, and more on individuals who have grievances to express. In addition, an array of "expert commentators" from the ranks of academia, think tanks, and polling organizations is called upon to provide quotes to fuel controversies. Gopnik contends that the use of these commentators places intellectual differences on the same level as personal squabbles.[46]

The overwhelming negativity in the news can have serious consequences. The constant barrage of bad news gives citizens the impression that political leaders are dishonest, government institutions are dysfunctional, and elections are a charade. These messages are reinforced in both old and new media. Newspapers and newscasts most often lead with stories highlighting some failure of the political system. Pundits thrive by casting aspersions at political leaders and policy decisions. Talk radio hosts and callers engage in hostile dialogue about lying politicians and unresponsive government. Television news magazines portray citizens as the unwitting victims of government scams and corporate rip-offs.[47] Some scholars fear that the net result of this unbridled negativity in the news is to undermine public faith in government and the political process.[48] Citizens, disgusted and worn down by the continual bad news bombardment, may withdraw from the political realm.[49]

The negative banter that occurs on talk radio and in other new media forums feeds this cycle of bad news. Adding the public's own voices to the chorus of negativity serves to reinforce and even enhance the problem.

The effects of negative reporting also can be felt at the elite level. The pool of political leaders and public servants has diminished, as qualified individuals refrain from entering government fearing media scrutiny of their private lives. In addition to the personal costs, the financial burden of even low-profile government officials has increased with the need to hire attorneys and media managers in the event a "feeding frenzy" to which they are even tangentially connected breaks out. People who served during the Bush and Clinton administrations ran up debts of hundreds of thousands of dollars protecting their reputations. Government officials often are required to hand over personal letters and diaries, which become fair game for the media. Former Clinton advisor George Stephanopoulos remarked, "I would advise anyone who comes into my job to make sure you have a lawyer on retainer from the day you walk in." President Clinton admonished the press for its role in this process.[50]

Some journalists defend the negative tone of news, stating that it reflects the gatekeeping function of the press. Exposure of scandal is the first step toward reform. Further, they argue that all politicians are fair game and receive equal scrutiny, although there is some disagreement on this point. Finally, journalism must contain all of the elements of fact, analysis, and opinion. Aggressive journalism, defenders claim, achieves these goals.[51]

The Tabloid News Agenda

In the current media environment, the mainstream press increasingly finds itself in the position of reporting sensational stories that have broken in the new media, including the tabloids. The *Washington Post*'s Howard Kurtz states, "The established media is [sic] increasingly covering the same sorts of things as the tabloids and finding the supermarket papers are often better at the game."[52]

A precedent-setting incident occurred in April 1991, when NBC News justified its broadcasting of the name of the alleged rape victim in the William Kennedy Smith case by citing the *Globe* tabloid as its source. The *New York Times,* in turn, printed the name based on the NBC newscast.[53]

During the 1996 presidential campaign, members of the mainstream press corps, including the *Washington Post*'s Bob Woodward, praised the *Star* and the *National Enquirer* tabloids for breaking the story of Bill Clinton's advisor Dick Morris's relationships with a high-priced Virginia call girl, Sherry Rowlands, and a Texas mistress, as well as his out-of-wedlock child. The tabloids even provided photographic evidence of Morris cavorting with the prostitute on a

Washington hotel balcony. Morris admitted to his relationship with Rowlands, and the White House confirmed the stories about the child. Subsequently, Morris received a $2 million book contract. *Newsweek's* Evan Thomas stated, "The *Star* has broken more news than the *Chicago Tribune.* In the last two campaigns, they have broken two of the biggest stories. It's embarrassing that a supermarket tabloid is breaking these big stories. On the other hand, the establishment press doesn't like to be first on these sorts of stories."[54]

While the mainstream press may not like covering these types of stories, their options are becoming increasingly limited. A news organization avoids these tabloid-originated stories at their peril. When politicians answer the charges levied in the tabloids, which is often the case, it is difficult for even the most high minded of news media to ignore the story. Thus, as Evan Thomas describes, the process by which personal scandals stories reach the mainstream press is far from protracted. "There is a media food chain which goes from supermarket tabloid, to New York tabloid, to CNN, to the mainstream press—in about 15 minutes."[55]

Mainstream news organizations can adopt a variety of strategies when reporting tabloid-generated political news. They can downplay the more sordid elements of the story, such as the details of the particular scandal, and cast the report in terms of its relevance to public policy or political decision making.[56] For example, the political press justified its coverage of the Dick Morris scandal on the basis of the "character issue" that plagued both Clinton campaigns for president.[57] A more stringent application of this rule is to cover only those elements of a story that are directly relevant to the individual's performance in office or in the public realm.[58]

Some journalists have proposed ethical criteria for reporting personal news about politicians or candidates of the kind that tabloids have featured. Reporters need to ask whether a "predicate"—a specific reason for wanting to know the answer to a particular question—exists before they consider using the material. It is not the role of the press to go on a fishing expedition to determine whether or not politicians are hiding past transgressions. The public purposes served by reporting on individuals' personal lives must be balanced against a respect for rights of privacy and human fellowship.[59]

A final perspective advocates for the mainstream press to actively pursue scandal stories before the tabloids get to them. In this way, news organizations can control the flow and content of information. They also can impose strong standards of accuracy. The media should refrain from making judgments and allow the public to decide the relevance of story on their own.[60] The 1996 presidential contest provides an example of the mainstream press holding back on reporting a tabloid-style story. The *National Enquirer* had uncovered evidence that Republican candidate Bob Dole had an extramarital affair that began in 1968 while he was married to his first wife. The *Washington*

Post and *Time* magazine investigated the story and conducted extensive interviews with the woman involved. These publications decided not to print the information they had gathered on the basis that a twenty-eight-year-old story was not news. The story appeared in the *National Enquirer* during the last week in October. In response, the *Washington Post* buried the allegations inside a lengthy campaign story, which indicated that the paper had investigated the incident and considered it irrelevant to the election. Few mainstream news organizations gave the story much play before election day, and many, including CNN, mentioned it only briefly or ignored it altogether, as was the case for all three major television networks.[61] The vague informal rules governing the mainstream press' coverage of tabloid topics in tabloid style were abandoned entirely during the Bill Clinton/ Monica Lewinsky feeding frenzy. The traditional and new media alike rushed to cover the story using the same tactics, and displaying the same disregard for professional journalistic norms. The differences between mainstream and tabloid media were not just blurred in their coverage of this situation, they were annihilated.

Obsessive Reporting

With the proliferation of news outlets, one would think that the news agenda would be highly varied—that a wider range of stories would be covered. This, however, has not been the case. The new media focus an inordinate amount of coverage on a small number of high-profile stories. Instead of breeding diversity, an abundance of media fosters conformity. Mainstream news organizations follow suit with the new media and play it safe, sticking with the same stories that are receiving widespread coverage. In this way, the old media minimize the risk of losing audience members to the new competition.

Coverage of the O. J. Simpson case, the death of Princess Diana, and the alleged Clinton/Lewinsky affair epitomize concentration of news focus on sensational stories. Television news programs, including CNN and the networks, initially set the agenda for reporting on this story by providing live coverage of the infamous Bronco chase. Print sources kept pace with electronic media. For example, a single day's coverage of the Simpson preliminary hearing in the *Los Angeles Times* commanded more inches of copy than all other national and international news combined.[62] This dramatic event sparked public interest in the case, which the media sought to sustain through months of legal battles. The entertainment component of the Simpson case increased its news value in the current media market. As *Los Angeles Times* correspondent Sam Fulwood III states, the Simpson case "is the perfect news story. . . . [It has] race, sex, money, power, athletes, beautiful women, layabouts, police, courts, chase, mystery weapons. I can't think of a theme or subplot in any movie that has all this."[63]

Some news organizations justify the obsessive focus on a relatively small number of stories, even when it means that important political information is not conveyed to the public. Decisions to cover these stories are based largely on ratings, which some observers, including "Nightline's" Ted Koppel, interpret as a form of public opinion. From this perspective, the members of the public are getting the news they want as consumers, even if they are not necessarily getting the news that they need to make informed political decisions as citizens.

The News Value of New Media

The new media themselves also have warranted coverage by the traditional press, constituting a new category of news. In the 1990s, stories have proliferated on the influence talk radio, the tabloid press, and cybermedia cast on the political, social, and cultural fabric of the United States. In addition, new media stars command attention in old media venues for their political roles. For example, talk radio host Don Imus commandeered headlines for several days for his controversial speech at a 1996 National Press Club dinner honoring President Clinton. It is interesting to note that coverage of particular new media tends to fade as they become more fully integrated into the media system. While talk radio was a hot mainstream media topic during the 1992 campaign, it was superseded by discussions of the Internet's role in the political process during the 1996 contest.

Updating Old Media

One response of the old media to the new media revolution appears to be "if you can't beat 'em, join 'em." At the most benign level, mainstream media have updated their look to be less formal and more eye-catching. Yet the traditional media have taken even greater strides toward integrating new media formats and technologies into their existing structures. In some cases, new innovations have been incorporated into old media standbys. For example, network news broadcasts ask for viewer input on stories via electronic mail. In other instances, news organizations have developed new media products to supplement their traditional offerings. Online versions of newspapers ranging in size and prestige from the *Washington Post* and the *New York Times* to the *Nantucket Inquirer and Mirror* populate the Internet.

The *Washington Post,* for instance, has spent millions of dollars on its online information service, *Digital Ink.* News consumers have access to the daily paper, articles dating back to 1986, discussion groups with *Post* editors, writers, and columnists, job listing, classified ads, sports scores, book and movie reviews, and a host of other features. Background information about stories is also available, including the full texts of speeches and survey results. *Digital Ink* also offers links to related sites on the World Wide Web. Questions and comments can be registered with the *Post*'s ombudsman.[64]

Some old-line media personalities have launched new careers in the uncharted waters of cyberspace. Michael Kinsley, former editor of the *New Republic* and a talk show anchor on CNN, left the traditional media world to become editor of *Slate,* Microsoft's online magazine. Each issue of *Slate* includes a wide variety of departments and features. Analyses of elections, public policy issues, and the media themselves, staples of political magazines, abound in *Slate.* The difference is that some articles are quite lengthy and include technologically driven bonuses, such as video downloads of political ads. Early editions of *Slate* were free to Internet browsers, although it was subsequently offered by subscription at a rate of approximately twenty dollars per year for the online version and slightly more for the paper equivalent.[65] *Slate* was not successful in gaining enough paid subscribers to sustain itself as an independent entity, and has become affiliated with America Online.

Cybernews creates some dilemmas for print journalism. Its benefits lie in the fact that it allows print formats to compete with broadcast media in the dissemination of real time news. Information can be updated frequently and distribution is instantaneous. Sidebars and cross-referencing provide more detailed information for interested users. In addition, the material is presented in exciting visual and even audio formats. The technology accommodates online news discussion groups.

In spite of these advantages, Internet news is not problem-free. Many of the stories, especially some of the extensive pieces like those that appear on *Slate,* are more easily consumed after being printed out, which mitigates the interactive component of the medium. Further, newspapers are reluctant to scoop their print versions, and so they do not update their most important stories, which include information that their reporters have uncovered, until the newspaper goes to press. Instead, they run wire service versions of the stories. The bottom line is that Web sites are not yet profitable, and they attract only a small fraction of the audience for newspapers.

It is, however, only a matter of time before these problems are turned around, and the potential of cybernews can be more fully realized. Some newspapers and magazines have established a separate reporting staff to write stories and commentary exclusively for online consumers of their Web site. *The Wall Street Journal,* which has gone farther than most publications in integrating the newspaper and the Web site, reorganized its news room so that the hard copy and online reporters share space.[66]

Television news also has entered the cyberage. Network and local news programs, CNN, and news magazine programs all have Web sites. Some, such as CNN, offer audience members free Internet software. MSNBC is the merger of Microsoft and NBC News. The twenty-four-hour cable news station promises to combine new technology with old-style reporting expertise and provide viewers with what Bill Gates has termed "an integrated media experience."[67] As such, MSNBC has hired journalists from mainstream media, including the *New York Times,* and regularly employs commentators from publications such as the *National Review, Time,* and *The Nation.* In addition, the station has its own Web site and invites viewer commentary via e-mail. A nightly segment called, "The Site," highlights technological news and the latest hot Web sites.

MSNBC and other attempts at combining television and computer technologies, such as "Talkback Live," have been criticized for promising more than they deliver via new technology. In the case of MSNBC, television already provides the mechanism for instantaneous news broadcasts, so the Internet component is largely superfluous and redundant. The interactive segments are limited and largely conform to the traditional question and answer prototype, which can just as easily be conducted with phone calls. It is actually the new-style television reporting that makes MSNBC different than its predecessors. The set is designed to create a warm and friendly atmosphere for viewers; with its exposed brick and modern furniture, it has a New York loft type feel. News segments do not conform to the tradition block format and instead use quick cutaways to on-site video or interviews. Features target specific segments of the viewing audience, such as Generation X, and the "talent" is wide-ranging, including talk radio host Don Imus, cybercritic Cliff Stoll, and television talk show host Dick Cavett, in addition to NBC News regulars such as Tom Brokaw and Jane Pauley.[68]

Implications

The new media's effect on the old media has been magnified by commercial incentives. The assumption that entertainment news draws a larger audience than serious news has caused the mainstream press to shift its values in line with those of the new media. In addition, the new media have helped to foster a journalistic star system that is driven by individuals' desire for personal wealth and fame.

Journalistic norms are highly malleable, and at present they are being eroded by market forces. As long as news organizations' incentives are profit-driven, there is little reason to believe that news will become much more than entertainment fare. New style news programs such as MSNBC are packaged in order to maximize their fun-loving and light-hearted credentials. This trend appears likely to continue into the future.

Critics are concerned that the new media norms have the potential to severely undermine the credibility of the mainstream press. The media lack internal and external checks on their veracity. Neither the new nor the old media can be counted on to report the "facts" accurately, given the competition to be first and most dramatic. Further, the public lacks the interest in politics and the inclination to demand that the media behave differently. The result is that the infiltration of tabloid stories into the mainstream press agenda will persist.

However, the personalization of news engendered by entertainment-infused reporting may not be an entirely destructive trend. Tabloid stories can foster a sense of intimacy with the public, which may attract audience members to news programs. They also provide a collective base of knowledge that can foster interpersonal communication in a society which has become increasingly atomized.

Economic considerations also pervade decisions about how to employ new technologies in the media industry. The news industry is still adapting to the presence of new technologies, especially with regard to how changes in the way news is reported and received will influence the existing financial structure.

As has traditionally been the case, technological potential exceeds its practical application. *New York Times* commentator Frank Rich notes that the Internet at present is like television news was in its infancy. Experimentation with the content is required before a technological innovation can make a notable difference as a communications medium. As Rich states, "[The Internet] repackages print and television journalism with interactive sideshows much as networks of the early '50s dressed up recycled print and radio reportage with primitive visuals." In the near future, however, old and new media will be more fully integrated.

At the same time, the habits of the media audience will change markedly. We have noted in chapter 6 the decline in network television news viewership and the dispersion of the audience among new media formats. A 1996 study conducted by Forrester Research concluded that newspapers will lose as much as 14 percent of their circulation to electronic publications by 2001. In addition, the Internet is cutting into television's audience, which may precipitate a shift back to a more print-oriented culture, whether it be in hard copy or online.[69]

Shaping Presidential Campaigns

In presidential electoral politics, strategies that are novel and innovative in one campaign quickly become part of the established campaign tactical arsenal. During Campaign '96, the presidential candidates pursued the new media routes that were forged in 1992, such as appearing on interview programs and participating in electronic town meetings. In addition, candidates stepped up their use of the Internet in the election, a political technological innovation that was nascent in the previous contest. In fact, candidates who did not make use of available new media outlets in 1996 faced criticism that was unheard of in 1988. Bob Dole, who actually made widespread use of new media tactics, was chided by Republican leaders and talk show hosts for not making enough use of the talk radio airwaves in his quest for the White House, a situation he quickly remedied.

The 1992 presidential election was a watershed for the mass media campaign. As is the norm, candidates and their campaign organizations worked hard to manage the mainstream media in an effort to gain strategic advantage. Yet candidates had come to the realization that they were losing ground to journalists in the bid to control the campaign agenda.[1] Thus the presidential candidates attempted to circumvent the conventional journalistic routes by turning to alternative media to get their messages across. The new media, especially talk radio, television talk programs, news magazines, and electronic town meetings, provided the opportunity for candidates to work outside of established press norms and gatekeeping practices. The new media were vehicles for fresh and novel campaign tactics, where candidates could speak to the mass public on a more personal, "intimate," informal, and direct level. Further, new media allowed the public to participate more openly in the campaign media spectacle.

The new media's foray into campaign politics in 1992 had several implications. First, they caused a dilemma for the mainstream press, which had to make decisions about whether or not to cover events that occurred or were reported first in new media venues. In addition, the new media had significant popular appeal, turning electoral politics, at least for the moment, into the "new American spectator sport." Finally, the new media contributed to the heavy infusion of entertainment into the campaign media mix and an increased tabloidization of campaign news stories. The new media's presence was credited, at least in part, with the increase in voter interest, enthusiasm, and even participation in the 1992 presidential contest.[2] By all indications, the stage was set for the new media to perform similar functions during the 1996 campaign.

In this chapter, we will examine the evolution of the mass media campaign in light of the new media's role in the process. We begin with a discussion of some trends in the modern day mass media campaign that established the context within which the new media became part of the election scene. We then examine some of the primary components of the new media campaign. These include the talk-show campaign, MTV's electoral role, and the election in cyberspace. We conclude the chapter with a discussion of the implications of the new media's role in elections, and some speculations about the future.

Trends in the Modern Mass Media Election

The origins of the modern mass media campaign can be traced to the mass media's technological roots. The introduction of broadcast technologies into the electoral process forever altered the relationship between candidates, journalists, and the mass public. Television emerged as the dominant force, structuring the course of campaigns. With its wide audience reach and its striking visual style, the television campaign is the cornerstone of presidential elections. Each electoral contest can be viewed as a struggle between journalists and candidates to be the masters of the medium. With each campaign, new strategies are devised by journalists to manage candidates and by candidates to handle the media.

At the onset of the 1992 campaign, it was clear that journalists had gained the upper hand in the election game. The press had become the chief intermediary between candidates and voters. In the process, the media had placed the spotlight on itself and had compromised the candidates' ability to reach their constituents on their own terms.

A number of conditions opened the door for new media to enter the electoral arena. The heavy emphasis in mainstream news reports on presidential candidates' personalities, personal lives, and campaign strategies prompted candidates to seek alternative outlets for gaining control of the news agenda. The new media, with their entertainment focus, are susceptible to these kinds of stories. However, new media forums, such as lengthy candidate interviews on television news magazines and talk programs, allow candidates the opportunity to present personal issues in their own words, and to issue rebuttals and engage in damage control.

In addition, mainstream news coverage featured more sound bites and less detailed discussion of candidates' issue positions and qualifications for office. Candidates welcome the opportunities that new media offer to speak for themselves and to converse directly with the public outside the boundaries of journalistic gatekeepers. Voters also prefer to listen to candidates speak and enjoy the greater direct access to presidential contenders that new media forums extend.

Personalities and Personal Lives

The style and substance of campaign reporting has changed dramatically during the latter part of this century. These changes are largely in response to the more intrusive role of television in the process. They are also a result of journalistic practices that have converted investigative reporting into attack journalism. In the wake of Watergate, aggressive reporting has manifested itself in a "feeding frenzy" mentality among journalists. According to political scientist Larry J. Sabato, since about 1974, reporters have engaged in "junkyard dog journalism," in which private lives of public persons have been defined as newsworthy by the press. "Every aspect of private life potentially becomes fair game for scrutiny as a new, almost 'anything goes' philosophy takes hold."[3]

Accompanying the rise in this mentality among reporters has been an explosion in the scope of the press' coverage of presidential campaigns. According to Theodore White, who chronicled campaigns during the 1950s through the 1970s, only six print reporters covered the New Hampshire primary in the 1950s.[4] Today, the number of journalists, broadcast technicians, and producers is in the thousands. But the big difference above and beyond the size of the press corps was that candidates in the past had been allowed to present themselves and to define each other. Personality profiles resulting from investigative reporting by the press were lacking. However, this new style of reporting placed journalists in the position of defining candidates.

This change can be traced to journalistic reaction to the series of Theodore White's successful books on presidential campaigns. Commencing with *The Making of the President 1960,* White followed four campaigns using a new and previously unknown journalistic technique of interpreting and critiquing the candidates' personality and style. Although White was not writing as a daily reporter, his work had a profound effect on journalistic approaches to covering candidates. Increasingly journalists moved beyond the recording of campaign rhetoric to speculating about the underlying motivations of candidates. Using this approach, flippant, off-hand comments by candidates became more newsworthy than lengthy, prepared speeches because they revealed the candidate's character. As a result, reporting began to focus on ways to reveal character, especially character flaws.

One of the first victims of this approach was 1968 Republican presidential candidate George Romney, whose remark about being "brainwashed" during the Vietnam War was interpreted by journalists as a sign that he lacked the gravity to serve as president.[5] Later examples include Gerald Ford's assertion in a 1976 debate that Poland was not under Soviet domination, Jimmy Carter's comment that he saw nothing wrong with various communities "trying to maintain the ethnic purity of their neighborhoods,"[6] and Jesse Jackson's 1984 "Hymietown" remark. Ford's remark was portrayed as providing evidence to support Lyndon Johnson's joke about Ford that he could not walk and chew gum at the same time. Carter's comment suggested to reporters that he still carried the racial prejudices of the South. Jackson's comment was viewed as proof that he was anti-Semitic.

The shift toward coverage of such gaffes was dramatic. According to one study, in 1968 network news coverage mentioned only one such incident, whereas in 1988, twenty-nine reports discussed them.[7] The new approach was legitimized by the journalists as a reaction to the character flaws of presidents such as Lyndon Johnson and Richard Nixon. Given the problems that could result from having a president with acute personality flaws, the press willingly adopted the role of scrutinizer of candidates. The media couches the character issue in terms of leadership, when in actuality what they cover are personal failings. Gary Hart's elimination from the 1988 presidential contest as a result of the press' revelations of his relationship with Donna Rice is an example of this phenomenon. Aside from coverage of this affair, very little attention was given to issues of Hart's character in the press. Similarly, in 1992, the majority of character coverage of Bill Clinton focused on his alleged affair with Gennifer Flowers. In fact, during the general election when the Flowers story had faded into the background, only 2 percent of Clinton's network news coverage dealt with his character.[8]

Strategies and the "Horse Race"

In addition to their focus on "character," the press spends an inordinate amount of time covering campaign strategies. The "horse race" analogy has become a mainstay of campaign reporting.[9] The media concentrate on campaign tactics and the relative position of the candidates in the race, often to the exclusion of issue information. The focus on the horse race is an outgrowth of the poll-driven reporting that has proliferated in the news business in recent years. The amount of poll-generated news has increased radically as the sources of polling information have proliferated. News organizations often employ their own pollsters, while polling data are available additionally from independent research institutes, think tanks, interest groups, academia, and even the candidates' organizations.

Candidates, especially those trailing in the polls, object to "horse race" coverage on the grounds that it is not meaningful or substantive. Polls themselves may be inaccurate, and stories that employ poll results may be misleading. Poll stories are not real events, but constitute manufactured news. Reporters must create a story around polling data. Given the fact that action and drama are central to television news' presentational style, reporters often link shifts in the polls to campaign events, although the connection may be spurious.

Voters, too, are dissatisfied with horse race coverage. A 1996 *Washington Post* postelection survey found that a majority of the electorate felt that the media made too much use of polls telling which candidate is ahead. Thirty-two percent of the respondents felt that the media should report fewer polls, while 26 percent preferred no polling data at all. Thirty-four percent of voters believed that the current level of "horse race" coverage is satisfactory, and 6 percent wanted more poll results.[10]

Telling Their Story in Their Own Words

One of the primary impetuses for candidates' use of the new media is their desire to tell their story in their own words. Sound bites are a characteristic of campaign reporting in the television age. The size of sound bites has shrunk precipitously in recent years. In the mainstream press, journalists now speak more often for candidates than candidates speak for themselves. The prevalence of celebrity journalists who thrive by keeping themselves in the public eye, as we discussed in chapter 8, has exacerbated this situation.

Political scientist Thomas Patterson tracked the shrinking television news sound bite over more than two decades of campaigns. In 1968 the average sound bite was forty-two seconds in length. Eighty-four percent of the time, candidates' images were on the screen while they were speaking. By 1988 the average sound bite was less than ten seconds long. Candidates increasingly provided the silent, pictorial backdrop for reporters' commentary. For every one minute the candidates spoke on television, journalists provided six minutes of their own analysis. Similarly, newspaper reports of candidates' words also have been truncated. In 1960 the front page of the *New York Times* averaged fourteen quoted lines of the candidates' words. This number had fallen to six lines by 1992.[11] These trends continued in 1996. The Center for Media and Public Affairs found that the average sound bite was approximately eight seconds long. For every eight-second sound bite, reporters made fifty-two seconds worth of observations. Commentary by reporters and anchors made up more than 72 percent of stories. Other actors, including voters, experts, campaign personnel, and interest groups provided further commentary. Very little network television air time—less than 28 percent—was devoted to comments by the presidential candidates themselves.[12]

Politicians, particularly presidential candidates, are well aware of the shrinking sound bite. The themes of campaigns have always been simple, but now the more detailed messages must be simple and succinct as well. Candidate appeals must conform to the expectations and desires of journalists. Cameras and pencils are directed toward those who know how to master the sound bite. One of the premier sound bite producers is Jesse Jackson, who once described his calculation in using sound bites to express his ideas:

> If there is anything I have developed over a period of time, it is to speak in epigrams. . . . So we say, 'we're going to have demonstrations without hesitation and jail without bail.' . . . I know if I take a minute and a half to say, 'We're going to demonstrate this afternoon, and we're not going to think about it any longer, and we're willing to go to jail and will not pay the price of the bail and bond,' there is no telling whether that would get picked out."[13]

Candidates who have resisted speaking in sound bite form have been disadvantaged in campaigns. Many others have accepted the new mode of communication, but dislike it.

Candidates are often in a tenuous situation in relation to the press when they address issues. The need to speak in sound bites forces candidates to dramatically oversimplify issues, which earns criticism from the press. At the same time, candidates are surprised that journalists can launch such attacks while ignoring the full texts of their speeches and the detailed position papers that every campaign prepares.[14] Presidential candidate Gary Hart began his first campaign for president in 1984 with a lengthy stump speech filled with specific proposals on energy conservation, military reform, and foreign trade. Few news organizations reported Hart's proposals. For example, according to one study of two newspapers' coverage of Hart early in the 1984 campaign, less than 3 percent of stories about Hart mentioned his job and training programs. The job programs were the most widely covered of Hart's proposals.[15] Not surprisingly, later in the campaign when Hart was accused by opponent Walter Mondale of having no specific proposals, the charge readily stuck in the public mind. Following his aborted 1988 campaign, Hart complained that he had not been able to get his message across. "I proposed a national course of strategic investments of public and private resources to ensure opportunity and a stable living standard for our children. But few have heard of these ideas," Hart lamented.[16]

A sound bite saturated campaign does not guarantee victory, however. During the 1992 presidential contest, Bill Clinton, while heavily pursuing a new media strategy, provided fewer sound bites than George Bush and, as a consequence, received less network television news coverage. Most of the prominent sound bites were uttered by Bush—"those two bozos," "Ozone Man," "the failed governor of a small state," and "not right for Arkansas, and not right for America."

Like candidates, voters are not especially fond of sound bite journalism or of having candidates' messages translated for them by reporters, commentators, and pundits. A *Washington Post* survey conducted during the 1996 presidential contest revealed that 77 percent of citizens would rather see candidates themselves giving their positions on issues, while only 16 percent preferred to see more of the news devoted to reporters explaining where candidates stand.[18]

In addition, when journalists interpret candidates' words instead of letting them speak for themselves, the result is a more negative discourse than the candidates themselves intend. In a study of campaign discourse from the 1960 to the 1992 presidential campaigns, the Annenberg Public Policy Center found that statements made by candidates in speeches, debates, and ads are more positive than negative. Candidates are more inclined to emphasize their own views or provide a contrast with the opponent than to go on the attack. The press tends to cull inflammatory remarks by candidates, such as name-calling and unsubstantiated attacks, from the large amount of material available, and report it to the exclusion of more positive statements.[19]

Enter New Media

The upshot of these trends is that mainstream media coverage of elections has become increasingly mediacentric, negative, and trivial. Traditional media coverage of campaigns, while extensive, often can bewilder and frustrate voters.[20] In 1992 presidential candidates Bill Clinton and Ross Perot retaliated by making the risky move of gearing a significant portion of their campaign efforts toward new media—a gamble that paid off. Voters responded, prompting the new media to assume greater levels of political involvement.

The Talk-Show Campaign

The rise of the talk-show campaign coincides with a drop in nightly news coverage of presidential campaigns that began in 1992 and continued in 1996. In 1992 there was a 30 percent drop in nightly news coverage compared to 1988.[21] Broadcast news coverage of the campaign declined even further in 1996, down 60 percent from 1992. Print news coverage also fell precipitously. The number of front page stories in the *New York Times, Washington Post,* and *Los Angeles Times* was down 59 percent from the previous election, and the coverage measured in words declined by 45 percent. The amount of issue and policy information reported in these sources also was down.[22]

While mainstream news coverage of presidential contests declined, the overall amount of mediated campaign discourse increased. Talk shows are largely responsible for picking up the slack. As Edwin Diamond and Robert Silverman note, new media have transformed the sound bite campaign into the "sound *glut*" campaign. Candidates have more than ample opportunities to speak to the public at length via new media venues. Journalists and pundits continue to fill the campaign airwaves with commentary and banter. Add the public to the mix, and the sound of American national elections can be deafening.

The talk show component of a presidential campaign takes a variety of forms. Call-in talk radio programs, television talk shows, interview segments on television news programs, and electronic town meetings all break away from the trend of short, quick, encapsulated news and allow for less structured, and more informal conversations about politics to take place.

It is not the case that talk show formats have never been used in campaigns before. Televised interviews with candidates have been part of the campaigning process since the 1950s.[23] Innovative uses of interview programs have occurred in past contests. In the 1976 campaign, for example, President Gerald Ford appeared on six half-hour talk television shows hosted by "Today Show" correspondent Joe Garagiola. However, as recently as 1988, candidates turned down invitations to appear on television talk shows, such as "Donahue," and rarely went on national talk radio programs.[24] All this changed dramatically in 1992. Between September 1 and October 19, 1992, candidates conducted 39 in-depth interviews on "Larry King Live," morning talk programs, public television, cable, and call-in shows.[25] Between January 26 and election day in November, the presidential candidates and their running mates participated in 254 interviews on 42 different programs, which run the gamut from "Nightline" and "60 Minutes" to "Letterman."[26] These trends were repeated during the 1996 contest. Further, candidates orchestrated their own electronic town hall meetings. Bill Clinton, for example, bought a half hour of time on NBC to host "America Speaks," a town hall meeting in Pittsburgh, which was also run on C-SPAN.

Devising a successful talk show strategy involves careful calculations by campaign organizations. While appearing on talk shows, candidates must be careful to maintain a requisite amount of dignity and seriousness in order to avoid charges that they are trivializing the electoral process. The decision is especially tricky for incumbent presidents. President George Bush appeared far less frequently on talk shows than rivals Bill Clinton and Ross Perot. His talk show appearances were a continual source of debate among staffers, who wanted to make sure that he maintained a "presidential" image. President Bush, a veteran of old-style media campaigning, was not comfortable performing in talk show settings. In 1996 President Clinton made the talk show rounds, even though his campaign was more low key than it had been four years prior. The television generation president was well-suited to a talk-show campaign, but he did not want to be viewed as demeaning the presidency.

Candidates also must take stock of the host of talk programs before they make a decision to appear. The conventional wisdom states that talk shows are a friendlier forum because they allow candidates to have greater control over the agenda. It is believed that hosts and audience members ask questions that steer clear of embarrassing personal issues and are more likely to focus on policy concerns. Yet there are times when these assumptions are flawed. In 1992, for example, when Bill Clinton was a guest on "Donahue," Phil Donahue grilled him about the Gennifer Flowers affair and allegations of draft evasion. Donahue continued this line of questioning even though the candidate and the audience protested.[27] In addition, candidates must decide whether or not to be associated with a particularly controversial host who may have a substantial following, but who also may have many detractors. Talk jocks, such as Don Imus and Howard Stern, have hosted presidential aspirants on their programs, in spite of their reputations for off-color commentary. The unpredictability of these talk radio hosts makes the decision to go on their programs a tough call for candidates.

There is evidence to suggest that the talk-show campaign in its many forms has had some favorable repercussions for voters. Some analysts contend that the addition of the talk-show campaign to the electoral process redefined political news for the better by making coverage broader and access to information easier. Communication scholar Jannette Dates observed,

> There has been a great opening up; there are different voices being heard today, and I think Perot helped that to occur when he went directly to the "Larry King Live" show. I did think that the new voices addressing these concerns, getting them into the popular culture, have been helpful because a lot of the populace is not listening

to the normal, journalistic sources of information. But they *are* watching "Arsenio Hall" and "Murphy Brown." They are involved with things that are happening on the popular front and so having those voices come through the system has been helpful to the discourse.[28]

Studies of voters' reactions to the talk-show campaign support these contentions. *Crosstalk*, a comprehensive study of campaign communication in 1992 by a distinguished team of researchers, concluded, "Beginning in 1992, citizens took a more direct role in campaign crosstalk, through call-in interview programs, town meetings, and the 'citizens' debate—prodding candidates and journalists toward a more substantive engagement with the issues."[29] In addition to analyses of news coverage and ads, the study included research on candidate interview programs. The findings indicate that while the mainstream press emphasized the horse race aspect of the campaign in 1992 and was frequently negative, talk shows provided an opportunity for substantive dialogue to take place between voters and the candidates. A content analysis of candidate interview programs demonstrated empirically that the public had more of a chance to hear candidates tell their own stories on interview programs than on network news. The average answer to a question was twenty-one seconds in length, more than twice as long as a news sound bite. Further, candidates spoke for an average of eight to twelve minutes per interview. Thus they received substantially more exposure in these venues than on network news.

The study also found that the public was receptive to the candidate interview format. Citizens responded to the "unfiltered" communication offered in these interviews, and the fact that journalists and expert commentary was lacking. They also identified more with interviewers, such as Larry King and Katie Couric, than with mainstream journalists.[30]

In addition to voters reporting that they liked candidate interview programs, there is evidence that they learned from them as well. Paying attention to appearances of candidates on television interview/talk shows improved citizens' knowledge of the issue positions of candidates. Voters who tend to have lower knowledge levels of candidates, such as members of the MTV generation, are likely to learn from these programs.[31]

On balance, reaction to candidate interview programs is positive. Assessments of talk radio's campaign role are more mixed. On the plus side, talk radio listeners claim that they learn things about the campaign that they don't get in other places. The views expressed on talk radio tend to be different, more outspoken, and more wide-ranging than those articulated in the mainstream press.[32] However, public satisfaction with talk radio during campaigns is not especially high. Only 6 percent of citizens asked to evaluate the quality of the job done by talk radio hosts in 1996 gave them a grade of A, 15 percent B, 25 percent C, 13 percent D, 16 percent F, and 25 percent did not know. These evaluations are substantially lower than the grades given in 1992, where 10 percent gave an A, 29 percent a B, 25 percent a C, 8 percent a D, 9 percent an F, and 19 percent did not know.[33] Talk show hosts are even more critical of their role in campaigns than is the general public. Twenty-six percent of hosts included in a Times Mirror Center study indicated that the shows have a negative effect on the electoral process. Hosts admitted that the format does not allow for the exposition of entire issues, as follow-up questions are rarely asked, and the quality of discussion is low. Programs frequently degenerate into free-for-alls. In addition, the profit and entertainment agendas of talk shows preclude learning.[34]

There is one additional aspect of the talk-show campaign that deserves mention. Television talk programs have become a fertile source of campaign humor, and monologues have become a political platform. Popular late night television talk shows hosted by David Letterman, Jay Leno, and Conan O'Brien frequently featured jokes about the candidates. For some voters, especially young people who are not attentive to campaigns, talk show humor has become a source of political information. In fact, the Pew Research Center found that 25 percent of the public learned something about the campaign from late-night comedians.[35] The impression of candidates that is left by this form of humor is not likely to be favorable, and perhaps may breed cynicism. In 1996 the tone of late night jokes was especially visceral and personal. Conan O'Brien, however, believes that jokes can inform the public because they usually focus on the day's news or something that is an issue in the campaign. Examples of O'Brien's humor show that jokes may tap into campaign issues, but they are heavily infused with personal attacks.

> *President Clinton's* videotaped testimony was shown at the Whitewater trial. . . . Yeah, the first thing Clinton did was remind the jurors that the camera adds 10 pounds. *Bob Dole*, believe it or not, took a lap around the Charlotte Motor Speedway. . . . You could tell it was Dole because he had his blinker on the whole time.[36]

MTV's Electoral Role

MTV's foray into the political world in the late 1980s was sparked by Republican politicians taking issue with rap music lyrics. Using this issue to test the waters, MTV realized that it was possible to arouse the political interest of young people. MTV discovered that politics provided another mechanism for marketing its music product and quickly expanded its political role, establishing a news division in 1984.[37] Politics proved to be quite good for business, as advertising revenues increased as MTV included more political and public service content in its programming.

Aware that tinkering with a successful music formula to accommodate politics is a risky proposition, MTV is more cautious in its political than its artistic role, where controversial videos are a staple on the agenda. The network does not want to saturate programming with too much politics or political content that is too dogmatic ideologically and, therefore, risk alienating young viewers who just want music. Yet MTV regularly will take positions on a range of issues, including protecting the environment, drug abuse, crime, and free speech. The station's internationally broadcast "Free Your Mind" campaign, designed to "foster an understanding of people's differences to help overcome intolerance," has run programs opposing ethnic and racial stereotyping and supporting gays in the military.[38] MTV will not endorse candidates, however.

MTV uses its platform on an ongoing basis to provide political information through regular news programs and specials, promote concern for issues through concerts and special events, and facilitate volunteerism through a range of public service programs. In fact, MTV coined the phrase that might well summarize Generation X's political outlook, "Think globally, act locally."

Politicians dismiss MTV's political clout at their own risk. MTV claims to reach more people between the ages of eighteen and thirty-four in a single day than any other media outlet. Its audience in the United States alone consists of over 60 million people. On a given day, MTV news can outdraw CNN's news coverage, as it is broadcast approximately twenty times a day and it is viewed by more than a million people. MTV special campaign reports have attracted more than 8 million viewers to a single broadcast.[39] It is during presidential election season that MTV's political presence becomes most apparent. Approximately 25 percent of its daily and weekend newscasts are devoted to the campaign.[40]

Long before MTV assumed a formal role in the electoral process, political analysts realized that the station offered a major source of clues about the political tastes of young people. During the 1984 presidential election, Lee Atwater, a strategist for the Reagan-Bush campaign, called MTV to request a copy of a John Cougar Mellencamp video to screen for President Reagan. MTV V-Jays regularly reported the request, and flashed a picture of Reagan while asking, "Does this man like MTV?" Atwater found that this impromptu MTV strategy struck a cord. "We got a lot of calls from MTV watchers saying, 'We didn't realize how cool Reagan was."[41]

In 1990 members of the recording industry formed Rock the Vote, a Los Angeles based nonprofit, nonpartisan organization. Rock the Vote is "dedicated to protecting freedom of speech, educating young people about the issues that affect us and motivating young people to participate by registering, voting, and speaking out."[42] Rock the Vote established a formal linkage with MTV for the 1992 campaign, and over time has expanded its MTV-supported role. Contrary to popular belief, Rock the Vote is not funded primarily by MTV, but by the Recording Industry Association of America.[43]

By 1996 Rock the Vote had devised a carefully orchestrated, multifaceted, multimedia campaign agenda. Rock the Vote worked with MTV to promote the "Choose or Lose" bus tour, which traveled the country registering voters, and coordinated the Youth Vote, Black Youth Vote, and Latino Vote campaigns. These voter registration drives were organized in conjunction with music-related appeals to young voters, including the Country Rocks the Vote drive and the Hip Hop Coalition targeted at urban minorities. Rock the Vote's 800 number for phone-in voter registration received over 200,000 calls in a two-hour period that corresponded with an MTV advertising effort. Radio also was employed as part of the outreach drive, including "Radio Rocks the Vote," a prime time call-in program kicked off by representatives Jesse Jackson (D-IL) and John Kasich (R-OH). Rock the Vote also ran trailers before major youth-oriented motion pictures and ran ads in magazines. Young people from MTV's "Real World" program, which features group house living, urged viewers to vote. Rock the Vote distributed over a half a million copies of a manual it prepared on citizenship, voting, and participation.

A visible, and somewhat controversial, aspect of Rock the Vote's registration drive is the ads/videos run on MTV. In 1992 over fifty stars taped spots for MTV. Rapper Ice-T proclaimed, "Either vote or hostile takeover. I'm down with either one. We're youth; and we have to change things." A scantily clothed Madonna wrapped in an American flag urged MTV viewers to "Vote!" to the tune of her song, "Vogue."[44]

In 1992 MTV spent $1 million on its Choose or Lose campaign. The Rock the Vote drive was quite successful, although it was initially greeted skeptically both within and outside the MTV ranks. Half of the people working for Rock the Vote were not registered themselves.[45] Estimates of the number of new voters registered vary widely. In 1992 Rock the Vote claims to have registered over 2 million new voters.[46] Other sources place the figure at half that number, which is still sizable. In addition, 78 percent of voters registered via the Rock the Vote campaign actually voted.[47] The number of new voters added to the rolls in 1996 through Rock the Vote drives is estimated at over 1 million.

During the 1996 campaign, Rock the Vote initiated the first Internet site for registering voters. The Rock the Vote Web site (www.rockthevote.org) was inaugurated in a promotion that featured founding members of the Congressional Internet Caucus, Senator Patrick Leahy (D-VT), Representative Bill Luther (DFL-MN), Representative Rick White (R-WA), rocker Sheryl Crow, and MCI. The site featured detailed information about the presidential election. Over five thousand voters were registered online in the first week that the site was in operation. Users could find out about the congressional campaigns in their districts and information about how to become involved in the election in their local communities by entering their zip code. E-mail correspondence could be addressed to rock-thevote@aol.com.[48]

In addition to voter registration drives, Rock the Vote also produces issue-based programming targeted at eighteen- to twenty-four-year-olds, some of which has won critical acclaim. A series of six short dramas on health issues, "Out of Order: Rock the Vote Targets Health," dealt with problems such as violence, drug abuse, eating disorders, sexually transmitted diseases, suicide, and the lack of health insurance among the young. Issues are presented in a dramatic, personalized style in keeping with traditional MTV fare to attract and keep audience attention, including advice for handling problems and information on other reaources.[49]

MTV's own brand of campaign coverage includes lengthy candidate profiles and interviews as well as its own polls. MTV political correspondents have become minor celebrities in their own right as they place their own unique stamp on coverage. Lead correspondent Tabitha Soren, who was twenty-five years old during the 1992 campaign, also appeared on the "Today" show as a contributing correspondent.[50] MTV also employs musicians as correspondents. For example, rocker Ted Nugent, a Republican, was assigned to cover his party's bid for the presidency. Although MTV reporters were greeted with some skepticism by politicians, parties, and the mainstream press in 1992, by 1996 they were considered serious journalists in the election.[51] Their 1992 coverage had earned a Peabody Award. The change in the level of respect granted to MTV is evidenced by their treatment at the national nominating conventions. In 1992 MTV reporters were relegated to the "nosebleed" sections—the cheap concert seats—in both the Democratic and Republican convention venues.[52] By 1996 MTV was given prime locations at both conventions.

MTV's general attitude in reporting the campaign differs in some respects from traditional new media. MTV does not ask very tough questions of candidates, and it shies away from many controversial issues. The trademark is its presentation style. Editing and cutting can have dramatic effects that can mesmerize the viewers.

MTV takes a nontraditional approach to remaining "objective" during the presidential campaign. "MTV News" lead anchor, Kurt Loder, a veteran of *Rolling Stone* magazine, makes a point of taking an equal number of swipes at each candidate. In spite of reports that MTV campaign coverage has a Democratic bias, reporters' political orientations span the spectrum. They openly state their partisan, ideological, and candidate preferences, and use these lenses to color their coverage. Popular veejay Kennedy, for example, is an outspoken conservative Republican whose support of her party's nominee is made clear on MTV in other media venues.

In 1992 candidates Bill Clinton and Al Gore appeared on MTV's televised town meetings, answering questions from an in-studio audience. The move was considered unprecedented at the time and earned Clinton and Gore substantial mainstream media coverage. Their appearance on MTV is thought to have given their campaign a boost, as they tailored their message to reach Gen Xers who were fearing for their future, especially the lack of jobs.[53] The Democratic candidates discussed issues, including gay rights and AIDS education, that were not addressed in other campaign forums, although they were criticized for providing easy answers to hard social problems.[54] Al Gore sought to solidify his credentials with the MTV set further by proclaiming himself a "Deadhead" and posing in a tie designed by Jerry Garcia, the late lead guitarist for the Grateful Dead.[55] George Bush, in contrast, was reluctant to appear on MTV, although his aides stressed that it would be a good idea. In July, he emphasized his position by stating that he would not be going on "the teeny bopper network."[56] By the end of the campaign, Bush realized that this was a mistake and made a reluctant appearance.

Bob Dole did not make a similar error in 1996 and courted MTV from the start. He held a series of interviews with Tabitha Soren on the Choose or Lose bus in an effort to connect with people two generations removed from himself. He answered questions about gay rights, abortion, assault weapons, and affirmative action. Bill Clinton, Steve Forbes, and other candidates also were interviewed by Soren.[57]

The impact of MTV on the campaign process for young people is apparent, especially by virtue of the success of the voter registration drive. It is difficult, however, to attribute definitively the increase in the youth vote that occurred in 1992 to MTV and Rock the Vote, but the circumstantial evidence is substantial. The youth vote had fallen to an all-time low in 1988, as only 36 percent of eighteen- to twenty-four-year-olds turned out.[58] The 1992 campaign boasted the largest turnout among this group since 1972. A postelection poll indicated that 12 percent of eighteen- to twenty-nine-year-olds were influenced by MTV to vote.[59]

At the end of Campaign '92, President Clinton and Vice President Gore acknowledged that MTV had helped their cause. In fact, young voters made up 22 percent of the electorate, and 44 percent cast their vote for Clinton, 34 percent for Bush, and 22 percent for Perot.[60] Clinton and Gore arrived first at the MTV Inaugural Ball, where Al Gore proclaimed to a televised audience, "Thank you, MTV! Thank you for winning this election. You did it!"[61] In addition, President Clinton held his first nationally televised interview after the campaign with MTV correspondent Tabitha Soren.

In 1996 the youth vote, in keeping with the national trend, was once again depressed. Young people did not connect with seventy-two-year-old Bob Dole, in spite of his MTV appearances. Generation Xers felt let down by President Clinton, whom they did not believe had kept the promises he had made to them about protecting their interests in economic matters, including Social Security, which he had made on MTV and elsewhere.[62]

Assessments of MTV's political role range from strong praise to harsh criticism. MTV has been lauded for igniting interest in politics among those who have been alienated. MTV has invigorated activism through its voter registration and awareness campaigns. In addition, MTV over time has emerged as a platform for debating issues in a forum that provides the opportunity for heated discussion. This is often accomplished because MTV fosters an oppositional forum. For example, the hedonistic world of the economic haves is juxtaposed with images of crime and poverty in videos and film commentary, while young people present their opinions. Working-class and minority faces, voices, and scenes appear on MTV in ways that are positive. Minority voters are portrayed as role models.[63]

MTV's political coverage has not gone without its critics. Many believe that the overt commercialism that drives MTV's political programming overshadows any positive role that it can play. Of all new media, MTV most blatantly obliterates the lines between advertising, entertainment, and information.[64] Even in its political coverage, MTV makes sure to keep the musicians and products it promotes out front, featuring them as correspondents, in political ads, or as opinion leaders. Media scholar Mark Crispin Miller believes that MTV's political coverage "celebrates the egoistic, selfish materialism of American culture." David Rosenthal, an editor of media books, characterizes it as, "guilt programming," "giving a little politics to a generation whom MTV has helped to lobotomize. Many of these kids are so spaced out they would think that test patterns are groovy."[65]

Another criticism is aimed at what has been termed "pop patriotism." MTV may be trivializing the electoral process by using star quality to influence political behavior. Instead of being truly informed about politics and elections, MTV viewers are voting because a rocker tells them to do so.[66]

Other critics challenge MTV's claims of objective campaign coverage, alleging that it adopts a clear liberal and Democratic partisan agenda. During the 1992 campaign, in particular, the Clinton/Gore campaign allegedly received more positive coverage than did the Bush/Quayle campaign. The impact of this biased coverage is enhanced by the fact that the MTV audience is young and malleable, and many of its members do not receive political news from other sources. These people do not view MTV news with the same skepticism as other news sources. In addition, underlying MTV's political reporting is the message that to assume a particular, MTV-sanctioned position on an issue or a candidate is to be "cool," to gain acceptance among peers.[67]

The success of the MTV model in the United States has not gone without notice in other parts of the world where the station has made major inroads. Versions of MTV International are available in close to one hundred countries in Latin America, Eastern and Western Europe, and Asia, where programming is tailored to the tastes of the audiences. In fact, MTV has more viewers in Europe than in the United States.[68] MTV Latino has been identified as the most important factor in the growth of cable in Latin America.[69] MTV's political style has been exported along with the station's other programming options and has raised controversy in its wake. In 1996 Boris Yeltsin borrowed strategies from American-style campaigning when he ran for president of Russia. He launched his own "Vote or You Will Lose" advertising campaign, which was almost indistinguishable from MTV's American counterpart. He appeared on television dancing to rock music with young voters.[70]

The Campaign in Cyberspace

If 1992 is going to be remembered as the year of the talk-show campaign, 1996 initiated the presidential election in cyberspace. Candidates used the World Wide Web as a marketing tool. Journalists both gained and disseminated information via the Internet. News organizations hosted forums to facilitate the exchange of public opinion. Reporters also made extensive use of e-mail for communicating and filing stories. Voters used online media to gain information, to express their views, to learn what others were thinking, and for pleasure. During the lackluster 1996 election, the cybercampaign offered the one fresh and dynamic diversion.

Candidates and political parties made extensive use of Web pages to promote their cause. The style and sophistication of these pages varied greatly, as we discussed in chapter 5. In addition to general appeals, candidates' Web sites were aimed at target audiences, such as Jewish, Latino, Asian, and gay and lesbian voters. E-mail communication also was used extensively by candidates. People who signed up for Ross Perot's e-mail service were inundated with messages daily. The major party candidates were more judicious in their use of mass e-mail communications.

In addition to their advertising function, candidate and political party Web sites are used to compile lists of supporters. The Web allows candidates to find out a wide range of information about voters, such as their main source of political information, their annual income, credit history, musical tastes, driving record, and other factors via online exchanges.[71]

Political parties used the Web extensively to communicate with activists, providing them with up-to-date information. The Republicans were especially good at maintaining cyberconnections with supporters, and with providing them with online material that was good for their cause and bad for the Democrats. Regional and local party organizations were able to use Web sites to quickly and inexpensively access position papers and press releases as well as artwork for posters, buttons, and bumper stickers. The Democrats packaged these materials in a "grass-roots action kit." The kit provided such campaign materials as electronic postcards that could be used to persuade other online users to vote for Bill Clinton.[72]

The press found that covering and reporting on the campaign in cyberspace offered challenges and opportunities. Technical tools available to journalists altered the dynamics of reporting somewhat. A study conducted during the 1992 campaign found that 90 percent of reporters and producers of news programs used laptop computers while on the campaign trail; 84 percent used modems to connect with other computers, and 25 percent used commercial databases for research.[73] The percentage of journalists relying on commercial databases and the World Wide Web for research purposes undoubtably was much higher during the 1996 contest, keeping pace with the evolving technology and the greater availability of information sources. Fax machines, beepers, and cellular phones also were prevalent. These tools greatly enhance journalists' capacity for covering campaigns. Stories can be researched, revised, and updated with increased speed.

Yet some people in the news business point to the downside of campaign coverage that is more technology driven. Reporters and producers felt overwhelmed by the technology and inundated with material. Instead of simplifying their job, technology has created more choices and forces reporters to make many more decisions about how to cover the campaign than were necessary in the past. Some journalists feel that the technology contributes to a "herd mentality," as everyone is using the same resources and is linked together electronically.[74] This instantaneous communications ability also has influenced the content of stories, as well as hastened the pace of campaigns. Reporters are able to more quickly identify candidates' misstatements, factual errors, and exaggerations. They can check facts online or reach out to sources via e-mail, fax, and portable phone. Further, candidates are expected to provide reporters with information and responses on demand. If allegations are made against a presidential contender, or if a candidate is attacked by his/her opponent, reporters expect an immediate response. Charges and countercharges are presented in the same news report.[75] This places increased pressure on candidates, who in the past had more time to contemplate strategies for dealing with potential crises. In addition, this situation contributes to the more negative campaign coverage we have experienced in recent years as a greater number of allegations and attacks are lodged and reported in an effort to keep fresh news in the public eye.

The news product presented online in 1996 was a mix of old-style communications transferred to a new technology and actual innovations. Much online campaign information failed to exploit the capabilities of the technology. Some offerings were cyberversions of newspapers and magazines, differing little from their print counterparts. Other sites, however, were creative and ground-breaking, and took advantage of the unique characteristics of the medium. CNN/*Time* AllPolitics' Web site, for example, allowed users to run a campaign by creating a fictional online election. MSNBC's site contained a multimedia history of elections. The *Boston Globe's* site has earned a reputation for fostering lively online discussions using an interactive New England town meeting forum.[76] The most popular sites for political information during the 1996 campaign were AllPolitics, the now defunct PoliticsNow, and ABC News/*National Journal/Washington Post/ Newsweek* site.[77] Candidates' Web sites were substantially less popular among online election seekers than the national news organization sites. Users' evaluations of the quality of the sites were modest, although positive, as approximately 25 percent rated them "very useful." Candidate sites were rated slightly lower.[78]

Assessments of the number of people who used the Internet to follow the 1996 campaign vary widely. The Pew Research Center reported that less than one in ten Internet users employed the Internet as a tool for acquiring information during the presidential contest. Only 3 percent of the public tracked the campaign online once a week or more, while another 2 percent logged on with lesser frequency.[79] However, the National Exit Poll found that 26 percent of voters used the Internet regularly. A survey conducted by the *Washington Post/* Harvard University/Kaiser Foundation revealed that 7 percent of voters considered the World Wide Web to be a major source of campaign information, while 26 percent viewed it as a minor source.[80] A Freedom Forum survey conducted in September 1996 and repeated after the election found that 28 percent of the public went online at some point during the campaign, 11 percent of all voters had used Web sites published by news organizations such as CBS, the *New York Times*, and PoliticsNow, and 8 percent accessed candidate and political party Web sites.[81]

There are a number of indications of online communications' popularity beyond these attempts to identify the size of the audience. At the time of the 1996 convention, there were more than sixty thousand political Web sites. Some of these sites received substantial traffic. The Republican National Committee site handled 3.5 million hits during the four days of the National Convention in San Diego. A significant number of citizens registered to vote online, as forty-three thousand new voters signed up via NetVote '96 alone.[82] Online access services were unprepared for the deluge of persons seeking to log on for election return information on election night in 1996. The system was overloaded, and many users could not get access to the major political sites that had promised up-to-the-minute information. One user exclaimed that "this is a defining moment for the Web as a part of public discourse."[83]

While the online audience for the campaign may have been small in size, it was composed of people that candidates and parties wanted to reach. As political scientist Michael Delli Carpini observed, the online campaign reached the technical elite, which "disproportionately consists of community leaders, campaign contributors, and likely voters, making them especially valuable."[84]

As we saw in chapter 6, online users are disproportionately from higher socioeconomic status groups. This profile of the cyberaudience for campaign communication has raised concerns among some observers. A report of the Aspen Institute compiled by Anthony Corrado and Charles Firestone urges caution when considering the contribution of cyberelections to democratic governance. The report notes that cyberspace creates a dilemma for the political process, as there is a potential for "increasing disparity between the 'haves' and the 'have nots' in society, and the misuses and abuse of technology by unscrupulous candidates and citizens alike."[85]

Others fear that more than any other form of campaign communication, online media contribute to the depersonalization of politics. Further, like television, online media may be a more attractive and exploitable format for some types of candidates than for others. We may be in store for a new era of cybersavvy candidates who campaign well online, limiting the pool of potential leaders.[86]

One thing is clear about the cybercampaign: 1996 was just a taste of what is to come in the future. The presidential election in 2000 promises more extensive and sophisticated online campaign applications.

Implications

Even as the new media were making inroads in 1992 and 1996, campaign coverage on network news, CNN, and in newspapers changed little in substance and tone from the era of the mass media election. Stories are framed in the familiar "horse race" format, and character eclipses issues and ideas.[87] Reporters talk at voters and for candidates rather than including them in a campaign dialogue. The traditional media treat candidates and voters like uninvited guests at their own party. Given these dynamics, what might we expect in future campaigns?

The new media have become a legitimate alternative to mainstream campaign media fare. As Doris Graber notes, new media edge a little closer to making campaigns more "user friendly." They attract audience members, they provide useful data and information to voters, and they communicate in a way that is more agreeable to many citizens than the media politics as usual.[88]

The new media will provide an established communication option for candidates. A premium will be placed on candidates who can operate effectively in both old and new media venues. Traditional media management skills differ substantially from those required to successfully negotiate the new media's terrain. Mastering old media management techniques is difficult enough. Combining the differing sets of skills required to negotiate a campaign situation where both old and new media feature prominently is a formidable challenge. Mainstream media management techniques emphasize the candidate's ability to perform effectively in carefully staged productions. Well-crafted sound bites are an essential component of these techniques. The new media, in contrast, require candidates to react spontaneously to media hosts and audience members. Candidates often are required to sustain a dialogue for a substantial amount of time for either live broadcasts or programs presented in their entirety. While the traditional media often create a distance between the candidate and voters, new media foster an impression of personal intimacy. The best new media candidates are those who are able to generate a psychological bond between themselves and audience members.[89]

The new media will not eclipse the mainstream press in the campaign arena. Television news and newspapers remain the most popular sources of campaign information.[90] Voters are now relying on a more diverse array of communication sources in elections. The distressing fact is that with more choice and more information has not come greater satisfaction with campaign coverage.

Shaping the Policy Agenda

In December 1988, a presidential commission appointed by Ronald Reagan announced a recommendation for a 51 percent pay increase for members of Congress. The recommendation also proposed salary increases for all other federal employees as well.

The commission's recommendation quickly filtered out to news media and radio talk show hosts. Talk show hosts around the nation immediately began discussing the news on the air and received angry phone calls from listeners who objected to the increase.

One listener to a talk show in Detroit, noting the 215th anniversary of the Boston Tea Party, suggested to the host that citizens send tea bags to members of Congress to register their protest over the proposed increase. The talk show host, Roy Fox, decided to adopt the idea and began to urge his colleagues around the country to join a national campaign. The Tetley Tea company even joined in, offering listeners a month's worth of free tea if they would join the protest.

The protest, known as the Teabag Revolution, caught on quickly. Many talk show hosts urged their listeners to register their opposition by mailing tea bags to members of Congress.[1] Democratic members of Congress meeting in a resort in West Virginia were so overwhelmed by the faxes that the resort shut down its machines. One hundred and sixty thousand tea bags were dumped by pay raise opponents in front of the White House.[2]

The teabag protest is the most dramatic example of talk radio's impact on policy, but new media impact on public policy did not stop there. Talk radio became an important venue for opposition to the confirmation of attorney-general designate Zoe Baird in early 1993. Support for Baird evaporated when senators began to hear that talk radio callers were disgruntled about Baird's actions in hiring illegal aliens for childcare. Many members of Congress and their staffers chose talk radio as the most influential medium in the health care reform debate.[3] In 1995 talk radio became important in opposition to a counter-terrorism bill.

Talk radio has not been alone among new media as a factor in public policy making. Television talk shows have played such a role. And the Internet also has become a forum for individuals and groups to influence policy making.

The new media role is not necessarily independent of others. In fact, much of the content of talk radio, for instance, is the product of efforts by public officials, interest groups, corporations, and others with specific agendas. To a great extent, new media offer a forum for the current clash of group interests in American politics. "Larry King Live" became a forum for the NAFTA debate between 1992 presidential candidate Ross Perot and Vice-President Al Gore.

Because other forms of new media are less political, talk radio, television talk, and the Internet are the most common platforms for discussing public policy. The television public affairs programs, especially on Sunday mornings, are frequently used for announcing policy shifts. The policy role of the new media usually is driven by external forces, but sometimes the new media, particularly talk radio, will conduct a more independent role in shaping policy.

Policy or Entertainment

Not all of the new media play a policy role, either as a forum for others or as an independent force. For most new media, entertainment is the objective and the introduction of politics is rarely in the form of policy discussion.

Other forms of new media serve image-making purposes. "Late Night with David Letterman" served this function for Vice President Al Gore when he appeared on the show with his list of ten best things about holding the office. President Clinton had a similar goal when answering questions on an MTV program with teens.

Some talk radio hosts are unabashed in their actions in favor of or against policy. Jerry Williams admitted, "I'm not doing journalism here, I'm doing an activist talk show."[4] Another such host is Mike Siegel, who hosts a statewide program in Washington state. Siegel considers his show to be primarily directed at policy activism. Siegel describes what he does on air in explicit activism terms. He says his show is "about empowering people to take back control of the government."[5] And Michael Reagan urges listeners to get paper and pen ready to write down information needed for policy involvement.

Actually, such policy activism is rare among talk show hosts. Many hosts consider the congressional pay raise to be their last major role in political activism. Others point to some isolated, highly infrequent incidents of policy activism. Even those hosts who view themselves primarily as social commentators eschew such activism in favor of just offering "food for thought."[6] One says he has "no particular stake" in what listeners decide to do with the information they receive from his show.[7] Others go even further and call themselves pure entertainers. Judy Jarvis claims her purpose is to "provoke entertaining conversation."[8] Tom Leykis is even more blunt: "My role with listeners is not to get them to send tea leaves to Congress or to show up at noon for a rally. My goal is to entertain them. . . . I'm not there as a proselytizer or an evangelist as much as I am an entertainer."[9]

The entertainers are uninterested in political activism, except as it feeds audience ratings. "I'm not going to get on the air day after day saying do this, do that, do the other. I happen to think that's extremely boring radio. I wouldn't listen to it."[10] And still others point to their sole objective of profit. Tom Leykis: "I have one agenda—my agenda is to get the most people listening to the radio between 3 and 7 Pacific time, as I can get. So that we can jack up the advertising rates as high as we can get them to go."[11]

This lack of activism is apparent in our analysis of talk radio content. Few explicit calls to action to listeners were made by hosts in the content analysis of nine hosts. Out of eighty-one hours of programming only fourteen efforts at mobilization were made by hosts. Four of the hosts (Bohannon, Colmes, Limbaugh, and Majors) made no such requests of listeners at all.

All such requests urged listeners to contact members of Congress. In all cases, the host not only suggested contact on a particular issue, but recommended specifically what listeners should urge the members to do. For example, G. Gordon Liddy exhorted listeners to tell their representatives to oppose recognizing Vietnam, oppose counterterrorism legislation, and support the B-2 bomber. But even these mobilization efforts are short-lived. Liddy was rare among the hosts because he continued his campaign against counter-terrorism legislation for two days in a row. Not all such mobilizations are designed to register opposition to lawmakers' efforts. Michael Reagan encouraged listeners to write to Senator Jesse Helms of North Carolina to voice support for a Helms' position.

But in most cases where such efforts at listener mobilization were made, the reference was to general legislation, that is, recognition of

Vietnam or anti-terrorism legislation. But listeners may not be as capable as others of actually voicing support or opposition as others without references to specific bills. Only Michael Reagan provided specific bill numbers for listeners to use in their correspondence with representatives. From interviews with hosts, it is clear that Reagan's approach of following specific legislation and urging listener support or rejection of particular bills is uncommon.

Although hosts only rarely explicitly urged listeners to take specific actions, one might expect they would seek to stimulate listener mobilization by discussing specific bills such as the Clinton administration's health care reform proposal or the Endangered Species Act or at least policy options such as opposition to affirmative action or the prochoice position on abortion. However, the talk radio content analyzed did not include much specific discussion of legislation or policy options. As Table 10.1 demonstrates, these talk radio hosts frequently discussed individuals, institutions, or organizations, but rarely moved beyond personal or general references to discussions of specific policy options or positions or even particular pieces of legislation currently before Congress. The most common references were to individuals such as Bill Clinton, Newt Gingrich, Bob Dole, or Phil Gramm. Institution or organization references included Congress, the Democrats, the religious right, among others. However, the discussion of specific policy options was rare.

There were significant differences between the approaches of hosts such as Liddy and Reagan, whose discussions were more substantive in policy terms and included more reference to current legislation, and those of Bohannon, Colmes, and Leykis, who raised social problems or emphasized discussion of current events such as the O. J. Simpson trial.

But for the vast majority of content, there was no explicit mobilization message. There were few specific calls to do anything, and there was even little discussion of distinct pieces of legislation or even particular policy options.

As a result, listeners hear much discussion of individuals—including political figures such as Newt Gingrich, Bill and Hillary Clinton, and Bob Dole, as well as nonpoliticians such as O. J. Simpson and Michael Jackson—and organizations such as Congress, the Supreme

TABLE 10.1 Category of Host Reference

Host	Bohannon	Colmes	Harder	Leykis	Liddy	Limbaugh	Majors	Reagan	Total
Bill	1.8	2.4	0.8	—	5.7	—	0.9	6.6	2.8
Ideology	4.1	4.7	0.8	—	3.4	0.9	5.1	2.0	3.0
Indiv/Organ	85.8	86.7	86.3	100.0	84.0	97.3	84.3	83.2	86.5
Policy	8.3	6.2	12.1	—	6.9	1.8	9.7	8.2	7.8
Total	100%	100%	100%	100%	100%	100%	100%	100%	100%

Court, environmentalists, and the Democratic party. And opinions are often given by hosts concerning them. For the conservative hosts, the Clinton administration routinely makes bad decisions and includes incompetent or immoral individuals, while the more liberal hosts take verbal jabs at the Republican-controlled Congress.

However, hosts do not move beyond such discussions to advocate explicit actions on policy or even detail the policy choices these individuals or organizations address. General discontent with current individuals or organizations usually does not result in further explanation of options for listener activism.

Rather than mobilize voters, perhaps talk radio content promotes cynicism and disinterest in political involvement. Early research on the talk radio audience suggested talk radio listeners were more socially and politically alienated than nonlisteners.[12]

Talk radio has been lambasted by critics, particularly traditional journalists and commentators and some politicians, for intense negativity. Yet more current studies link talk radio listenership with political interest and activism.[13]

The content of the nine programs studied confirms the more current research. Talk content, at least for those programs studied, is not strongly negative, as critics have suggested. As Table 10.2 shows, most talk hosts made as many favorable as unfavorable references to current events, issues, and individuals. The two exceptions were G. Gordon Liddy and Chuck Harder. Forty-six percent of Liddy's references were negative, while Harder's negative references topped 70 percent. Chuck Harder's high negativity is not surprising given his self-proclaimed title as the "king of the conspiracy theorists."

As Table 10.2 demonstrates, the most negative references were made in allusion to policy positions. The conservative hosts' negative references generally related to Clinton administration initiatives, such as health care reform, NAFTA, and GATT. The hosts were far less negative toward individuals and organizations and were most positive (34 percent of references) toward bills. The positive reference to bills undoubtedly was due to Republican control of the 104th Congress, which produced actions many of the hosts (especially Reagan, Limbaugh, North, and Liddy) agreed with.

The muted negativity generally, compared with the political rhetoric of critics concerning talk radio, also can be attributed to Republican control of Congress. It is possible that talk radio content had been more negative prior to the 1994 elections because of Democratic control of both houses of Congress and the presidency.

But it is significant that during this period most of the hosts spent time also discussing favorable topics to them. For the conservative hosts these included topics such as Newt Gingrich, the 104th Congress, the Contract with America, and the flat tax. The host who spoke in the most positive vein was Jim Bohannon. In keeping with his

TABLE 10.2 Category of Reference by Tone

Category	Bill	Ideology	Indiv/Organiz	Policy	Total
Favorable	34.2	26.8	25.7	29.0	26.2
Unfavorable	26.3	39.0	34.5	49.5	35.6
Neutral/Mixed	39.5	34.1	39.8	21.5	38.2
Total	100%	100%	100%	100%	100%

centrist image, Bohannon at various times spoke favorably of Jimmy Carter, Bob Dole, George McGovern, and Rush Limbaugh. But Bohannon's references also included frequent discussion of nonpolitical topics such as sports and entertainment.

It is possible the timing of the study affected the result. There was no high-profile topic, such as the O. J. Simpson murders or the Oklahoma City bombing or some unpopular administration decision that might have excited hosts and callers toward negativism. Conversely, there also was no event or topic that would have led the hosts to be more favorable than normal. This finding suggests that criticism of talk radio's negative content focuses on particular hosts and ignores the hosts' use of this platform to express support for individuals or policies they approve of.

Factors in New Media Agenda Setting

The congressional pay increase example mentioned at the beginning of this chapter illustrates the type of issue that can be influenced by new media, that is, a valence issue simply framed (such as a large pay increase) with positions that are clearly dichotomous. In these cases, few listeners would be inclined to object to the host's position or his or her activism on the issue.

Moreover, activism is easier to pursue in opposition than in support. Talk radio hosts have a more difficult time initiating policy, rather than defeating it. For example, less successful efforts at the national level by talk radio hosts include health care reform, campaign finance reform, and welfare reform. These issues demand more complex solutions and the various proposed options cannot be easily described as populist or antiestablishment. Speaking of campaign finance reform, one talk show host admitted that "this won't produce the public outcry as the pay raise push for the simple reason that it's not as clear cut and gut level an issue."[14]

Admittedly, national campaigns by hosts can be influential. However, as stated earlier, these have been rare. Not only must the issue meet the foregoing criteria, but there must be some gain for the host. If hosts do not perceive the campaign will benefit their program, they lack much incentive to participate. In fact, they run the risk of alienating listeners if the issue stance is not overwhelmingly popular. But the fact of their rarity does not mean they cannot be repeated under the right circumstances with great effect.

The Mechanics of Policy Influence

It bears repeating that most hosts do not goad listeners into taking specific political action on public policy. But for those minority of hosts who do routinely engage in direct activism, a common set of techniques can be identified. Although these techniques may apply regularly to only a few hosts, and usually in local areas, they can also be applicable to the rare, large-scale effort.

One familiar method is the broadcasting of the phone or fax numbers of elected officials or Internet distribution of government e-mail addresses. These efforts, particularly in the midst of the policy formulation process, are designed to provide listeners, viewers, or Internet users with a target for their discontent.

In the midst of the debate over gays in the military in early 1993, Pat Robertson's "700 Club" television program repeatedly flashed the switchboard number for the U.S. Capitol on the screen to urge viewers to call their own members of Congress. By the end of the day, the switchboard had logged ten times the daily average, most of them opposed to the policy.[15]

The Children's Defense Fund sent a press release out via Internet e-mail subscription lists urging recipients to lobby the president to oppose changes in Medicaid proposed by the 104th Congress. The organization included the e-mail message of the White House to facilitate electronic lobbying by supporters. It also urged recipients of the message to send the organization their e-mail number so that the fund could send them flyers to distribute. These newsgroup messages have the advantage of reaching large numbers of individuals who are already interested in the topic and familiar with e-mail.

Another method is requesting the listeners, viewers, or Internet users take some other dramatic kind of action, such as mailing certain items to an elected official or a corporate executive. These are acts that are unmistakably the work of the host. Hence, they are more persuasive in reinforcing the talk show hosts' role since the action can be clearly attributed to the host. By contrast, encouraging listeners to send faxes or letters produces more nebulous results. One does not know whether the talk host's call produced those specific results. It also places the responsibility on the recipients to acknowledge a response and attribute it to the talk program.

One example occurred in 1989, following the Exxon Valdez spill. Seattle host Mike Siegel organized a boycott of Exxon by urging listeners to cut up their Exxon credit cards and send them to Siegel. Siegel then displayed more than one thousand letters with cut-up credit cards.[16]

Another example of Siegel's mobilization was the "tennis shoe brigade." Siegel led efforts in Washington state to increase punishment for sexual predators. He urged listeners to join the "tennis shoe brigade" by donating tennis shoes with attached notes from children asking the governor to change the laws. Ten thousand tennis shoes were delivered to the governor's office. Subsequently state laws were changed to double sexual predator sentences.[17]

Mobilization efforts usually focus on small acts, easily performed by individuals, but when multiplied by hundreds or thousands of listeners, demonstrate the power of the forum. Another Seattle host, Dave Ross, suggested that his listeners put a one dollar bill in an envelope and send it to a member of Congress who does something they approve of. Ross's first recipient was Representative Mike Castle of Delaware who had announced he would not use his franking privilege to send bulk mail to his constituents. In response, Ross conducted what he called an "on-air mailing party" where "I took out my dollar, put it in my envelope, and said I want you all to do the same, and at noon, the stroke of noon, drop those things in the mail."[18] Within a week, Castle's office received sixteen hundred letters with one-dollar bills from residents of a state nearly three thousand miles away from his own.

The Rainforest Action Network Web site offers a prewritten fax to officials of companies the group is boycotting protesting their actions. The user merely completes the form. The site also explains the locations of upcoming demonstrations where supporters can participate.

Tennis shoes with attached notes from children, torn credit cards, one dollar bills, or prewritten faxes not only are small acts listeners can easily perform, but they also do not require any independent research by the listener. Anyone can participate at minimal cost.

Still another form of mobilization is the mass rally. This is the same kind of mass protest common in the 1960s, which invariably attracts the notice of the mainstream media. Clearly, it is a highly dramatic form of mobilization well suited for press coverage. For example, the Rainforest Action Network Web site explains the locations of upcoming demonstrations where supporters can participate.

Talk show hosts also have initiated such rallies. In 1991 Connecticut talk show host Tom Scott mobilized at least forty thousand people to an anti–state income tax rally at the state capitol in Hartford.[19] On July 2, 1990, six thousand protestors in Trenton, New Jersey, attended a rally after a local radio station urged residents to participate in opposition to the implementation of a state sales tax increase. The idea for the rally came from a caller to a talk show.[20] In 1986 Boston talk radio host Jerry Williams helped get two thousand people to rally at the state capitol against a tax increase.

Even when there is a call to action, does it have any effect on the audience? Unfortunately, the evidence is mainly anecdotal. Tales of talk radio listeners' responses to these calls circulate. During the congressional check-bouncing scandal, when Rush Limbaugh urged outraged listeners to call Representative Newt Gingrich's office to complain about the scandal, congressional staffers admitted telephone lines were tied up for most of the rest of the day.[21] In another instance, a Massachusetts state legislator complained that the state legislature's phone lines were overloaded for hours during debates because Boston talker Jerry Williams repeatedly urged listeners to call their representative.[22] Tying up telephone lines or emptying fax machines of paper is a common example of new media's potential to mobilize listeners.

Policymakers sometimes directly provide weight to these rumors. Senator James Jeffords of Vermont, who has served in Congress for two decades, said his mail has increased dramatically in recent years and that talk radio is a significant reason.[23]

Members of Congress have seen a dramatic increase in the number of form e-mail messages, probably originating from groups using the Internet to mobilize members. The response from members is not necessarily positive. Representative Tom Campbell: "When [e-mail] came out it was great. . . . And then I began to get unsolicited e-mails, then the majority are unsolicited, then the majority are blast to a hundred people. And so it becomes less and less useful."[24]

Because they are more significant to local listeners and the numbers needed to suggest public support are smaller, local issues are easier for talk radio hosts to influence through mass mobilization. Local or state politicians are more affected by mobilization by hosts at that level.

When they occur at the national level, these mobilizations possess their own problems for public involvement in policymaking. As demonstrated in the dollar-bill incident, listeners may have little or no supplemental or confirming evidence before they act at the host's request. It is unlikely Seattle voters knew very much about Representative Castle of Delaware or his campaign finance policies. They may not know independently whether the cause is worthy or the specific action is accurately directed.

Also, when an issue is presented as being neatly divided between good and bad, elected officials may find it more difficult to adopt positions that result in sound policy. Few politicians would risk their political capital over issues that are seen to be unpopular, even if the information on which this public judgment is made is shallow and misleading. And the search for compromise is a more laborious journey when the two sides are painted so starkly.

Despite these drawbacks, such actions, absent other gauges of public opinion, become significant. Elected officials who lack more scientific means of measuring public opinion may be driven by such mobilization, which is allegedly reflective of public opinion.

Another form of policy influence is personal contact with policymakers. Online chats are providing that forum. On January 13, 1994, Vice President Al Gore was the first federal government official to conduct an online news conference with Internet users.[25] Other officials, including presidential candidates and state officials, have conducted similar sessions.[26]

Talk radio also has the potential for such unfiltered access. Unlike common citizens, many talk radio hosts have direct contact with many policymakers who appear as guests on their programs or occasionally become callers. These hosts often use their position to lobby policymakers directly, usually on the air. In such instances they are less concerned about mobilizing listeners or viewers than in urging their guests to adopt certain issue stances in full view of the public.

Sometimes they even propose specific policy solutions to their guests. One example is Bruce Dumont, who says he is "much more interested in exploring solutions than I am in hearing a recitation of the problem."[27] Dumont will propose solutions to his guests and sometimes attempt to get an on-air commitment from them about the idea.

At times this direct contact becomes oddly joined when the policymaker and the new media host are one and the same person. Governors, senators, and mayors are becoming frequent hosts or cohosts of their own radio or cable television programs, sometimes taking calls from listeners or viewers. Such venues are used primarily to acquire public support for the official's policy.

In spite of the many ways that new media can influence policymakers, traditional media still hold one large advantage: Policymakers are far less likely to attend to the new media for political purposes than they are to the traditional media. While policymakers will read newspapers and catch snippets of television news programs, especially CNN, talk radio listening is less common. Because talk radio and television talk, particularly, can be time-consuming, policymakers do not take much time with them.

But two trends suggest more direct policymaker attention to new media content. A new growth industry of daily or weekly faxed summaries or compilations of talk radio programs may minimize time costs and increase elites' attention to the medium.[28] Also print media, such as news magazines and daily newspapers, make reference to talk radio content as traditional journalists increasingly appear to be listening and using the medium as a gauge for public opinion.

Who Sets the New Media's Agenda?

Talk show hosts tend to minimize their influence over policy issues. Whatever influence they have, they modestly admit, is merely a reflection of public opinion. Ken Hamblin said he does not have any influence except for the "ability to bring Americans together to focus on something that we all agree is worthy."[29] One host claims "talk radio merely airs what the American people have to say."[30] Listeners, they claim, set the agenda.

But, quite clearly, the hosts do play a role in determining the agenda for their programs (see chapter 3). However, they are correct in asserting that the agendas of their programs cannot stray far from audience interests. Not unlike the politicians they often malign, talk show hosts also face the difficulty of deciding whether to pursue an issue that may be of importance to them but which their constituents do not find very significant. One host claimed talk show hosts cannot create audience interest. "If the person listening doesn't already have a strong, passionate feeling about an issue, the talk show host isn't going to give it to him."[31]

But some see their role as educators seeking to inform their listeners by presenting both sides of an issue or engaging points of view. Such hosts are more likely to attempt to find topics that may not be of great interest, but the host believes is important. However, there are limits even to the pursuit of such topics. Seattle host Mike Siegel admits that he varies the objects of his political activism in order not to lose segments of his audience disinterested or actually in disagreement with his position on a single issue. Others, however, do not seek to veer into any areas not of interest to listeners. Tom Leykis: "I'm not in the 'let's educate the public and tell them that this is really important even though they don't think it's important' business."[32]

What is even more difficult is for the host to take a position that is unpopular with the public. Tom Leykis joined other hosts' opposition to the congressional pay increase because it was a universally popular position. But supporting something less popular would "drive my ratings into the ground."[33] Nonetheless the agenda-setting role is still vital even if it is conducted under the aegis of public interest. The determination of that interest at any given time is within the realm of the host.

Hosts often face listeners who would like to propose a competing agenda. As discussed in chapter 3, callers who intend to veer from the program's agenda often are not allowed to join the discussion.

If hosts set the agenda, what are the antecedents of the hosts' agenda choices? Those antecedents are not limited to those discussed in chapter 3, such as the host's or the producer's perceptions of audience interest or the interests of executives. Forces external to the new media also seek to shape the new media's agenda. Not surprisingly, these forces, including both government and nongovernmental actors, are usually the very subjects of the new media's content. Obviously, such actors seek to influence the new media's agenda to shape the content about themselves.

Such a practice is hardly new. Traditional news media outlets long have been subject to the same pressure. Journalists routinely receive mountains of faxes from various interest groups, candidates, and governmental offices.

And not unlike their approach to the traditional news media, policymakers have adopted carrot and stick approaches to the new media. On one hand, talk radio has prompted responses from those who are often targets of talk radio or television talk hosts. For example, upset with a drumbeat of talk radio criticism, then Massachusetts governor Michael Dukakis commented, "I am disappointed in all of us who have let the talkmasters and columnists define our values."[34]

The Clinton administration also has used the "stick" approach. President Clinton has lashed out at new media hosts calling talk radio "a constant, unremitting drumbeat of negativism and cynicism."[35] White House counselor George Stephanopoulos at one point threatened to seek to revive the Fairness Doctrine to rein in talk radio's "'tear it down' mentality."[36]

At other times, policymakers have tried more private approaches. Clinton administration officials chastised talk radio station management after a talk radio interview the officials viewed as too harsh.[37] One member of Congress contacted a local talk radio host's relative, who was a friend of the member, to pass on the message that the host should not be so tough on him.[38]

But such complaints have been less frequent than more positive attempts to influence its content through inducements. These inducements include availability for guest interviews and accessibility for information.

The Clinton administration began its tenure reaching out to embrace talk radio. In fact, Clinton was even friendly with talk radio during the 1992 campaign (see chapter 9). In September 1993, the administration invited talk show hosts to participate in a mass broadcast from the South Lawn of the White House. The White House set up tables and access to telephone lines. But even more important was access to the administration. The White House instructed cabinet officers, such as Health and Human Services Secretary Donna Shalala, Labor Secretary Robert Reich, and Deputy Treasury Secretary Richard Rubin, to walk from host to host for brief consecutive interviews. Administration officials were offering hosts rare access—on-site, in-person interviews—that enhanced the hosts' reputation back home. The White House also hosted a press conference for the hosts. They were treated with cordiality and respect similar to other media practitioners.

White House courting was designed to curry favor with the hosts while allowing the administration to express its viewpoint across many talk radio programs simultaneously. By meeting talk radio's imperatives—access to the president, the perception of power, in-person interviews with cabinet members—the administration hoped to achieve its own policy-related goal of increased support for Mrs. Clinton's health care reform proposal.

Although the effect was positive in the short-run, it had little long-lasting impact. The White House did not repeat that effort. In fact, the administration became increasingly despairing of its ability to influence talk radio's content through ingratiation. And it subsequently alternated back to the stick.

The Republican-dominated 104th Congress took a page from the administration's book when it invited talk show hosts to set up broadcast booths in the basement of the Capitol building for the inaugural day of the new Congress. Local hosts from across the country sat next to each other at card tables while they broadcast back to their respective local audiences. Although cramped by the space shortage and limited technical facilities, the hosts were pleased to be invited. One host called it "the biggest story in my lifetime."[39] Although the technical conditions were poor, the hosts appreciated the access to members of Congress and the national press corps, who spoke with the hosts about their role in the elections and the advent of the new Congress. And unlike the administration's efforts, the Congress continued to maintain the separate facilities for talk radio and extended the positive coverage beyond one day.

Individual members also have employed the new media route to press legislative agendas. In September 1993, one member of Congress used talk radio to lobby for a change in a House rule allowing signers of discharge petitions to remain anonymous.[40] The lopsided vote on the rule followed an intensive radio talk show campaign by the member, in conjunction with United We Stand, Ross Perot's organization.[41]

The next month some members of the House even attempted to change Senate rules via talk shows. Three House Democrats held a news conference to urge talk show hosts and editorial writers to institute a public campaign against the Senate rule allowing filibusters.[42]

Despite the frequent anti-incumbent rhetoric, elected officials find many new media venues willing to entertain them as guests and provide a forum for the politician's agenda. Internet chat rooms for America Online or Prodigy, television talk programs, and talk radio shows routinely invite politicians to appear. Even though many hosts are self-described as populists and argue that their programs are opportunities for common citizens to express their opinions, the hosts provide this forum to policymakers because they believe it enhances the reputation of their shows.

Speaking of a program airing on the day the state attorney general issued a report on child abuse, Seattle host Mike Siegel commented: "I think it's a tribute to the program that the attorney general came out with this report this morning and then chose to call us to come on this program first."[43] When policymakers are interested in appearing, it demonstrates the program's prestige.

One caveat is the ideological bias of hosts. Policymaker guests on talk radio programs are likely to reflect the ideology of the host, as discussed in chapter 3. But the linkage between hosts and some policymakers of similar ideological persuasions raises questions about credibility. Are hosts turning over their programs to favored politicians?

Tom Leykis, who has not been accused of this practice, does not view it as a problem because talk radio is held to a different, some might say lower, standard. "Credibility is not as important to talk radio as it is to the news media. We're the op-ed page, not the front page."[44]

Elected officials and candidates are not the only willing participants in seeking to forge the agenda of the new media. The party organizations have become active in seeking to shape the agenda of the new media, with the Republicans moving farther and faster. The Republican National Committee hosts a visually attractive Web site that is linked to many other megasites political activist Internet users are likely to frequent. The Republican National Committee daily sends to talk radio hosts a report including lists of possible topics, quotable comments, and suggestions for guests complete with phone numbers. The GOP chair's take on the political scene, then, can get daily exposure on talk shows around the nation. The faxes are geared toward talk radio. One, for example, issued in December 1995 contained a ditty titled "Won't You Come Home, Bill Clinton?" (sung to the tune of "Bill Bailey") that, ideally, talk radio hosts would sing on the air.

The House Republican Conference issues a daily fax especially designed for talk radio hosts. Also Republicans offer hosts easy access to GOP congressional leaders. According to one local host, "The Republicans make available [House Majority Leader] Dick Armey, Newt Gingrich, anybody you want."[45]

The Democrats have been laggards in meeting talk radio needs. Even though the Democratic National Committee now has a radio talk service, it is viewed as incompetent. "They're still trying to get into the editorial pages of the daily newspaper," one host complains. "It's a different attitude."[46] But the Democratic National Committee has effectively carried its message on occasion.

The Democrats have relied on the success of sympathetic hosts such as former Democratic elected officials Jim Hightower and Mario Cuomo. However, Hightower's exit as a host and Cuomo's inability to attract affiliates has doomed that effort.

In another stark contrast, the Republicans ran a weekly cable talk show long before the Democrats even considered their own alternative. One year after its first broadcast, the GOP program, called "Rising Tide," was being carried on more than two thousand cable systems reaching 55 million households.[47]

Policymakers and party organizations are joined by other pleaders seeking entrance at the new media's gates. A key player in talk radio's role in the 1989 pay raise issue was not a talk radio personality or a public official, but an interest group adept at influencing talk radio.

Public Citizen's Congress Watch, a group lobbying for congressional reform, successfully worked with talk radio programs both in 1987 and again in 1989 to scuttle the proposed congressional pay raise. Because of group founder Ralph Nader's role as a celebrity, talk show hosts were anxious to book him as a guest. In fact, Nader even appeared on the programs of many conservative hosts who noted their disagreement with the consumer activist on many other issues. But those appearances enhanced the salience of the stance since it demonstrated its appeal across ideological lines.

Nader's talk show appearances were hardly random. Public Citizen placed particular emphasis on scheduling Nader in congressional districts of party leaders.[48]

Increasingly, groups are sending faxes to talk radio hosts and calling producers to gain time on a show. One group, Citizens United, thrice weekly sends "ClintonWatch" bulletins to radio talk hosts.[49] The bulletins are particularly useful for hosts already hostile to the president. Hosts searching for topics to fill two-, three-, or four-hour blocks of time often use the faxes for ideas for topics, facts to mention on the air, or guest lists. Interest groups are now major sources of the talk radio agenda.

External Players as Guests

Groups can most effectively relay their positions by placing group representatives as guests on talk shows. Guests are usually accorded a distinct status from callers. They are given opportunities to offer opinions at length, usually uninterrupted and unchallenged. The groups must compete with publishing houses seeking recognition for authors of recent books, public officials, and the talk show hosts' penchant for interviewing media representatives.

Guest spots are easier to obtain on local stations where there is greater demand for, but less supply of, available guests. Talk radio interviews of national guests are most likely to be conducted by telephone, while television talk usually occurs in the studio. For example, during the Robert Bork confirmation process in 1987, the Leadership Council on Civil Rights, which opposed Bork's nomination, scheduled its Washington, D.C.-based speakers on approximately a hundred talk radio programs around the country.[50] Since hosts and producers prefer in-studio interviews, groups often attempt to meet that need by sending local representatives to the station for an in-studio interview or scheduling a national figure for talk radio interviews during a tour of a local area.

Some groups use public relations firms to schedule guests for talk shows. Others, such as the association of pharmaceutical research companies, the American Legion, and the AFL-CIO, actually promote their guest availability through advertisements in *Talkers*, the talk radio industry publication.

Some external players shy away from new media because of the entertainment imperatives. The executive director of one interest group said he avoids talk radio because "they don't want analysis. They just want you to rant and rave. It's an unpleasant environment."[51]

But another reason for avoidance is potential "broadcast abuse" from producers who invite participants on the program only to subject them to verbal harassment on the air. As David Kusnet, former director of communications for People For the American Way, explains, guests can play the role as "a tribune of the people, speaking out for the average citizen against some enemy or problem, or as one more target of populist wrath, to be grilled by the host and the call-ins."[52]

Obviously, guests are far less likely to want to do the latter. Thus a group that has become the current "public enemy number one" is more cautious about placing group representatives on talk radio programs. It is easier when the group or individual appears to be outside the establishment. But if they are too far outside they will probably not have the public relations apparatus to launch publicity campaigns replete with available guests. Such avoidance, or at least gravitation toward sympathetic hosts, coupled with scheduling preferences toward favorable guests, helps produce the high level of guest/host agreement discussed in chapter 3.

The relationship between new media and external forces clearly is one of a symbiotic interaction. Individuals or groups are seeking to have the forum of a talk program, while producers are searching for interesting guests. But the interaction is not necessarily equal. For a national figure such as Ross Perot, a national forum, such as "Larry King Live," is more attractive than a program in a local market.

"Larry King Live" is one example of explicit usage by external forces. In most cases the usage is favorable because it produces the desired outcome, a positive portrayal of the guest. Larry King has been eager to allow his program to be used as a forum for political actors to play their various parts. A regular, Ross Perot appeared on the program six times during the 1992 campaign. In 1993 he appeared with Vice President Al Gore in a debate on NAFTA. Then, in September 1995 he used the show to announce the formation of his third party. "Larry King Live" became a popular forum for 1996 presidential candidates. King even sponsored a forum with the minor party candidates.

On the other hand, national figures with agendas may pursue a strategy including local markets because of the perception that local hosts will be more friendly because they are honored to host a nationally known figure. For example, President Clinton agreed to appear on the talk show of St. Louis host Charles Brennan. The interview made news, but the White House complained that Brennan's questions were too harsh.[53] Such complaints bolster the impression that the White House expected a softball interview from a local host.

Information Source

New media outlets usually possess small staffs and little research support, making them far more dependent on external forces for information than, say, national news media outlets. The need is especially acute because of the long blocks of time some hosts (particularly talk radio) must fill and the requirement to appear better informed than their listeners.

Interest groups and major party organizations are well aware of this dependency and have proactively moved to meet it. One example is the Heritage Foundation, which has become a talk radio—friendly Washington, D.C., think tank. It provides space for talk show broadcasts and sponsors conferences for the talk radio industry. It generates position papers and press releases, which are freely distributed to talk radio shows in major markets. One Denver talk show host readily displayed to one of the authors the Heritage Foundation reports he routinely cites on his program.

Talk show hosts receive reams of press releases from various interest groups. The Christian Coalition faxes releases on their legislative agenda. Industry groups, trade associations, nonprofit organizations all join the effort to set the agenda of the new media. It is hoped the information in the press releases, particularly statistical data, will be used in the program.

In turn, new media gravitate to those meeting their imperatives. Talk radio producers come to rely on certain groups, such as the Heritage Foundation, as regular information sources and routinely contact them for more data when focusing on particular issues. According to a media coordinator for the National Rifle Association, about one-third of the organization's daily inquiries from the media come from talk radio.[54] A host often will ask the producer or another staffer to contact the group for clarifications or additional information on a topic to be dealt with on the show, thus allowing another opportunity for the group to spin its story.

Many elected officials, party organizations, and interest groups have met the new media's demand for rapid delivery of information, continual ideas for new topics, and the ready availability of guests who will address those topics. Their ability to influence the new media's agenda is the result of their skill at meeting the imperatives of the new media.

Clearly, understanding and meeting those imperatives is a prerequisite for helping set the new media's agenda. But not everyone comprehends this point. The story of the three House members seeking to change the Senate's filibuster rule is a good example of the failure of such an attempt. An overt appeal to talk show hosts is doomed to failure as compared to more subtle methods such as availability as guests, regular faxes, and issuance of reports the host can use in his or her own monologue.

Using and Being Used

The relationship with interest groups challenges new media's supposed populist leanings. The Internet ostensibly offers anyone the opportunity to become a self-publisher to the world. Talk radio's appeal is the perception that it "gives the common person a place to voice his or her opinion."[55] Yet, for the most part, the voices given priority on new media tend to be those of individuals and groups who also are heard on traditional media.

Interest groups and traditional media organizations have moved their communication efforts onto the Internet. Media organizations such as NBC, CNN, *Time*, and the *National Journal* have created megasites such as MSNBC, AllPolitics, and Politics Now, which provide a structure for users who are repelled by the anarchy of the Internet. As a result, as the news audience moves from print or broadcast versions to the Internet, they maintain their loyalty to traditional media.

Some talk show hosts have become advocates and therefore handmaidens for particular causes and groups. This is true for individual hosts such as Rush Limbaugh, who has been accused of being an apologist for the Republican party.

But it also applies to hosts generally. When an education bill amendment required that home-school parents be certified, the Home School Legal Defense Fund swung into action to kill the legislation. However, unlike most groups, this one received the almost immediate support of many conservative talk radio hosts across the nation. As one host described it, "We kept our program packed with critiques from politicians, home-school leaders, and religious freedom lawyers."[56]

At least some talk show hosts seem quite willing to hand over their programs to groups they favor. Speaking approvingly of this practice, one host admitted that "when Christian or conservative leaders have a message to get out, they can access—and mobilize—literally millions of listeners in minutes."[57]

The line becomes even more blurred when groups and hosts are indistinguishable. At least two hosts have formed their own interest groups. Mike Siegel formed a group called Washington Watch, which takes positions on issues, lobbies on legislation, and supports candidates. Stan Solomon, a Republican talk radio host in Indianapolis, created a political action committee that raises funds to help elect favored candidates as well as defeat Democrats.[58]

Michael Harrison, editor of *Talkers,* does not view this as a problem because the marketplace will intervene. "If they get too co-opted by the groups, they're going to lose their ratings, and they're not going to be on the radio for long, which is the balancing factor."[59]

But is this weeding out process Harrison describes done quickly or even at all? Even though Rush Limbaugh's numbers dropped during 1995 as he was defending the Republican-controlled 104th Congress, he was still the number-one talk show host in the country. One host has suggested that the audience usually remains unaware of the decisions made that affect content on the air.[60] Thus the market seems a poor weapon against such tactics.

Running for Office

Some new media practitioners have moved from commenting on politics to actual candidacy for office. The 1994 elections became a milestone for talk radio not only as a factor in mobilizing voters, but also in supplying candidates. The best-known candidacy, although short-lived, was that of Howard Stern, the "shock jock" who announced he would run for governor of New York on the Libertarian ticket. Although Stern was welcomed by the Libertarians, who needed a minimum threshold of votes to become a fixture on the New York state ballot, the bid was never viewed as serious and Stern eventually dropped out of the race.

Seven talk show hosts actually ran for elective office that year. Four ran for Congress. Two women hosts, Janet Jeghelian in Massachusetts and Ronna Romney in Michigan, ran for the U.S. Senate, although both failed to win their party nominations. None were elected. Others were touted as potential candidates, but opted not to run. Seattle talk host and policy activist Mike Siegel considered running for the U.S. Senate from Washington, but decided against it.[61] Connecticut talk show host Tom Scott spearheaded an anti–income tax campaign in Connecticut following the passage of the first state income tax. He then ran for Congress as a Republican in 1992 and received 34 percent of the vote, and two years later ran for governor as an independent, garnering 11 percent of the vote.

Although candidates drawn from the new media would enjoy apparent advantages in name recognition and populist identification, their failure to succeed in electoral politics suggests those advantages are not enough. Moreover, other disadvantages inhere from their pre-candidacy careers. They may be unable to alter positions widely known to the electorate, thus limiting their appeal beyond a faithful, but small core of listeners. Their negative ratings may be high among nonlisteners who reject their on-air messages. And hosts like Howard Stern attract notoriety but are not taken seriously as candidates for elective office.

Despite the high name recognition, talk radio hosts attempting to move into electoral politics will find as many drawbacks as advantages. The exceptions may be those who enter talk radio with a background in political office.

Fulfilling the Policy Agenda

For some talk show hosts, the 1994 elections served as a dramatic turning point to sane government. As conservatives, they applauded the rise of the new Republican Congress. Their role shifted from critic to apologist.

But for others, the election of a new Congress only switched the focus of criticism. The same occurs when a new administration takes office. While President Clinton took a back seat to the 104th Congress, some talk radio hosts quickly moved into the opposition, even to a group whose election they had just encouraged a few months earlier. Hosts such as Chuck Harder view even many Republicans as part of government conspiracies.

Michael Harrison warned that talk radio's ire will be directed at practically anyone in office predicting that "even if the next president of the United States is a squeaky-clean, God-fearing conservative Republican, you can be sure that he or she will continue to take the bashing being endured by Mr. Clinton." This will occur because talk radio reflects a movement that is "disgusted with the kind of president the system continues to serve up."[62]

That tension between the two camps reveals differing visions about the role of talk radio as a political forum. The former camp is seeking alterations in policy through personnel change in government, while the latter camp maintains a deep-seated hostility to all incumbents and their policies. The former group can become satisfied by election results and changes in policies, but the latter will never be satisfied and adopts the permanent and persistent critic role.

The cynicism of the latter camp can lead to governance difficulties. In a precursor to the aftermath of the Oklahoma City bombing, talk radio in Boston in 1989 and 1990 came under criticism for contributing to an atmosphere of "poisoned politics" in Massachusetts.[63] In an unusual response to talk radio content, in a series of articles, the *Boston Globe* attacked talk radio as the cause for an inability for policymakers to govern.[64]

Some talk radio hosts feed the climate of cynicism through unrealistic expectations of government. According to Michael Harrison, intense criticism of those in power will continue "until we have people in government that are really sensitive to the needs of the people and to honesty and truth and to decency."[65]

Despite the difficulty of determining when those objectives have been met, talk radio has no incentive to stop its attacks on politicians. The entertainment value of such criticism argues for continuance, while the content of the message itself conforms to many Americans' cynicism about politics and those who engage in it. Only if the marketing value of cynicism dims will talk radio change. When listeners tire of cynicism, talk radio will switch or die.

There is nothing inherent in new media that leans toward cynicism, despite its supposed populist origins. Cynicism is currently popular. New media could become as much cheerleaders for a popular administration or policy.

Cynicism itself could become a taboo expression. In fact, the tide already may have turned with increasing attention to excesses in the new media. "I talk to enough listeners," explained Michael Harrison, "to know that they say, 'I'm sick of that guy beating up on this guy. I'm sick of hearing that everyday, the same thing.'"[66]

New Media as a Forum for Policy

New media, like traditional media, do not possess enormous, independent power to shape the public's agenda. Although the audience is large and real, it is not necessarily ripe for conversion. As discussed in chapter 7, the new media are not necessarily more persuasive than the traditional news media.

There are significant differences between traditional media and new media in approaches to public policy and hence their impact. New media practitioners are not limited by journalistic standards of objectivity. They are not interested in presenting a neutral perspective of issues or events. This would seem to increase their ability to affect their audiences.

However, new media practitioners are more keenly governed by the dictates of commercialism than are journalists. Talk radio and television hosts with broadcast backgrounds are more likely to have emerged from the entertainment world rather than the news function of broadcasting. Their familiarity with measuring ratings and employing techniques for increasing audiences spills over into their talk format. Also they are not cushioned by layers of editors or news executives as are journalists at major news operations. The profitability of their program is directly laid on their shoulders. In fact, they are often involved in the solicitation of advertisers.

Hence, the new media are more concerned about how their agenda broadens their audience rather than with the political implications of that agenda. This obsession with audience makes it more difficult for them to sustain a campaign aimed at altering public policy unless it serves commercial interests.

It is true that the traditional media's approach to public policy coverage also is tied to public interest. It is rare, for example, for traditional news media outlets to maintain stories that readers have no interest in. However, there are few direct measures of public reaction to news agendas.

Talk radio hosts, on the other hand, can gauge public reaction to their agenda through the open mike method. But most eschew such a format, except occasionally. However, they can determine public interest immediately by the number of calls to the programming. A topic such as a coup in a Latin American nation is likely to attract empty phone lines, while discussion of the O. J. Simpson trial or flag burning will flood the phone bank. So, although the host is the agenda setter, the agenda can be rejected by the audience as uninteresting or unimportant, leaving the host pursuing a lengthy monologue and eventually another occupation.

The host is the agenda setter not only through the topics chosen, but also the guests allowed on the show. Encouraging guests to appear is not a problem for nationally syndicated radio or television talk shows. It has become less problematic even for local hosts of well-established regional stations. The competition for program time has become more intense as various groups have recognized the audience of these programs. While in the past it was common for hosts to choose topics according to who would appear on the program, today the host can pick an issue and usually find the personalities who will speak to it.

However, choice of topic and guests depends to a great extent again on their entertainment value and far less on their political value. Hence, authors of popular new books, whether political or not, are more frequent guests than public officials. "This is the whole thing about taking talk shows as a springboard for policy," complains Seattle host Dave Ross. "There are so many artificialities in it."[67]

The tragedy for the audience may be the expectation that the new media are primarily policy oriented and discuss politics for public service. Speaking of the audience, Victoria Jones of WRC (Washington, D.C.) explained that "it's a show. And it's hard for some people to grasp that. And when some people do grasp it, they actually get quite angry, and they feel they've been conned because they thought it was purely public service."[68]

Conclusion

Popular Voice or Demagogic Tool

The term *new media* will get old quickly, but the new media forms to which the term now applies will not be disappearing. The new media are new, but not ephemeral. As our discussion demonstrates, new media have garnered substantial audiences. Political talk radio has a core of loyal followers; television tabloids, although experiencing ebbs and flows of popularity, command a steady viewership; and Internet use is expanding. Further, the political role of new media is now established and promises to expand. In the future, we can anticipate fresh media trends coinciding with creative applications of innovations in communications technologies.

If the new media look toward a bright future in terms of audience, revenue, and political influence, what does that future hold for a democratic society affected by these mediums? Is it similarly bright? Proponents and critics of new media have contemplated the effects of new media on the body politic. Visions of the future differ widely, as we will discuss shortly.

It is our contention that the new media's populist bent and democratizing influence are more accidental than deliberate, more elusive than real. While there is a potential for new media to facilitate democratic discourse and to foster participant norms, there is no guiding principle that is leading toward these goals. In fact, when the governing ideals are commercial, even democratic by-products should be subject to scrutiny.

Taking Stock of the Evidence

Before we debate what the new media means for democracy, we summarize some of the key findings of our investigation.

A Period of Adolescence

New media are trumpeted as an alternative to traditional media because they are viewed as free from the forces dictating traditional media. They are not bound by even the remnants of a prior code of public service imperatives or professional ethics. They generally do not have the close, symbiotic ties to sources that are characteristic of the mainstream political press. As we have learned, new media impose their own values, which are often far more entertainment oriented than those of the traditional news media. At times, there is an "anything goes" quality to new media. As NPR's Ray Suarez notes, talk radio "doesn't impose journalistic values or thresholds."[1]

New media's novelty, as well as its commercial ambition, has given it a "frontier" quality. There has not been an agreed-upon code of ethics in new media, as was true in the past for journalists, editors, publishers, and broadcast executives. Television news magazines have been criticized for their overwhelming attention to sleaze. Talk radio standards for objectivity or accuracy are low or nonexistent. One host admitted that "the only code of ethics is the one you impose upon yourself, and each of us imposes a different code."[2] In essence, there is no code independent of making a profit. "Talk radio's code of ethics is basically driven by the marketplace," concludes Michael Harrison.[3]

New media are governed as much, if not more, by commercial imperatives than entertainment values. Even when there is an attempt to produce a not-for-profit mass communication medium, it is quickly overtaken by commercial interests. The Internet began its life as a noncommercial entity, but has quickly shed that quality.

New media are still in an adolescent stage in their political development, although the novelty of particular formats may be somewhat short-lived. Thus, it is possible that codes of ethics may appear in the future, as they did with traditional journalism a century ago, although they are not likely to emerge soon. Nor is there much guarantee that ethical guidelines will be followed or enforced. Ethical considerations are eclipsed by economic incentives. In the realm of talk radio, for example, the struggle will be between those who would like to use talk shows to illuminate public discourse, stimulate greater political participation, and achieve public policy change, and those who are interested in making money. The balance is lopsidedly in favor of commerce over discourse, as those who control the airwaves overwhelmingly emphasize profit above all else.

Similar to the attitude of the penny press toward the established partisan press of a previous century, new media have acquired a tone of David versus Goliath. The new media are taking on large, entrenched media organizations and audience habits. This attitude has sparked an "us versus them" approach to politics. The traditional media are treated to verbal barrages by many in the new media. Ironically, the traditional media are the mainstays of information for much new media fare. The new media frequently appropriate their political agenda items from the mainstream press. As we demonstrated in chapter 3, major talk radio hosts rely on the traditional media for their discussion topics. News magazine segments are frequently lengthier accounts of evening new program reports. Even Internet discussion groups primarily take their lead from the mainstream press agenda.

In addition to the anti–old media rhetoric, there is a strong propopulist edge. "We are fine no matter who wins the next election because we serve the little guy and the little guy is awakening to the fact that he has very, very few friends," explains Chuck Harder. "We are his friend. We want the very best for Mr. and Mrs. America."[4] This populist tone, however, may be more self-serving than genuine. Like the entertainment focus, new media populism may well be yet another manifestation of the profit motive.

Influencing Old Media, Elections, and Public Policy

This book has provided substantial empirical evidence describing the new media as they operate today and the actual effects of the new media's role on American politics. We have shown that the new media have reshaped traditional media. Traditional media's presentational style and even news values have changed in response to the existence of competing new media. The new media have sparked debates within the newsroom and the boardroom about what journalism means. The definition of news itself is currently in flux, and the new media have contributed to the confusion.

We have demonstrated that new media now perform roles in electoral campaigns that used to be played by traditional journalists. Talk radio, television news magazines, print tabloids, and electronic town meetings all came of age during the 1992 campaign. The Internet had a similar birth in 1996. These communication forms became components of campaign strategy for reaching voters that will be employed routinely in elections to come. More important, voters do gain information from new media sources. Talk shows, candidate interview programs, and the Internet can be rich sources of more detailed information with less intervention from journalist gatekeepers. As such, the new media contribute to a more "user-friendly" campaign.

We also have shown that the new media have had some impact on policy decisions. Certain policy issues—uncomplicated, nontechnical, bipolar—are more prone to influence by new media because citizens are able to assert a clear vocal position about them.

However, the extent to which these new media formats are enhancing democratic participation—both in electoral campaigns and the policy process—is questionable. As we have demonstrated, certain types of new media, such as talk radio and the Internet, have attracted a politically interested audience. What we do not know is whether new media have produced political interest or whether that interest already existed. It may be a combination of both. But the evidence does not support the theory of a revolution in public participation, a point to which we will return shortly.

One point that bears emphasis is that there is wide variation in new media, and the differences between media are important. The extent of political interest and activity depends on the type of new media we are discussing. Internet users and talk radio listeners are more politically interested than television news magazine viewers. Television is the most passive of these media and is likely to attract a broader audience. Those who are politically interested and motivated to acquire information should be more active in seeking to acquire that information, suggesting that the interested audience is selecting the appropriate medium rather than the medium transforming the audience.

In sum, we have seen a new media that can affect the political agenda, and even the nature of electoral campaigns and public policy. The effects, however, are not as large as either the proponents promote or the critics fear. Depending on the medium, the extent of those effects vary. We have questioned whether new media actually stimulate political activity. That is still unknown. We have shown that the audience for new media formats is not monolithic; as common sense would dictate, audiences vary with the media. We have seen that the greatest effect may well be on a nongovernmental institution, the traditional media. Given these findings, what is the influence of the new media on democracy?

New Media and Democracy

In addressing these questions, it is important to establish what kind of a democratic vision has been associated with speculations about new media. The most optimistic, and perhaps most unrealistic, perspective sees new media as a force in a democratic revolution, with new media stimulating political interest and activism among citizens. Media populism abounds, as ordinary citizens work their way into a political arena that once was primarily the domain of elites. A successful, strong democracy in this vain, as Benjamin Barber observes, is characterized by thoughtful deliberation and debate among citizens.[5] A concrete manifestation of this perspective is offered by James Fishkin's deliberative public opinion polls and the accompanying town meetings that are designed to reinvigorate meaningful interchange.[6]

More modest claims are that new media provide the opportunity for a more informed citizenry. They make politics more interesting and accessible to nonelites. New media formats are conducive to generating lengthier, more detailed, higher quality discussions of issues. They provide information to citizens that they cannot get elsewhere.

Some observers, especially those working in the new media industry, claim that new media have taken democratic discourse in these directions, if the goals have not been met entirely. The 1992 presidential contest, which was characterized by an inordinate amount of public discussion facilitated by new media and was marked by a surge in turnout, is cited as an example of a movement toward greater participatory democracy. By virtue of providing the public an accessible forum for expressing opinions, viewpoints, and discontent, the new media serve democratic ideals. Speaking specifically of talk radio, talk show host Alan Colmes called the medium "a national town meeting where people have an opportunity to just let their frustrations out and vent, and that I think is when the medium performs its highest calling.[7]

W. Russell Neuman takes an optimistic view of a future where computer networks play a meaningful role in fostering democratic ideals. He predicts that over time there will be a horizontal integration of individuals using computer networks that will facilitate discussions among citizens and between citizens and elites.[8] There are some indications that this view is not misguided. For example, online users are having an impact on the journalists who report in cyberspace, which may eventually carry over into other media. Web journalists find that they must respond almost instantaneously to the comments and criticisms of their readers. In a sense, a story is not completed when it is filed by the reporter. Instead, the story becomes the catalyst for an ongoing dialogue.[9] Further, the general public is becoming a greater resource for news stories, as journalists for noncyber media go online with ideas and solicit citizens' reactions.

David Thelen's contention that people want to take part in public dialogue seems to be correct: Journalists report that when requests for information go out to the public the response from average citizens is overwhelming. People in small communities, which tend to be overlooked by national journalists, are making their views and activities known via the Internet. Thus there is some evidence that the public's role in agenda setting may be growing.

The realization of a truly democratic vision of public discourse facilitated via the new media, however, will require a large-scale societal commitment to change. While new media, especially interactive forums, are expanding their horizons in terms of their reach, they are not necessarily fostering more and better democracy.

Roderick Hart contends that the increase in political information available to citizens today has created an illusion. Rather than stimulating participation and interest, the media discourage citizen action. Writing about television, Hart feels that watching governance has become the equivalent of engaging in governance. People now believe that they can fulfill their citizenship obligations by simply monitoring politics. He argues further that politics became more confusing in the television age. Television leaves citizens with the false impression that they are close to politicians, especially as much coverage focuses on the personal side of political figures. Yet, the illusion of proximity to leaders ultimately is unsatisfying, and furthers public political impotence.[10]

It is not unreasonable to argue that politics in the new media age has become even more mystifying and unsettling for the public. The new media do much to further the illusion of a public proximity to poiltics that is far from being realized. The actual effectiveness of talk radio rantings, town meeting discussions, and Internet postings is contingent upon political leaders tuning into these forums, taking the information that the public makes available there seriously, and using it when making decisions. Evidence that this occurs with even modest regularity is far from overwhelming.

David Thelen argues that talk radio and other new media communication forums constitute separate spheres confined to their own participants, and that their effects are limited because they do not permeate society at large.[11] Further, there is a dearth of alternative voices represented in new media. Although there are some exceptions, such as black talk radio, the new media have not worked to noticeably expand the public sphere by giving voice to excluded groups, as our discussion of the new media audiences reveals. New technologies, especially, create accessibility challenges. Online sources and the necessary skills to engage them must be made available to everyone, not just those with economic means. The prospects for accomplishing this are daunting. Some scholars go so far as to contend that new media undermine democratic ideals. As Benjamin Barber observes, the kind of turbulent, virulent, unconsidered drone and banter that is offered by much new media does not come close to fulfilling these criteria.[12] America's new "public square" breeds faction, discontent, and noncooperation.

We began this project with open minds. We intended to leave the question of the democratizing influence of new media open for debate, reasoning that the answer would become clear over time. However, the preponderance of the evidence we collected indicates that the new media are not the new democratic facilitators. Instead, the profit motive that drives all new media and structures the discourse in these channels compromises the new media's ability to provide genuine and meaningful citizenship initiatives. Until these economic imperatives are held in check or counterbalanced, we believe new media are a democratic resource that is not only untapped, by gone awry.

In addition, changes have to be initiated on the cultural front. American society in general, and political discourse in particular, has become increasingly uncivil. Citizens injure and kill one another by aggressive driving, trash one another on tell-all television shows, and deface public property. Political leaders in Congress and the executive branch bicker openly, further promoting the atmosphere of incivility. Similarly, the tone and style of political discourse reflects these aggressive, nasty, intolerant trends. While cultural changes are often slow to take shape, some proactive initiatives are needed to reorient the tenor and content of political discourse. In the new media environment, the impetus lies with all citizens—journalists, leaders, and the public—to work against these trends. Even adopting simple etiquette and practices of common courtesy for talk radio and Internet use might be a step in the right direction. Moving away from attack journalism and a bad news definition of news is another step.

Finally, the technological frontier is filled with new and vastly untapped resources. Educational programs that provide younger generations with technical tools and instill a healthy respect for the political potential of new communications forms will help to make technological transitions in the future less random and more positive. Making the technology and skills widely available can also work to bridge economic, educational, cultural, and ethnic divides.

Reform Movements

The current state of the mass media enterprise has sparked reform movements designed to seek changes in the news product and stop the increased tendency toward tabloidization of news and infotainment politics. These reformers fear that the old media have come to resemble the new media too much. One group of reformers has targeted the media for substantial role change. Represented most visibly by the "civic journalism" movement, the goal is to emphasize the importance of responsibility in reporting, while downplaying the role of entertainment. As Tom Rosenstiel states, "Technology is democratizing the American political landscape. But it is also lowering the standards of American journalism."[13] Other reformers disagree with Rosenstiel about the democratizing effects of new media. They focus on targeting the audience, hoping to create more informed media consumers through education programs.

The goal of the civic journalism movement is to provide the public with more meaningful information about politics while allowing for greater citizen input into the process. Civic journalism assumes that the media are responsible for eroding the public trust and seeks to use the press to restore faith in government. Proponents emphasize that citizens and journalists join forces to foster deliberation about politics in the public sphere. For example, civic journalism advocates believe that deemphasizing horse-race coverage of political campaigns and focusing more directly on issues is one way of working to restore citizen confidence in the political process. In addition, instead of filtering the opinions of politicians through journalists, civic journalists advocate citizen panels, such as those employed during electronic town hall meetings, to ask questions directly to political leaders.[14]

Foundations, most notably the Pew Charitable Trusts, have been providing lucrative grants to media and outside organizations to promote civic journalism. These grants sponsor public radio programs, including National Public Radio; help organize town meetings; and underwrite polling and focus group exercises. Since 1993, the Pew Charitable Trusts have donated approximately $12.2 million to media enterprises, with at lease $6.4 million going to civic journalism projects.[15] Foundations, such as Ford, Kaiser, Knight, and Robert Wood Johnson, also sponsor civic journalism projects.

The civic journalism movement is not without its critics. At best, opponents believe that civic journalism is unnecessary; they argue there is plenty of communication between reporters, political leaders, and average citizens as it is, especially given the rise of new media. Former *New York Times* executive editor Max Frankel questions the need for civic journalism. "I've never understood it. I've read all the theory on it. Some of it sounds like good old fashioned reporting. Some of its sounds like getting in bed with the promotion department, and that's unfortunate. Some of it sounds downright political."[16]

At worse, critics contend that civic journalism represents a serious problem for the ideal of a free and independent media. Some fear that "civic journalism" substitutes ideology for accuracy. *Boston Globe* columnist David Warsh considers the "Outsiders," as he refers to the foundations who fund civic journalism, "a downright ominous threat to the integrity of the press." Warsh contends that civic journalism promotes its own agenda at the expense of the public's interest and that editors' judgment about what the public wants to know is the best aspect of the newspaper business. Under the guise of providing better-quality information, the foundations underwriting civic journalism use the tools of the trade, such as polling exercises, as they seek "to tell editors what readers are thinking." However, it is unclear whether the opinions that are reported are those of the public or what the elites within the foundation would like public opinion to be.[17]

Instead of focusing on the news producers, other reform efforts are aimed at the media consumers, that is, creating more discriminating consumers of media fare. "Media literacy" programs seek to provide audience members with the skills to make informed decisions about what media to consume and how to evaluate media messages that are conveyed to them. The movement, which has been in existence for almost three decades, gained momentum when the surgeon general released a report in 1972 linking television viewing with anti-social behavior. Formal organizations, such as the Center for Media Literacy in Los Angeles, have been formed.

Media literacy programs have been instituted in public middle and high schools across the country. In addition, workshops sponsored by organizations such as the National PTA, the United Methodist Church, the Junior League, and the White House Office of National Drug Control Policy are held for adults. In-school programs and workshops are designed to help people assess the underlying values that drive mass communications, including the profit motive and Hollywood's influence on the media product. The programs examine the stock storytelling techniques employed by the media and the technical tricks of the trade. By revealing trade secrets to the public, media literacy advocates hope to stimulate critical evaluation of media products. In addition, parents are encouraged to take an active role in developing their children's media use habits. They are inspired to watch television with their children and discuss what they see.

Critics of media literacy contend that this movement lets the communications industry off the hook and places all of the responsibility on the audience. They point to the fact that the television and cable industries fund many media literacy projects, including those run by the PTA. The TV industry may be using the media literacy movement as a way of justifying their desire to present what some people consider objectionable material on the air. Further, TV companies oppose the V-CHIP, a special microchip that allows parents to screen programming. Nonetheless, mandatory installation of the V-CHIP and a ratings system for television programs based on violent content has been authorized by Congress and approved by President Clinton.[18]

Also, a spate of media watchdog organizations has formed whose goal is to publicize what they perceive as problems with the press. These organizations can have an ideological agenda, such as the conservative Accuracy in Media, whose newsletter, *Media Watch*, catalogues the liberal media's weekly sins. In addition to keeping lists and writing newsletters, media watchdog organizations sometimes employ other, more aggressive tactics. They will organize boycotts of products or programs based on their objections to programming content.

The Unpredictable Future

As Lawrence Grossman notes, new communications technologies—the electronic republic—are already redefining traditional citizenship and leadership roles.[19] These changes are occurring at an accelerated pace. It is important to carefully consider the consequences of new communications technologies on society, as their implications are wide ranging, consequential, and potentially detrimental to democratic ideals.

While reform movements, such as the ones described above, are accompanied by their own agendas, the specter of reform is a signal to society that there is an opportunity to change the media system for the better. These changes need to occur simultaneously in the economic, cultural, and technological realms.

Optimists anticipate the opportunities for public discouse presented by new communications formats, especially the more interactive ones such as call-in programs and online forums.[20] But others wonder whether the nature of these media prevents such a role from ever evolving. The question is whether the rules of the media game, being in a state of flux, can be rewritten to incorporate a more honestly democratic and populist societal communication flow. Can the new media's role be transformed so that it truly serves democratic goals of providing quality information for citizen decision-making, sparking public awareness, and fostering a political environment which encourages participation? Ultimately the new media and the public will have to answer that question.

Notes

Chapter 1

1. Maureen Grope, "Talk-Radio Hosts Decide to Go Off the Air and On the Ballot," *CQ Weekly Report*, April 9, 1994, pp. 852–854.

2. See, for example, Sam Howe Verhovek, "Out of Politics But Still Talking, Radio Style," *New York Times*, March 13, 1995, p. A1.

3. Louis Bolce, Gerald De Maio, and Douglas Muzzio, "Dial-In Democracy: Talk Radio and the 1994 Election," *Political Science Quarterly*, vol. 111, no. 3, pp. 457–482; Timothy Egan, "Triumph Leaves Talk-Radio Pondering Its Next Targets," *New York Times*, January 1, 1995, p. A1.

4. Steven W. Colford, "On the Electronic Campaign Trail," *Advertising Age*, August 29, 1994, p. 14.

5. Francis X. Clines, "Cool to Dole's Campaigning, Talk Radio Tries to Start Fire, *New York Times*, September 17, 1996, p. A1; and Ellen Ratner, "The Elections and Talk Radio, the Dust Settles," *Talkers*, November 1996, p. 21.

6. James Bennet, "Did You Hear the One about the '96 Campaign?" *New York Times*, July 9, 1996, p. A12.

7. Edmund L. Andrews, "The '96 Race on the Internet: Surfer Beware," *New York Times*, October 23, 1995, p. A1; Mike Allen, "A Web Guide for Election Enthusiasts," *New York Times*, November 4, 1996, p. C7.

8. Kim McAvoy, "White House Woos Local News Outlets," *Broadcasting & Cable*, September 27, 1993, p. 54.

9. See debate transcript at ttp://iir1.uwaterloo.ca/MOTW96/Gore Perot–Debate.html.

10. *Talkers*, mid-Summer 1994, pp. 12–13.

11. Katharine Q. Seeley, "G.O.P. Starts Expanding TV Coverage," *New York Times*, January 3, 1995, p. A17.

12. Egan, "Triumph."

13. Timothy Egan, "On the Angry Airwaves, The Response to the Budget Vote Is Underwhelming," *New York Times*, March 2, 1995, p. B8.

14. Elizabeth Kolbert, "My Next Guest's Policy Opens Today!" *New York Times*, September 10, 1993, p. A18; and Elizabeth Kolbert, "Frank Talk by Clinton to MTV Generation," *New York Times*, April 20, 1994, p. A14.

15. Ann Devroy and Kevin Merida, "Angry President Assails Radio Talk Shows, Press," *Washington Post*, June 25, 1994, p. A1; and President Bill Clinton, Speech to American Association of Community Colleges, Minneapolis, Minnesota, April 23, 1995.

16. Donna Petrozzello, "Talk Still Going Strong," *Broadcasting & Cable*, January 23, 1995, p. 162; and Donna Petrozzello, "Country Still King, But Slipping," *Broadcasting & Cable*, February 5, 1996, p. 41.

17. "Technology in the American Household," Times Mirror Center for the People & the Press, May 1994, p. 4. See American Internet User Survey, http://etrg.findsvp.com/Internet/hightlights.html; and O'Reilly Research, "Defining the Internet Opportunity," http://www.ora.com/research/; and "Internet Market Share Size and Demographics," Survey by Wirthlin Worldwide and WSI, September 1996.

18. Doris A. Graber, "Media as Opinion Resources: Are the 1990s a New Ball Game?" in Barbara Norander and Clyde Wilcox, eds., *Understanding Public Opinion* (Washington, DC: CQ Press, 1997), pp. 69–87.

19. See, for example, Edward W. Chester, *Radio, Television, and American Politics* (New York: Sheed and Ward, 1969); Eric Barnouw, *A Tower in Babel* (New York: Oxford University Press, 1966).

20. See Paul C. Colford, *The Rush Limbaugh Story* (New York: St. Martin's, 1993).

21. Robert Suro, "The Youth Vote; Democrats Court Youngest Voters," *New York Times*, October 30, 1992, p. A18.

22. For recent trends in talk and news radio formats, see recent issues of Andrew Grabois, ed., *Broadcasting and Cable Yearbook* (New Providence, NJ: R. R. Bowker, 1993), p. B-524.

23. Francis Chase, Jr., *Sound and Fury: An Informal History of Broadcasting* (New York: Harper & Brothers, 1942), p. 288.

24. Chase, p. 128.

25. See Charles J. Tull, *Father Coughlin and the New Deal* (Syracuse, NY: Syracuse University Press, 1965); and Alan Brinkley, *Voices of Protest: Huey Long, Father Coughlin, and the Great Depression* (New York: Alfred A. Knopf, 1982).

26. Brinkley, *Voices of Protest*, p. 169.

27. Chase, *Sound and Fury*, p. 121.

28. Bruce McCabe, "AM Radio Heating Up the Airwaves," *Boston Globe*, February 10, 1989, p. 41.

29. Donna Petrozzello, "Talk Still Going Strong," *Broadcasting & Cable*, January 23, 1995, p. 162.

30. McCabe, "AM Radio Heating Up the Airwaves," p. 41.

31. Murray B. Levin, *Talk Radio and the American Dream* (Lexington, MA: D. C. Heath, 1987), p. 15; and Ellen Ratner, "Talk Radio Responds; Our 'Back Fence'" *Los Angeles Times*, April 27, 1995, p. B7.

32. Jerry Springer, a former mayor of Cincinnati, Ohio, briefly appeared as a commentator on a local television news program in that city. He resigned the position amid controversy and the resignation of a popular anchor.

33. Donald Kellerman and Andrew Kohut, "The Press, The People and Politics: Campaign '92," Times Mirror Center for the People & the Press, Survey 12, Part 2, 1992.

34. Tom Rosenstiel, *Strange Bedfellows: How Television and the Presidential Candidates Changed American Politics* (New York: Hyperion, 1994); Diana Owen and Stephen J. Farnsworth, "Public Support for Electronic Town Meetings," paper presented at the Annual Meeting of the Southern Political Science Association, Atlanta, Georgia, November, 1995.

35. Jeffrey B. Abramson and Charles M. Firestone, *Democratic Designs for Electronic Town Meetings* (Washington, DC: The Aspen Institute, 1993).

36. Ted Becker, "Teledemocracy: Gathering Momentum in State and Local Governance," *Spectrum: The Journal of State Government*, vol. 66, Spring 1993, pp. 14–19; Duane Elgin, "Revitalizing Democracy Through Electronic Town Meetings," *Spectrum: The Journal of State Government*, vol. 66, Spring 1993, pp. 6–13.

37. Marc Gunther, "Prime-Time News Blues: Magazine Shows Try to Regroup After a Bad Year," *Washington Post*, September 17, 1995, p. G7.

38. See Gunther, "Prime-Time News Blues," p. G7; and Jeff MacGregor, "Diluting the News Into Soft Half-Truths," *New York Times*, June 4, 1995, p. H25.

39. See, for example, "Justice Marshall's Regrettable Comments," (editorial) *Hartford Current*, July 29, 1990.

40. Marc Levinson, "Rock Around the World," *Newsweek*, April 24, 1995, p. 65.

41. Megan Rosenfeld, "MTV, Facing the Music on Teen Health," *Washington Post*, May 15, 1995, B1, B5.

42. Joel L. Swerdlow, "Information Revolution," *National Geographic*, October 1995, pp. 5–36.

43. This burgeoning political communication and information industry raises issues about regulation that are staggering. For example, should computer network use be monitored during political campaigns? Is there any type of material that should be banned from the Web? If so, who should be responsible for monitoring this information? The answers raise complex constitutional issues. For example, Virginia Tech University disciplined a student for posting a message of hate on a gay men's Internet home page, although this action may violate the free speech provision of the Constitution.

44. Chris McConnell, "High-tech Talking for CNN," *Broadcasting & Cable*, August 22, 1994, p. 37.

45. Michael Schudson, *Discovering the News* (New York: Basic Books, 1978).

46. W. Lance Bennett, *News: The Politics of Illusion* (New York: Longman, 1995).

47. "TV News Viewership Declines," The Pew Research Center for the

People & The Press, May 13, 1996; "Fewer Favor Media Scrutiny of Political Leaders," Washington, DC: The Pew Research Center for the People & The Press, March 21, 1997.

48. Jon Katz, "The Plugged-In Voter: The New News Has Reconnected People and Politics," *Rolling Stone,* December 10–24, 1992, p. 115.

49. Eric Morgenthaler, "Dittoheads All Over Make Rush Limbaugh Superstar of the Right," *Wall Street Journal,* June 28, 1993, p. A1.

50. Peter Viles, "Hosts, Callers Trash Clinton on Talk Radio," *Broadcasting & Cable,* July 12, 1993, p. 43.

51. Booknotes, C-SPAN, December 15, 1996, President Clinton interview with Brian Lamb.

52. For a discussion on public perceptions of media bias, see Kellerman and Kohut, "The People & the Press," p. 28.

53. Adam Shell (ed.), "Perot, Talk Shows and the 'New Media,'" *Public Relations Journal,* vol. 66, September 1992, p. 8.

54. David Brudnoy, Raoul Lowrey Contreras, Blanquita Cullum, Marlin Madoux, Jon Matthews, Mike Rosen, Mike Siegel, Errol Smith, and Armstrong Williams, "Gurus of Gab," *Policy Review,* vol. 69, Summer 1994, p. 65.

55. For a sample of the literature on this interaction, see Timothy Crouse, *The Boys on the Bus* (New York: Ballentine, 1973); Michael Grossman and Martha Joynt Kumar, *Portraying the President: The White House and the News Media* (Baltimore, MD: Johns Hopkins University Press, 1981); Timothy E. Cook, *Making Laws and Making News: Media Strategies in the U.S. House of Representatives* (Washington, DC: Brookings, 1989); and Richard Davis, *Decisions and Images: The Supreme Court and the Press* (Englewood Cliffs, NJ: Prentice Hall, 1994).

56. Diana Owen, "Talk Radio and Evaluations of President Clinton," *Political Communication,* vol. 14, no. 3, July–September, pp. 333–354.

57. "1994—The Year in Review," *Media Monitor,* January/February 1995, p. 2.

58. Howard Kurtz, "Reports on Clinton Pose Quandary for Journalists," *Washington Post,* January 30, 1992, p. A14.

59. Tom Rosensteil, *The Beat Goes On* (New York: The Twentieth Century Fund Press, 1994), p. 37.

60. Rosensteil, p. 37.

61. Rosensteil, p. 38.

62. Andrew Kohut, "The Vocal Minority in American Politics," Times Mirror Center for the People & the Press, July 16, 1993; an analysis of the 1996 American National Election Study reveals that approximately 38 percent of the population tunes in to talk radio.

63. *The 1993 Media Encyclopedia,* vol. 2 (Chicago: The National Research Bureau, 1993).

64. Diedre A. Depke, "Talk-Show Campaigning Helps Candidates Connect," *Business Week,* October 26, 1992, p. 34.

65. Quoted in Christopher Georges, "Mock the Vote," *Washington Monthly,* May 1993, p. 30.

66. John Tierney, "On the Inside, Looking Surprised," *New York Times,* February 22, 1995, p. B1.

67. Benjamin Ginsburg, *The Captive Public,* New York, NY: Basic Books,

1986; Daniel Yankelovich, *Coming to Public Judgment,* Syracuse, NY: Syracuse University Press, 1991.

68. That a similar pattern of participation did not occur during the 1996 presidential contest is attributed to lackluster campaigning, a strong economy, and a host of non-new media related explanations.

Chapter 2

1. Michael Schudson, *Discovering the News* (New York: Basic Books, 1978).

2. Schudson, 1978, p. 35.

3. Schudson, 1978.

4. Michael Schudson, *The Power of News* (Cambridge, MA: Harvard University Press, 1995).

5. Daniel C. Hallin, *The "Uncensored War": The Media and Vietnam* (New York: Oxford, 1986).

6. Daniel Yankelovich, *Coming to Public Judgment* (Syracuse, NY: Syracuse University Press, 1991).

7. "The People and the Press," Times Mirror Center for the People & the Press, January 1986, pp. 14–15.

8. Thomas E. Patterson, *Out of Order* (New York: Knopf, 1993), pp. 79–82.

9. Patterson, 1993, p. 114.

10. James D. Squires, *Read All About It!* (New York: Random House, 1993).

11. Robin D. Shatz, "All News, Almost All Profit, All the Time," *New York Times,* June 24, 1996, p. D7.

12. Squires, *Read All About It!,* p. 6.

13. James Fallows, *Breaking the News* (New York: Pantheon, 1996).

14. Squires, *Read All About It!,* p. 21.

15. Leo Bogart, "The State of the Industry," in Philip S. Cook, Douglas Gomery, and Lawrence W. Lichty, *The Future of News: Television-Newspapers-Wire Services-Newsmagazines* (Washington, DC: The Woodrow Wilson Center Press, 1992).

16. Squires, *Read All About It!*

17. William B. Blankenburg, "Unbundling the Daily Newspaper," in Philip S. Cook, Douglas Gomery, and Lawrence W. Lichty, *The Future of News: Television-Newspapers-Wire Services-Newsmagazines* (Washington, D.C.: The Woodrow Wilson Center Press, 1992).

18. Squires, *Read All About It!*

19. Bogart, "The State of the Industry."

20. Squires, *Read All About It!*

21. Edwin Diamond, *The Media Show* (Cambridge, MA: The MIT Press, 1991).

22. Jon Katz, "Say Goodnight, Dan," *Rolling Stone,* June 27, 1991, pp. 81–84.

23. Diamond, *The Media Show.*

24. Katz, "Say Goodnight, Dan."

25. Lawrence W. Lichty and Douglas Gomery, "More Is Less," in Philip S. Cook, Douglas Gomery, and Lawrence W. Lichty, eds., *The Future of*

News: Television-Newspapers-Wire Services-Newsmagazines (Washington, DC: The Woodrow Wilson Center Press, 1992).

26. An exception to this rule was the FCC's antiobscenity crusade waged largely against talk jock Howard Stern in the late 1980s. The FCC expanded the definition of "indecent" speech to include "patently offensive" discussion of "sexual or excretory activities and organs." Stern's employer, Infinity Entertainment, was assessed fines amounting to $1.7 million. The issue was debated on First Amendment grounds, and Stern gained in popularity. Infinity ultimately paid the fine. See Howard Kurtz, *Hot Air: All Talk All the Time* (New York: Times Books, 1996), pp. 275–278.

27. Kurtz, 1996.

28. Quoted in Bruce McCabe, "AM Radio Heating Up the Airwaves," *Boston Globe*, February 10, 1989, p. 41.

29. Katz, "Say Goodnight, Dan," pp. 81–84.

30. *Statistical Abstract of the United States 1994* (Washington, DC: U.S. Government Printing Office, 1994), p. 1005.

31. Fallows, *Breaking the News.*

32. See Ray Hiebert, Donald Ungarait, and Thomas Bohn, *Mass Media VI* (White Plains, NY: Longman, 1991), chap. 11.

33. Philip S. Cook, Douglas Gomery, and Lawrence W. Lichty, *The Future of News: Television-Newspapers-Wire Services-Newsmagazines* (Washington, D.C.: The Woodrow Wilson Center Press, 1992).

34. William C. Spragens, *Electronic Magazines* (Westport, CT: Praeger, 1995).

35. Susan Herbst, "On Electronic Public Space: Talk Shows in Theoretical Perspective," *Political Communication*, vol. 12, no. 3, July–September 1995, pp. 263–274.

36. Larry J. Sabato, *Feeding Frenzy* (New York: Free Press, 1993).

37. Patterson, *Out of Order.*

38. Astrid Schutz, "Entertainers, Experts, or Public Servants? Politicians' Self-Presentation on Television Talk Shows," *Political Communication*, vol. 12, no. 2, April–June 1995, pp. 211–222.

39. "TV News Viewership Declines," Pew Research Center for the People & the Press, May 13, 1996.

40. "The People, the Press, & Their Leaders 1995," Times Mirror Center for the People & the Press, pp. 9–12; and "The Year in Figures 1994," Times Mirror Center for the People & the Press, 1994, p. 1.

41. "The People, the Press, & Their Leaders 1995," pp. 24–28.

42. Speech at the University of California, Riverside, February 12, 1991. Quoted in Philip Meyer, "The Media Reformation," in Michael Nelson, ed. *The Elections of 1992* (Washington, DC: CQ Press, 1993), p. 91.

43. "The People, the Press, & Their Leaders 1995," p. 15.

44. Raymond L. Carroll, "Blurring Distinctions: Network and Local News," in Philip S. Cook, Douglas Gomery, and Lawrence W. Lichty, eds., *The Future of News: Television-Newspapers-Wire Services-Newsmagazines* (Washington, DC: The Woodrow Wilson Center Press, 1992).

45. "The People & the Press," p. 28.

46. "The People, the Press, & Their Leaders 1995," pp. 24–25.

47. "The People, the Press, & Their Leaders 1995," pp. 35–37.

48. Susan Herbst, "On Electronic Public Space: Talk Shows in Theoretical Perspective," pp. 263–274.

49. Andrew Kohut, "The Age of Indifference: A Study of Young Americans and How They View the News," Times Mirror Center for the People & the Press, June 28, 1990, p. 20.

50. "The Age of Indifference," p. 23.

51. Andrew Kohut, "The Vocal Minority in American Politics," Times Mirror Center for The People & The Press, July 16, 1993.

52. Sonia Livingstone and Peter Lunt, *Talk On Television* (New York: Routledge, 1994).

53. Schudson, *The Power of News*, p. 193.

54. "The Vocal Minority in American Politics."

Chapter 3

1. The nine hosts selected were Jim Bohannon, Alan Colmes, Chuck Harder, Tom Leykis, Rush Limbaugh, G. Gordon Liddy, Stan Majors, Oliver North, and Michael Reagan. These hosts are among the most popular in national syndication. According to one listener survey, Limbaugh alone is listened to by 37 percent of talk radio listeners. Limbaugh, Liddy, Leykis, Harder, North, and Reagan combined are tuned in regularly by 56 percent of listeners according to *Talk Daily*, a talk radio industry publication by Adams Research. Ideological balance was sought in the selection of hosts rather than concentration on the most popular hosts, which would have limited the study to conservatives almost exclusively. Six of the nine hosts are conservative and two (Colmes and Leykis) are left of center. Bohannon is a political centrist. The one-week period studied was June 12–16, 1995. It was designed to be a typical week with no unusual topics. Such a method also would allow comparison across programs of treatment of similar topics and events. The programs were taped off-air from local affiliates with the exception of Colmes's shows, which were obtained from Alan Colmes himself. Two hours of each program were recorded daily. Two exceptions were the Rush Limbaugh program on Friday, June 16, 1995, which was preempted for one of the two hours by the news story of the announcement of the site for the 2002 Winter Olympics, and the Chuck Harder program, part of which was preempted by a sports event on one day.

2. The authors are aware that much of talk radio features content that is not political, such as psychological self-help, social relations, and financial advice. However, when talk radio is discussed in this book, political talk is the focus.

3. Telephone interview with Michael Harrison, editor, *Talkers*, September 18, 1995.

4. Telephone interview with Ray Suarez, National Public Radio host, October 17, 1995.

5. Michael Oneal, "Everybody's Talkin' at Us," *Business Week*, May 22, 1995, p. 106.

6. See, for example, Marjorie Coeyman, "Talk Is Cheap," *Restaurant Business*, July 1, 1995, p. 44.

7. Oneal, "Everybody's Talkin' at Us," p. 106.

8. Donna Petrozzello, "O. J. Doubles Ratings for News/Talk Stations," *Broadcasting & Cable*, May 1, 1995, p. 33.

9. Telephone interview with Michael Harrison, editor of *Talkers*, September 18, 1995.

10. Susan Herbst, "On Electronic Public Space: Talk Shows in Theoretical Perspective," *Political Communication*, vol. 12 (July–September 1995), p. 270.

11. Bill Miller and John McCarty, *You're on Open Line! Inside the Wacky World of Late-Night Talk Radio* (Brattleboro, VT: The Stephen Greene Press, 1978), p. 24.

12. Ellen Ratner, "Talk Radio Responds; Our 'Back Fence,'" *Los Angeles Times*, April 27, 1995, p. B7.

13. Telephone interview with Tom Leykis, October 6, 1995.

14. Howard Kurtz, "Talking Back: Radio Hosts Stir Up Fires and Bask in Newfound Glow," *Washington Post*, June 22, 1996, pp. D1, D4.

15. Kurtz, p. D4.

16. Kurtz, p. D1.

17. Mensah Dean, "Freedom to Speak at Radio Awards," *Washington Times*, June 24, 1996, p. C10.

18. Telephone interview with Alan Colmes, Major Radio Network host, October 4, 1995.

19. Interview with Greg Dobbs KOA (Denver) talk show host, August 22, 1995.

20. Oneal, "Everybody's Talkin' at Us," p. 104.

21. Rush Limbaugh, *The Way Things Ought to Be* (New York: Pocket Books, 1992), p. 21.

22. Rush H. Limbaugh, *See, I Told You So* (New York: Pocket Books, 1993), p. xiv.

23. Adams Research, "Talk Daily 1995 Talk Radio Survey," July/August 1995.

24. Paul Starobin, "Bob Who?" *National Journal*, April 27, 1996, pp. 922–926.

25. Ann Devroy and Kevin Merida, "Angry President Assails Radio Talk Shows, Press," *Washington Post*, June 25, 1994, p. A1.

26. Richard Cohen, "The Salute That Wasn't," *Washington Post*, May 4, 1995, p. A21.

27. Howard Kurtz, *Hot Air: All Talk All the Time* (New York: Times Books, 1996), p. 268.

28. Tom Gorman, "Radio Station Drops Liddy Show, Gets Threats," *Los Angeles Times*, April 27, 1995, p. A16.

29. Tim Weiner, "Oliver North on Airwaves: Definitely Not Modulated," *New York Times*, March 17, 1995, p. A14.

30. Kurtz, *Hot Air*, p. 326.

31. John Tierney, "On the Inside, Looking Surprised," *New York Times*, February 22, 1995, p. A1.

32. Telephone interview with Tom Leykis, Westwood One Network host, October 6, 1995.

33. Quoted in "The Gurus of Gab," *Policy Review*, Summer 1994, pp. 61–62.

34. Marc Cooper, "The Paranoid Style," *The Nation*, April 10, 1995, p. 490.

35. Adams Research, "Talk Daily 1995 Talk Radio Survey," July/August 1995.

36. Telephone interview with Victoria Jones, United Stations Talk Network talk host, November 15, 1995.

37. Interview with Alan Colmes, October 4, 1995

38. The best known nationally syndicated female host, Dr. Laura Schlesinger, is not politically oriented.

39. Interview with Erin Hart, KTLK (Denver) talk host, August 23, 1995.

40. Telephone interview with Victoria Jones, November 15, 1995.

41. Telephone interview with Victoria Jones, November 15, 1995.

42. Telephone interview with Victoria Jones, November 15, 1995.

43. Telephone interview with Judy Jarvis, Talk America Radio Network host, September 18, 1995.

44. William E. Schmidt, "Black Talk Radio: A Vital Force Is Emerging to Mobilize Opinion," *New York Times*, March 31, 1989, p. A1.

45. "The Avenger," *People*, December 12, 1994, p. 105; and Joseph Kearned, "Talk Radio's 'Black Avenger' Ken Hamblin," *Destiny Magazine*, (April 1994): 15–16.

46. Amy Bernstein, "Black Conservatives Will Find an Audience," *U.S. News & World Report*, December 26–January 2, 1995, p. 75.

47. Telephone interview with Alan Colmes, Major Radio Network host, October 4, 1995.

48. Telephone interview with Victoria Jones, November 15, 1995.

49. Kurtz, *Hot Air*, pp. 327–328.

50. Kurtz, *Hot Air*, p. 331.

51. Interview with Dave Ross, KIRO (Seattle) talk host, September 8, 1995.

52. Quoted in Kurtz, *Hot Air*, p. 325.

53. Kurtz, *Hot Air*, p. 286.

54. Michael Wilke, "Liberal Talk Radio Lacking Sponsors," *Advertising Age*, January 16, 1995, p. 25.

55. Steve Bates, "Wilder's Radio Show Going Off the Air," *Washington Post*, August 23, 1995, p. D3.

56. Donna Petrozzello, "Conservative Talk Shows Drown Out Liberal Voice," *Broadcasting & Cable*, June 19, 1995, p. 22.

57. Wayne Munson, *All Talk: The Talk Show in Media Culture* (Philadelphia: Temple University Press, 1993), p. 100.

58. Interview with Dave Ross, KIRO (Seattle) talk host, September 8, 1995.

59. Interview with Greg Dobbs, KOA (Denver) talk host, August 22, 1995.

60. Ted Byrne, "We Buy Advertising, We Don't Buy Controversy," *Talkers Magazine*, March 1996, p. 15.

61. Telephone interview with Judy Jarvis, September 18, 1995.

62. Telephone interview with Tom Leykis, Westwood One Network host, October 6, 1995.

63. Telephone interview with Michael Harrison, editor, *Talkers*, September 18, 1995.

64. Interview with Dave Ross, KIRO (Seattle) talk host, September 8, 1995.

65. Interview with Greg Dobbs, KOA (Denver) talk host, August 22, 1995.

66. Margaret Carlson, "My Dinner with Rush," *Time*, January 23, 1995, p. 26.

67. Telephone interview with Victoria Jones, November 15, 1995.

68. Interview with Dave Ross, KIRO (Seattle) talk host, September 8, 1995.

69. Interview with Erin Hart, KTLK (Denver) talk host, August 23, 1995.

70. Munson, *All Talk*, p. 150.

71. Interview with Erin Hart, August 23, 1995.

72. Mike Hoyt, "Talk Radio: Turning Up the Volume," *Columbia Journalism Review*, November/December 1992, p. 45.

73. Limbaugh, *The Way Things Ought to Be*, pp. 27–28.

74. Quoted in Brudnoy et al., "The Gurus of Gab," pp. 62.

75. Quoted in Brudnoy et al., "The Gurus of Gab," p. 60.

76. Limor Peer and Susan Herbst, "Talk Shows as Electronic Salons: The Nature of Discourse in a Rational Public Sphere," paper presented at the annual meeting of the American Political Science Association, Chicago, IL, August 30–September 3, 1995.

77. Telephone interview with Michael Harrison, September 18, 1995.

78. Murray B. Levin, *Talk Radio and the American Dream* (Lexington, MA: D. C. Heath, 1987), p. 17.

79. Quoted in Howard Fineman, "The Power of Talk," *Newsweek*, February 8, 1993, pp. 24–25.

80. Interview with Dave Ross, KIRO (Seattle) talk show host, September 8, 1995.

81. Interview with Greg Dobbs, KOA (Denver) talk show host, August 22, 1995.

82. Limbaugh, *The Way Things Ought to Be*, p. ix.; and Limbaugh, *See, I Told You*, p. 105.

83. Telephone interview with Michael Harrison, editor, *Talkers*, September 18, 1995.

84. Telephone interview with Ray Suarez, October 17, 1995.

85. Interview with Mike Siegel, former, KVI (Seattle) talk show host, September 8, 1995.

86. Telephone interview with Alan Colmes, October 4, 1995.

87. Interview with Greg Dobbs, August 22, 1995.

88. Telephone interview with Bruce Dumont, "Beyond the Beltway" host, September 21, 1995.

89. Telephone interview with Ray Suarez, October 17, 1995.

90. Telephone interview with Victoria Jones, November 15, 1995.

91. Donna Petrozzello, "Talk Still Going Strong," *Broadcasting & Cable*, January 23, 1995, p. 162.

92. Interview with Mike Rosen, KOA (Denver) talk host, August 23, 1995.

93. Telephone interview with Charles Brennan, KMOX (St. Louis) talk host, November 15, 1995.

94. Telephone interview with Bruce Dumont, September 21, 1995.

95. Telephone interview with Tom Leykis, Westwood One Network host, October 6, 1995.

96. Telephone interview with Judy Jarvis, September 18, 1995.

97. Telephone interview with Victoria Jones, November 15, 1995.

98. Telephone interview with Charles Brennan, November 15, 1995.

99. Telephone interview with Charles Brennan, November 15, 1995.

100. See Pat Aufderheide and Jeffrey Chester, "Talk Radio: Who's Talking? Who's Listening?" Benton Foundation Strategic Communications for Nonprofits, 1992.

101. Limbaugh, *See I Told You*, p. 3.

102. Telephone interview with Charles Brennan, November 15, 1995.

103. Telephone interview with Michael Harrison, September 18, 1995.

104. Interview with Greg Dobbs, KOA (Denver) talk host, August 22, 1995.

105. Interview with Mike Rosen, August 23, 1995.

106. Bruce W. Marr, "Talk Radio Programming," in Susan Tyler Eastman et al., eds., *Broadcast/Cable Programming*, 3d ed. (Belmont, CA: Wadsworth, 1989), pp. 451–452.

107. Interview with Mike Rosen, KOA (Denver) talk host, August 23, 1995.

108. Miller and McCarty, *You're on Open Line!*, p. ix.

109. Munson, *All Talk*, p. 95.

110. Donna Petrozzello, "ABC Drops Hightower Show," *Broadcasting & Cable*, October 2, 1995, p. 39.

111. Telephone interview with Charles Brennan, November 15, 1995.

112. Telephone interview with Charles Brennan, November 15, 1995.

113. Telephone interview with Charles Brennan, November 15, 1995.

114. Limbaugh, *The Way Things Ought to Be*, p. 21.

115. Telephone interview with Michael Harrison, September 18, 1995.

116. Andrew Kohut, "The Vocal Minority in American Politics," Times Mirror Center for the People & the Press, July 16, 1993.

117. See, for example, *Talkers Magazine*, October 1995, p. 7; Adams Research, *Talk Daily* July/August 1995 Survey; and C. Richard Hofstetter, "Situational Involvement and Political Mobilization: Political Talk Radio and Political Action," paper presented at the annual meeting of the Midwest Political Science Association, Chicago, IL, April 18–20, 1996.

118. See Kohut, "The Vocal Minority in American Politics," and Susan Herbst, "On Electronic Public Space: Talk Shows in Theoretical Perspective," *Political Communication,* vol. 12 (July–September 1995), 267.

119. Copy in author's possession.

120. Telephone interview with Victoria Jones, November 15, 1995.

121. Telephone interview with Tom Leykis, October 6, 1995.

122. Marr, "Talk Radio Programming," p. 454.

123. Interview with Mike Rosen, August 23, 1995.

124. Telephone interview with Blanquita Cullum, nationally syndicated host, October 6, 1995.

125. Interview with Greg Dobbs, August 22, 1995.

126. Munson, *All Talk*, p. 47.

127. Telephone interview with Michael Harrison, September 18, 1995.

128. Interview with Dave Ross, KIRO(Seattle) talk show host, September 8, 1995.

129. Interview with Mike Rosen, KOA (Denver) talk show host, August 23, 1995.

130. Interview with Mike Rosen, August 23, 1995.

131. Ratner, "Talk Radio Responds; Our 'Back Fence'"; and Interview with Ken Hamblin, nationally syndicated talk show host, August 22, 1995.

132. Kurtz, *Hot Air*, p. 371.

133. Alan Dershowitz, "My First Amendment Battle with WABC," *Talkers*, April 1996, p. 1.

134. Quoted in Brudnoy et al., "The Gurus of Gab," 60.

135. Telephone interview with Alan Colmes, October 4, 1995.

136. Interview with Ken Hamblin, August 22, 1995.

137. Interview with Erin Hart, KTLK (Denver) talk show host, August 23, 1995.

Chapter 4

1. Neil Postman, *Amusing Ourselves to Death* (New York: Viking Penguin, 1985).

2. Ron Dorfman, "Peeping Watchdogs," *The Quill*, June 1987, pp. 14–16.

3. Donald L. Shaw and John W. Slater, "In the Eye of the Beholder? Sensationalism in American Press News, 1820–1860," *Journalism History*, vol. 12, nos. 3–4, Winter–Autumn 1985, pp. 86–91.

4. Michael Schudson, *Discovering the News* (New York: Basic Books, 1978).

5. Sue Hubbell, "Rare Glimpse Inside Tabloid World Reveals Editor is Mad Dog," *Smithsonian*, October 1993, pp. 71–80.

6. Hubbell, "Rare Glimpse Inside Tabloid World"; Elizabeth S. Bird, *For Enquiring Minds* (Knoxville, TN: University of Tennessee Press, 1992).

7. John D. Stevens, "Sensationalism in Perspective," *Journalism History*, vol. 12, nos. 3–4, Winter–Autumn 1985, p. 78.

8. C. Richard Hofstetter and David M. Dozier, "Useful News, Sensational News: Quality, Sensationalism and Local TV News," *Journalism Quarterly*, vol. 63, Winter 1986, pp. 815–820, 853.

9. Hofstetter and Dozier, "Useful News, Sensational News"; William C. Adams, "Local Public Affairs Content of TV News," *Journalism Quarterly*, vol. 55, 1978, pp. 690–695; Jung S. Ryu, "Public Affairs and Sensationalism in Local TV News Programs," *Journalism Quarterly*, vol. 59, 1982.

10. Shaw and Slater, "In the Eye of the Beholder?" 1985, pp. 86–91.

11. Shaw and Slater, 1985, pp. 86–91.

12. Warren Franke, "Sensationalism and the Development of 19th-Century Reporting: The Broom Sweeps Sensory Details," *Journalism History*, vol. 12, nos. 3–4, Winter–Autumn 1985, pp. 80–85.

13. Bruce Selcraig, "Buying News," *Columbia Journalism Review*, July/August 1994, pp. 45–46.

14. Jeffrey Toobin, "Buying Headlines," *The Quill*, November/December 1994, pp. 21–23.

15. Hubbell, "Rare Glimpse Inside Tabloid World," pp. 71–80.

16. Christopher Clausen, "Reading the Supermarket Tabloids," *New Leader*, September 7, 1992, pp. 10–13.

17. Hubbell, "Rare Glimpse Inside Tabloid World," 1993, pp. 71–80.

18. Hubbell, 1993, pp. 71–80.

19. Clausen, "Reading the Supermarket Tabloids," pp. 10–13.

20. Hubbell, "Rare Glimpse Inside Tabloid World," pp. 71–80.

21. "Who Reads Supermarket Tabs?" *American Journalism Review*, vol. 15, September 1993, pp. 14–15.

22. Clausen, "Reading the Supermarket Tabloids," 1992, p. 13.

23. Clausen, 1992, p. 13.

24. Hubbell, "Rare Glimpse Inside Tabloid World," pp. 71–80.

25. "2-Headed Tots, Nazi Astronauts & Gennifer," *U.S. News and World Report*, February 10, 1995, p. 16.

26. Clausen, "Reading the Supermarket Tabloids," pp. 10–13.

27. Howard Kurtz, "Tabs Gag Employees," *Washington Post*, May 3, 1996, pp. D1, D3.

28. Kurtz, p. D3.

29. Clausen, "Reading the Supermarket Tabloids," pp. 10–13.

30. John Morton, "Feeding Readers' Tabloid Appetites," *American Journalism Review*, vol. 16, September 1994, p. 60.

31. Jonathan Alter, "America Goes Tabloid," *Newsweek*, December 26, 1995, pp. 34–36.

32. Teresa Keller, "Trash TV," *Journal of Popular Culture*, vol. 26, no. 4, Spring 1993, pp. 195–206.

33. Erica Goode and Katia Hetter, "The Selling of Reality," *U.S. News and World Report*, July 25, 1994, pp. 49–56.

34. Edwin Diamond, "TV's Lower Common Denominator," *New York*, March 14, 1994, pp. 18–20.

35. Richard Zoglin, "A Walk on the Seamy Side," *Time*, October 31, 1988, p. 78; Harry F. Waters, "Trash TV," *Newsweek*, November 14, 1988, pp. 72–78.

36. Martha Brant and Nina Archer Biddle, "Cheap Thrills: Where Less is More," *Newsweek*, April 11, 1994, pp. 64–65.

37. Ernest Sander, "A TV Tabloid Vows to Clean Up Its Act," *Columbia Journalism Review*, vol. 16, May 1994, p. 15.

38. "A Current Affair" was not renewed for the 1996–97 season. This flagship tabloid television program was squeezed out by the competition glut.

39. Keller, "Trash TV," pp. 196–206.

40. Sander, "A TV Tabloid Vows to Clean Up Its Act," p. 15.

41. Keller, "Trash TV," pp. 195–206.

42. Jeffrey Ressner, "Easing the Sleaze," *Time*, December 6, 1993, pp. 72–74.

43. Keller, "Trash TV," pp. 195–206.

44. James Fallows, *Breaking the News* (New York: Pantheon Books, 1996).

45. Elayne Rapping, "Tabloid TV and Social Reality," *Progressive*, August 1992, pp. 35–37.

46. Stevens, "Sensationalism in Perspective," p. 78.

47. Joshua Gamson, "Incredible News," *American Prospect*, Fall 1994, pp. 28–35.

48. Philip Weiss, "Bad Rap for TV Tabs," *Columbia Journalism Re-*

view, May/June, 1989, pp. 38–42; Brant and Archer, "Cheap Thrills," pp. 64–65.

49. "Who Reads Supermarket Tabs?" p. 15.

50. Keller, "Trash TV," pp. 195–206.

51. Weiss, "Bad Rap for TV Tabs," p. 38.

52. Larry Reibstein, "The Battle of the TV News Magazine Shows," *Newsweek*, April 11, 1994, pp. 61–65; Brant and Archer Biddle, "Cheap Thrills," pp. 64–65.

53. Mike Tharp and Betsy Streisand, "Tabloid TV's Blood Lust," *U.S. News and World Report*, July 25, 1994, pp. 47–48.

54. Alter, "America Goes Tabloid," pp. 34–36.

55. Christopher Hanson, "The Triumph of Fuzz and Wuzz," *Columbia Journalism Review*, November/December 1994, p. 23.

56. Waters, "Trash TV," p. 75.

57. Gamson, "Incredible News," pp. 28–35.

58. Goode and Hetter, "The Selling of Reality," pp. 49–55.

59. Tharp and Streisand, "Tabloid TV's Blood Lust," pp. 47–48.

60. Zoglin, "A Walk on the Seamy Side," p. 78.

61. Keller, "Trash TV," pp. 195–206.

62. Howard Kurtz, "Violence on TV: A Lot of It Is on the Network News," *The Washington Post*, August 12, 1997, p. D1.

63. Rapping, "Tabloid TV and Social Reality," pp. 35–37.

64. Goode and Hetter, "The Selling of Reality," 1994, pp. 49–56.

65. Goode and Hetter, 1994 pp. 49–56.

66. Waters, "Trash TV," pp. 72–78.

67. Diamond, "TV's Lower Common Denominator," pp. 18–19.

68. Jonathan Alter, "It Isn't All Junk Food," *Newsweek*, April 11, 1994, p. 66.

69. Weiss, "Bad Rap for TV Tabs," pp. 38–42.

70. Peter Shaw, "Reliable Sources," *National Review*, June 21, 1993, pp. 63–64.

71. Alter, "America Goes Tabloid," pp. 34–36.

72. John D. Stevens, "Social Utility of Sensational News: Murder and Divorce in the 1920s," *Journalism Quarterly*, vol. 62, no. 1, Spring 1985, pp. 53–58; Jack Levin, Amita Mody-Desbareau, and Arnold Arluke, "The Gossip Tabloid As Agent of Social Control," *Journalism Quarterly*, vol. 65, no. 2, Summer 1988, pp. 514–517.

73. Goode and Hetter, "The Selling of Reality," pp. 49–56.

74. Alter, "America Goes Tabloid," pp. 34–36.

75. Stevens, "Social Utility of Sensational News," pp. 53–58; Stevens, "Sensationalism in Perspective," p. 78.

76. Tom Rosenstiel, "U.S. Press: Paying for Its Sins," *The Washington Post*, September 14, 1997, C3.

77. Max Hastings, "The British Press: Sinning for Its Pay," *The Washington Post*, September 14, 1997, C3.

78. Jonathan Alter, "Dying for the Age of Diana," *Newsweek*, September 8, 1997, p. 39

79. Howard Kurtz, "Now Here's a News Bite: Mainstream Media Leap at Marv Albert Trial," *The Washington Post*, September 24, 1997, D1, D4.

80. Rae Corelli and William Lowther, "Packaging the News," *Maclean's*, October 30, 1989, pp. 82–83.

Chapter 5

1. For a brief discussion of the history of the Internet, see Robert E. Kahn, "The Role of the Government in the Evolution of the Internet," in National Academy of Engineering, *Revolution in the U.S. Information Structure* (Washington, DC: National Academy Press, 1995), pp. 13–24; and *Realizing the Information Future: The Internet and Beyond* (Washington, DC: National Academy Press, 1994), pp. 20–30.

2. The CommerceNet/Nielsen Internet Demographics Survey, Executive Summary. Survey results are available at http://www.nielsenmedia.com; and "6th WWW User Survey," Graphic, Visualization, & Usability Center, Georgia Tech University, December 1996.

3. "6th WWW User Survey," Graphic, Visualization, & Usability Center, Georgia Tech University, December 1996, at http://www.cc.gatech.edu/gvu/user–surveys/survey-10-1996/#exec.

4. "Internet Market Share Size and Demographics," A Survey by Wirthlin Worldwide and WSI, September 1996.

5. See CyberAtlas Market Size at http://www.cyberatlas.com/market.html.

6. "6th WWW User Survey," Graphic, Visualization, & Usability Center, Georgia Tech University, December 1996.

7. Peter H. Lewis, "Follow-Up Survey Reports Growth in Internet Users," *New York Times*, August 14, 1996, p. A20.

8. Quoted in Graeme Browning, "Return to Sender," *National Journal*, April 1, 1995, p. 795.

9. Joe Abernathy, "Casting the Internet; A New Tool for Electronic News Gathering," *Columbia Journalism Review*, January/February 1993, p. 56.

10. Telephone interview with Charles D. Benjamin, White House associate director of Information Systems and Technology Division, August 18, 1996.

11. *Congressional Record*, January 4, 1995, vol. 141, no 1, p. 1400.

12. Mark Lewyn and John Carey, "Will America Log on to Internewt?" *Business Week*, December 5, 1994, p. 38.

13. Kevin W. Hula, "Linking the Network: Interest Group Electronic Coalitions in the Policy Process," paper presented at the annual meeting of the Southern Political Science Association, November 1–4, 1995, Tampa, Florida.

14. Hula, p. 15.

15. Hula, p. 15.

16. The Web site lists were Project Vote Smart 96 at http://www.votesmart.org/campaign–96/cong–links.html; GTE.Net at http://www.gte.net/election96/; and Campaign 96 Online at http://96.com/cc.htm. Duplicate listings across the three lists were deleted.

17. Edmund L. Andrews, "The '96 Race on the Internet: Surfer Beware," *New York Times*, October 23, 1995, p. A1.

18. Walter B. Mossberg, "Accountability Is Key to Democracy In the On-Line World," *Wall Street Journal*, January 26, 1995, p. B1.

19. Gary Chapman, "Sending a Message to the White House," *Technology Review*, July 1993, p. 16.

20. Chapman, p. 17.

21. Lorien Golaski, "Taking the Cyber Plunge: White House Sets Good Example," *Business Marketing*, April 1995, p. T-2.

22. Edmund L. Andrews, "The 104th Congress: The Internet; Mr. Smith Goes to Cyberspace," *New York Times*, January 6, 1995, p. A22.

23. Browning, "Return to Sender," 1995, p. 794.

24. Browning, 1995 p. 797.

25. Quoted in "What If They're Right," *Economist*, February 12, 1994, p. 56.

26. Mossberg, "Accountability Is Key."

27. The CommerceNet/Nielsen Internet Demographics Survey, Executive Summary. Survey results are available at http://www.nielsenmedia.com./news/hotech-summary.html.

28. David Kirkpatrick, "As the Internet Sizzles, Online Services Battle for Stakes," *Fortune*, May 1, 1995, p. 89.

29. "6th WWW User Survey," Graphic, Visualization, & Usability Center, Georgia Tech University, December 1996, at http://www.cc.gatech.edu/gvu/user-surveys/survey-10-1996/#exec.; and SurveyNet, October 1996, at http://www.survey.net/info.htm.

30. See All Things Political at http://www.federal.com/Political. html; and "Survey Profiles Voters' Use of Media," Media Studies Center, Freedom Forum News Advisory at http://www.mediastudies.org/new.html. For an opposing view, see Douglas Muzzio and David Birdsell, "The 1996 'Net Voter," *The Public Perspective*, December/January 1997, pp. 42–43.

31. Kirkpatrick, "As the Internet Sizzles," p. 89.

32. Steve Lohr, "Adapting 60's Sensibilities to the Internet," *New York Times*, June 19, 1995, p. D3.

33. Gene S. Bartlow, "Associations and the Internet," *Association Management*, June 1995, p. 78.

34. Hula, "Linking the Network," p. 18.

35. Golaski, "Taking the Cyber Plunge."

Chapter 6

1. James G. Webster, "Audience Behavior in the New Media Environment," *Journal of Communication*, vol. 36, Summer 1996, pp. 77–91.

2. For an overview of the ways that the concept of the audience has been treated in classic mass communication research, see Shearon A. Lowery and Melvin L. DeFleur, *Milestones in Mass Communication Research*, 3d ed. (White Plains, NY: Longman Publishers, 1995).

3. Dennis McQuail and Sven Windahl, *Communication Models for the Study of Mass Communications* (New York: Longman, 1981); Robert Escarpit, "The Concept of 'Mass'," *Journal of Communication*, vol. 1, 1977, pp. 44–47.

4. Dean E. Hewes and Sally Planalp, "The Individual's Place in Communication Science," in Charles R. Berger and Steven H. Chaffee, eds., *Handbook of Communication Science* (Newbury Park, CA: Sage, 1987), pp. 146–

183; Jay G. Blumler, "The Social Character of Media Gratifications," in Karl Erik Rosengren, Lawrence A. Wenner, and Philip Palmgreen, *Media Gratifications Research: Current Perspectives* (Beverly Hills, CA: Sage Publications, 1985), pp. 41–59.

5. Blumler, "The Social Character of Media Gratifications."

6. Karl Erik Rosengren and Sven Windahl, "Mass Media Consumption as a Functional Alternative," in Denis McQuail, ed., *Sociology of Mass Communications* (Baltimore, MD: Penguin Books, 1972), pp. 166–194; Jack M. McLeod, Gerald M. Kosicki, and Douglas M. McLeod, "The Expanding Boundaries of Political Communication Effects," in Jennings Bryant and Dolf Zillman, eds., *Media Effects: Advances in Theory and Research* (Hillsdale, NJ: Lawrence Erlbaum Associates, 1994), pp. 123–162.

7. Michael Traugott, Adam Berinsky, Katherine Cramer, Margaret Howard, Russell Mayer, Harvey Prieto Schuckman, David Tewksbury, and Margaret Young, "The Impact of Talk Radio on Its Audience," paper presented at the Annual Meeting of the International Society of Political Psychology, Washington, DC, July 1996.

8. The wording of the questions tapping media exposure differ, even within surveys. We have tried to be as consistent as possible in identifying the people we consider to be regular audience members. We employ the response category that indicates the most frequently or highest level of exposure.

9. "TV News Viewership Declines," The Pew Research Center for the People & The Press, May 13, 1996. A study conducted by the Roper Center for Public Opinion Research in January 1977 indicates that 25 percent of the public listens to a talk radio program at least once a week.

10. "New Attracts Most Internet Users," The Pew Research Center for the People & The Press, December 16, 1996.

11. Judith Valente, "Do You Believe What Newspeople Tell You?" *Parade Magazine*, March 2, 1997, pp. 4–6.

12. "TV News Viewership Declines," The Pew Research Center for the People & The Press, May 13, 1996.

13. Ronald Berman, *How Television Sees Its Audience* (Newbury Park, CA: Sage, 1987).

14. George Comstock, *Television in America* (Beverly Hills, CA: Sage, 1980).

15. "TV News Viewership Declines," The Pew Research Center for the People & The Press, May 13, 1996.

16. Roper Center for Public Opinion Research survey, January 1997.

17. "Press 'Unfair, Inaccurate and Pushy,'" The Pew Research Center for the People & The Press, March 21, 1997.

18. Pew Research Center, May 13, 1996.

19. Table 6B presents the rotated factor loadings for the analysis. A principal components analysis with a varimax rotation was performed. Loadings indicate the degree to which a variable is associated with a particular factor. We have followed convention and consider loadings of .300 or better to indicate that a variable is part of a particular factor.

20. The figure for print tabloids may be inflated, as these people may consider their reading of tabloids as part of their daily newspaper habit.

21. It may be the case that people who listen to talk radio regularly are not distinguishing between talk programs with a call-in component and news radio programs, even though the survey questions make this distinction. Thus the reported proportion of talk radio listeners who also regularly listen to radio news may be exaggerated.

22. Howard Kurtz, "Tuning Out Traditional News: With More Coverage Available, the Public Seems Interested In Less," *Washington Post*, May 15, 1995, pp. A1, A6.

23. Joseph Turow, "Talk Radio as Interpersonal Communication," *Journal of Broadcasting*, vol. 18, 1974, pp. 171–179; Jeffrey Bierig and John Dimmick, "The Late Night Radio Talk Show as Interpersonal Communication, *Journalism Quarterly*, vol. 56, 1979, pp. 92–99; Harriet Trammers and Leo W. Jeffres, "Talk Radio–Form and Companion," *Journal of Broadcasting*, vol. 27, 1983, pp. 297–300; Cameron B. Armstrong and Alan M. Rubin, "Talk Radio as Interpersonal Communication," *Journal of Communication*, vol. 39, 1989, pp. 84–94.

24. Diana Owen, "Who's Talking? Who's Listening? The New Politics of Radio Talk Shows," in Stephen C. Craig, ed., *Broken Contract: Changing Relationships Between Americans and Their Government* (Boulder, CO: Westview, 1996), pp. 127–146.

25. Alyssa L. Fallwell, "The Politics of Talk Radio: Differences Between Public and Commercial Stations," Washington, D.C.: Georgetown University (unpublished manuscript).

26. The Pew Research Center survey did not ask specifically about talk programs on NPR, but instead asked about listening to NPR in general. In spite of the limitations of this variable, it provides us with some indication of the differences between radio show listeners.

27. Traugott et al., "The Impact of Talk Radio on Its Audience," 1996.

28. A study of talk radio conducted by the Annenberg Public Policy Center found that 18 percent of the adult population listens to at least one call-in political talk program at least twice a week. Four percent of these listeners listen to Rush Limbaugh and at least one other host, while 7 percent listen to only Limbaugh. (Joseph N. Cappella, Joseph Turow, and Kathleen Hall Jamieson, "Call-In Political Talk Radio: Background, Content, Audiences, Portrayal in Mainstream Media," The Annenberg Public Policy Center of the University of Pennsylvania, 1996.)

29. Cynthia M. Long, "The Roles Assigned to Females and Males in Non-Music Radio Programming, *Sex Roles*, vol. 22, nos. 9/10, pp. 661–668.

30. Owen, "Who's Talking? Who's Listening?"

31. Richard Corliss, "Look Who's Talking," *Time*, January 23, 1995, pp. 22–25; James Hamilton, "Bull Rush," *Vanity Fair*, May 1992, pp. 155–160, 205–209.

32. Blayne Cutler, "Mature Audiences Only," *American Demographics*, October 1989, pp. 20–26.

33. William E. Schmidt, "Black Talk Radio: A Vital Force is Emerging to Mobilize Opinion," *New York Times*, March 31, 1989, pp. A1, A12; James Warren, "Talk About Clout: When Black Talk Radio Speaks, Chicago's Politicians Listen," *Chicago Tribune*, March 23, 1989, sec. 5, pp. 1, 15.

34. Owen, "Who's Talking? Who's Listening?"

35. The data for talk shows in general and "Larry King Live" are from the Americans Talk Security Foundation survey of 1,000 adults conducted by National Opinion Surveys in March 1993, which is available through the Roper Center. The questions are not direct measures of media use, but indicate how positively disposed people are toward viewing these shows. The data for daytime talk shows were collected by the Pew Research Center, May 1996.

36. Jeffrey B. Abramson, F. Christopher Arterton, and Gary R. Orren, *The Electronic Commonwealth* (New York: Basic Books, 1988).

37. Judith Miller, "But Can You Dance to It? MTV Turns to News," *New York Times*, October 11, 1992, p. 31.

38. Miller, p. 31.

39. Analysis of Pew Research Center, May 1996 survey data.

40. Peter H. Lewis, "Follow-Up Survey Reports Growth in Internet Users," *New York Times*, August 14, 1996, p. 20.

41. "News Attracts Most Internet Users," The Pew Research Center for the People & The Press, December 16, 1996. Data from this 1996 Pew Research Center Survey of Technology was analyzed to create Table 6–11 and the related demographic analysis. The study was a reinterview telephone survey of 1,003 adults who were identified in previous surveys as online users. The questionnaire was administered between October 21 and October 31, 1996.

42. Paul F. Lazarsfeld, *Radio and the Printed Page* (New York: Duell, Sloan, and Pearce, 1940); Herta Herzog, "What Do We Really Know About Daytime Serial Listeners?" in Paul F. Lazarsfeld and Frank N. Stanton, eds., *Radio Research 1942–1943* (New York: Duell, Sloan, and Pearce, 1944), pp. 3–33; Bernard Berelson, "What 'Missing the Newspaper' Means," in Paul F. Lazarsfeld and Frank N. Stanton, eds., *Communication Research 1948–1949* (New York: Harper, 1949), pp. 111–129.

43. Wilbur Schramm, Jack Lyle, and Edwin Parker, *Television in the Lives of Our Children* (Palo Alto, CA: Stanford University Press, 1961); Elihu Katz, Michael Gurevitch, and Hadasah Haas, "On the Use of Mass Media for Important Things," *American Sociological Review*, vol. 38, 1973, pp. 164–181.

44. Elihu Katz, Jay G. Blumler, and Michael Gurevitch, "Utilization of Mass Communication by the Individual," in Jay G. Blumler and Elihu Katz, eds., *The Uses of Mass Communications: Current Perspectives on Gratifications Research* (Beverly Hills, CA: Sage, 1979), p. 20.

45. S. Finn, "Television Addiction? An Evaluation of Four Competing Media Use Models," *Journalism Quarterly*, vol. 69, pp. 422–435.

46. The uses and gratifications paradigm is not without its critics. Many of the criticisms of the approach are linked to perceived vagaries in the theoretical underpinnings, concepts, and indicators. For example, uses and gratifications approaches are not linked to any specific sociological or psychological theory, such as Freudian psychology. The categories of needs, such as surveillance, may be too broad to be meaningful. In addition, uses and gratifications approaches are focused largely on individual media consumption and may overlook group dynamics. For a discussion of the critiques of uses and gratifications perspectives, see Alan M. Rubin, "Media Uses and Effects: A Uses-and-Gratifications Perspective" in Jennings Bryant and Dolf Zillmann

(eds.), *Media Effects: Advances in Theory and Research* (Hillsdale, NJ: Lawrence Erlbaum Associates,1994), pp. 417–436; Mark R. Levy and Sven Windahl, "Audience Activity and Gratifications: A Conceptual Clarification and Exploration," *Communication Research*, vol. 11, 1984, pp. 51–78.

47. Tatiana Schneiterman Boncompagni, "Updating the Uses and Gratifications Model: Why CNN's Legal Issues Talk Show *Burden of Proof* Is on the Cutting Edge" Washington, DC: Georgetown University (unpublished), 1997; Che Baysinger, "Race in American Conversation: Can the Internet Help Us Cross the Racial Divide?" paper presented at the Annual Meeting of the International Communication Association, May 1997.

48. J. D. Rayburn II and Philip Palmgreen, "Merging Uses and Gratifications and Expectancy-Value Theory," *Communication Research*, vol. 11, 1984, pp. 537–562; Lawrence A. Wenner, "Model Specification and Theoretical Development in Gratifications Sought and Obtained Research: A Comparison of Discrepancy and Transactional Approaches," *Communication Monographs*, vol. 53, 1984, pp. 160–179.

49. Jack M. McLeod, Gerald M. Kosicki, and Douglas M. McLeod, "The Expanding Boundaries of Political Communication Effects," in Jennings Bryant and Dolf Zillmann, eds., *Media Effects: Advances in Theory and Research* (Hillsdale, NJ: Lawrence Erlbaum Associates, 1994), pp. 123–162.

50. Richard C. Hofstetter, Mark C. Donovan, Melville R. Klauber, Alexandra Cole, Carolyn J. Juie, and Toshiyuki Yuasa, "Political Talk Radio: A Stereotype Reconsidered," *Political Research Quarterly*, vol. 47, no. 2, 1994, pp. 467–479; Diana Owen, "Talk Radio and Evaluations of President Clinton," *Political Communication*, Summer 1997 (in press).

51. Owen, "Who's Talking? Who's Listening?" pp. 127–146.

52. Rosengren and Windahl, "Media Consumption as a Functional Alternative," pp. 166–194; John E. Newhagen, "Interactivity as a Factor in the Assessment of Political Call-in Programs," College Park, MD: University of Maryland, College of Journalism, 1996 (unpublished manuscript).

53. Byron Reeves and Clifford Nass, *The Media Equation* (New York: Cambridge University Press, 1996).

54. Susan Herbst, "On Electronic Public Space: Talk Shows in Theoretical Perspective," *Political Communication*, vol. 12, 1995, pp. 263–274.

55. Ian Hutchby, "The Pursuit of Controversy: Routine Skepticism in Talk on 'Talk Radio,'" *Sociology*, vol. 26, no. 4, November 1992, pp. 673–694.

56. Joseph Turow, "Talk Show Radio as Interpersonal Communication," *Journal of Broadcasting*, vol. 18, no. 2, Spring 1974, pp. 171–179; Bierig and Dimmick, "The Late Night Radio Talk Show as Interpersonal Communication," pp. 92–96; Trammers and Jeffres, "Talk Radio–Forum and Companion," pp. 297–300; Armstrong and Rubin, "Talk Radio as Interpersonal Communication," pp. 84–94.

57. Frederick Williams, Sharon Strover, and August E. Grant, "Social Aspects of New Media Technologies," in Jennings Bryant and Dolf Zillmann, eds., *Media Effects: Advances in Theory and Research* (Hillsdale, NJ: Lawrence Erlbaum Associates, 1994), pp. 463–482.

58. Daniel Yankelovich, *Coming to Public Judgment* (Syracuse, NY: Syracuse University Press, 1991).

59. David Thelen, *Becoming Citizens in the Age of Television* (Chicago: University of Chicago Press, 1996).

60. Roderick P. Hart, "Citizens' Attitudes and the Need to Communicate: A Survey of Political Energy," paper presented at the Annual Meeting of the American Political Science Association, New York, NY, August 1994.

61. Michelle Jaconi, "Cyberpundits and the American Media: Political Bulletin Boards at WWW.AllPolitics.Com," Washington, DC: Georgetown University, Communication, Culture, and Technology Program (unpublished manuscript), 1997.

62. Richard Davis, Diana Owen, and Vincent James Strickler, "Congress and the Internet," paper presented at the Annual Meeting of the International Communication Association, Montreal, May 1997.

Chapter 7

1. C. Richard Hofstetter, Mark C. Donovan, Melville R. Klauber, Alexandra Cole, Carolyn J. Huie, and Toshiyuki Yuasa, "Political Talk Radio: A Stereotype Reconsidered," *Political Research Quarterly*, vol. 47, no. 2, 1994, pp. 467–479; Susan Herbst, "On Electronic Public Space: Talk Shows in Theoretical Perspective," *Political Communication*, vol. 12, no. 3, 1995, pp. 467–479.

2. We examined demographic data for the ANES talk radio, television news magazine, and online media audiences, and found the same patterns as for the Pew Research Center data employed in chapter 6. The Pew data base did not contain all of the political variables that we wanted to explore here in chapter 7. The ANES survey did not include the range of new media variables that the Pew study contained, which facilitated our analysis in chapter 6.

3. A better question for our purposes is one that asks the frequency with which the individual accessed online sources, especially for political information. While other data bases, such as the 1996 Pew Research Center Technology Study, included such a question, we employed the ANES in order to maintain consistency in our analysis. Further, the ANES contained many attitude and participation items that were not included in other studies. Finally, the ANES asked if people went online to get information specifically about the election campaign. We compared the results of the analysis for this variable with the general online item we employ here, and the findings were similar, if not identical, in most cases.

4. Michael X. Delli Carpini and Scott Keeter, *What Americans Know About Politics and Why It Matters* (New Haven, CT: Yale University Press, 1996).

5. W. Russell Neuman, *The Paradox of Mass Politics* (Cambridge, MA: Harvard University Press, 1986); Jack M. McLeod, Gerald M. Kosicki, and Douglas M. McLeod, "The Expanding Boundaries of Political Communication Effects," in Jennnings Bryant and Dolf Zillmann, eds., *Media Effects: Advances in Theory and Research* (Hillsdale, NJ: Lawrence Erlbaum Associates, 1994), pp. 123–162.

6. W. Lance Bennett, *News: The Politics of Illusion*, 3d ed. (New York: Longman, 1996).

7. For the regression analysis, the dependent variable is an additive index constructed from the six political knowledge questions. It ranges from a high score of six, where the respondent answered every question correctly, to

a low score of zero. The demographic controls consist of age (in years), sex (coded with the high score representing female), education (highest level achieved), family income, and race (a dichotomy with white as the high value). The results are summarized in the following table:

Variable	Standardized Coefficient	Significance Level
Age	.138	.000
Sex	−.112	.000
Education	.329	.000
Income	.094	.001
Race	.171	.000
Talk Radio	.062	.008
TV News Magazine	−.048	.037
Online Sources	.098	.000

n=1449
Adjusted R^2=.263

8. Diana Owen, "Who's Talking? Who's Listening? The New Politics of Radio Talk Shows," in Stephen C. Craig, *Broken Contract: Changing Relationships Between Americans and Their Government* (Boulder, CO: Westview Press, 1996), pp. 127–146.

9. The 1996 Pew Research Center Technology Study of online users included a weighted sampled to reflect the age, sex, and educational distribution of the online population. Using this sample, the Pew data show a similar patterns to the ANES data. Pew found an equal percentage of Republicans (31 percent) and Democrats (31 percent) among online users, and approximately 35 percent Independents. ("News Attracts Most Internet Users," The Pew Research Center for the People & The Press, December 16, 1991.)

10. Diana Owen and Jack Dennis, "Anti-partyism in the USA and Support for Ross Perot," *European Journal of Political Research*, vol. 29, April 1996, pp. 383–400; Jack Dennis and Diana Owen, "Dimensions of Antipartyism in the United States," paper presented at the Annual Meeting of the Midwest Political Science Association, Chicago, IL, April 1977.

11. Thomas E. Patterson, *The Mass Media Election* (New York: Praeger, 1980); Walter Dean Burnham, *The Current Crisis in American Politics* (New York: Oxford University Press, 1982); Austin Ranney, *Channels of Power* (New York: Basic Books, 1983).

12. It is interesting to note the paucity of press coverage of efforts by members of Congress to achieve bipartisan cooperation. For example, a series of four congressional hearings designed to explore means of fostering bipartisanship sponsored by the Democratic Caucus and chaired by Congressman Ben Cardin (D-MD) in the summer of 1996 received scant attention from the media beyond Washington insider publications, such as *Roll Call* and *The Hill*. Even C-SPAN passed on the opportunity to cover these events, which were well-publicized to the press.

13. Stephen C. Craig, "The Angry Voter: Politics and Popular Discontent in the 1990s," in Stephen C. Craig, ed., *Broken Contract: Changing Relationships Between Americans and Their Government* (Boulder, CO: Westview, 1996), pp. 46–66.

14. Ronald Inglehart, "The Renaissance of Political Culture," *American Political Science Review*, vol. 82, no. 4, 1988, pp. 1203–30; Robert Putnam, "Bowling Alone: America's Declining Social Capital," *Journal of Democracy*, vol. 6, no. 1, 1995, pp. 65–78.

15. Kettering Foundation, *Citizens and Politics: A View from Main Street America* (Dayton, OH: Kettering Foundation, 1991).

16. Stephen C. Craig, *The Malevolent Leaders: Popular Discontent in America* (Boulder, CO: Westview, 1993).

17. Putnam, "Bowling Alone: America's Declining Social Capital," 1995; Matthew Robert Kerbel, *Remote and Controlled* (Boulder, CO; Westview Press, 1996); Bennett, *News: The Politics of Illusion*.

18. Joseph N. Cappella and Kathleen Hall Jamieson, *Spiral of Cynicism: The Press and the Public Good* (New York, NY: Oxford University Press, 1997).

19. David S. Broder, "Frustrated Clinton Assails Falwell and Limbaugh," *Los Angeles Times*, June 25, 1994, p. A21; Howard Rosenberg, "His Rush to Judgment," *Los Angeles Times*, June 29, 1994, p. F1.

20. Steven E. Finkel, "Reciprocal Effects of Participation and Political Efficacy: A Panel Analysis," *American Journal of Political Science*, vol. 29, November 1985, pp. 891–913.

21. Paul R. Abramson, *Political Attitudes in America* (San Francisco, CA: W. H. Freeman, 1983).

22. Stephen C. Craig, Richard G. Niemi, and Glenn E. Silver, "Political Efficacy and Trust: A Report on the NES Pilot Study Items," *Political Behavior*, vol. 12, September 1990, pp. 289–314; Seymour Martin Lipset and William Schneider, "The Decline in Confidence in American Institutions," *Political Science Quarterly*, vol. 98, 1983, pp. 379–402.

23. John E. Newhagen, "Self-Efficacy and Call-in Political Television Show Use," *Communication Research*, vol. 21, no. 3, June 1994, pp. 366–379.

24. Owen, "Who's Talking? Who's Listening? pp. 127–146. The data employed for the analysis in this research were from Andrew Kohut, "The Vocal Minority in Politics," Times Mirror Center for the People & the Press, May 1993.

25. Owen, "Who's Talking? Who's Listening?"" pp. 127–146.

26. The candidate preferences of the specific new media audiences differed notably. According to the ANES , the talk radio audience preferred Bob Dole (48 percent) slightly to Bill Clinton (45 percent), with a small percentage (6 percent) supporting Ross Perot. In 1992, the talk radio audience disproportionately fell in line behind Perot when he looked more legitimately like an outsider candidate waging a more serious campaign. News magazine viewers favored Bill Clinton (55 percent) over Bob Dole (36 percent) and Ross Perot (9 percent). The online media audience was not as strong in its support of Bill Clinton as news magazine viewers (48 percent). Forty-one percent of online users cast their ballots for Bob Dole and 9 percent for Perot.

27. Owen, Who's Talking? Who's Listening?" pp. 127–146.

Chapter 8

1. Thanks to James Hettleman for this insight.

2. Larry J. Sabato, *Feeding Frenzy* (New York: The Free Press, 1993), p. 1.

3. An interesting, and apparently deliberate, departure from this trend occurred on the "CBS Evening News" on January 6, 1997, the day that House Speaker Newt Gingrich was reelected while ethics charges against him were still pending. Anchor Dan Rather, who has been critical of reporters interpreting the news without providing the opportunity for the public to judge political leaders' actions for themselves, began the newscast by stating that clips from the speaker's acceptance speech would be run without commentary so that citizens could form their own opinions. Commentary from Washington correspondents came later in the broadcast.

4. Stanley Cloud and Lynn Olson, *The Murrow Boys* (New York: Houghton Mifflin, 1996).

5. Cloud and Olson, 1996.

6. Stanley Cloud and Lynn Olson, "Modern Celebrity Journalism is Born," *The American Enterprise*, March/April 1996, pp. 32–33.

7. Howard Kurtz, "Thinking Out Loud," *Washington Post*, October 4, 1994, pp. E1, E6.

8. James Fallows, *Breaking the News* (New York: Pantheon Press, 1996).

9. Fallows, 1996.

10. Howard Kurtz, "Money Talks," *Washington Post Magazine*, January 21, 1996, pp. 11–15, 22–25.

11. Lloyd Grove, "The News Hawk: Editor James Fallows Declares War on Journalism's Status Quo," *Washington Post*, March 5, 1997, pp. D1, D6.

12. Kurtz, Money Talks," pp. 11–15, 22–25.

13. Fallows, *Breaking the News*.

14. Kurtz, "Thinking Out Loud," p. E6.

15. Kurtz, "Money Talks," p. 13.

16. Fallows, *Breaking the News*.

17. Kurtz, "Money Talks," 1996, pp. 11–15, 22–25.

18. Kurtz, "Money Talks," 1996.

19. David S. Broder, "How Pundits' Partisanship Subverts Democracy," *Boston Globe*, January 6, 1997, A21.

20. Charity Vogel and Michael Kranish, "Molinari's Move to TV Has Pundits Tuning In," *Boston Globe*, May 29, 1997, p. A3; Jonathan Alter, "Lost in the Big Blur," *Newsweek*, June 9, 1997, p.43.

21. Broder, "How Pundits' Partisanship Subverts Democracy," A21.

22. Jeffrey Toobin, "Buying Headlines," *Quill*, November/December, 1994, pp. 21–23.

23. Toobin, 1994, pp. 21–23.

24. Lou Prato, "Tabloids Force All To Pay for News," *American Journalism Review*, vol. 16, September 1994, p. 56.

25. Toobin, "Buying Headlines," pp. 21–23.

26. Richard Ben Cramer and Thomas Lennon, "Tabloid Truth: The Michael Jackson Story," *Frontline*, February 15, 1994.

27. Prato, "Tabloids Force All To Pay for News," p. 56.

28. Bruce Selcraig, "Buying News," *Columbia Journalism Review*, July/August, 1994, pp. 45–46.

29. Selcraig, 1994, pp. 45–46.

30. Prato, "Tabloids Force All To Pay for News," p. 56.

31. Toobin, "Buying Headlines," 1994, pp. 21–23.

32. Toobin, 1994.

33. Toobin, 1994.

34. Prato, "Tabloids Force All To Pay for News," p. 56.

35. Toobin, "Buying Headlines," pp. 21–23.

36. Selcraig, "Buying News," pp. 45–46.

37. Toobin, "Buying Headlines," 1994, pp. 21–23.

38. Toobin, 1994.

39. Selcraig, "Buying News," pp. 45–46.

40. Louise Mengelkoch, "When Checkbook Journalism Does God's Work," *Columbia Journalism Review*, November/December 1994, pp. 35–38.

41. Jon Katz, "Say Goodnight, Dan," *Rolling Stone*, June 27, 1991, pp. 81–84.

42. Mark Hosenball, "The Anatomy of a Rumor," *Newsweek*, September 23, 1996, p. 43.

43. Sabato, *Feeding Frenzy*.

44. Adam Gopnik, "Read All About It," *New Yorker*, December 12, 1994, pp. 82–102.

45. Gopnik, 1994.

46. Gopnik, 1994.

47. Jeff MacGregor, "Diluting the News Into Soft Half-Truths," *New York Times*, June 4, 1995, pp. H25, H32.

48. Joseph N. Cappella and Kathleen Hall Jamieson, *Spiral of Cynicism: The Press and the Public Good* (New York: Oxford University Press, 1997).

49. See W. Lance Bennett, *News: The Politics of Illusion*, 3d ed. (White Plains, NY: Longman, 1996); Matthew Robert Kerbel, *Remote and Controlled* (Boulder, CO: Westview, 1996).

50. Judy Bachrach, "They Who Serve and Suffer," *Vanity Fair*, December 1996, pp. 128–134, 141–156.

51. Max Frankel, "Word and Image: Journalism 101," *New York Times*, January 22, 1995, Sec. 6, p. 18.

52. J. Peder Zane, "Liz's Love Life! Oprah's Diet! Dole's Foreign Policy!," *New York Times*, September 29, 1996, p. D1.

53. Todd Gitlin, "Media Lemmings Run Amok!," *Washington Journalism Review*, April 1992, vol. 14, pp. 28–32.

54. Howard Kurtz, "Tabloid Journalism's Scoops for Scandal," *Washington Post*, September 16, 1996, pp. D1–D2.

55. A quote by Evan Thomas on *Inside Washington*, November 16, 1996, when discussing the issue of media "feeding frenzies."

56. Christopher Hansen, "How to Handle Dirty Stories (And Still Feel Clean)," *Columbia Journalism Review*, March/April 1994, pp. 14–16.

57. Kurtz, "Tabloid Journalism's Scoops for Scandal," pp. D1–D2.

58. Hansen, "How to Handle Dirty Stories," pp. 14–16.

59. Ron Dorfman, "Peeping Watchdogs," *The Quill*, June 1987, pp. 14–16.

60. Hansen, "How to Handle Dirty Stories," pp. 14–16.

61. Howard Kurtz, "A Big Story—But Only Behind the Scenes," *Washington Post*, November 13, 1996, pp. D1, D6.

62. Thomas B. Rosenstiel, "To Journalists, Technology Is a Blessing—and a Curse," *Los Angeles Times*, September 24, 1994, p. A1.

63. Jacqueline Sharkey, "Judgment Calls," *American Journalism Review*, September 1994, vol. 16, p. 21.

64. Jennifer E. Kerslake, "The Traditional Media: Dealing with the 'New Media,'" unpublished manuscript, Georgetown University, 1996.

65. Howard Kurtz, "Kinsley's Slate Serves Up A Full Plate," *Washington Post*, June 24, 1996, pp. D1, D4.

66. Laurence Zuckerman, "Don't Stop the Presses!" *New York Times*, January 6, 1997, pp. D1, D7.

67. Frank Rich, "Cybernews Is No News," *New York Times*, July 24, 1996. OP-ED.

68. James Wolcott, "Only Disconnect," *New Yorker*, September 16, 1996, pp. 104–106.

69. Zuckerman, January 6, 1997, pp. D1, D7.

Chapter 9

1. Thomas E. Patterson, *Out of Order* (New York: Knopf, 1994).

2. Edwin Diamond and Robert A. Silverman, *White House to Your House: Media and Politics in Virtual America* (Cambridge, MA: MIT Press, 1995).

3. Larry J. Sabato, *Feeding Frenzy* (New York: The Free Press, 1993), p. 26.

4. John D. Callaway et al., *Campaigning on Cue* (Chicago: William Benton Fellowships Program, 1988), pp. 1–2.

5. For a discussion of the incident, see Theodore H. White, *The Making of the President 1968* (New York: Atheneum, 1969), pp. 54–60.

6. Peter Goldman et al., "Carter's Trip of the Tongue," *Newsweek*, April 19, 1976, p. 14.

7. Kiku Adatto, "Sound Bite Democracy: Network Evening News Presidential Campaign Coverage, 1968 and 1988," Joan Shorenstein Barone Center on the Press, Politics and Public Policy, Research Paper R-2, John F. Kennedy School of Government, Harvard University, Cambridge, MA, June 1990.

8. Patterson, *Out of Order*, p. 195.

9. Thomas E. Patterson, *The Mass Media Election: How Americans Choose Their President* (New York: Praeger, 1980).

10. *Washington Post*/Harvard University/Kaiser Foundation, *Politics 96 Poll Results*, November 15, 1996.

11. Patterson, *Out of Order*, pp. 73–75.

12. Robert S. Lichter and Linda S. Lichter, "Take This Campaign—Please," *Media Monitor*, vol. 10, no. 5, September/October, Washington, D.C.: Center for Media and Public Affairs, 1996.

13. Callaway et al, *Campaigning on Cue*, p. 165.

14. Patterson, *Out of Order*.

15. Thomas E. Patterson and Richard Davis, "The Media Campaign: Struggle for the Agenda," in Michael Nelson, ed., *The Elections of 1984* (Washington: CQ Press, 1985), pp. 116–118.

16. "Gary Hart on Why Our Media Miss the Message," *Washington Post*, December 20, 1987, p. C1.

17. Patterson, *Out of Order*, pp. 160–161.

18. *Washington Post*/Kaiser Foundation, *Politics 96 Poll Results*, November 15, 1996.

19. Campaign Discourse Mapping Project, "Assessing the Quality of Campaign Discourse–1960, 1980, 1988, 1992," The Annenberg Public Policy Center of the University of Pennsylvania, 1996, (http://www.asc.upenn.edu/appc/campmapp/assesing/index.html). "Tracking the Quality of Campaign Discourse," The Annenberg Public Policy Center of the University of Pennsylvania, 1996.

20. Marion R. Just, Ann N. Crigler, Dean E. Alger, Timothy E. Cook, Montague Kern, Darrell M. West, *Crosstalk: Citizens, Candidates, and the Media in a Presidential Campaign* (Chicago: University of Chicago Press, 1996).

21. Dirk Smillie, "Talking to America: The Rise of Talk Shows in the '92 Campaign," in *An Uncertain Season: Reporting in the Postprimary Period* (New York: The Freedom Forum Media Studies Center, Columbia University, 1992), pp. 17–27.

22. "Tracking the Quality of Campaign Discourse: News Coverage Down from '92," Annenberg Public Policy Center of the University of Pennsylvania, no. 12, October 15, 1996.

23. Just et al., *Crosstalk.*

24. Smillie, "Talking to America," pp. 17–27.

25. Diamond and Silverman, *White House to Your House.*

26. Just et al., *Crosstalk.*

27. Smillie, "Talking to America," pp. 17–27.

28. Edward C. Pease, "'New' Media Voices Challenging the 'Old' Media Status Quo," in *The Homestretch: New Politics, New Media, New Voters?* (New York: The Freedom Forum Media Studies Center, Columbia University, 1992) p. 100.

29. Just et al., *Crosstalk,* 1996, p. 7.

30. Just et al., 1996.

31. Steven H. Chaffee, Xinshu Zhao, and Glenn Leshner, "Political Knowledge and the Campaign Media of 1992," *Communication Research,* vol. 21, no. 3, June 1994, pp. 305–324.

32. Times Mirror Center for the People & the Press, "The Press And Campaign '92: A Self-Assessment," *Columbia Journalism Review Supplement,* March/April 1993.

33. "Campaign '96 Gets Lower Grades From Voters," The Pew Research Center for the People & The Press, November 15, 1996.

34. "The Press And Campaign '92: A Self-Assessment," Times Mirror Center for the People & the Press, 1993.

35. "Dole Can't Cash in on Mixed View of Clinton," The Pew Research Center for the People & The Press, October 4, 1996.

36. James Bennett, "Did You Hear the One About the '96 Campaign?" *New York Times,* July 9, 1996, A17.

37. Michael Lewis, "The Herd of Independent Minds," *New Republic,* June 3, 1996, pp. 20–22, 26; Manny Howard, "Why Don't We Do It on the Road," *George,* April/May 1996, pp. 74–80.

38. Phyllis Zagano, "Beavis and Butt-head, Free Your Minds," *America,* March 5, 1994, vol. 170, no. 8, pp. 6–7.

39. Christopher Georges, "Mock the Vote: What's Wrong With MTV's Hot New Political Coverage," *Washington Monthly,* May 1993, vol. 25, no. 5, pp. 30–35.

40. Judith Miller, "But Can You Dance to It? MTV Turns to News," *New York Times*, October 11, 1992, p. 31.

41. Maureen Dowd, "Why Are All the Politicians Watching Rock Video," *New York Times*, April 19, 1985, p. 18A.

42. Rock the Vote promotional packet, May 1996.

43. Correspondence to members of Congress from Hilary B. Rosen, president and chief operating officer, Recording Industry Association of America, May 28, 1996.

44. Janice C. Simpson, "Rock Vote," *Time*, June 15, 1992, pp. 66–67.

45. Miller, "But Can You Dance to It?" p. 31.

46. Rock the Vote promotional material, May 1996.

47. "The Campaign: Rockers and Rappers," *Economist*, June 20, 1993, p. 25.

48. Rock the Vote Election 1996 Program Plan, May 24, 1996.

49. Megan Rosenfeld, "MTV, Facing the Music on Teen Health," *Washington Post*, May 15, 1995, p. B2.

50. Elizabeth Kolbert, "From MTV to NBC," *New York Times*, March 14, 1992, p. 1G.

51. David Zurawik, "MTV is a Player in the Election," *Baltimore Sun*, June 10, 1996, pp. 1D, 3D.

52. Miller, "But Can You Dance to It? p. 31.

53. Joshua Hammer, "Not Just Hit Videos Anymore: MTV Energizes a Young—and Powerful—Electorate," *Newsweek*, November 2, 1992, p. 93.

54. Gloria Borger, "Setting Words to Music Over Values," *U.S. News & World Report*, June 29, 1992, pp. 8–9; Kim Neely, "I Want the MTV Vote," *Rolling Stone*, August 6, 1992, p. 22.

55. Maureen Dowd and Frank Rich, "The New Presidency: The Boomers' Ball," *New York Times*, January 17, 1993, p. 18A.

56. Miller, "But Can You Dance to It?" p. 31.

57. Brett Atwood, "MTV Renews 'Choose or Lose,'" *Billboard*, February 3, 1996, pp. 20, 85.

58. Roxanne Roberts, "Voting: Not Their Primary Thing," *Washington Post*, March 3, 1992, p. B1.

59. Georges, "Mock the Vote," pp. 30–35.

60. Donatella Lorch, "Young Voters, Diverse and Disillusioned, Are Unpredictable in '96 Race," *New York Times*, March 30, 1996, p. 8A.

61. Georges, "Mock the Vote," pp. 30–35.

62. Eric Alterman, "The Vote Clinton Rocked is Rocking Him," *Sacramento Bee*, February 19, 1995, p. F6.

63. "Sex, Commercials, Rock 'n' Roll," *Progressive*, July 1993, vol. 57, no. 7, pp. 36–38.

64. John Seabrook, "Rocking in Shangri-la," *New Yorker*, October 10, 1994, pp. 64–78.

65. Miller, "But Can You Dance to It?" p. 31.

66. Simpson, "Rock Vote," pp. 66–67.

67. Georges, "Mock the Vote," pp. 30–35.

68. Marc Levinson, "Rock Around the World," *Newsweek*, April 24, 1995, p. 65.

69. "Latin American Television: Yo Quiero Mi MTV," *Economist*, February 25, 1995, p. 67.

70. Jonathan Alter, "Pitching the President," *Newsweek*, June 17, 1996.

71. Mark Hall, "One-to-One Politics in Cyberspace," *Media Studies Journal*, Winter 1997 (http://www.mediastudies.org/cov96/hall.html).

72. Hall, "One-to-One Politics in Cyberspace," 1997.

73. Mark Thalhimer, "The 'Virtual Newsroom': New Technologies Create a Newsroom Without Walls," in *The Homestretch: New Politics, New Media, New Voters?* (New York: The Freedom Forum Media Studies Center, Columbia University, 1992), pp. 70–81.

74. Everette E. Dennis, "Executive Summary," in *The Homestretch: New Politics, New Media, New Voters?* (New York: The Freedom Forum Media Studies Center, Columbia University, 1992), pp. 1–16.

75. Dennis, "Executive Summary," 1992, pp. 1–16.

76. Hall, "One-to-One Politics in Cyberspace."

77. "News Attracts Most Internet Users," The Pew Research Center for the People & The Press, December 16, 1996.

78. Renee Beutner, "Elections in Cyberspace: A New Form of Political Communication," Washington, DC: Georgetown University (unpublished manuscript). Data analysis relied on the 1996 Pew Research Center Technology survey.

79. "Survey Profiles Voters' Use of Media," Media Studies Center, Freedom Forum News Advisory at http://www.mediastudies.org/new.html; and "Campaign '96 Gets Lower Grades From Voters," The Pew Research Center for the People & The Press, November 1996 Post-Election Survey.

80. *Washington Post*/Harvard University/Kaiser Foundation, *Politics '96 Poll Results*, November 15, 1996.

81. Adam Clayton Powell, III, *Campaign '96 On Line: Findings from the Freedom Forum's Digital Democracy Project* (New York: The Freedom Forum, Columbia University, 1996), http://www.fac.org/publicat/campaign/lth96powon.html).

82. Hall, "One-to-One Politics in Cyberspace."

83. See "Election Crush Creates Internet Logjam," CNN Interactive at http://cnn.com/TECH9611/06/Internet.crush.ap/index.html.

84. Hall, "One-to-One Politics in Cyberspace." p. 2.

85. Anthony Corrado and Charles M. Firestone, eds., *Elections in Cyberspace: Toward a New Era in American Politics* (Washington, DC: The Aspen Institute, 1996), p. vii.

86. Howard Fineman, "Who Needs Washington," *Newsweek*, January 27, 1997, pp. 50–52.

87. Matthew R. Kerbel, "Old Wine in More Bottles: Coverage of the 1992 Presidential Election on Broadcast and Cable Television," paper presented at the Annual Meeting of the American Political Science Association, New York, NY, September, 1994.

88. Doris A. Graber, "Making Campaign News User Friendly," *American Behavioral Scientist*, vol. 37, no. 2, November 1993, pp. 328–336.

89. W. Lance Bennett, "The Clueless Public: Bill Clinton Meets the New American Voter in Campaign '92," in Stanley A. Renshon, ed., *The Clinton Presidency: Campaigning, Governing, and the Psychology of Leadership* (Boulder, CO: Westview Press, 1995), pp. 95–112.

90. *Washington Post*/Harvard University/Kaiser Foundation, *Politics '96 Poll Results*, November 15, 1996.

Chapter 10

1. "Talk Hosts Steer Listeners into Political Process," *Broadcasting*, May 14, 1990, pp. 48–50.

2. Howard Kurtz, *Hot Air: All Talk, All the Time* (New York: Times Books, 1996), pp. 295–296.

3. Kurtz, 1996, pp. 293–294.

4. Susan F. Rasky, "Fury Over Lawmakers' Raise Finds an Outlet on the Radio," *New York Times*, February 6, 1989, p. A1.

5. Interview with Mike Siegel, former KVI (Seattle) talk host, September 8, 1995.

6. Interview with Greg Dobbs, KOA (Denver) talk host, August 22, 1995.

7. Telephone interview with Ray Suarez, National Public Radio host, October 17, 1995.

8. Telephone interview with Judy Jarvis, Talk America Radio Network host, September 18, 1995.

9. Telephone interview with Alan Colmes, Major Radio Network host, October 4, 1995.

10. Telephone interview with Victoria Jones, WRC (Washington) talk host, November 15, 1995.

11. Telephone interview with Tom Leykis, Westwood One Network host, October 6, 1995.

12. See, for example, Joseph Turow, "Talk Radio as Interpersonal Communication," *Journal of Broadcasting*, vol. 18, 1974, pp. 171–179; Jeffrey Bierg and John Dimmick, "The Late Night Radio Talk Show as Interpersonal Communication," *Journalism Quarterly*, vol. 56, Spring 1979, pp. 92–96; and Cameron B. Armstrong and Alan M. Rubin, "Talk Radio as Interpersonal Communication," *Journal of Communication*, vol. 39, Spring 1989, pp. 89–94.

13. C. Richard Hofstetter et al, "Political Talk Radio: A Stereotype Reconsidered," *Political Research Quarterly*, vol. 47, June 1994, pp. 467–480.

14. "Talk Hosts Steer Listeners into Political Process," p. 48–50.

15. Bill Turque, "Press '1' for the Christian Right," *Newsweek*, February 8, 1993, p. 28.

16. "Radio Hosts Urging Exxon Boycott," *New York Times*, April 17, 1989, p. D11.

17. Interview with Mike Siegel, September 8, 1995.

18. Interview with Dave Ross, KIRO (Seattle) talk host, September 8, 1995.

19. Mark Pazniokas, "40,000–or 70,000–Showed Up," *Hartford Courant*, October 6, 1991, p. A8.

20. Anthony DePalma, "Anti-Tax Protesters Demand Florio's Recall, for Starters," *New York Times*, July 2, 1990, p. B4.

21. Peter Viles, "Talkers Let Fly on Check-Bouncing Scandal," *Broadcasting*, March 23, 1992, p. 76.

22. Scott Lehigh, "'Governors' on the Airwaves Spread Cynicism," *Boston Globe*, November 20, 1989, p. 1.

23. Elizabeth Kolbert, "The People Are Heard, at Least Those Who Call Talk Radio," *New York Times*, January 29, 1993, p. A12

24. Interview with Representative Tom Campbell (R-California), December 19, 1996.

25. John V. Pavlik, *New Media Technology: Cultural and Commercial Perspectives* (Boston: Allyn and Bacon, 1996),pp. 168–169. Gore has gravitated toward such new media firsts. He was the first member of the House of Representatives to give a speech on C-SPAN in 1979, as well as the first member of the Senate to do so when C-SPAN was introduced there in 1986. Stephen Frantzich and John Sullivan, *The C-SPAN Revolution* (Norman: University of Oklahoma Press, 1996), p. 60.

26. See, for example, "Voters Can Take Chat with Candidates Via Cyberspace, *Miami Herald*, October 22, 1995; and "Schools, Libraries Access the Internet, *Hartford Courant*, October 3, 1996.

27. Telephone interview with Bruce Dumont, "Beyond the Beltway" host, September 21, 1995.

28. One example of such a daily service is *Talk Daily* published by Adams Research in Arlington, Virginia. Another is the compilation service offered by former direct mail guru Richard Vigurie.

29. Interview with Ken Hamblin, nationally syndicated talk host, August 22, 1995.

30. Ellen Ratner, "Talk Radio Responds; Our 'Back Fence,'" *Los Angeles Times*, April 27, 1995, p. B7.

31. "Talk Hosts Steer Listeners into Political Process," p. 48–50.

32. Telephone interview with Tom Leykis, October 6, 1995.

33. Telephone interview with Tom Leykis, October 6, 1995.

34. Lehigh, "'Governors' on the Airwaves Spread Cynicism."

35. Remarks by the president in telephone call to KMOX Radio Station, St. Louis, Office of the Press Secretary, The White House, June 24, 1994.

36. Michael Harrison, "The Voice of America," *New York Times*, July 9, 1994, section 1, p. 19.

37. Telephone interview with Charles Brennan, KMOX (St. Louis) talk show host, November 15, 1995.

38. Telephone interview with Charles Brennan, November 15, 1995.

39. Telephone interview with Judy Jarvis, September 18, 1995.

40. The discharge petition is a tool used by members to force committees to release bills for floor action. Since a discharge petition often angers committee chairs and party leaders who seek to control the floor agenda, the secrecy of the signers originally was designed to avoid retribution by the leadership as well as lobbying efforts by interest groups while a discharge petition drive was still short of the required 218 signatures. Opponents of the secrecy provision argued that it allowed members publicly to claim support of a bill while secretly refusing to sign a discharge petition to free it from the jurisdiction of a committee.

41. "Outflanked by Talk Shows, House Drops Secrecy Rule," *Chicago Tribune*, September 29, 1993, p. 6.

42. Adam Clymer, "House Members Seek Senate Change," *New York Times*, October 21, 1993, p. A13.

43. Interview with Mike Siegel, September 8, 1995.

44. Telephone interview with Tom Leykis, October 6, 1995.

45. Telephone interview with Charles Brennan, November 15, 1995.

46. Telephone interview with Charles Brennan, November 15, 1995.

47. Rick Wartzman, "Democrats Try to Play Catch-Up on Talk Radio," *The Wall Street Journal*, February 8, 1995, p. B1.

48. Pat Aufderheide and Jeffrey Chester, "Talk Radio: Who's Talking? Who's Listening?" Benton Foundation Strategic Communications for Non-profits report, 1992.

49. Erik Eckholm, "From Right, a Rain of Anti-Clinton Salvos," *New York Times*, June 26, 1994, section 1, p. 1.

50. Aufderheide and Chester, "Talk Radio: Who's Talking? Who's Listening?" 1992

51. Aufderheide and Chester, 1992.

52. Aufderheide and Chester, 1992.

53. Telephone interview with Charles Brennan, November 15, 1995.

54. Aufderheide and Chester, "Talk Radio: Who's Talking? Who's Listening?"

55. Telephone interview with Ray Suarez, October 17, 1995.

56. Quoted in Brudnoy et al., "The Gurus of Gab," *Policy Review* (Summer 1994), p. 62.

57. Brudnoy et al., "The Gurus of Gab," 1994, p. 62.

58. Maureen Grope, "Talk-Radio Hosts Decide to Go Off the Air and On the Ballot," *CQ Weekly Report*, April 9, 1994, pp. 852–854.

59. Telephone interview with Michael Harrison, September 18, 1995.

60. Bill Miller and John McCarty, *You're on Open Line! Inside the Wacky World of Late-Night Talk Radio* (Brattleboro, VT: The Stephen Greene Press, 1978), p. 10.

61. Grope, "Talk-Radio Hosts Decide to Go Off the Air and On the Ballot."

62. Michael Harrison, "The Voice of America," *New York Times*, July 9, 1994, section 1, p. 19.

63. Wayne Munson, *All Talk: The Talk Show in Media Culture* (Philadelphia: Temple University Press, 1993), p. 96.

64. See, for example, Lehigh, "'Governors' on the Airwaves Spread Cynicism," p. 1.

65. Telephone interview with Michael Harrison, September 18, 1995.

66. Telephone interview with Michael Harrison, September 18, 1995.

67. Interview with Dave Ross, KIRO (Seattle) talk show host, September 8, 1995.

68. Telephone interview with Victoria Jones, WRC (Washington) talk show host, November 15, 1995.

Conclusion

1. Telephone interview with Ray Suarez, National Public Radio host, October 17, 1995.

2. Telephone interview with Charles Brennan, KMOX (St. Louis) talk host, November 15, 1995.

3. Interview with Greg Dobbs, KOA (Denver) talk show host, August 22, 1995.

4. Telephone interview with Michael Harrison, editor, *Talkers*, September 18, 1995

5. Benjamin Barber, *Strong Democracy,* Berkley, CA: University of California Press, 1984.

6. James S. Fishkin, *The Voice of the People,* New Haven, CT: Yale University Press, 1995.

7. This corresponds to endnote 6 in the original text.

8. Telephone interview with Alan Colmes, Major Radio Network host, October 4, 1995.

9. W. Russell Neuman, *The Future of the Mass Audience* (New York: Cambridge University Press, 1991).

10. Roderick P. Hart, *Seducing America,* New York, NY: Oxford University Press, 1984.

11. Michelle Jaconi, "An Online Discussion: The Future of Cyberjournalism?" Washington, DC: Georgetown University, Communication, Culture, and Technology Program, (unpublished manuscript), 1997.

12. Paul Starobin, "On the Square," *National Journal,* May 25, 1996, pp. 1145–1149.

13. David Thelen, *Becoming Citizens in the Age of Television* (Chicago: University of Chicago Press, 1996).

14. Tom Rosenstiel, *Strange Bedfellows* (New York: Hyperion, 1993).

15. Peter Levine, "Public Journalism and Deliberation," *Report from the Institute for Philosophy and Public Policy,* vol. 16, no. 1, Winter 1996, pp. 1–5.

16. Alicia C. Shepard, "The Pew Connection," *American Journalism Review,* April 1996, pp. 24–29.

17. Shepard, 1996, p. 28.

18. David Warsh, "The Newspapers are Downsizing, But So What?" *Boston Sunday Globe,* April 14, 1996, pp. 91, 93.

19. Paul Farhi, "Turning the Tables on TV Violence," *Washington Post,* June 21, 1995, pp. F1–2.

20. Lawrence K. Grossman, *The Electronic Commonwealth* (New York: Penguin Books, 1995).

Index

20/20 13, 151
48 Hours 13, 151, 192
60 Minutes 13, 24, 95, 101–102, 135, 151, 217
700 Club 237

A Current Affair 94, 99–100, 195, 197
ABC 13, 21, 23, 53, 67, 75, 80, 114, 228
Accuracy in Media 261
advertising 51–53, 57, 61, 66, 72, 80, 89
AFL-CIO 120–121
agenda setting 75–79, 236–237, 240–249
  and hosts 75–79, 236–237, 240
  and interest groups 244–249
  and political parties 244–245
Alexander, Lamar 122
AllPolitics 228
Allred, Gloria 55, 62

Alter, Jonathan 107
AM Radio 53
America Online 15, 110, 112, 124, 200, 243
Armey, Richard 244
Arsenio 219
Atwater, Lee 221
audience 133–185
  attitudes 164–185
  attitudes toward parties 171–173
  attitudes toward government 165, 173–177
  and campaign involvement 181–183
  and community involvement 183–184
  electronic town meeting 149–151
  ideology of 167–170
  Internet 141, 144, 155–157
  mobilization of 233, 234, 238, 239
  MTV 141, 144, 154–155

audience (*continued*)
  overlapping 140–144
  partisanship of 170–171
  and political activity 181–184
  and political efficacy 177–180
  and political interest 180–181
  and political knowledge 165–167
  and political orientations 167–184
  print tabloid 141, 144, 154–155
  profile of 144–157
  talk radio 141–148
  television news magazine 141,
    144, 154–155
  television tabloid 141, 144,
    154–155
  television talk show 141, 144,
    148–149
  use of mass media 135–138
  and uses and gratifications 157–
    163

"bad news" 201–203
Baird, Zoe 232
Barber, Benjamin 258
Bird, Elizabeth 103
Bobbitt, Lorena 102, 195
Bohannon, Jim 10, 68, 73, 82, 233,
  235–236
Blumler, Jay 157
Bradley, Bill 55
Boortz, Neal 10, 147
Bork, Robert 87, 245
Boston Globe 12, 19, 250, 260
Brennan, Charles 77, 247
Broder, David 44, 194
Brokaw, Tom 13, 192, 208
Brown, Jerry 4
Brudnoy, David 40
Buchanan, Pat 57, 122–123
Burden of Proof 158
Bureau of Alcohol, Tobacco, and
  Firearms 59
Burns, Gene 66
Bush, George 4, 14, 216, 218, 221,
  224–225
Byrd, Robert 203

Cal Thomas Show 11
callers 51, 58, 69, 70, 72, 73, 75,
  76, 79, 81–90

age of 82–84
agreement with host 84–87
gender of 82–84
Campbell, Tom 239
candidate(s) 121–123, 171,
  213–220, 223–230
  and the Internet 121–123,
    226–229
  and MTV 220–226
  and soundbites 214–216
  and talk shows 217–220
  -centered campaigns 171
Carlson, Margaret 193
Carter, Jimmy 54, 236
Castle, Mike 238, 239
CBS 8, 11, 32, 101, 108
celebrity journalism 190–194
censorship of new media content
  80–81
Charles Grodin Show 11
checkbook journalism 96, 196–198
Chicago Tribune 204
Choose or Lose 222, 224
Christian Coalition 247
civic journalism 259–261
civility 55, 90
Clinton, Bill 4, 12, 14, 15, 21, 22,
  42, 43, 55, 57–60, 67, 73, 100,
  106, 108, 148, 156, 193, 202–
  204, 206, 213, 216–218, 220,
  223–227, 232, 234–235, 242–
  245, 247, 250
Clinton, Hillary 14, 147
Clinton administration 116, 125,
  235–236, 242
CNBC 8, 11
CNN 37, 40, 106, 136, 139, 141–
  144, 162, 228, 229, 240, 248
Colmes, Alan 60, 61, 66, 68, 82, 83,
  85, 87, 90, 115, 233–235
Comedy Central 15
CompuServe 110, 112
Congress 6, 16, 38, 59, 72, 73, 89,
  117–118, 231–235, 237–239,
  242, 243, 245, 249, 250, 258,
  261
Congressional Internet Caucus 222
Congressional Quarterly 123
congressional pay raise 232, 233,
  236, 245

Congress Watch 235
Contract with America 244
Corrado, Anthony 229
Coughlin, Father Charles 9, 65
Couric, Katie 219
Crispin, Mark 225
Cronkite, Walter 32, 196
Crosstalk 219
Crow, Sheryl 222
C-SPAN 12, 19, 22, 115–123, 218
Cullum, Blanquita 61, 62, 64, 67
Cuomo, Mario 4, 59, 64–66, 244
cynicism 235, 242, 250–251

Dallas Morning News 114
Dateline NBC 13, 24, 136, 151, 192
Dave 192
Day One 13
definition of new media 7
Delli Carpini, Michael 229
Democratic 55, 58, 166, 223, 225,
    229, 244
democracy 126–130, 253–262
    and the Internet 126–130
Denver Post 63
Department of Defense (DOD) 111
Diamond, Edwin 36, 37, 217
Digital Ink 206
Disney 36, 55, 80
Dobbs, Greg 69, 75, 85
Dole, Bob 5–6, 11, 55, 57, 58, 122,
    204, 210, 220, 224
Donahue, Phil 6, 11, 99, 100,
    217–218
Donaldson, Sam 192–193
Dornan, Bob 64, 122
Dukakis, Michael 242
Duke, David 65
Dumont, Bruce 68, 240

Elders, Jocelyn 56, 63, 64
electronic town meetings 12–13,
    149–151, 159
e-mail 8, 15–17, 155–156, 162
Equal Time 11
entertainment 70–72, 137, 139,
    143, 148, 158–160, 202, 208,
    232–236, 254
executive branch 116–117, 259
Eye to Eye 13, 101, 104

Fairness Doctrine 38–39, 77, 89
Fallows, James 102
Federal Communications Commis-
    sion (FCC) 37–38
"feeding frenzies" 201–203, 212
Ferraro, Geraldine 32
Firestone, Charles 229
Flowers, Gennifer 93, 96, 223–225
FM Radio 53, 54, 56
Forbes, Steve 224
Forrester Research 209
Fox, Roy 231
Frankel, Max 260
Free Congress 79
Freedom Forum 216–218, 226–227
Frontline 114

Gamson, Joshua 103, 104
Gannett Company 36
Garagiola, Joe 216
Gates, Bill 207
Gates, Daryl 65
Gejdenson, Sam 126
General Electric 35
General Motors 13
Generation X 152
Gephardt, Richard 55, 80
Geraldo 11, 99–100
Gergen, David 193
Gill, Jonathan 130
Gingrich, Newt 6, 57, 117–118,
    123, 166, 172, 180, 234, 235,
    244
Gitlin, Todd 105
Good Morning America 8, 11
GOPAC 55
Gopnik, Adam 201
Gore, Al 6, 25, 166, 229, 232, 240,
    246
Graber, Doris 228
Gramm, Phil 234
Grant, Bob 55
Great Depression 39, 42
Greenfield, Jeff 105
Grossman, Lawrence 261
guests 86–88, 247–249
    agreement with host 86–87
    and interest groups 247–249
Gulf War 40–43, 46, 199
Gurevitch, Michael 157

Hall, Arsenio 4, 22
Hamblin, Ken 63, 85, 88, 90, 115, 240
Hard Copy 15, 99–101, 136, 142
Harder, Chuck 60, 66, 73, 83–84, 87, 235, 250, 255
Harrison, Michael 19, 52, 63, 65, 68, 71, 73, 249–251, 254
Hart, Gary 15, 23, 93, 219
Harvard University 222
Hedgecock, Roger 64
Helms, Jesse 233
Heritage Foundation 247
Hightower, Jim 66, 80, 244
"horse race" coverage 214
Houston Chronicle 114

Ice-T 222
ideology 65–69, 80, 167–170
Illustrated Daily News 93
Imus, Don 62, 77, 88, 192, 206, 208, 218
Inside Edition 15, 100–101, 106, 197
interest groups 66, 87, 110, 118, 120–121, 232, 244–249
    and guests 245–247
    as information source 247–248
    and Internet 110, 120–121
    lobbying 118, 120
    relationship with new media 248–249
Internet 4–7, 15–16, 40–43, 46, 110–130, 141, 144, 155–157, 164–165, 200, 206–209, 210, 222, 226, 228, 232, 237, 239, 243, 248, 253–258
    audience 141, 144, 155–157
    candidate use of 121–123
    Congressional use of 117–118
    and democracy 126–130
    executive branch use of 116–117
    as information source 113–116
    interest group use of 110, 120–121
    as linking mechanism 116–123
    local government use of 118–120
    news 206–208
    origins of 111–113
    as political discussion forum 123–125
    and political participation 127–130
    presidential use of 116–117
    state government use of 118–120
    surveys 127
    and traditional media 113–115, 206–208
investigative reporting 30–31, 36, 212
issue discussion 73–81, 85–88

Jackson, Jesse 215
Jackson, Jesse Jr. 222
Jackson, Michael 10, 102, 189, 196, 197
Jarvis, Judy 61, 62, 65, 68, 77, 233
Jeffords, James 239
Jennings, Peter 192, 200
Jewell, Richard 138
John Birch Society 121
Johnson, Lyndon 213
Jones, Jenny 148
Jones, Victoria 61, 62, 69, 78, 252

Kaiser Foundation 228
Kasich, John 222
Kaelin, Kato 107, 197
Katz, Elihu 157
Katz, Jon 37, 152, 199
Kennedy 223
Keyes, Alan 122
King, Larry 43, 56, 64, 71
Kinsley, Michael 206
Koch, Ed 4, 61
Koppel, Ted 149, 192, 206
Kramer, Marcia 200
Kurtz, Howard 88, 143, 203

Lamb, Brian 11, 192
Larry King Live 4–6, 10, 18, 22, 148, 172, 217, 218, 232, 246
Late Night with Conan O'Brien 115
Leahy, Patrick 222
Lehrer, Jim 166, 192
Leno, Jay 99, 220
Levin, Murray 71
Leykis, Tom 54, 59, 60, 61, 66, 68, 83, 84, 90, 233, 241, 244
Letterman, David 6, 11, 17, 99–100, 115, 217, 220

Liddy, G. Gordon 8, 53–55, 58, 59, 60, 61, 62, 68, 73, 77, 78, 81, 83–84, 95, 123, 174, 234–235
Limbaugh, Rush 4, 6, 8–10, 17, 19, 21, 24, 56–58, 60–62, 65, 66, 69, 70, 72, 73, 74, 77, 78, 81, 84–88, 91, 115, 123, 146–147, 174, 233, 236, 239, 248
local governments 22, 118–120
Los Angeles Times 198, 205, 217
Lugar, Richard 122
Luther, Bill 222

MacNeil, Robert 108
Madonna 222
Maher, Bill 11
Majors, Stan 233
McGovern, George 236
McGrory, Mary 162
Media Watch 261
Meet the Press 166, 191
Miami Herald 23, 93
Microsoft 206
midterm election 76
Million Man March 158
mobilization of the audience 233, 234, 238, 239
Mondale, Walter 216
Morning Edition 114
Morris, Dick 15, 204
MSNBC 37, 114, 207–208
MTV 3–4, 6, 14–15, 24–25, 41, 45, 134, 136, 139–144, 152–153, 219–226
Murphy Brown 219
Murrow, Edward R. 191

NAACP 63
Nader, Ralph 245
Nass, Clifford 160
National Aeronautics and Space Administration (NASA) 111, 117
National Association of Radio Talk Show Hosts (NARTSH) 54–55, 58
National Public Radio (NPR) 114, 145–147, 254, 260
NBC 218

National Enquirer 15, 24, 96–99, 197, 204, 205
National Exit Poll 228
National Journal 123, 228, 248
National Organization for Women 120
National Rifle Association 55, 121, 247
National Science Foundation 111
negativity 235–236
Neuharth, Alan 35
Neuman, W. Russell 257
new media effect on traditional media 189–209
  news agenda 201–206
  news values 206–208
  reporting techniques 198–201
  saturation coverage 205–206
New Republic 206
New York Times 78, 194, 203, 204, 206–209, 215, 217, 228
news business 29–33, 34, 36
  evolution of 29–33
Newsweek 17, 24, 135, 142, 228
Nightline 11, 149, 217
North, Oliver 4, 57, 59, 64, 73, 75, 82–84, 87
Nugent, Ted 223

Oklahoma City bombing 11, 121, 174, 236, 250
Oprah 11, 99–100, 136, 148

Patterson, Thomas 32, 214
People 29, 31, 35–36, 41, 43–46, 97–98
Perot, Ross 4–6, 12, 45, 57, 64, 123, 172, 216, 218, 224, 232, 245, 246
personalization of news stories 166, 212–213
Pew Research Center 136–138, 145, 155, 220, 228
Police Gazette 93
political participation 253–262
Politically Incorrect 11
Pope, Generoso Paul 96
populism 23–24, 43–46
Postman, Neil 92
Powell, Colin 122–123

Prodigy 110, 112, 124, 243
presidential campaigns 121–123,
    210–230
  1980 195
  1992 36, 43, 45, 114, 122, 172,
    178, 180–181, 194, 206, 210–
    211, 213–220, 221–229
  1996 112, 117, 121, 123, 128,
    165, 168, 179–182, 189, 203–
    206, 209–211, 214–229
  and coverage of personalities
    212–213
  trends 211–216
Presley, Lisa Marie 189
Prime Time Live 13, 14, 165, 192
print tabloids 15, 93–107, 141, 144,
    154–155
profit 33–38, 52–54, 64, 69, 84, 89,
    91
public policy 232–251
  policy influence 237–240
  policy success 250–251
public dissatisfaction with media
    43–45
pundits 194–195

Quivvers, Robin 62

Rainforest Action Network 121, 238
Rapping, Elayne 104
Rather, Dan 13, 104, 192
Ratner, Ellen 88
Reagan, Michael 8, 21, 56, 59, 60,
    64, 68, 77, 82, 83, 115, 233–
    234
Reagan, Ronald 194–195, 221, 231
Real World 222
reality programs 102
Recording Industry Association 222
Rehm, Diane 62
Rehnquist, William 166
Reich, Robert 242
religious right 234
Republican 58, 79, 166, 170, 171,
    210, 220, 223, 228, 235, 243,
    244, 248–250
Reeves, Byron 160
"revolving door" 64–65, 194–195
Rice, Donna 23, 93, 213
Rising Sun 192

Rizzo, Frank 66
Robb, Chuck 59
Roberts, Cokie 192
Rock the Vote 14–15, 25, 221–224
Romney, George 213
Roper Center 136–138
Rosen, Mike 76, 79, 84
Rosenstiel, Tom 259
Rosenthal, David 225
Ross, Dave 85, 238, 252

Sabato, Larry 212
Salinger, Pierre 200
San Francisco Chronicle 114
San Jose Mercury News 114
Saturday Night Live 11
Sawyer, David 19
Sawyer, Diane 103
Schieffer, Bob 192
Schudson, Michael 29–30, 45
Schwartzenegger, Arnold 41
scoops 196, 199, 207
Scott, Tom 238, 249
Selene 53
Siegel, Mike 10, 20, 65, 67, 77, 233,
    237, 238, 241, 243, 249
Silverman, Robert 217
Simpson, O. J. 11, 13, 21, 22, 53,
    75, 76, 195, 197, 200, 205, 234,
    236, 252
Slate 16, 207
sleaze 254
Smith, Howard K. 191
Smith, William Kennedy 22, 53,
    197, 203
social change 40–42
Socialist Party 121
Socks 116
Soren, Tabitha 14, 222–224
soundbite 165, 213–216, 219
Squires, James 34
Specter, Arlen 122
Springer, Jerry 11, 148
Star 15, 93, 96–98, 137, 203–204
State Department 112, 117
state governments 118–120
Stephanopoulos, George 55, 194,
    203
Stern, Howard 52–54, 62, 67, 115,
    218, 249

Stringer, Howard 103
Suarez, Ray 52, 76, 145, 254

tabloid journalism 92–109, 189,
    192, 195–197, 201, 203–206,
    208–209
  appeal of 102–107
  benefits of 105–107
  debate over 103–107
  definition of 94–96
  history of 93–94
  print 96–99
  television 99–102
Talk of the Nation 52
talk radio 9–10, 51–91, 115, 127,
    134, 137, 140–148, 158–163,
    173–175, 178–185, 190, 199,
    202, 206, 208, 210–211, 217–
    219, 232–251, 253–258
  advertising 72
  agenda setting 75–79
  call screener 81
  callers 51, 58, 69, 70, 72, 73, 75,
    76, 79, 81–90
  characteristics 90–91
  format 72
  guests 87–88
  as medium for discourse 88–91
  and profit 52–54
  as vehicle for expression 54
talk radio content 73–81, 85–88,
    235–236
  issue discussion 73–81, 85–88
  negativity 235–236
  newspaper stories as sources of
    78
talk radio hosts 56–73, 231–251
  agreement with callers 84–87
  agreement with guests 86–87
  black 62–64
  as former politicians 64–65
  ideological bias 65–69
  local 53, 54, 56, 57, 61, 62, 63,
    65, 67, 69, 72, 73, 77, 78, 79, 80
  opening monologue 72–73
  organization 54–55
  personality 69–70
  as political activists 233–237
  running for political office
    249–250

syndicated 56–60
  women 61–63
Talkback Live 17
Talkers 19, 60, 246, 249
technological change 39–40
television news magazines 13–14,
    100–102, 141, 144, 154–155,
    253–258
television tabloids 15, 92–107, 141,
    144, 154–155, 253–258
television talk shows 10–12, 70, 83,
    99–100, 115, 127, 141, 144,
    148–149, 211, 217, 220, 232,
    240, 242, 243, 245, 252,
    253–258
terrorism 232, 233
The Capital Gang 191–193
The Comedy Channel 8
Thelen, David 161, 258
THOMAS 118, 120
Thomas, Clarence 63
Thomas, Evan 204
Thurmond, Strom 63
Tim Russert Show 10
Time 17, 24, 114, 135, 138, 140,
    142, 162, 193, 205, 248
Times Mirror Center 179, 220
Today 8, 11, 217, 222
Tonight Show 11, 115
traditional media 17–23, 77, 78, 90,
    113–115, 165, 173, 175, 177,
    206–208, 240, 248, 251,
    259–261
  differences with new media 17–23
  and Internet 113–115, 206–208
  reform 259–261
Treasury Department 117
trust 165, 173, 175, 177

United Methodist Church 261
U.S. News and World Report
    192
USA Today 78, 114
uses and gratifications 157–162

V-CHIP 261
Vietnam War 31–32

Wall Street Journal 78, 116, 194,
    207

Walters, Barbara 32, 101, 106
Ward, Bernie 63
Warsh, David 260
Washington Post 17, 23, 78, 143,
    194, 203, 205–206, 214–217,
    228
Washington Times 55, 78
Watergate 31, 58, 60, 212
Weekly World News 97–98
Westwood One 54, 59, 67
White House 5,6,14, 116–117
White House intern scandal
    93

White House Office of National
    Drug Control Policy 261
White, Rick 222
White, Theodore 212
Whitewater 60, 106, 220
Wilder, Douglas 63, 64, 66
Will, George 162, 194
Williams, Armstrong 63
Williams, Jerry 65, 80, 232, 238
Williams, Montel 11
Woodward, Bob 23

Yeltsin, Boris 166